EDITION 3

Meeting the
Ethical
Challenges
of Leadership

To my students

EDITION 3

Meeting the
Ethical
Challenges
of Leadership

Casting Light or Shadow

Craig E. Johnson
George Fox University

Los Angeles • London • New Delhi • Singapore

For information:

SAGE Publications, Inc.
2455 Teller Road
Thousand Oaks,
    California 91320
E-mail: order@sagepub.com

SAGE Publications India Pvt. Ltd.
B 1/I 1 Mohan Cooperative Industrial Area
Mathura Road, New Delhi 110 044
India

SAGE Publications Ltd.
1 Oliver's Yard
55 City Road
London EC1Y 1SP
United Kingdom

SAGE Publications Asia-Pacific Pte. Ltd.
33 Pekin Street #02–01
Far East Square
Singapore 048763

Printed in the United States of America

Library of Congress Cataloging-in-Publication Data

Johnson, Craig E. (Craig Edward), 1952–
Meeting the ethical challenges of leadership: Casting light or shadow / Craig E. Johnson. —3rd ed.
    p. cm.
Includes bibliographical references and index.
ISBN 978-1-4129-6481-4 (pbk.)
    1. Leadership—Moral and ethical aspects. I. Title.

HM1261.J64 2009
303.3´4—dc22   2008011830

This book is printed on acid-free paper.

10   11   12   11   10   9   8   7   6   5   4   3

Acquisitions Editor:	Al Bruckner
Editorial Assistant:	MaryAnn Vail
Production Editor:	Diane S. Foster
Copy Editor:	Carol Anne Peschke
Typesetter:	C&M Digitals (P) Ltd.
Proofreader:	Dennis W. Webb
Indexer:	Diggs Publication Services
Cover Designer:	Gail Buschman
Marketing Manager:	Jennifer Reed Banando

Contents

Acknowledgments

Colleagues and students provided practical and emotional support during the writing of the third edition of this text, just as they did for the first two. Research librarians Janis Tyhurst and Louise Newswanger helped locate sources and double-check facts. Richard Engnell and Phil Smith helped clarify my understanding of Rawls's justice-as-fairness theory. Student assistants, ably supervised by Kelly Borror, Colleen Huffman, and Sandee Robinson, located articles and photocopied materials. Those enrolled in my leadership seminar, doctoral leadership seminar, and leadership communication classes helped shape this third edition by responding to chapter content, exercises, and cases. My special thanks go to instructors from around the country who adopted the first two editions of *Meeting the Ethical Challenges of Leadership* for classroom use and then provided me with feedback. (Some of their students have also been kind enough to send me their thoughts.) Roger Smitter, executive director of the National Communication Association, sent cases and examples for the last edition, many of which are incorporated in this edition as well. Three anonymous reviewers provided feedback that helped guide my revisions. Kristina Findley, Mark Reed, and Dana Miller supplied material for chapter end scenarios. Editor Al Bruckner continues to be the advocate for this project at Sage. For that I am grateful. Finally, I want to once again thank my wife, Mary, who is a steady source of encouragement.

Introduction

"This might not be ethical. Is that a problem for anybody?"

Fallen Leaders

The modern landscape is littered with fallen leaders. Wherever we turn—business, military, politics, medicine, education, and religion—we find leaders toppled by ethical scandals. Nearly all have sacrificed their positions of leadership and their reputations. Many face civil lawsuits, criminal charges, and jail time. The costs can be even greater for followers. Consider the following:

- Investors lost billions when leaders at AIG Insurance, Quest, the Fannie Mae loan corporation, Finova, HealthSouth, and other companies engaged in shady financial practices.

- Thousands of former Enron and WorldCom employees may never recover from the loss of their jobs and their retirement savings.
- Thousands of homeowners were threatened with foreclosure after unscrupulous lenders sold them mortgages they couldn't afford to repay.
- Detainees at Iraq's Abu Ghraib prison were physically and psychologically abused and sexually humiliated by their captors. Photos of the abuse enraged viewers around the world.
- Hundreds of children suffered sexual abuse at the hands of Catholic clergy. Victims' lawsuits bankrupted some dioceses.
- Students overpaid for college loans when financial aid directors steered them to lenders in return for kickbacks.
- Homeless patients at some Los Angeles hospitals were allegedly "dumped" back on the street after treatment.
- Millions have been driven from their homes in Western Africa. They face permanent displacement and starvation because world leaders hesitate to intervene.
- Public confidence in the American and British governments dropped because of allegations that administrations in both countries overstated the risk posed by Saddam Hussein and Al Qaeda in order to justify the invasion of Iraq.

The misery caused by unethical leaders drives home an important point: Ethics is at the heart of leadership.[1] When we assume the benefits of leadership, we also assume ethical burdens. I believe that we must make every effort to act in such a way as to benefit rather than damage others, to cast light instead of shadow. Doing so will significantly reduce the likelihood that we will join the future ranks of fallen leaders. Furthermore, providing ethical leadership produces a number of positive outcomes for our groups and organizations.[2] These include lower stress levels, turnover, and absenteeism; higher employee job satisfaction, commitment, and willingness to give extra effort; better decision making; greater levels of trust and collaboration; positive public image; and, in many cases, higher performance (productivity, profitability).[3]

You should find this book helpful if you are a leader or an aspiring leader who (1) acknowledges that there are ethical consequences associated with exercising influence over others, (2) seeks to develop your capacity to make more informed ethical choices and to follow through on your decisions, and (3) wants to foster ethical behavior in others. You'll also find useful insights if you are a follower who wants to behave ethically and bring out the best in your leaders.

There is no guarantee that after reading this book you will act in a more ethical fashion in every situation. Nor can you be sure that others will reach the same conclusions as you do about what is the best answer to an ethical dilemma or that you will succeed in improving the ethical climate of your group or organization. Nevertheless, you can increase your ethical competence and encourage others to do the same. This book is dedicated to that end.

Whatever the specific context, leaders face similar kinds of ethical choices. For that reason, I draw examples from a wide variety of settings: business, coaching, education, government, nonprofit organizations, and the military. Most are based on actual events, but I don't hesitate to draw from fictional sources as well. Literature and drama can give us rich insights into reality. Cases continue to play an important role in this edition. A case is included in the body of each chapter along with two case studies at the end of each chapter (with the exception of Chapter 7). Many of the cases from earlier editions have been replaced. You'll find new stories about backdated stock options, the death of Pat Tillman, the student loan scandal, organ donation, Google, Vivendi Universal, the Jena Six, genocide in Darfur, reformer William Wilberforce, and former Hewlett Packard CEO Carly Fiorina. Other cases have been updated. For example, the *Columbia* crash (Chapter 8) and Air Force Academy (Chapter 9) cases have been revised to reflect the fact that both NASA and military leaders have successfully instituted ethical reforms.

Once again, you'll also find a feature called "Leadership Ethics at the Movies." Each of these short summaries introduces a feature film (new to this edition) that brings important concepts to life. Analyzing these films on your own or, better yet, in a group will deepen your understanding of leadership ethics. You may want to follow this three-step format: (1) Identify the important ethical principles portrayed in the film, (2) analyze and evaluate how the characters respond to moral dilemmas, and (3) draw ethical implications and applications from the movie.

Four other features are also found in every chapter. The first, "Focus on Follower Ethics," is new to this edition and addresses the ethical challenges facing followers. I've added this feature in recognition of the fact that followers play an important role in supporting ethical leaders and creating ethical environments. (I'll have more to say about the partnership between leaders and followers later in the Introduction.) The second feature, "Self-Assessment," measures your performance on an important behavior, skill, or concept discussed in the chapter. The third, "Implications and Applications," reviews key ideas and their ramifications for you as a leader. The fourth, "For Further Exploration, Challenge, and Assessment," encourages you to engage in extended reflection and self-analysis.

Readers of the second edition will note that a reference section has been added at the end of this edition. In the pages to come, you'll find new and expanded coverage of the shadow side of leadership, unhealthy motivations, character, evil, moral development and decision making, authentic leadership, fostering ethical accountability in small groups, the leader as ethical role model, ethical organizational climates, and promoting diversity.

The first two chapters focus on the dark side of leadership in the belief that the first step in mastering the ethical challenges of leadership is to recognize their existence. Chapter 1 outlines common shadows cast by leaders: abuse of power and privilege, mismanagement of information, misplaced and broken loyalties, inconsistency, and irresponsibility. Chapter 2 explores the reasons why leaders often cause more harm than good and introduces the Ethical

Capacity Model. At the end of the second chapter, we'll pause to preview the remainder of the text. You can read the chapters in any order you wish, but they are designed to build on one another.

Defining Terms

Because this is a book about leadership ethics, we need to clarify what both of these terms mean. Leadership is the exercise of influence in a group context.[4] Want to know who the leaders are? Look for the people having the greatest impact on the group or organization. Leaders are change agents engaged in furthering the needs, wants, and goals of leaders and followers alike. They are found wherever humans associate with one another, whether in a social movement, sports team, task force, nonprofit agency, state legislature, military unit, or corporation.

No definition of leadership is complete without distinguishing between leading and following. Generally leaders get the most press. The newfound success of a college football team is a case in point. A head coach gets most of the credit for changing a losing team into a winner, but the turnaround is really the result of the efforts of many followers. Assistant coaches work with offensive and defensive lines, quarterbacks, and kicking teams; trainers tend to injuries; academic tutors keep players in school; athletic department staff solicit contributions for training facilities; and sports information personnel draw attention to the team's accomplishments.

In truth, leaders and followers function collaboratively, working together toward shared objectives. They are relational partners who play complementary roles.[5] Whereas leaders exert a greater degree of influence and take more responsibility for the overall direction of the group, followers are more involved in implementing plans and doing the work. During the course of a day or week, we typically shift between leader and follower roles, heading up a project team at work, for example, while taking the position of follower as a student in a night class. As a result, we need to know how to behave ethically as both leaders and followers.

Moving from a follower role to a leadership role brings with it a shift in expectations. Important leader functions include establishing direction, organizing, coordinating activities and resources, motivating, and managing conflicts. Important follower functions include carrying out group and organizational tasks (engineering, social work, teaching, accounting), generating new ideas about how to get jobs done, teamwork, and providing feedback.[6]

Viewing leadership as a role should put to rest the notion that leaders are born, not made. The fact that nearly all of us will function as leaders if we haven't already done so means that leadership is not limited to those with the proper genetic background, income level, or education. Many ordinary people emerged as leaders during the horrific events of September 11, 2001, for example. Office workers in the World Trade Center calmed victims and bandaged their wounds. They formed human chains to walk down the stairs in the smoke and darkness, assisting those who had difficulty navigating the steps. While these workers were headed down, firefighters of all ranks were rushing up the staircases to help. A paramedic driving near the Pentagon took his bag out of his car, doused burn victims with saline, and got others to drag victims to safety. Passengers on hijacked United Flight 93 rushed the attackers and prevented the plane from striking its intended target.

Leadership should not be confused with position, although leaders often occupy positions of authority. Those designated as leaders, such as a disillusioned manager nearing retirement, don't always exert much influence. On the other hand, those without the benefit of a title on the organizational chart can have a significant impact. Lech Walesa was an electrician in a Polish plant. Nonetheless, he went on to lead a revolution that led to the overthrow of the nation's communist government.

Human leadership differs in important ways from the pattern of dominance and submission that characterizes animal societies. The dominant female hyena or male chimpanzee rules over the pack or troop through pure physical strength. Each maintains authority until some stronger rival (often seeking mates) comes along. Unlike other animals, which seem to be driven largely by instinct, humans consciously choose how they want to influence others. We can rely on persuasion, rewards, punishments, emotional appeals, rules, and a host of other means to get our way. Freedom of choice makes ethical considerations an important part of any discussion of leadership. The term *ethics* refers to judgments about whether human behavior is right or wrong. We may be repulsed by the idea that a male lion will kill the offspring of the previous dominant male when he takes control of the pride. Yet we cannot label his actions as unethical because he is driven by a genetic drive to start his own bloodline. We can and do condemn the actions of leaders who decide to lie, belittle followers, and enrich themselves at the expense of the less fortunate.

Some philosophers distinguish between *ethics,* which they define as the systematic study of the principles of right or wrong behavior, and *morals,* which they describe as specific standards of right and wrong ("thou shall not steal," "do unto others as they would do unto you"). Just as many scholars appear to use these terms interchangeably. I will follow the latter course.

The practice of *ethical leadership* is a two-part process involving personal moral behavior and moral influence.[7] Ethical leaders earn that label when they act morally as they carry out their duties and shape the ethical contexts of their groups, organizations, and societies. Both components are essential. Leaders must demonstrate such character traits as justice, humility, optimism, courage, and compassion; make wise choices; and master the ethical challenges of their roles. In addition, they are also responsible for the ethical behavior of others.

These dual responsibilities intertwine. As we'll see in Chapter 9, leaders act as role models for the rest of the organization. How followers behave depends in large part on the example set by leaders. Conversely, leaders become products of their own creations. Ethical climates promote the moral development of leaders as well as followers, fostering their character and improving their ability to make and follow through ethical choices. Ethical environments have safeguards that keep both leaders and followers from engaging in destructive behaviors.

With these preliminaries out of the way, we're now ready to take a closer look at some of the ethical hurdles faced by leaders.

Notes

1. See Ciulla, J. (Ed.). (2004). *Ethics: The heart of leadership.* Westport, CT: Praeger.

2. Johnson, C. E. (2007). Best practices in ethical leadership. In J. A. Conger & R. E. Riggio (Eds.), *The practice of leadership: Developing the next generation of leaders* (pp. 150–171). San Francisco: Jossey-Bass; Brown, M. E., Trevino, L. K., & Harrison, D. A. (2005). Ethical leadership: A social learning perspective for construct development and testing. *Organizational Behavior and Human Decision Processes, 97,* 117–134.

3. See Waddock, S. A., & Graves, S. B. (1997). The corporate social performance–financial performance link. *Strategic Management Journal, 18,* 303–319.

4. Bass, B. M. (1990). *Bass and Stogdill's handbook of leadership* (3rd ed.). New York: Free Press.

5. Hollander, E. P. (1992, April). The essential interdependence of leadership and followership. *Current Directions in Psychological Science,* 71–75.

6. Johnson, C. E., & Hackman, M. Z. (1997). *Rediscovering the power of followership in the leadership communication text.* Paper presented at the National Communication Association convention, Chicago.

7. Brown, M. E., & Trevino, L. K. (2006). Ethical leadership: A review and future directions. *The Leadership Quarterly, 17,* 595–616.

Part I

The Shadow Side of Leadership

1

The Leader's Light or Shadow

We know where light is coming from by looking at the shadows.

—Humanities scholar Paul Woodruff

What's Ahead

This chapter introduces the dark (bad, toxic) side of leadership as the first step in promoting good or ethical leadership. The metaphor of light and shadow dramatizes the differences between moral and immoral leaders. Leaders have the power to illuminate the lives of followers or to cover them in darkness. They cast shadows when they fail to meet the ethical challenges of the leadership role by (1) abusing power, (2) hoarding privileges, (3) mismanaging information, (4) acting inconsistently, (5) misplacing or betraying loyalties, and (6) failing to assume responsibilities.

A Dramatic Difference

In an influential essay titled "Leading From Within," educational writer and consultant Parker Palmer introduces a powerful metaphor to dramatize the distinction between ethical and unethical leadership. According to Palmer, the difference between moral and immoral leaders is as sharp as the contrast between light and darkness, between heaven and hell.

> A leader is a person who has an unusual degree of power to create the conditions under which other people must live and move and have their being, conditions

3

that can be either as illuminating as heaven or as shadowy as hell. A leader must take special responsibility for what's going on inside his or her own self, inside his or her consciousness, lest the act of leadership create more harm than good.[1]

Psychotherapist Carl Jung was the first social scientist to identify the shadow side of the personality. He used the term to refer to the subconscious, which could include both negative (greed, fear, hatred) and positive (creativity, desire for achievement) elements.[2] Unlike Jung and other researchers who use the shadow label to refer to the hidden part of the personality, both good and bad, Palmer equates shadow with destruction. However, Palmer and Jungian psychologists agree on one point: *If we want to manage or master the dark forces inside us, we must first acknowledge that they exist.* For this reason, Palmer urges us to pay more attention to the shadow side of leadership. Political figures, classroom teachers, parents, clergy, and business executives have the potential to cast as much shadow as they do light. Refusing to face the dark side of leadership makes abuse more likely. All too often, leaders "do not even know they are making a choice, let alone how to reflect on the process of choosing."[3]

Recently other scholars have joined Palmer in urging us to pay more attention to the dark or negative dimension of leadership. Claremont University professor Jean Lipman-Blumen uses the term *toxic leaders* to describe those who engage in destructive behaviors and who exhibit dysfunctional personal characteristics.[4] These behaviors and qualities (summarized in Table 1.1) cause significant harm to followers and organizations.

Harvard professor Barbara Kellerman objects to the positive bias of those who study and practice leadership.[5] Leadership in American society is assumed to be good. However, limiting leadership solely to good leadership ignores the reality that a great many leaders engage in destructive behaviors. Overlooking that fact, Kellerman says, undermines our attempts to promote good leadership: "I take it as a given that we promote good leadership not by ignoring bad leadership, nor by presuming that it is immutable, but rather by attacking it as we would a disease that is always pernicious and sometimes deadly."[6]

According to professor Kellerman, bad leaders can be ineffective, unethical, or both. She identifies seven types of bad leaders:

Incompetent. These leaders don't have the motivation or ability to sustain effective action. They may lack emotional or academic intelligence, for example, or be careless, distracted, or sloppy. Some can't function under stress, and their communication and decisions suffer as a result. Former International Olympic Committee president Juan Antonio Samaranch (1961–2000) is one example of an incompetent leader. Toward the end of his tenure he turned a blind eye to commercialism, drug scandals, and corruption in the Olympic movement.

Table 1.1   The Behaviors and Personal Characteristics of Toxic Leaders

Destructive Behaviors	Toxic Qualities
Leaving followers worse off	Lack of integrity
Violating human rights	Insatiable ambition
Feeding followers' illusions; creating dependence	Enormous egos
Playing to the basest fears and needs of followers	Arrogance
Stifling criticism; enforcing compliance	Amorality (unable to discern right from wrong)
Misleading followers	Avarice (greed)
Subverting ethical organizational structures and processes	Reckless disregard for the costs of their actions
Engaging in unethical, illegal, and criminal acts	Cowardice (won't make tough choices)
Building totalitarian regimes	Failure to understand problems
Failing to nurture followers, including successors	Incompetent in key leadership situations
Setting constituents against one another	
Encouraging followers to hate or destroy others	
Identifying scapegoats	
Making themselves indispensable	
Ignoring or promoting incompetence, cronyism, and corruption	

SOURCE: Adapted from Lipman-Blumen, J. (2005). *The allure of toxic leaders: Why we follow destructive bosses and corrupt politicians—and how we can survive them.* Oxford, UK: Oxford University Press, pp. 19–23.

Rigid. Rigid leaders may be competent, but they are unyielding, unable to accept new ideas, new information, or changing conditions. Morgan Stanley Dean Witter financial analyst Mary Meeker was one such leader. During the technology boom of the 1990s, she promoted Internet stocks such as Yahoo!, Netscape, and AOL. Millions of investors followed her advice. However, when the Internet bubble burst at the beginning of the new millennium, she continued to promote online stocks even as their values plummeted.

Intemperate. Intemperate leaders lack self-control and are enabled by followers who don't want to intervene or can't. Marion Barry Jr.'s political career demonstrates intemperate leadership in action. Barry served as mayor of Washington, DC, from 1979 to 1991. He ignored widespread corruption in his administration, perhaps in part because he was busy cheating on his wife and doing drugs. Barry was convicted of possessing crack cocaine and served 6 months in jail. After being released from prison, he was elected to the city council in 1992 and was reelected as mayor in 1994. During his administrations, the district's schools and public services deteriorated while the murder rate soared.

Callous. The callous leader is uncaring or unkind, ignoring or downplaying the needs, wants, and wishes of followers. Former hotel magnate Leona Helmsley personified the callous leader. She earned the title "The Queen of Mean" by screaming at employees and firing them for minor infractions such as having dirty fingernails. Helmsley later served time for tax evasion. (She once quipped, "Only the little people pay taxes.")

Corrupt. These leaders and at least some of their followers lie, cheat, and steal. They put self-interest ahead of public interest. Former United Way of America chief William Aramony was an exemplar of this type of leader. Aramony used United Way funds to buy and furnish an apartment for his girlfriend and to pay for vacations. His top financial officers helped him hide his illegal actions. Aramony and his colleagues were convicted on fraud-related charges.

Insular. The insular leader draws a clear boundary between the welfare of his or her immediate group or organization and outsiders. Former President Bill Clinton behaved in an insular manner when he didn't intervene in the Rwandan genocide that took the lives of 800,000 in 1994. He later traveled to Africa to apologize for failing to act even though he had reliable information describing how thousands of Tutsis were being hacked to death by their Hutu neighbors.

Evil. Evil leaders commit atrocities, using their power to inflict severe physical or psychological harm. Former Cambodian dictator Pol Pot was one of modern history's most evil leaders. During his 3 years in absolute power in the

1970s, Pol Pot's Khmer Rouge army terrorized the populace through slavery, torture, execution, and murder. He was responsible for the deaths of more than 1.7 million people—one-third of the Cambodian population.

The Leader's Shadows

When we function as leaders, we take on a unique set of ethical burdens in addition to a set of expectations and tasks. These dilemmas involve issues of power, privilege, information, consistency, loyalty, and responsibility. How we handle the challenges of leadership determines whether we cause more harm than good or, to return to Palmer's metaphor, whether we cast light or shadow. Unless we're careful, we're likely to cast one or more of the shadows described in this section.

THE SHADOW OF POWER

Power is the foundation for influence attempts. The more power we have, the more likely others are to comply with our wishes. Power comes from a variety of sources. The most popular power classification system identifies five power bases.[7] *Coercive power* is based on penalties or punishments such as physical force, salary reductions, student suspensions, or embargoes against national enemies. *Reward power* depends on being able to deliver something of value to others, whether tangible (bonuses, health insurance, grades) or intangible (praise, trust, cooperation). *Legitimate power* resides in the position, not the person. Supervisors, judges, police officers, instructors, and parents have the right to control our behavior within certain limits. A boss can require us to carry out certain tasks at work, for example, but in most cases he or she has no say in what we do in our free time. In contrast to legitimate power, *expert power* is based on the characteristics of the individual regardless of his or her official position. Knowledge, skills, education, and certification all build expert power. *Referent (role model) power* rests on the admiration one person has for another. We're more likely to do favors for a supervisor we admire or to buy a product promoted by our favorite sports hero.

Leaders typically draw on more than one power source. The manager who is appointed to lead a task force is granted legitimate power that enables her to reward or punish. Yet in order to be successful, she'll have to demonstrate her knowledge of the topic, skillfully direct the group process, and earn the respect of task force members through hard work and commitment to the group.

There are advantages and disadvantages of using each power type. For instance, rewards are widely accepted in Western culture but can be counterproductive if they promote the wrong behaviors (see Chapter 9) or go to the wrong people. Researchers report that U.S. workers are more satisfied and productive when their leaders rely on forms of power that are tied to the person (expert and referent) rather than on forms of power that are linked to the position (coercive, reward, and legitimate).[8] In addition, positional power is more susceptible to abuse. Coercive tactics have the potential to do the most damage, threatening the dignity as well as the physical and mental health of followers. Leaders, then, have important decisions to make about the types of power they use and when.

The fact that leadership cannot exist without power makes some Americans uncomfortable. Harvard business professor Rosabeth Kanter goes so far as to declare that power is "America's last dirty word."[9] She believes that for many of us talking about money and sex is easier than discussing power. We admire powerful leaders who act decisively but can be reluctant to admit that we have and use power.

Our refusal to face up to the reality of power can make us more vulnerable to the shadow side of leadership. Cult leader Jim Jones presided over the suicide–murder of more than 900 followers in the jungles of Guyana (see the "Leadership Ethics at the Movies" case in Box 1.1 for more information about Jones and his Peoples Temple). Perhaps this tragedy could have been avoided if cult members and outside observers had challenged Jones's abuse of power.[10] Conversely, ignoring the topic of power prevents the attainment of worthy objectives, leaving followers in darkness. Consider the case of the community activist who wants to build a new shelter for homeless families. He can't help these families unless he skillfully wields power to enlist the support of local groups, overcome resistance of opponents, raise funds, and secure building permits.

I suspect that we treat power as a dirty word because we recognize that power has a corrosive effect on those who possess it. We've seen how Richard Nixon used the power of his office to order illegal acts against his enemies and how corporate executives often intimidate their subordinates. Many of us are uneasy about new powers, such as the authority to conduct secret searches and monitor library records, that have been given to law enforcement officials to fight terrorism.

Unfortunately, abuse of power is an all too common fact of life in modern organizations. In one survey, 90% of those responding reported that they had experienced disrespect from a boss some time during their working careers. Twenty percent of the sample said they currently work for an abusive leader. (Complete the "Self-Assessment" in Box 1.2 to determine whether your supervisor is abusive or just tough.) "Brutal" bosses regularly engage in the following behaviors, some of which will be discussed in more detail later in the chapter.[11]

- *Deceit.* Lying and giving false or misleading information.
- *Constraint.* Restricting followers' activities outside work, such as telling them whom they can befriend, where they can live, with whom they can live, and the civic activities they can participate in.

Box 1.1

Leadership Ethics at the Movies

JONESTOWN: THE LIFE AND DEATH OF PEOPLES TEMPLE

Key Cast Members: Jim Jones, Jim Jones Jr., former Temple members and relatives

Synopsis: On November 18, 1978, 910 members of the Peoples Temple died in Guyana after drinking Kool-Aid laced with cyanide. This documentary reveals how the group's leader, Jim Jones, convinced so many to participate in mass murder–suicide. Jones started out as a social reformer, promoting racial harmony and social justice, but became increasingly paranoid and delusional. Claiming deity, he sexually exploited Temple members, controlled every aspect of their lives, and humiliated anyone who broke the rules. The film includes footage from the Jonestown compound and interviews with two members who survived the slaughter by fleeing into the jungle.

Rating: Not rated but contains mature content, disturbing images, and adult language

Themes: the shadow side of leadership, evil, the dark side of followership

---

- *Coercion.* Inappropriate or excessive threats for not complying with the leader's directives.
- *Selfishness.* Blaming subordinates and making them scapegoats.
- *Inequity.* Supplying unequal benefits or punishments based on favoritism or criteria unrelated to the job.
- *Cruelty.* Harming subordinates in such illegitimate ways as name calling or public humiliation.
- *Disregard.* Ignoring normal standards of politeness; obvious disregard for what is happening in the lives of followers.
- *Deification.* Creating a master–servant relationship in which bosses can do whatever they want because they feel superior.

The greater a leader's power, the greater the potential for abuse. This prompted Britain's Lord Acton to observe that "power corrupts, and absolute power corrupts absolutely." The long shadow cast by absolute power, as in the case of Pol Pot, can be seen in torture, death, starvation, and imprisonment. Psychologists offer several explanations for why concentrated power is so dangerous. First, power makes it easier for impulsive, selfish people to pursue their goals without considering the needs of others. They are likely to justify their

Box 1.2

Self-Assessment

THE BRUTAL BOSS QUESTIONNAIRE

For an assessment of your current experience of abuse by superior(s) and its possible consequences for your health, well-being, and work productivity, complete the questionnaire that follows. Then find your personal rating using the scoring information, which is provided on the reverse side.

Rate your boss on the following behaviors and actions. If you agree that a statement categorizes your boss, write a number from 5 to 8, depending on the extent of your agreement. If you disagree with a statement in reference to your boss, write a number from 1 to 4, depending on the extent of your disagreement.

1	2	3	4	5	6	7	8
Strongly Disagree							Strongly Agree

1. My boss deliberately provides me with false or misleading information. _2_

2. My boss treats me unfairly at times for no apparent reason. _2_

3. My boss deceives me sometimes. _5_

4. My boss deliberately withholds information from me that I need to perform my job. _2_

5. My boss criticizes low-quality work from me. _2_

6. My boss tells me how I should be spending my time when not at work. _1_

7. My boss will "get" me if I don't comply with her or his wishes. _1_

8. My boss humiliates me in public. _1_

9. My boss calls me unflattering names. _1_

10. My boss requires that her or his standards be met before giving a compliment. _2_

11. My boss believes that I am generally inferior and blames me whenever something goes wrong. _3_

12. My boss acts as if she or he can do as she or he pleases to me, because she or he is the boss. _2_

the world's haves and have-nots?" We'll never reach complete agreement on these issues, but the fact remains that privilege is a significant ethical burden associated with leadership. Leaders must give questions of privilege the same careful consideration as questions of power. The shadow cast by the abuse of privilege can be as long and dark as that cast by the misuse of power.

THE SHADOW OF MISMANAGED INFORMATION

Leaders have more access to information than do others in an organization. They are more likely to participate in the decision-making processes, network with managers in other units, have access to personnel files, and formulate long-term plans. Knowledge is a mixed blessing. Leaders must be in the information loop in order to carry out their tasks, but possessing knowledge makes life more complicated. Do they reveal that they are in the know? When should they release information and to whom? How much do they tell? Is it ever right for them to lie?

No wonder leaders are tempted to think ignorance is bliss! If all these challenges weren't enough, leaders face the very real temptation to lie or hide the truth to protect themselves. For instance, tobacco executives swore before Congress that smoking was safe even though they had sponsored research that said otherwise. Prominent pastor Ted Haggard tried to salvage his ministry by denying that he had sex with a male prostitute. (Case Study 1.1 describes another example of how leaders tried to cover up the truth.)

The issues surrounding access to information are broader than deciding whether to lie or to tell the truth. Although leaders often decide between lying and truth telling, they are just as likely to be faced with the questions related to the release of information. Take the case of a middle manager who has learned about an upcoming merger that will mean layoffs. Her superiors have asked her to keep this information to herself for a couple of weeks until the deal is completed. In the interim, employees may make financial commitments (home and car purchases) that they would postpone if they knew that major changes were in the works. Should she voluntarily share information about the merger despite her orders? What happens when a member of her department asks her to confirm or deny the rumor that the company is about to merge?

Privacy issues raise additional ethical concerns. E-commerce firms routinely track the activity of Internet surfers, collecting and selling information that will allow marketers to better target their advertisements. Supermarkets use courtesy cards to track the purchases of shoppers. Employers monitor employee computer keystrokes, phone calls, and e-mail messages. Hundreds of thousands of video cameras track our movements at automated teller machines, parking lots, stores, and other public places. Videotapes made for security purposes have shown up on Web sites.[18]

In sum, leaders cast shadows not only when they lie but also when they mismanage information and engage in deceptive practices. Unethical leaders

- Deny having knowledge that is in their possession
- Withhold information that followers need
- Use information solely for personal benefit
- Violate the privacy rights of followers
- Release information to the wrong people
- Put followers in ethical binds by preventing them from releasing information that others have a legitimate right to know

SOURCE: Scott Adams/United Features Syndicate.

CASE STUDY 1.1

Hiding the Truth

Friendly Fire and the Death of Pat Tillman

In war, truth is the first casualty.

—Greek playwright Aeschylus

Former National Football League star Pat Tillman was an authentic American hero. Tillman turned down a 3-year, $3.6-million contract extension with the Arizona Cardinals to join the Army with his brother Kevin after the September 11 terrorist attacks. His determination to defend his country earned him a letter of thanks from then–Secretary of Defense Donald Rumsfeld and praise from talk show hosts and ordinary citizens.

Tillman took part in the invasion of Iraq and then was transferred to Afghanistan. On April 22, 2004, the two Tillman brothers were part of a patrol that came under enemy fire in a canyon in southeastern Afghanistan. The unit split into two sections (Kevin in one group, Pat in the other) during the battle. In the confusion, soldiers from Kevin's section began firing at Pat's group. Pat Tillman was killed while trying to stop the shooting.

Attempts to cover up the fact that Tillman died due to friendly fire began almost immediately. Fellow soldiers were ordered not to tell Kevin what happened and to burn Pat's equipment, including his protective vest. (These items are supposed to be preserved as evidence in friendly fire cases.) After the first reports about the incident went out on military radio, phone and Internet service were cut off to prevent anyone from discussing the incident. The initial casualty report said that Tillman died by enemy fire. A doctor at a field hospital reported that Tillman received cardiopulmonary resuscitation and intensive care before his life ended (even though the bullets had gone through his head). The initial press release implied that enemy forces had killed the Army Ranger, claiming that he died "when his patrol vehicle came under attack."[1]

The most blatant distortions came in Tillman's Silver Star commendation, the third most prestigious military honor. "Above the din of battle, Cpl. Tillman was heard issuing fire commands to take the fight to the enemy," the recommendation claims.[2] It also praises Tillman for getting his group through the ambush, which ignores the fact that Tillman and another soldier were killed while two others were wounded. At Tillman's well-publicized funeral, top military officials kept silent as speakers declared that the former football star had died at the hands of the Taliban.

Eventually the truth about Tillman's death came out. Army coroners refused to certify that the death was from enemy fire and asked Army criminal investigators to examine the case. The Tillman family began pressing for the facts. An Army inspector general's investigation found a "series of mistakes" in how the incident was reported but no organized attempt at a cover-up. Four soldiers were given minor punishments, and one had his military pay reduced. The inspector general criticized three generals for their actions. In congressional hearings on the matter, House committee members released an e-mail suggesting that the top-ranking general in Iraq and Afghanistan, General John Abizaid, as well as Secretary Rumsfeld, knew the true cause of Tillman's death within days.

Tillman perished at a bad time for the military, which is probably what prompted the deceit. The war in Iraq was going badly, and the prison abuse scandal at Abu Ghraib was headline news. Officials apparently hoped to stir up patriotism and support for the war while avoiding bad publicity. They used the story of Private Jessica Lynch in much the same way. The Pentagon claimed that Lynch fought back when captured by Iraqi forces and was rescued in a dramatic hospital raid. In truth, she never fired a shot (she was knocked unconscious by the crash of her vehicle), and hospital staff offered no resistance. "The story of the little girl Rambo from the hills who went down fighting is not true," Lynch says. "The bottom line is, the American people are capable of determining their own ideas for heroes, and they don't need to be told elaborate lies."[3]

Pat Tillman's Silver Star medal will not be taken back, although the wording of the commendation will be rewritten. A Pentagon spokesperson acknowledged mistakes in the case and has apologized on behalf the U.S. Army. However, the Tillman family remains bitter about the Pentagon's dishonesty and how the tragedy of Pat's death was turned into an "inspirational message" designed to bolster U.S. foreign policy.[4]

DISCUSSION PROBES

1. Were Army leaders justified in trying to conceal the real cause of Tillman's death? Why or why not?

2. Does Pat Tillman remain a hero despite the fact that he died by friendly fire?

3. Was this a case of a series of mistakes by Army officials or an organized cover up?

4. Would you punish high-ranking officers and officials, including the Secretary of Defense, for what happened in this case?

5. What leadership ethics lessons do you take from this case?

NOTES

    1. Colle, Z. (2007, April 21). Evidence of cover-up key to Tillman hearings. *The San Francisco Chronicle,* p. A1. Retrieved June 5, 2007, from LexisNexis Academic database.

    2. Colle, Z., & Collier, R. (2007, April 25). Lawmakers see cover-up, vow to probe Tillman death. *The San Francisco Chronicle,* p. A1. Retrieved June 5, 2007, from LexisNexis Academic database.

    3. Cornwell, R. (2007, April 26). Secrets and lies: How war heroes returned to haunt Pentagon. *The Independent* (London). Retrieved June 5, 2007, from LexisNexis Academic database, para. 7.

    4. Collier, R., & Epstein, E. (2007, March 27). Tillmans assail Pentagon report. *The San Francisco Chronicle,* p. A1. Retrieved June 5, 2007, from LexisNexis Academic database.

Patterns of deception, whether they take the form of outright lies or hiding or distorting information, destroy the trust that binds leaders and followers together. Consider the popularity of conspiracy theories, for example. Many citizens are convinced that the Air Force is hiding the fact that aliens landed in Roswell, New Mexico. They also believe that law enforcement officials are deliberately ignoring evidence that John F. Kennedy and Martin Luther King, Jr., were the victims of elaborate assassination plots. These theories may seem illogical, but they flourish in part because government leaders have created a shadow atmosphere through deceit. It wasn't until after the first Gulf War that we learned that our "smart bombs" weren't really so smart and missed their targets. The president and other cabinet officials apparently overstated the danger posed by Saddam Hussein in order to rally support for the second Gulf War.

Leaders must also consider ethical issues related to the image they hope to project to followers. In order to earn their positions and to achieve their objectives, leaders carefully manage the impressions they make on others. Impression management can be compared to a performance on a stage.[19] Leader–actors carefully manage everything from the setting to their words and nonverbal behaviors in order to have the desired effect on their follower audiences. For example, presidential staffers make sure that the chief executive is framed by visual images (Mt. Rushmore, the Oval Office) that reinforce his messages and his presidential standing. Like politicians, leaders in charge of such high-risk activities as mountain climbing and whitewater kayaking also work hard to project the desired impressions. In order to appear confident and competent, they stand up straight, look others in the eye, and use an authoritative tone of voice.

Impression management is integral to effective leadership because followers have images of ideal leaders called prototypes.[20] We expect that the mountain climbing guide will be confident (otherwise we would cancel the trip!), that the small-group leader will be active in group discussions, that the military leader will stay calm under fire. The closer the person is to the ideal, the more likely it is that we will select that person as leader and accept her or his influence. Nonetheless, a number of students find impression management ethically troubling. They value integrity and see role playing as insincere because the leader may have to disguise his or her true feelings in order to be successful.

There is no doubt that impression management can be used to reach immoral ends. Many demagogues, such as Huey Long and George Wallace, have used public speaking performances to rally audiences to destructive causes. It would be impossible to eliminate this form of influence, however. To begin, others form impressions of us, whether we are conscious of that fact or not. They judge our personality and values by what we wear, for instance, even if we don't give much thought to what we put on in the morning. Most of us use impression management to accurately convey our identities, not to conceal them or to manipulate others.

When considering the morality of impression management, we need to consider its end products. Ethical impression managers meet group wants and needs, not just the leader's. They spur followers toward highly moral ends. These leaders use impression management to accurately convey information, to build positive interpersonal relationships, and to facilitate good decisions. Unethical impression managers produce the opposite effects, subverting group wishes and lowering purpose and aspiration. These leaders use dysfunctional impression management to send deceptive messages, undermine relationships, and distort information, which leads to poor conclusions and decisions.[21]

THE SHADOW OF INCONSISTENCY

Leaders deal with a variety of constituencies, each with its own set of abilities, needs, and interests. In addition, they like some followers better than others. The Leader–Member Exchange (LMX) theory is based on the notion that leaders develop closer relationships with one group of followers.[22] Members of the "in-group" become advisors, assistants, and lieutenants. High levels of trust, mutual influence, and support characterize their exchanges with the leader. Members of the "out-group" are expected to carry out the basic requirements of their jobs. Their communication with the leader is not as trusting and supportive. Not surprisingly, members of in-groups are more satisfied and productive than members of out-groups. For that reason, LMX theorists have begun to explore ways in which leaders can develop close relationships with all of their followers.

Situational variables also complicate leader–follower interactions. Guidelines that work in ordinary times may break down under stressful conditions. A professor may state in her syllabus that five absences will result in flunking a class, for instance. However, she may have to loosen her standard if a flu epidemic strikes the campus.

Diverse followers, varying levels of relationships, and elements of the situation make consistency an ethical burden of leadership. Should all followers be treated equally even if some are more skilled and committed or closer to us than others? When should we bend the rules and for whom? Shadows arise when leaders appear to act arbitrarily and unfairly when faced with questions such as these, as in the case of a resident assistant who enforces dormitory rules for some students but ignores infractions committed by friends. Of course, determining whether a leader is casting light or shadow may depend on where you stand as a follower. When Michael Jordan played for the Chicago Bulls, Coach Phil Jackson allowed him more freedom than other players. Jordan was comfortable with this arrangement, but his teammates weren't as enthusiastic.

Issues of inconsistency can also arise in a leader's relationships with those outside the immediate group or organization. For example, until recent reforms, Merrill Lynch and other investment banks provided important clients with benefits denied ordinary investors. Investment banks manage the stock offerings of companies going public for the first time. Bankers gave executives doing business with their firms the opportunity to buy initial public offering (IPO) shares before the general public could. During the stock market boom of the 1990s, IPO stocks often increased dramatically in value in a matter of hours or days, creating a financial windfall for these privileged insiders.[23]

Misgivings about the current system of financing political elections stem from the fact that large donors can buy access to elected officials and influence their votes. Laws often favor those who have contributed the most, as in the case of the nation's oil companies. Critics charge that congressional representatives who receive more money from oil companies oppose legislation that would reduce demand for oil or increase clean energy supplies.[24]

THE SHADOW OF MISPLACED AND BROKEN LOYALTIES

Leaders must weigh a host of loyalties or duties when making choices. In addition to their duties to employees and stockholders, they must consider their obligations to their families, local communities, professions, larger society, and the environment. Noteworthy leaders put the needs of the larger community above selfish interests. For example, outdoor clothing manufacturer Timberland receives praise for its commitment to community service and social responsibility. Company leaders pay employees for volunteer service, partner with community groups, and support nonprofit organizations through the sale of selected products. In contrast, those who appear to put their interests first are worthy of condemnation. Executives at United Airlines were harshly criticized for profiting at the expense of employees and travelers. The company filed for bankruptcy, which allowed executives to dump pension funds, void labor contracts, and cut costs. A quarter of the workforce was laid off, and those remaining took significant pay cuts. Customer service suffered as a result. When United emerged from bankruptcy, 400 executives (some of whom had helped mismanage the airline into bankruptcy) ended up with 8% of the new firm, estimated to be worth more than $300 million. CEO Glenn Tilton alone received $40 million in stock and stock options.[25] (For another example of how the few benefited at the expense of the many, see the "It Pays to Be an Executive" case study at the end of this chapter.)

Loyalties can be broken as well as misplaced. If anything, we heap more scorn on those who betray our trust than on those who misplace their loyalties. Many of history's villains are traitors: Judas Iscariot, Benedict Arnold, Vidkun Quisling (he sold out his fellow Norwegians to the Nazis), and Tokyo Rose, a U.S. citizen who broadcast to American troops on behalf of the Japanese in World War II. Enron CEO Ken Lay is a contemporary example of a leader who violated the trust of followers (see Case Study 1.2). Lay betrayed employees by assuring them that the firm was in good shape even as it was headed towards collapse.

Mergers and acquisitions are common forms of corporate betrayal. Executives of the new conglomerate typically assure consumers that they will benefit from the merger. Quality and service will improve, not suffer, they claim. Employees are told that the best elements of their current companies will be maintained. Sadly, these promises are broken more often than not. Quality and service decline as the new firm cuts costs to pay for its expansion. Important corporate values such as family support and social responsibility are lost and benefits slashed. As egregious as these corporate examples of betrayal appear, they pale in comparison to cases of Catholic priests who sexually abused children in their care. As you'll see in Chapter 4, clergy in Boston, Portland, New Mexico, and elsewhere used their positions as respected spiritual authorities to gain access to young parishioners for sexual gratification. Bishops and cardinals failed to stop the abusers. In far too many cases, they let offending priests continue to minister and to have contact with children. Often church officials transferred pedophiles without warning their new congregations about these priests' troubled pasts.

The fact that I've placed the loyalty shadow after such concerns as power and privilege should not diminish its importance. Philosopher George Fletcher argues that we define ourselves through our loyalties to families, sports franchises, companies, and other groups and organizations.[26] Political strategist James Carville points out that the significance of loyalty is reflected in the central role it plays in drama. "Take apart any great story," he claims, "and there's loyalty at its heart."[27] As evidence of this fact, he points to Shakespeare's *Romeo and Juliet, The Godfather* trilogy, the HBO series *The Sopranos,* and even episodes of *The Andy Griffith Show* (Carville doesn't claim to have excellent taste).

You may think that Carville overstates his case but the fact remains that loyalty is a significant burden placed on leaders. In fact, well-placed loyalty can make a significant moral statement. Such was the case with Pee Wee Reese. The Brooklyn Dodger never wavered in his loyalty to Jackie Robinson, the first black player in the major leagues. In front of one especially hostile crowd in Cincinnati, Reese put his arm around Robinson's shoulders in a display of support.[28]

Pay particular attention to the shadow of loyalty as you analyze the feature films highlighted in each chapter. In most of these movies, leaders struggle with where to place their loyalties and how to honor the trust others have placed in them.

THE SHADOW OF IRRESPONSIBILITY

Earlier we noted that the breadth of responsibility is one of the factors distinguishing between the leader and follower roles. Followers are largely responsible for their own actions or, in the case of a self-directed work team, for their peers. This is not the case for leaders. They are held accountable for the performance of their entire department or unit. However, determining the extent of a leader's responsibility is far from easy. Can we blame a college coach for the misdeeds of team members during the off season or for the excesses of the university's athletic booster club? Are clothing executives responsible for the actions of their overseas contractors who force workers to work in sweatshops? Do employers owe employees a minimum wage level, a certain degree of job security, and safe working conditions? If military officers are punished for following unethical orders, should their supervisors receive the same or harsher penalties? Rabbis and pastors encourage members of their congregations to build strong marriages. Should they lose their jobs when they have affairs?

Leaders act irresponsibly when they fail to make reasonable efforts to prevent followers' misdeeds, ignore or deny ethical problems, don't shoulder responsibility for the consequences of their directives, deny their duties to followers, or hold followers to higher standards than themselves. We don't hold coaches responsible for everything their players do. Nonetheless, we want them to encourage their athletes to obey the law and to punish any misbehavior. Most of us expect the Gap, Nike, and Banana Republic to make every effort to treat their overseas labor force fairly, convinced that the companies owe their workers (even the ones employed by subcontractors) decent wages and working conditions. We generally believe that officers giving orders are as culpable as those carrying them out, and we have little tolerance for religious figures and others who violate their own ethical standards. For that reason, conservative talk show host Rush Limbaugh came under attack for urging harsh punishments for drug users at the same time he was addicted to prescription painkillers.[29]

Many corporate scandals demonstrate what can happen when boards of directors fail to live up to their responsibilities. Far too many boards in the past were rubber stamps. Made up largely of friends of the CEO and those doing business with the firm, they were quick to approve executive pay increases and other management proposals. Some directors appeared interested only in collecting their fees and made little effort to understand the company's operations or finances. Other board members were well intentioned but lacked expertise. Now federal regulations require that the chair of the audit committee be a financial expert. The compensation, audit, and nominating committees must be made up of people who have no financial ties to the organization. These requirements should help prevent future abuses, but only if directors take their responsibilities seriously.

These, then, are some of the common shadows cast by leaders faced with the ethical challenges of leadership. Identifying these shadows raises an important question: *Why is it, when faced with the same ethical challenges, that some leaders cast light and others cast shadows?* In the next chapter, we'll explore the forces that contribute to the shadow side of leadership. But first read Box 1.3 to learn about the ethical demands facing followers.

Implications and Applications

- Understanding the dark (bad, toxic) side of leadership is the first step in promoting good or ethical leadership.
- The contrast between ethical and unethical leadership is as dramatic as the contrast between light and darkness.
- "Toxic" or "bad" leaders engage in destructive behaviors. They may be ineffective, unethical, or both. Common types of bad leaders include incompetent, rigid, intemperate, callous, corrupt, insular, and evil.
- Certain ethical challenges or dilemmas are inherent in the leadership role. If you choose to become a leader, recognize that you accept ethical burdens along with new tasks, expectations, and rewards.

Box 1.3

Focus on Follower Ethics

THE DARK SIDE OF FOLLOWERSHIP

There is a dark side to followership, just as there is to leadership. Followers walk on the dark side when they fail to meet the moral responsibilities of their roles. Important ethical challenges confronted by followers include the following.

The Challenge of Obligation. Followers contribute to a shadowy atmosphere when they fail to fulfill their minimal responsibilities by coming to work late, taking extended breaks, not carrying out assignments, undermining the authority of their leaders, stealing supplies, and so on. However, they can also contribute to an unethical climate by taking on too many obligations. Employees forced to work mandatory overtime and salaried staff at many technology and consulting firms work 70–80 hours a week, leaving little time for family and personal interests. They experience stress and burnout, and their family relationships suffer.

Followers also have ethical duties to outsiders. Carpenters and other tradespeople have an obligation to buyers to build high-quality homes and to meet construction deadlines, for example. Government employees owe it to taxpayers to spend their money wisely by working hard while keeping expenses down.

These questions can help sort out the obligations we owe as followers.

- Am I doing all I reasonably can to carry out my tasks and further the mission of my organization? What more could I do?
- Am I fulfilling my obligations to outsiders (clients, neighbors, community, customers)? Are there any additional steps I should take?
- Am I giving back to the group or organization as much as I am taking from it?
- Am I carrying my fair share of the workload?
- Am I serving the needs of my leaders?
- Am I earning the salary and benefits I receive?
- Can I fulfill my organizational obligations and, at the same time, maintain a healthy personal life and productive relationships? If not, what can I do to bring my work and personal life into balance?

The Challenge of Obedience. Groups and organizations couldn't function if members refused to obey orders or adhere to policies, even the ones they don't like. As a result, followers have an ethical duty to obey. However, blindly following authority can drive followers to engage in illegal and immoral activities that they would never participate in on their own.

Obeying orders is no excuse for unethical behavior. Therefore, deciding when to disobey is critical. To make this determination, consider the following factors: Does this order appear to call for unethical behavior? Would I engage in this course of action if I weren't ordered to? What are the potential consequences for others if these directions are followed? For myself? Does obedience threaten the mission and health of the organization as a whole? What steps should I take if I decide to disobey?

The Challenge of Cynicism. There is a difference between healthy skepticism, which prevents followers from being exploited, and unhealthy cynicism, which undermines individual and group performance. Followers darken the atmosphere when

---

Box 1.3 (Continued)

they become organizational cynics. That's because cynicism destroys commitment and undermines trust. Collective performance suffers as a result. Few give their best effort when they are disillusioned with the group. Cynical employees feel less identification with and commitment to their employers while being more resistant to change. The greater the degree of cynicism, the more effort is directed toward attacking the organization at the expense of completing the task at hand.

The Challenge of Dissent. Expressing disagreement is an important ethical duty of followership. Followers should take issue with policies and procedures that are inefficient, harmful, or costly and with leaders who harm others or put the organization at risk. Doing so serves the mission of the organization while protecting the rights of its members and the larger community. Although followers contribute to shadowy environment when they fail to speak up, they can go too far by generating a constant stream of complaints. Ethical followers know when to speak up (not every issue is worth contesting) and when to wait until a more important issue comes along. They must also determine whether the problem is significant enough to justify going outside the organization (becoming a whistleblower) if leaders don't respond.

The Challenge of Bad News. Delivering bad news is risky business. Followers who tell their bosses that the project is over budget, that sales are down, or that the software doesn't work as promised may be verbally abused, demoted, or fired.

Organizations and leaders pay a high price when followers hide or cover up bad news, deny responsibility, or shift blame. Leaders can't correct problems they don't know exist. Failure to address serious deficiencies such as accounting fraud, cost overruns, and product contamination can destroy an organization. Leaders who don't get feedback about their ineffective habits (micromanaging, poor listening skills, indecisiveness) can't address these behaviors. Denying accountability and shifting blame undermine trust and shift people's focus from solving problems to defending themselves.

To avoid contributing to a shadow environment, followers must deliver bad news and accept responsibility for their actions. They also need to pay close attention to how they deliver bad tidings, selecting the right time, place, and message channel. Significant problems should be brought to the leader's attention immediately, when he or she is most receptive, and delivered face to face whenever possible, not through e-mail, faxes, and other less personal channels.

SOURCE: Adapted from Johnson, C. E. (2007). *Ethics in the workplace: Tools and tactics for organizational transformation.* Thousand Oaks, CA: Sage, Ch. 7.

Additional Sources

Bedian, A. G. (2007). Even if the tower is "ivory," it isn't "white": Understanding the consequences of faculty cynicism. *Academy of Management Learning and Education, 6,* 9–32.

Dean, J. W., Brandes, P., & Dharwadkar, R. (1998). Organizational cynicism. *Academy of Management Review, 23,* 341–352.

Roloff, M. E., & Paulson, G. D. (2001). Confronting organizational transgressions. In J. M. Darley, D. M. Messick, & T. R. Tyler (Eds.), *Social influences on ethical behavior in organizations* (pp. 53–68). Mahwah, NJ: Erlbaum.

Stanley, D. J., Meyer, J. P., & Topolnytsky, L. (2005). Employee cynicism and resistance to organizational change. *Journal of Business and Psychology, 19,* 429–459.

- *Power* may not be a dirty word, but it can have a corrosive effect on values and behavior. You must determine how much power to accumulate, what forms of power to use, and how much power to give to followers.
- Abuse of privilege is the evil twin of power. If you abuse power, you'll generally overlook the needs of followers as you take advantage of the perks that come with your position.
- Leaders have access to more information than followers. In addition to deciding whether or not to tell the truth, you'll have to determine when to reveal what you know and to whom, how to gather and use information, and so on.
- A certain degree of inconsistency is probably inevitable in leadership roles, but you'll cast shadows if you are seen as acting arbitrarily and unfairly.
- As a leader you'll have to balance your needs and the needs of your small group or organization with loyalties or duties to broader communities. Expect condemnation if you put narrow, selfish concerns first.
- Leadership brings a broader range of responsibility, but determining the limits of accountability may be difficult. You'll cast a shadow if you fail to make a reasonable attempt to prevent abuse or to shoulder the blame, deny that you have a duty to followers, or hold others to a higher ethical standard than you are willing to follow.

For Further Exploration, Challenge, and Self-Assessment

1. Create an ethics journal. In it, describe the ethical dilemmas you encounter as a leader and as a follower, how you resolved them, how you felt about the outcomes, and what you learned that will transfer to future ethical decisions. You may also want to include your observations about the moral choices made by public figures. Make periodic entries as you continue to read this text.

2. Rosabeth Kanter argues that "powerlessness corrupts and absolute powerlessness corrupts absolutely." Do you agree? What are some of the symptoms of powerlessness?

3. What factors do you consider when determining the extent of your loyalty to an individual, group, or organization?

4. Evaluate the work of a corporate or nonprofit board of directors. Is the board made up largely of outside members? Are directors qualified? Does the board fulfill its leadership responsibilities? Write up your findings.

5. Which shadow are you most likely to cast as a leader? Why? What can you do to cast light instead? Can you think of any other ethical shadows cast by leaders?

6. Look for examples of unethical leadership behavior in the news and classify them according to the six shadows. What patterns do you note?

7. What is the toughest ethical challenge of being a follower? How do you meet that challenge?

CASE STUDY 1.2

Chapter End Case: Casting Shadows at Enron

I n the 1990s, Enron was one of the fastest-growing, most admired companies in the United States. From its humble origins as a regional natural gas supplier, the Houston firm grew to become the seventh largest company of the *Fortune 500*. In 2000, the company employed 21,000 people, and its stock hit an all-time high of $90 per share.

Enron appeared regularly on lists of the nation's best companies, receiving accolades for its innovative climate. The firm focused on energy transportation, trading, and financing and developed new ways to market nontraditional commodities. Founder and CEO Kenneth Lay was profiled in a number of business magazines, gave generously to local charities, and golfed regularly with presidents Clinton and Bush.

Rising stock values and revenues were the glue that held the company together. To keep debt (which would lower the price of the stock by lowering earnings) off the books, chief financial officer Andrew Fastow created special purpose entities. These limited partnerships with outside investors enable firms to share risks while hiding deficits. Although special purpose entities are legal and used in many industries, Enron's partnerships didn't have enough outside investors. In essence, the company was insuring itself. Employees who managed these investments made millions while acting against the best interests of the firm.

In 2001, losses in overseas projects and a major subsidiary caused a financial meltdown. Enron's stock price dropped, and the company was unable to back its guarantees. Financial analysts and journalists who had previously sung the company's praises began to question Enron's financial statements. In the midst of the unfolding disaster, Chairman Lay repeatedly assured employees that the stock was solid. At one point he declared, "Our performance has never been stronger; our business model has never been more robust; our growth has never been more certain." At the same time he was making these optimistic pronouncements, Lay and other officials were calling Bush cabinet members to ask them to intervene on the firm's behalf. Arthur Andersen auditors then forced the company to restate earnings, and the Securities and Exchange Commission began to investigate.

Enron filed for bankruptcy in December 2001, and in January 2002 Lay resigned. Both Fastow and his deputy pled guilty for their roles in creating and managing the illegal partnerships. Enron energy traders also entered guilty pleas for manipulating electricity markets. In 2006, both Skilling and Lay were convicted of conspiracy and fraud for lying about the company's financial health and condoning illegal accounting practices. Lay died of a heart attack before entering jail. Skilling is currently serving a 24-year sentence. The government is seeking millions in restitution from Skilling and from Lay's estate and his wife, Linda.

Greed, pride, lack of internal controls, pressure to make quarterly earnings projections, and other factors all played a role in Enron's collapse. However, most of blame must go to the firm's executives, who failed to meet each of the challenges of leadership described in this chapter. Leaders at Enron cast shadows in the following ways:

Abuse of Power. Both Lay and Jeffrey Skilling (Lay's short-term replacement) wielded power ruthlessly. Lay routinely demoted vice-chairs who disagreed with him, and Skilling frequently intimidated subordinates.

Excess Privilege. Excess typified top management at Enron. Lay told a friend, "I don't want to be rich; I want to be world-class rich." At another point he joked that he had given his wife, Linda, a $2 million decorating budget for a new home in Houston, which she promptly exceeded. Lay and other executives were able to unload their shares even as the 401(k) accounts of employees (made up largely of Enron stock) were wiped out.

Mismanaged Information. Enron officials manipulated information to protect their interests and to deceive the public. Both executives and board members claimed that they weren't aware of the company's off-the-books partnerships and shaky financial standing. However, both Skilling and Lay were warned that the firm's accounting tactics were suspect, and the Senate Permanent Subcommittee on Investigations concluded, "Much that was wrong with Enron was known to the board."

Inconsistent Treatment of Internal and External Constituencies. Five hundred Enron officials received "retention bonuses" totaling $55 million after the firm filed for bankruptcy. At the same time, laid-off workers received only a fraction of the severance pay they had been promised. Outsiders also received inconsistent treatment. The company was generous with its friends. As the top contributor to the Bush campaign, Enron used this leverage to nominate friendly candidates to serve on the Securities and Exchange Commission and the Federal Energy Regulatory Commission. Company representatives also helped set federal energy policy that deregulated additional energy markets for Enron's benefit. In contrast, critics of the company could expect retribution. Investment bankers who expressed the least bit of doubt about Enron lost underwriting business from the firm. Critical stock analysts lost their jobs.

Misplaced and Broken Loyalties. Leaders at Enron put their loyalty to themselves above everyone else with a stake in the company's fate: stockholders, business partners, ratepayers, local communities, and foreign governments. They also abused the trust of those who worked for them. Employees felt betrayed in addition to losing their jobs and retirement savings.

Irresponsibility. Enron's leaders acted irresponsibly by failing to take needed action, failing to exercise proper oversight, and failing to shoulder responsibility for the ethical miscues of their organization. CEO Lay downplayed warnings of financial improprieties, and some board members didn't understand the company's finances or operations. Too often managers left employees to their own devices, encouraging them to achieve financial goals by any means possible. Neither CEO stepped forward to accept blame for what happened after the firm's collapse. Lay invoked Fifth Amendment privileges against self-incrimination; Skilling claimed ignorance.

DISCUSSION PROBES

1. Which attitudes and behaviors of Enron's leaders do you find most offensive? Why?

2. Did one shadow caster play a more important role than the others in causing the collapse of Enron? If so, which one and why?

3. How much responsibility should the board of directors assume for what happened at Enron?

4. What similarities do you see between what happened at Enron and at other well-known companies accused of ethical wrongdoing?

5. What can be done to prevent future Enrons?

6. What leadership ethics lessons do you draw from this case?

SOURCES: Adapted from Johnson, C. E. (2002). *Enron's ethical collapse: Lessons from the top.* Paper delivered at the National Communication Association convention, New Orleans, LA; Johnson, C. E. (2003). Enron's ethical collapse: Lessons for leadership educators. *Journal of Leadership Education, 2.* Retrieved February 7, 2004, from http://www.fhsu.edu/jole/issues/archive_index.html.

ADDITIONAL SOURCES

Hays, K. (2007, May 24). Linda Lay files against forfeiture. *The Houston Chronicle,* Business, p. 3. Retrieved June 19, 2007, from LexisNexis Academic database.

Mulligan, T. S. (2006, May 26). The Enron verdicts. *Los Angeles Times,* p. A1. Retrieved June 19, 2007, from LexisNexis Academic database.

Weidlich, T., & Calkins, L. B. (2006, October 24). Skilling jailed 24 years. *National Post,* p. FP1. Retrieved June 19, 2007, from LexisNexis Academic database.

CASE STUDY 1.3

Chapter End Case: It Pays to Be an Executive

The Stock Options Scandal

The 1990s saw the advent of stock options designed to tie executive compensation to company performance. Firms grant CEOs and other corporate officers the option to buy company stock at a set price. If the price of the stock goes up, the CEO and his or her colleagues can then sell their shares at the higher price, pocketing the difference. However, if the stock price goes down, the options lose their value.

CEOs soon found ways to manipulate stock options through a process called backdating. In backdating, the date of the stock option grant is shifted to increase the value of the options. Typically the new date falls when the share price was at a low point or just before the release of positive news that boosted the company's stock price. Undisclosed backdated options violate federal rules against false financial disclosures. They can inflate corporate profits and result in the underpayment of taxes. Earnings have to be reduced when backdating is uncovered, lowering the stock price and hurting investors.

The backdating scandal is still unfolding, but at last count more than one hundred publicly traded companies were under federal investigation, with others doing internal reviews. More than $5 billion in profits has been restated. A number of CEOs have been forced out, and executives at Brocade Communication Systems and Comverse Technology have been indicted. Backdating was particularly popular at high-tech companies (Mercury Interactive and McAfee are among the other technology firms under scrutiny) because executives in the Silicon Valley often sit on each other's boards. In this tightly knit social circle, the practice spread rapidly, and few were willing to challenge the behavior of their colleagues. However, questions have also been raised about the timing of stock options at Costco, Barnes & Noble, UnitedHealth Group, Staples, and Home Depot.

In some cases, CEOs changed the dates of the options on their own or recorded dates different from those set out by the board. In other cases, boards ordered the dates changed or gave executives the power to do so. Employees also played a role in the scandal. Members of the accounting and human resource departments, for example, recorded the date changes and helped in the cover up. At Brocade Communication Systems, maker of network storage switches, human resource managers altered the employment records of several new executives to it make appear that they joined the company later than they actually did. This inflated the value of their stock options because share prices had dropped since they were hired. Managers at other firms were asked to start employees as part timers so they could get options sooner as the stock price went up.

University of Iowa professor Erik Lie, who conducted the study that uncovered the widespread manipulation of stock options, believes that executives and boards knew that the practice was unethical. "A lot of executives thought that, although they knew it was not acceptable, they were not likely to be detected. In some cases [directors] got bad advice. In some cases they knew it was wrong. In most cases, people knew it was not quite ethical."[1]

DISCUSSION PROBES

1. What proportion of the blame for the scandal do you assign to the CEOs involved? The boards of directors? Employees?

2. How can future backdating scandals be prevented?

3. Do you think that the practice of granting stock options should be outlawed? Why? Why not?

4. How can corporations ensure that both leaders and followers are rewarded when companies perform well?

5. What can be done to encourage executives to put the interests of shareholders ahead of their own interests?

6. What leadership ethics lessons do you draw from this case?

NOTE

1. Stecklow, S. (2006, July 20). How one company played with timing of stock options. *Associated Press Financial Wire*. Retrieved June 20, 2007, from LexisNexis Academic database, para. 24.

SOURCES

Gordon, M. (2006, June 9). Role of directors is piece of puzzle as scandal over stock options widens. *Associated Press Financial Wire*. Retrieved June 20, 2007, from LexisNexis Academic database.

Gordon, M. (2006, December 12). Toll of options timing scandal heavy in 2006; more cases expected next year. *Associated Press Financial Wire*. Retrieved June 20, 2007, from LexisNexis Academic database.

Krugan, P. (2006, October 20). Incentives for the dead. *The New York Times,* p. A23. Retrieved June 20, 2007, from LexisNexis Academic database.

Liedtke, M. (2006, November 9). Chummy CEOs now part of Silicon Valley's backdating club. *Associated Press Financial Wire*. Retrieved June 20, 2007, from LexisNexis Academic database.

Phelps, D. (2006, October 6). A quiet Viking sniffed out a stock-option scandal. *Minneapolis Star Tribune*. Retrieved June 20, 2007, from LexisNexis Academic database.

Notes

1. Palmer, P. (1996). Leading from within. In L. C. Spears (Ed.), *Insights on leadership: Service, stewardship, spirit, and servant-leadership* (pp. 197–208). New York: Wiley, p. 200.

2. Jung, C. B. (1933). *Modern man in search of a soul.* New York: Harcourt.

3. Palmer, p. 200.

4. Lipman-Blumen, J. (2005). *The allure of toxic leaders: Why we follow destructive bosses and corrupt politicians—and how we can survive them.* Oxford, UK: Oxford University Press.

5. Kellerman, B. (2004). *Bad leadership: What it is, how it happens, why it matters.* Boston: Harvard Business School Press.

6. Kellerman, p. xvi.

7. French, R. P., & Raven, B. (1959). The bases of social power. In D. Cartwright, *Studies in social power* (pp. 150–167). Ann Arbor: University of Michigan, Institute for Social Research.

8. Hackman, M. Z., & Johnson, C. E. (2003). *Leadership: A communication perspective* (4th ed.). Prospect Heights, IL: Waveland, Ch. 5.

9. Kanter, R. M. (1979, July–August). Power failure in management circuits. *Harvard Business Review, 57,* 65–75.

10. Pfeffer, J. (1992, Winter). Understanding power in organizations. *California Management Review, 34,* (2), 29–50.

11. Hornstein, H. A. (1996). *Brutal bosses and their prey.* New York: Riverhead.

12. Keltner, D., Langner, C. A., & Allison, M. L. (2006). Power and moral leadership. In D. L. Rhode (Ed.), *Moral leadership: The theory and practice of power, judgment, and policy* (pp. 177–194). San Francisco: Jossey-Bass.

13. Fiske, S. T. (1993). Controlling other people: The impact of power on stereotyping. *American Psychologist, 48,* 621–628.

14. Lublin, J. S. (2006, October 12). Executive pay soars despite attempted restraints. *Associated Press Financial Wire.* Retrieved January 22, 2007, from LexisNexis Academic database.

15. Huffington, A. (2003). *Pigs at the trough: How corporate greed and political corruption are undermining America.* New York: Crown; Lublin, Executive pay soars; Grow, B., Foust, D., Thornton, E., Farzad, R., McGregor, J., Zegle, S., et al. (2007, January 15). Out at Home Depot. *Business Week,* pp. 56–62. Retrieved January 22, 2007, from Business Source Premiere database.

16. Bing, S. (2000). *What would Machiavelli do? The ends justify the meanness.* New York: HarperBusiness.

17. Income disparity statistic taken from Sachs, J. (2007, May 27). Sharing the wealth. *Time,* p. 81. Data about the AIDS epidemic taken from Seston, A. (2006, December 6). AIDS day draws attention to epidemic. *The Daily Cardinal.* Retrieved June 13, 2007, from LexisNexis Academic database.

18. Goodman, E. (2002, October 6). Freeze-frame nation. *The Oregonian,* p. C3.

19. Brissett, D., & Edgely, C. (Eds.). (1990). The dramaturgical perspective. In D. Brissett & C. Edgley (Eds.), *Life as theater: A dramaturgical sourcebook* (2nd ed., pp. 1–46). New York: Aldine de Gruyter.

20. Brown, D. J., Scott, K. A., & Lewis, H. (2004). Information processing and leadership. In J. Antonakis, A. T. Cianciolo, & R. J. Sternberg (Eds.), *The nature of leadership* (pp. 125–147). Thousand Oaks, CA: Sage.

21. Rosenfeld, P., Giacalone, R. A., & Riordan, C. A. (1995). *Impression management in organizations: Theory, measurement, practice.* London: Routledge.

22. For more information on LMX theory, see:

> Graen, G. B., & Cashman, J. F. (1975). A role-making model of leadership in formal organizations. In J. G. Hunt & L. L. Larson (Eds.), *Leadership frontiers* (pp. 143–165). Kent, OH: Kent State University Press.
>
> Graen, G. B., & Scandura, T. (1987). Toward a psychology of dyadic organizing. *Research in Organizational Behavior, 9,* 175–208.
>
> Graen, G. B., & Uhl-Bien, M. (1998). Relationship-based approach to leadership. Development of leader–member exchange (LMX) theory of leadership over 25 years: Applying a multi-level multi-domain perspective. In F. Dansereau & F. J. Yammarino (Eds.), *Leadership: The multiple-level approaches* (pp. 103–158). Stamford, CT: JAI Press.
>
> Vecchio, R. P. (1982). A further test of leadership effects due to between-group variation and in-group variation. *Journal of Applied Psychology, 67,* 200–208.

23. Time to outlaw sweetheart IPOs. (2003, May 16). *Rocky Mountain News,* p. 46A. Retrieved February 7, 2004, from LexisNexis Academic database.

24. Campaign contributions from big oil sharply influenced votes on clean energy. (2006, November 1). *U.S. Newswire.* Retrieved June 19, 2007, from LexisNexis Academic database.

25. Shared sacrifice? Not for these airline executives. (2006, February 2). *USA Today.* Retrieved June 9, 2007, from LexisNexis Academic database.

26. Fletcher, G. (1993). *Loyalty: An essay on the morality of relationships.* New York: Oxford University Press.

27. Carville, J. (2000). *Stickin': The case for loyalty.* New York: Simon & Schuster.

28. Rampersad, A. (1997). *Jackie Robinson.* New York: Alfred A. Knopf.

29. Skoloff, B. (2006, April 29). Both Limbaugh and prosecutors can declare victory in deal. *The Associated Press.* Retrieved June 18, 2007, from LexisNexis Academic database.

2

Shadow Casters

Darkness is most likely to get a "hold" when you are safely settled in the good and righteous position, where nothing can assail you. When you are absolutely right is the most dangerous position of all, because, most probably, the devil has already got you by the throat.

—Psychotherapist Edward Edinger

What's Ahead

In this chapter, we look at why leaders cast shadows instead of light. Shadow casters include (1) unhealthy motivations, (2) faulty decision making caused by errors in thinking, (3) an inactive or overactive moral imagination, (4) ethical deficiencies (ethical ignorance and ethical flabbiness that comes from a lack of moral exercise), and (5) contextual (group, organizational, societal) pressures that encourage people to set their personal standards aside. To address these shadow casters, we need to engage in development aimed at expanding our ethical capacity as leaders. Effective leader development programs incorporate assessment, challenge, and support and broaden our knowledge, skills, perspectives, and motivation.

Only humans seem to be troubled by the question "why?" Unlike other creatures, we analyze past events (particularly the painful ones) to determine their causes. The urge to understand and to account for the ethical failures of leaders has taken on added urgency with the recent spate of corporate scandals. Observers wonder, why would bright, talented CEOs steal from their companies, lie to investors, engage in insider trading, use corporate jets to move family furniture, and avoid taxes? Why can't multimillionaire executives be satisfied with what they already have? Why do they feel they need more? (See Box 2.1 for one set of answers to these questions.)

Coming up with an explanation provides a measure of comfort and control. If we can understand *why* something bad has happened (broken relationships, cruelty, betrayal), we may be able to put it behind us and move on. We are also better equipped to prevent something similar from happening again. Such is the case with shadows. Identifying the reasons for our ethical failures (what I'll call "shadow casters") is the first step to stepping out of the darkness they create.

As you read about the shadow casters, keep in mind that human behavior is seldom the product of just one factor. For example, leaders struggling with insecurities are particularly vulnerable to external pressures. Faulty decision making and inexperience often go hand in hand; we're more prone to make poor moral choices because we haven't had much practice.

Shadow Casters

UNHEALTHY MOTIVATIONS

Internal Enemies or Monsters

Parker Palmer believes that leaders project shadows out of their inner darkness. That's why he urges leaders to pay special attention to their motivations lest "the act of leadership create more harm than good." Palmer identifies five internal enemies or "monsters" living within leaders that produce unethical behavior.[1] I'll include one additional monster to round out the list.

Monster 1: Insecurity. Leaders often are deeply insecure people who mask their inner doubts through extroversion and by tying their identity to their roles as leaders. Who they are is inextricably bound to what they do. Leaders project their insecurities on others when they use followers to serve their selfish needs.

Monster 2: Battleground Mentality. Leaders often use military images when carrying out their tasks, speaking of "wins" and "losses," "allies" and "enemies," and "doing battle" with the competition. For example, former IBM chief Lou Gerstner inspired hatred of Microsoft by projecting a picture of Bill Gates on a large screen and telling his managers, "This man wakes up hating you."[2] Acting competitively becomes a self-fulfilling prophecy; competition begets competitive responses in return. This militaristic approach can be counterproductive. More often than not, cooperation is more productive than competition (see Chapter 8). Instead of pitting departments against each other, for instance, a growing number of companies use cross-functional project teams and task forces to boost productivity.

Box 2.1

The Warped Minds of Top CEOs

Writers at *USA Today* asked a group of corporate psychologists to describe the internal motivation of greedy top executives. The experts concluded that the seemingly insatiable desires of out-of-control CEOs have less to do with money and more to do with the following.

Poor Self-Image. Many CEOs (e.g., Martha Stewart) have low self-esteem and want to put their humble pasts behind them. They try to make up for their feelings of inadequacy by building monuments to themselves. Sadly, this strategy never works.

The "I Deserve It" Myth. Many C-level executives believe that they should get all the credit for their firms' success. This type of reasoning accounts for Jack Welch's belief that he deserved the lavish retirement package originally granted to him at retirement.

Unchecked Fantasies. The desires of most people are controlled by harsh reality. We don't have the money or power to make our dreams come true. Not so with some CEOs. Boards of directors or public opinion didn't rein them in, so they were free to do what they wanted, no matter how outrageous.

Society's Blessing. CEOs have gotten the message that they can do whatever they want as long as they produce results. The media have fueled this belief by making business executives heroes with the same status as sports stars.

Competitiveness Gone Awry. Corporate executives compete with their peers for higher and higher salaries and perks.

Lonesome Soldier Syndrome. People at the top find it hard to make friends because they fear that others are attracted only by their power. Expensive things then take the place of relationships.

Boredom. Many CEOs at the peak of their careers don't know what to do next. They may invent new challenges that put them in moral jeopardy.

Power Corrupts. Executives lose the sense of what is rightfully theirs and what isn't. They become like medieval kings, treating others like peasants and claiming all that they see.

SOURCE: Horovitz, B. (2002, October 11). Scandals grow out of CEOs warped mind-set. *USA Today,* pp. 1B–2B.

Monster 3: Functional Atheism. Functional atheism is a leader's belief that she or he has the ultimate responsibility for everything that happens in a group or organization. "It is the unconscious, unexamined conviction within us that if anything decent is going to happen here, I am the one who needs to make it happen."[3] This shadow destroys both leaders and followers. Symptoms include high stress, broken relationships and families, workaholism, burnout, and mindless activity.

Monster 4: Fear. Fear of chaos drives many leaders to stifle dissent and innovation. They emphasize rules and procedures instead of creativity and consolidate their power instead of sharing it with followers. (To see how fear motivates followers, see Box 2.2.)

Monster 5: Denying Death. Our culture as a whole denies the reality of death, and leaders, in particular, don't want to face the fact that projects and programs should die if they're no longer useful. Leaders also deny death through their fear of negative evaluation and public failure. Those who fail should be given an opportunity to learn from their mistakes, not be punished. Only a few executives display the wisdom of IBM founder Thomas Watson. A young executive entered his office after making a $10-million blunder and began the conversation by saying, "I guess you want my resignation." Watson answered, "You can't be serious. We've just spent $10 million educating you!"[4]

Monster 6: Evil. There are lots of other demons lurking in leaders and followers alike—jealousy, envy, rage—but I want to single out evil for special consideration. Palmer doesn't specifically mention evil as an internal monster, but it is hard to ignore the fact that some people seem driven by a force more powerful than anxiety or fear. Teenage insecurities and a desire to vanquish their enemies sparked the murderous rampage of Dylan Klebold and Eric Harris at Columbine High. However, these factors don't totally explain how these privileged suburban children became heartless killers. Evil may help us answer the question "why?" when we're confronted with monstrous shadows such as those cast by the Columbine shooters, the gunman at Virginia Tech University, or the terrorists who destroyed the World Trade Center.

Selfishness

A great deal of destructive leadership behavior is driven by self-centeredness, which manifests itself through pride, greed, and narcissism. Self-centered leaders are proud of themselves and their accomplishments. They lack empathy for others and can't see other points of view or learn from followers. They are too important to do "little things" such as making their own coffee or standing in line, so they hire others to handle these tasks for them.[5] Their focus is on defending their turf and maintaining their status instead of on cooperating with other groups to serve the common good. Ego-driven leaders ignore creative ideas and valuable data that come from outside their circle of influence.

Box 2.2

Focus on Follower Ethics

FOLLOWER MOTIVATIONS
AND THE DANGERS OF TOXIC LEADERSHIP

Leadership expert Jean Lipman-Blumen argues that followers have deep-seated psycho-logical needs and fears that make them seek leaders. However, we need to make sure that these motivations, which can drive us toward good leaders, don't drive us into the arms of toxic leaders instead.

A Need for Parent Figures. As children, we depend heavily on caretakers who have far more power than we do. Obedience to these authorities keeps us safe and feeling loved. As adults, we may look for other authority figures to meet our needs and obey their directives. If we haven't resolved our issues with our parents, we are likely to have similar issues with our leaders. Negative role models (authoritative, abusive, demeaning) often encourage follow-ers to seek out similar toxic leaders later in life.

Exchanging Freedom for Security. Reaching adulthood is both liberating and frightening. Freedom allows people to be themselves but can produce a sense of isolation. Insecure follow-ers often give up their freedom in order to join unethical leaders and destructive causes.

The Need to Feel Chosen. Feeling special is a powerful motivator. Bad leaders take advantage of that fact by convincing followers that they are part of a unique organization or cause that is better than all others. Joining with these leaders becomes "a route not simply to safety but to victory and glory" (p. 37). Driven by a feeling of superiority, group members may con-vert outsiders, dominate them, absorb them into the group, or even kill them.

The Need for Community. The need to belong is intertwined with the need to feel special. Humans are social animals, defined in large part by their communities. Group membership provides security and meaning and equips individuals to deal with their fears. People will sacrifice a great deal to maintain their group memberships. They will endure abusive treat-ment from their leaders, for instance, obey unethical orders, accept low wages, and so on.

Fear of Ostracism, Isolation, and Social Death. Speaking out against an unethical leader, organization, or cause brings ostracism ("social death") that keeps followers from dis-senting. Whistle blowers, those who go public with complaints or concerns, can expect a hostile reaction as peers, friends, and even family members turn against them. They may be demoted, fired, shunned by neighbors, threatened with violence, and so on.

A Sense of Personal Weakness and Powerlessness. Followers who otherwise feel competent find it intimidating to challenge a toxic leader. Instead, they try to adapt, change themselves, or escape from the situation, not realizing that expressing dissent might empower others to do the same. Toxic leaders play on follower fears by isolating dissenters and rewarding their backers. They reinforce their powerful images by mobilizing displays of support while attacking and eliminating those they identify as enemies.

SOURCE: Adapted from Lipman-Blumen, J. (2005). *The allure of toxic leaders: Why we follow destructive bosses and corrupt politicians—and how we can survive them.* Oxford, UK: Oxford University Press, Ch. 2.

Greed is another hallmark of self-oriented leaders. They are driven to earn more (no matter how much they are currently paid) and to accumulate additional perks. Greed focuses attention on making the numbers—generating more sales, increasing earnings, boosting the stock price, collecting more donations. In the process of reaching these financial goals, the few often benefit at the expense of the many, casting the shadow of privilege described in Chapter 1.

A great number of scandals can be attributed directly to greed. Salespeople at Lucent Technology pressured customers into buying products they couldn't afford, for instance.[6] Officials at insurance broker Marsh & McLennan rigged bids in return for kickbacks. Quest CEO Sam Nacchio enriched himself by stock trades based on inside information.[7] However, Martha Stewart may provide the most vivid example of the power of greed. Stewart served jail time and put her corporate empire at risk to save a few thousand dollars (just a small fraction of her billion-dollar net worth) on a stock sale and then lied to cover up her actions.[8]

Narcissism is the third manifestation of self-centeredness. The word *narcissism* has its origins in an ancient Greek fable. In this tale, Narcissus falls in love with the image of himself he sees reflected in a pond. Like their ancient namesake, modern-day narcissists are self-absorbed. They like attention and feel entitled to their power and positions. They also have an unrealistic sense of what they can accomplish.[9]

Narcissistic leaders engage in a wide range of unethical behaviors. They claim special privileges, demand obedience, abuse power for their personal ends, ignore the welfare of others, and have an autocratic leadership style. In extreme cases (Hitler and Stalin, for example), they can be hyperaggressive, exploitive, and sadistic. Narcissists put their groups, organizations, and countries at risk because their dreams and visions are unrealistic and can't be implemented. For example, Napoleon stretched France's resources beyond the breaking point. (Turn to Case Study 2.2 to read about another narcissistic French leader.)

FAULTY DECISION MAKING

Identifying dysfunctional motivations is a good first step in explaining the shadow side of leadership. Yet well-meaning, well-adjusted leaders can also cast shadows, as in the decision to storm the Branch Davidian compound in Waco, Texas, in 1993. Instead of waiting for the cult members to surrender peacefully (as they did 2 years later in the Montana Freemen case), FBI agents and other law enforcement officers launched a tank and tear gas attack. Eighty cult members, including some of the children whom officials were trying to protect, died. The failed mission fanned antigovernment sentiment.[10]

Blame for many ethical miscues can be placed on the way in which ethical decisions are made. Moral reasoning, though focused on issues of right and wrong, shares much in common with other forms of decision making. Making a wise ethical choice involves many of the same steps as making other important decisions: identifying the issue, gathering information, deciding on criteria, weighing options, and so on. A breakdown anywhere along the way can derail the process.

Decision-making experts David Messick and Max Bazerman speculate that many unethical business decisions aren't the product of greed or callousness but stem instead from widespread weaknesses in how people process information and make decisions. In particular, executives have faulty theories about how the world operates, about other people, and about themselves.[11]

Theories About How the World Operates. These assumptions have to do with determining the consequences of choices, judging risks, and identifying causes. Executives generally fail to take into account all the implications of their decisions (see Box 2.3). They overlook low-probability events, fail to consider all the affected parties, think they can hide their unethical behavior from the public, and downplay long-range consequences. In determining risk, decision-makers generally fail to acknowledge that many events happen by chance or are out of their control. America's involvement in Vietnam, for example, was predicated on the mistaken assumption that the United States could successfully impose its will in the region. Other times, leaders and followers misframe risks, thus minimizing the dangers. For instance, a new drug seems more desirable when it is described as working half of the time rather than as failing half of the time.

The perception of causes is the most important of all our theories about the world because determining responsibility is the first step to assigning blame or praise. In the United States, we're quick to criticize the person when larger systems are at fault. Consider the Sears automotive repair scandal, for example. Investigators discovered that Sears automotive technicians, who were paid commissions based on the number and cost of the repairs they ordered, charged customers for unnecessary work. Although the mechanics ought to be held accountable for their actions, the commission system was also at fault. Executives should be blamed for creating a program that rewarded dishonesty. Messick and Bazerman also point out that we're more likely to blame someone else for acting immorally than for failing to act. We condemn the executive who steals. However, we are less critical of the executive who doesn't disclose the fact that another manager is incompetent.

Theories About Other People. These are "our organized beliefs about how 'we' differ from 'they'" (competitors, suppliers, managers, employees, ethnic groups). Such beliefs, which we may not be aware of, influence how we treat other people. Ethnocentrism and stereotyping are particularly damaging. *Ethnocentrism* is the tendency to think that we are better than they, that our way of doing things is superior to theirs. We then seek out (socialize with, hire) others who look and act

Box 2.3

Decision-Making Biases

Theories of the World

- Ignoring low-probability events even when they could have serious consequences later
- Limiting the search for stakeholders and thus overlooking the needs of important groups
- Ignoring the possibility that the public will find out about an action
- Discounting the future by putting immediate needs ahead of long-term goals
- Underestimating the impact of a decision on a collective group (e.g., industry, city, profession)
- Acting as if the world is certain instead of unpredictable
- Failure to acknowledge and confront risk
- Framing risk differently from followers
- Blaming people when larger systems are at fault
- Excusing those who fail to act when they should

Theories About Other People

- Believing that our group is normal and ordinary (good) whereas others are strange and inferior (bad)
- Giving special consideration and aid to members of the in-group
- Judging and evaluating according to group membership (stereotyping)

Theories About Ourselves

- Rating ourselves more highly than other people
- Underestimating the likelihood that negative things will happen to us, such as divorce, illness, accidents, and addictions
- Believing that we can control random events
- Overestimating our contributions and the contributions of departments and organizations
- Overconfidence, which prevents us from learning more about a situation
- Concluding that the normal rules and obligations don't apply to us

SOURCE: Messick, D. M., & Bazerman, M. H. (1996, Winter). Ethical leadership and the psychology of decision making. *Sloan Management Review, 37*(2), 9–23. See also Bazerman, M. H. (1986). *Management in managerial decision making.* New York: Wiley. Table reprinted from Hackman, M. Z., & Johnson, C. E. (2008). *Leadership: A communication perspective* (5th ed.). Prospect Heights, IL: Waveland. Reprinted by permission.

like us. Military leaders often fall into the trap of ethnocentrism when they underestimate the ability of the enemy to resist hardships. For example, commanders have no trouble believing that their own citizens will survive repeated bombings but don't think that civilian populations in other nations can do the same. Such was the case in World War II. The British thought that bombing Berlin would break the spirit of the Germans, forgetting that earlier German air raids on London had failed to drive Britain out of the war. Similar reasoning fed into the decision to storm the Branch Davidian compound. FBI officers underestimated the commitment of Koresh and his followers to their cause. They thought that Koresh was afraid of physical harm and would surrender rather than risk injury. Instead, he led his followers in a mass suicide.[12]

Stereotypes, our beliefs about other groups of people, are closely related to ethnocentrism. These theories (women are weaker than men, the mentally challenged can't do productive work) can produce a host of unethical outcomes, including sexual and racial discrimination. (We'll take a closer look at ethnocentrism and stereotyping in Chapter 10.)

Theories About Ourselves. These faulty theories involve self-perceptions. Leaders need to have a degree of confidence to make tough decisions, but their self-images are often seriously distorted. Executives tend to think they (and their organizations) are superior, are immune to disasters, and can control events. No matter how fair they want to be, leaders tend to favor themselves when making decisions. Top-level managers argue that they deserve larger offices, more money, and stock options because their divisions contribute more to the success of the organization. Overconfidence is also a problem for decision makers because it seduces them into thinking that they have all the information they need, so they fail to learn more. Even when they do seek additional data, they're likely to interpret new information according to their existing biases.

Unrealistic self-perceptions of all types put leaders at ethical risk. Executives may claim that they have a "right" to steal company property because they are vital to the success of the corporation. Over time they may come to believe that they aren't subject to the same rules as everyone else. University of Richmond leadership studies professor Terry Price argues that leader immorality generally stems from such mistaken beliefs.[13] Leaders know right from wrong but often make exceptions for (justify) their own behavior. They are convinced that their leadership positions exempt them from following traffic laws or from showing up to meetings on time, for example. They may justify immoral behavior such as lying or intimidating followers on the grounds that it is the only way to protect the country or to save the company. Unethical leaders may also decide (with the support of followers) that the rules of morality apply only to the immediate group and not to outsiders. Excluding others from moral considerations (from moral membership) justified such unethical practices as slavery and colonization in the past. In recent times, this logic has been used to deny legal protections to suspected terrorists.

The loftier a leader's position, the greater the chances that he or she will overestimate his or her abilities. Powerful leaders are particularly likely to think they are godlike, believing they are omniscient (all knowing), omnipotent (all powerful), and invulnerable (safe from all harm).[14] Top leaders can mistakenly conclude they know everything because they have access to many different sources of information and followers look to them for answers. They believe that they can do whatever they want because they have so much power. Surrounded by an entourage of subservient staff members, these same officials are convinced that they will be protected from the consequences of their actions. Former President Clinton's affair with Monica Lewinsky demonstrates the impact of these delusions. Caught up in the power of his position, Clinton didn't expect to be found out or to face negative repercussions from his actions.

INACTIVE OR OVERACTIVE MORAL IMAGINATION

According to many ethicists, moral imagination—sensitivity to moral issues and options—is the key to ethical behavior.[15] University of Virginia professor Patricia Werhane offers an extended definition of moral imagination. Those with moral imagination are sensitive to ethical dilemmas, she argues, but can also detach themselves from the immediate situation in order to see the bigger picture. They recognize their typical ways of thinking and set aside these normal operating rules to come up with creative solutions that are "novel, economically viable, and morally justifiable."[16]

Werhane cites Merck CEO Roy Vagelos as one example of a leader with a vivid moral imagination. He proceeded with the development of the drug Mectizan, which treats the parasite that causes river blindness in Africa and South America, even though developing the product would be expensive with little hope that patients in poor countries could pay for it.[17] When relief agencies didn't step forward to fund and distribute the drug, Merck developed its own distribution systems in poor nations. Lost income from the drug totaled more than $200 million, but the number of victims (who are filled with globs of worms that cause blindness and death) dropped dramatically. In contrast, NASA engineer Roger Boisjoly recognized the ethical problem of launching the *Challenger* shuttle in cold weather in 1985 but failed to generate a creative strategy for preventing the launch. He stopped objecting and deferred to management (normal operating procedure). Boisjoly made no effort to go outside the chain of command to express his concerns to the agency director or to the press. The *Challenger* exploded upon liftoff, killing all seven aboard. (Turn to Chapter 8 for a description of the more recent *Columbia* shuttle disaster.)

Leaders fail to exercise moral imagination in large part because they are victims of their typical mental models or scripts. Scripts are mental shortcuts that enable decision makers to process data rapidly in order to make quick choices. We function easily in class, for instance, because we have well-developed scripts about how class periods are structured, what roles professors and students play, and so forth. Unfortunately, our scripts can leave out the ethical dimension of a situation. Consider the case of Ford Motor's failure to recall and repair the gas tanks on Pintos manufactured between 1970 and 1976. Gas tanks on these subcompacts were located behind the rear axle and ruptured during low-speed rear-end collisions. Sparks ignited the fuel, engulfing the car in flames. Fixing the problem would have only cost $11 per vehicle, but Ford refused to act. The firm believed that all small cars were inherently unsafe and that customers weren't interested in safety. Furthermore, Ford managers conducted a cost–benefit analysis and determined that the costs in human life were less than the costs to repair the problem.

The National Highway Traffic Safety Administration finally forced Ford to recall the Pinto in 1978. By that time the damage had been done. The company lost a major lawsuit brought by a burn victim. In a trial involving the deaths of three Indiana teens in a rear-end crash, Ford became the first major corporation to face criminal, not civil, charges for manufacturing faulty products. The automaker was later acquitted, but its image was severely tarnished.

Business professor Dennis Gioia, who served as Ford's recall coordinator from 1973 to 1975, blames moral blindness for the company's failure to act.[18] Ethical considerations weren't part of the safety committee's script. The group made decisions about recalls based on the number of incidents and cost–benefit analyses. Because there were only a few reports of gas tank explosions and the expense of the fixing the tank didn't seem justified, members decided not to act. At no point did Gioia and his colleagues question the morality of putting a dollar value on human life and of allowing customers to die in order to save the company money.

Werhane cautions that moral imagination can also become overactive when leaders and followers focus on creativity at the expense of ethical common sense. For example, managers and employees at personal computer disk manufacturer MiniScribe tried to meet impossible sales goals in the 1980s by double shipping to customers, making up accounts, altering auditors' reports, and, at one point, shipping bricks in disk drive cartons. These were highly creative but highly immoral responses to an ethical dilemma. Audi had to recall its 5000 series German automobile when drivers and the media claimed that the vehicle suffered from an acceleration problem. As it turned out, deaths linked to a mechanical defect were really the product of drivers accidentally putting their feet on the accelerator instead of the brake. Hyperactive moral imagination created a false scenario that cost Audi 80% of its market share.

ETHICAL DEFICIENCIES

Leaders may unintentionally cast shadows because they lack the necessary knowledge, skills, and experience. Not understanding how to go about making ethical decisions can be a problem. So can ignorance of ethical perspectives or frameworks that can be applied to ethical dilemmas. When I ask students to read and respond to Case Study 2.1, groups generally reach a consensus about whether Hanson was justified in exaggerating his statistics in order to raise money for this worthy cause. When I question them about the standards they used to reach their conclusions, however, they generally give me a blank look. Some teams make their decision based on personal feelings ("We don't like to be lied to, no matter how good the cause"). Other groups use a common ethical principle ("Lying is always wrong"; "It's okay to lie if more people are helped than hurt") in their deliberations but don't realize that they've done so.

It's possible to blunder into good ethical choices, but it's far more likely that we'll make wise decisions when we are guided by some widely used ethical principles and standards. These ethical theories help us define the problem, highlight important elements of the situation, force us to think systematically, encourage us to view the problem from a variety of perspectives, and strengthen our resolve to act responsibly.

CASE STUDY 2.1

The Multiplied Abused Children

S ave the Kids is a nonprofit group that pushes for tougher laws against those who sexually abuse children. Currently Save the Kids is in its biggest lobbying effort ever in an attempt to get the state legislature to pass a law that requires convicted sex offenders to register their whereabouts with local police departments. The organization's founder, Steve Hanson, is convinced that such a law can significantly reduce the number of child abuse cases in the state. Unfortunately, contributions aren't keeping up with expenses, and Save the Kids may have to drastically reduce its lobbying efforts just as the sex offender registration bill comes before the legislature. Chances are, this law will pass only if Save the Kids keeps up its lobbying campaign. Mr. Hanson is now raising money for Save the Kids through a series of speeches. To encourage contributions, Hanson knowingly exaggerates both the number of convicted sex offenders in the state and the number of children who are abused every year.

DISCUSSION PROBES

1. Do you agree with Hanson's decision to exaggerate in order to raise money for Save the Kids? Why or why not?

2. Does the amount of exaggeration make a difference in your evaluation of Hanson's action? What if he decides to exaggerate only slightly? What if he greatly inflates the figures?

3. Does the fact that Hanson intentionally lied make a difference in how you evaluate his decision? What if he exaggerated because he didn't check his facts carefully?

4. How do you determine whether someone is justified in lying? What standards do you use to determine whether you should tell the truth?

Making and implementing ethical decisions take both critical thinking and communication skills. We must be able to articulate our reasoning, convince other leaders of the wisdom of our position, and work with others to put the choice into place. A manager who wants to eliminate discriminatory hiring practices, for instance, will have to listen effectively, gather information, analyze and formulate arguments, appeal to moral principles, and build relationships. Failure to develop these skills will doom the reform effort.

In a book with the intriguing title *How Good People Make Tough Choices,* ethicist Rushworth Kidder encourages readers to develop their ethical fitness by putting their ethical commitments to work in real-life settings.[19] Kidder's exhortation implies that many of us are ethically unfit or flabby. Faulty decision making, ethical ignorance, and underdeveloped skills surely contribute to this condition, but lack of practice plays a role as well. Studying ethical theories and discussing ethical cases are essential to any ethical fitness program. Reasoning and communication skills can be sharpened during class. Ultimately, however, we need the first-hand experience that comes from tackling real-life leadership dilemmas.

CONTEXTUAL PRESSURES

Not all shadow casters come from within. Ethical failures are the product of group, organizational, and cultural forces as well. Conformity is a problem for many small groups. Members put a higher priority on cohesion than on coming up with a well-reasoned choice. They pressure dissenters, shield themselves from negative feedback, keep silent when they disagree, and so on.[20] Members of these shadowy groups engage in unhealthy communication patterns that generate negative emotions while undermining the reasoning process.

Organizations can also be shadow lands. For instance, car dealerships are known for their deceptive practices, and computer retailers are rapidly earning the same reputation. Although working in such environments makes moral behavior much more difficult, no organization is immune to ethical failure. Top managers at some organizations may fire employees who talk about ethical issues so that they can claim ignorance if followers do act unethically. This "don't ask, don't tell" atmosphere forces workers to make ethical choices on their own without the benefit of interaction. They seldom challenge the questionable decisions of others and assume that everyone supports the immoral acts. Division of labor allows low-level employees to assert that they just follow orders and upper-level employees to claim that they only set broad policies and therefore can't be held accountable for the illegal acts of their subordinates.[21] When tasks are broken down in small segments, workers may not even know that they are engaged in an improper activity. For example, the secretary who shreds documents may not realize that the papers are wanted in a civil or criminal investigation. The pressures of organizational moral decision making can create a kind of *ethical segregation*. Leaders and followers may have strong personal moral codes that regulate their personal lives but act much less ethically while at work.

Socialization is another process that encourages employees to set their personal codes aside. Organizations use orientation sessions, training seminars, mentors, and other means to help new hires identify with the group and absorb the group's culture. Loyalty to and knowledge of the organization are essential. Nonetheless, the socialization process may blind members to the consequences of their actions. This may have happened at Microsoft. A federal judge ruled that the company used unfair tactics in order to monopolize software and Web browser markets. Many Microsoft executives and employees refused to acknowledge any wrongdoing. Instead they claimed that the court's ruling was just the latest in a series of unfair attacks against the company.

There are organizations that deliberately use the socialization process to corrupt new members through co-option, incrementalism, and compromise.[22] In *co-option*, organizational leaders use rewards to reduce new employees' discomfort with immoral behaviors. Targets may not realize that these incentives are warping their judgment, making it easier to justify destructive behavior. For example, salespeople rewarded for selling expensive products (copiers, televisions, computers) with more features than consumers need may convince themselves that these items are good values. (The film described in Box 2.4 provides another example of co-option in action.) *Incrementalism* gradually leads new members up the "ladder of corruption." Newcomers are first persuaded to engage in a practice that is only mildly unethical, such as accepting free meals from company vendors. After the first practice becomes normal, employees are then encouraged to move on to increasingly more corrupt activities such as steering contracts to vendors in return for cash payments. Eventually they find themselves participating in acts that they would have rejected when they first joined the organization. *Compromise* backs members into corruption as they deal with dilemmas and conflicts. For instance, politicians enter into many compromises in order to secure votes for their pet projects. Cutting deals and forming political networks make it harder for them to take ethical stands. In the end they find themselves supporting causes and people they would normally avoid, which has led to the adage "Politics makes strange bedfellows."

Cultural differences, like group and organizational forces, can also encourage leaders to abandon their personal codes of conduct. (We'll examine this topic in more depth in Chapter 10.) A corporate manager from the United States may be personally opposed to bribery. Her company's ethics code forbids such payments, and so does federal law. However, she may bribe customs officials and government officials in her adopted country if such payments are an integral part of the national culture and appear to be the only way to achieve her company's goals.

Stepping Out of the Shadows: Expanding Our Ethical Capacity

Taking on the role of leader is a stretching experience. We must acquire additional skills to tackle broader responsibilities (see our discussion of the difference

---

Box 2.4

Leadership Ethics at the Movies

THE DEVIL WEARS PRADA

Key Cast Members: Meryl Streep, Anne Hathaway, Stanley Tucci, Emily Blunt

Synopsis: Fresh out of college, budding journalist Andy Sachs (Hathaway) lands a job as a personal assistant to New York's top fashion magazine editor, Miranda Priestly (Streep). Priestly is the "boss from hell." Arrogant, abusive, inconsistent, and demanding, she makes life difficult for her newest employee. However, with the help of a sympathetic coworker (Tucci), Andy succeeds in earning Priestly's grudging respect. But when the job threatens her relationships and values, Sachs must decide whether the price of her success is too high.

Rating: PG-13 for some sexuality

Themes: contextual pressures, corruption, socialization, character, unhealthy motivations, abuse of power and privilege, ethical followership, loyalty

---

between leading and following in Chapter 1) and master a new set of ethical dilemmas. This requires continuous leader development. Researchers at the Center for Creative Leadership (CCL) define leader development as "the expansion of a person's capacity to be effective in leadership roles and processes."[23] Leader development programs assume that people can expand their leadership competence and that the skills and knowledge they acquire will make them more effective in a wide variety of leadership situations, ranging from business and professional organizations to neighborhood groups, clubs, and churches.

The CCL researchers report that people develop a number of capacities in leader development programs, including (1) more effective ways to manage their emotions, thoughts, attitudes, and actions (self-management capabilities); (2) interpersonal and social skills such as relationship building and communication, which enable them to work with others in social systems (social capabilities); and (3) skills and perspectives (work facilitation capabilities) that promote the labor of individuals, groups, and units through goal setting, strategic thinking, creativity, and change management. We can and should expand our ethical capacity as well.

According to leadership development expert Bruce Avolio and his colleagues, leaders with heightened moral capacity believe that they have a responsibility to act morally in their positions and to set a high ethical standard for followers.[24]

They can take several different perspectives on an ethical dilemma, understand how others think and feel, and anticipate the consequences of their choices. All these factors help them deal with complex moral issues. Finally, leaders with expanded moral capacity have a base of experience that enables them to recognize the particular ethical problems they may encounter in their positions and equips them with the mental models or strategies they'll need to manage these dilemmas.

Business ethicist Lynn Sharp Paine describes moral thinking as "an essential capability" for organizational managers.[25] She contrasts *moral reasoning,* which is concerned with ethical principles and the consequences of choices, with *strategic* or result-based thinking, which focuses on reaching objectives such as increasing revenue, finding new distributors, or manufacturing products. Though distinct, these two strands of reasoning intertwine. Managers making strategic choices ought to consider important moral principles and weigh potential ethical consequences or outcomes. If they don't, their organizations may lose the right to operate in modern society. Conversely, managers must be good strategic thinkers in order to make wise moral decisions. They must understand how their groups operate, for example, in order to implement their ethical choices.

The same elements that go into developing other leadership competencies also go into building our ethical effectiveness. According to the CCL researchers, the three most important components of the leader development process are assessment, challenge, and support (see Figure 2.1).

Successful developmental programs provide plenty of feedback that lets participants know how they are doing and how others are responding to their leadership strategies. Assessment data provoke self-evaluation ("What am I doing well?" "How do I need to improve?") and provide information that helps answer these questions. Simply put, a leader learns to identify gaps between current performance and where he or she needs to be and then closes those gaps. The most powerful leadership experiences also stretch or challenge people. As long as people don't feel the need to change, they won't. Difficult and novel experiences, conflict situations, and high goals force leaders outside their comfort zones and give them the opportunity to practice new skills. To make the most of feedback and challenges, leaders need support. Supportive comments ("I appreciate the effort you're making to become a better listener"; "I'm confident that you can handle this new assignment") sustain the leader during the struggle to improve. The most common source of support is other people (family, coworkers, bosses), but developing leaders can also draw on organizational cultures and systems. Supportive organizations believe in continuous learning and staff development, provide funds for training, reward progress, and so on.

All three elements—assessment, challenge, and support—should be part of your plan to increase your ethical capacity. You need feedback about how well you handle ethical dilemmas, how others perceive your character, and how your

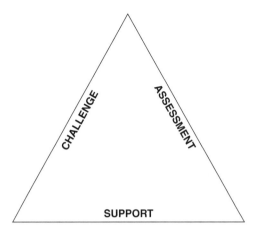

Figure 2.1   Developmental Components

decisions affect followers. You need the challenges and practice that come from moving into new leadership positions. Seek out opportunities to influence others by engaging in service projects, chairing committees, teaching children, or taking on a supervisory role. You also need the support of others to maximize your development. Talk with colleagues about ethical choices at work, draw on the insights of important thinkers, and find groups that will support your efforts to change.

Feedback, challenge, and support are incorporated into the design of this book. To encourage assessment, I ask you to reflect on and evaluate your own experiences and to get feedback from others. A self-assessment instrument is included in every chapter of this edition (see Box 2.5) along with additional self-analysis activities at the end of every chapter. To highlight challenge, I introduce a number of cases and encourage you to explore ideas further. To provide support, I gather and organize concepts from a variety of sources, identify additional resources, tell the stories of leaders, and encourage you to work with others (friends, small-group members, classmates) to increase your ethical competence. Make this text one part of a larger, ongoing program to develop your ethical capacity and other leadership abilities. Record your efforts in your ethics journal.

The remaining chapters are based on the foundation laid in these first two. Now that we have identified the leader's shadows and their causes, we're ready to expand our ethical capacity to better master them. Ethical capacity consists of knowledge, skills, perspectives, and motivations. You need to increase your understanding, sharpen your skills, broaden your worldview and perspective-

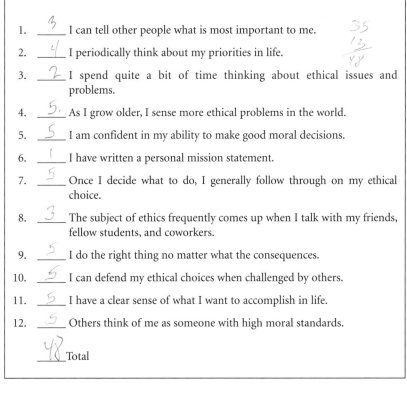

Box 2.5

Self-Assessment

ETHICAL SELF-AWARENESS INSTRUMENT

The following survey is designed to provide you with feedback about your ethical self-understanding. Respond to each of the following items on a scale of 1 (strongly disagree) to 5 (strongly agree). The higher your total score (maximum 60), the more aware you think you are of your ethical strengths and weaknesses, motivations, personal mission, values, and self-confidence. Pay particular attention to lower-ranked items. You may want to address these thoughts, feelings, and behaviors in your development plan in question 6, For Further Exploration, Challenge, and Self-Assessment, at the end of the chapter.

1. ___3___ I can tell other people what is most important to me.

2. ___4___ I periodically think about my priorities in life.

3. ___2___ I spend quite a bit of time thinking about ethical issues and problems.

4. ___5___ As I grow older, I sense more ethical problems in the world.

5. ___5___ I am confident in my ability to make good moral decisions.

6. ___1___ I have written a personal mission statement.

7. ___5___ Once I decide what to do, I generally follow through on my ethical choice.

8. ___3___ The subject of ethics frequently comes up when I talk with my friends, fellow students, and coworkers.

9. ___5___ I do the right thing no matter what the consequences.

10. ___5___ I can defend my ethical choices when challenged by others.

11. ___5___ I have a clear sense of what I want to accomplish in life.

12. ___5___ Others think of me as someone with high moral standards.

___48___ Total

taking ability, and strengthen your motivation to become more ethically competent. (A model of this process is found in Figure 2.2.) Expect to learn new terminology along with key principles, decision-making formats, and important elements of the ethical context. This information will be drawn from a number of different fields of study—philosophy, communication, theology, history, psychology, sociology, political science, and organizational behavior—because we need insights from many different disciplines if we're to step out of the shadows. You can anticipate reading about and then practicing a variety of skills, ranging from information gathering to listening and conflict management. Some material will encourage you to challenge your assumptions and to develop new perspectives on ethical problems. You'll also find that motivation is a central concern of this book. I'll touch on the "why" of ethics when discussing such topics as character, altruism, communitarianism, and servant leadership.

Part II, "Looking Inward," focuses on the inner dimension of leadership. Chapter 3 examines the role of character development in overcoming our internal enemies and faulty motivations, and Chapter 4 explores the nature of evil, forgiveness, and spirituality. Part III, "Ethical Standards and Strategies," addresses our ethical deficiencies by describing ethical theories and techniques that can be applied to ethical problem solving. Chapters 5 and 6 survey a wide range of perspectives, both general and leader focused, that can help us set moral priorities. Chapter 7 then describes the process of moral reasoning and systems or formats that we can use to make better ethical choices. Part IV, "Shaping Ethical Contexts," looks at ways in which leaders can shed light in a variety of situations. Chapter 8 examines ethical group decision making. Chapter 9 describes the creation of ethical organizational climates. Chapter 10 highlights the challenges of ethical diversity.

The ultimate goal of developing ethical capacity is to cast light rather than shadow, to exercise ethical leadership through moral behavior and moral influence. However, measuring your progress toward this goal is more difficult than, say, determining whether you are mastering the principles of accounting or learning computer skills. There is no one widely accepted ethics exam to tell you how you stack up against other leaders. Furthermore, ethical development, like other aspects of leadership development, never ends. We never reach a point at which we can say that we have reached full ethical capacity, that we have arrived as moral leaders. We can always develop further.

Marking our progress may be difficult for the reasons described here, but it is not impossible. You'll know that you are becoming more ethically competent if you note the following milestones.[26]

- *Greater self-awareness.* Feedback and personal reflection (particularly on the inner dimension of leadership) will deepen your self-understanding. You'll become more aware of your strengths, weaknesses, and motivations. You should develop a clearer grasp of your personal mission and your values. At the same time, you will probably become more aware of the purposes, values, and moral blind spots you share in common with others in your group or organization.

of ethical growth, we're ready to end the chapter by putting these elements together in the comprehensive model of ethical development found in Figure 2.3.

Implications and Applications

- Unethical or immoral behavior is the product of a number of factors, both internal and external. All of these elements must be addressed if you want to cast light rather than shadow.
- Unhealthy motivations that produce immoral behavior include internal enemies (insecurity, battleground mentality, functional atheism, fear, denial of death, evil) and selfishness (pride, ego, narcissism).
- "Good" leaders can and do make bad ethical decisions. Honorable intentions alone won't save you from casting shadows.
- Beware of faulty assumptions about how the world operates, other people, and yourself. These can lead you to underestimate risks and overestimate your abilities and value to your organization. Avoid the temptation to excuse or justify immoral behavior based on your leadership position.
- Exercise your moral imagination: Be sensitive to ethical issues, step outside your normal way of thinking, and come up with creative solutions. However, don't let your imagination become overactive, causing you to substitute creativity for sound reasoning and evidence.
- When it comes to ethics, ignorance is dangerous. Learning about ethical standards and principles is likely to help you make wiser ethical choices.
- Experience is vital. Put what you're learning to use in solving real-life ethical dilemmas.
- Never put cohesion first when making important group decisions.
- Your organization, no matter how high minded, may undermine your personal moral code by discouraging discussion of ethical issues, diffusing responsibility through division of labor, and promoting socialization processes that corrupt new members.
- Leader development (expansion of your capacity to be effective in leadership roles and processes) provides a useful framework for understanding ethical growth. You develop your ethical capacity (which is made up of knowledge, skills, perspectives, and motivations) in the same way that you develop your other leadership capacities: through assessment, challenge, and support.
- Ethical development is a lifelong process. You're making progress if you demonstrate one or more of the following:
  - Greater self-awareness and self-confidence
  - Ethical role modeling
  - Healthy moral imagination
  - Sound moral reasoning and better follow-through on choices
  - Resistance to group, organizational, and societal pressures to compromise personal standards
  - Creation of healthier ethical climates

For Further Exploration, Challenge, and Self-Assessment

1. In a group, identify unhealthy motivations to add to the list provided in the chapter.

2. Analyze a time when you cast a shadow as a leader. Which of the shadow casters led to your unethical behavior? Write up your analysis.

3. Does your employer pressure you to abandon your personal moral code of ethics? If so, how? What can you do to resist this pressure?

4. Describe a time when you exercised or failed to exercise moral imagination.

5. With a partner, develop a definition of ethical capacity. How would you measure ethical progress according to your definition?

6. Create a plan for expanding your ethical capacity that incorporates assessment, challenge, and support. Revisit your plan at the end of the course to determine how effective it has been.

CASE STUDY 2.2

Chapter End Case: Napoleon Marches Again

Jean-Marie Messier and Vivendi Universal

Jean-Marie Messier was named the director of General des Eaux, a French sewage and water company, in 1994. Soon Messier became bored with running a national utility firm and began a series of acquisitions designed to make him (and France) a major player in the world economy. He renamed his company Vivendi and then began building a media and telecommunication empire, purchasing stakes in cell phone companies, publishing firms, Internet ventures, and cable networks all over Europe. Messier set his sights on building the number one media and entertainment company in the world and spent $100 billion trying to reach this goal. His key purchase was Seagram's, the owner of Universal Studios and Universal Records. With this acquisition, Messier entered the North American entertainment market and began to compete with Disney's Michael Eisner and other Hollywood moguls.

Messier's buying spree didn't end with Seagram's. In 2001, he averaged one deal a month, including the purchase of MP3.com, Houghton Mifflin, Echostar, and USA Networks. *Business Week* proclaimed, "Not since Napoleon has France produced an empire builder as Jean-Marie Messier."[1]

Messier was hailed as a hero in his native country. He represented a new breed of French business leader who could stand up to American CEOs and beat them at their own game. As France's first celebrity executive, he routinely posed for magazine photos and appeared on television shows. All this attention fed Messier's already supersized ego. He encouraged shareholders to think of an investment in Vivendi as an investment in him. He ruled his empire autocratically, dismissing the input of his managers and hiding billions of dollars of debt from his board. Any outsiders who dared to criticize him would feel his wrath. Messier also lived like a modern-day Napoleon. He stayed in a $17.5-million Park Avenue apartment (renovated by France's leading architect), owned an extensive art collection and chateau outside Paris, and controlled a private air force that included a helicopter and seven planes.

Messier had little time to bask in his glory because investors soon lost confidence in him and his conglomerate. Messier paid well above market value for a number of his acquisitions. Losses from the company's Internet business mounted. Vivendi Universal appeared to be a bewildering collection of businesses, not an integrated media conglomerate. (At one point, 50 employees in the accounts department struggled to balance the books of more than 3,000 subsidiaries.) The firm owed much more than Messier admitted.

Troubles mounted when Vivendi Universal's share price, which had been used to finance acquisitions and pay down debt, dropped dramatically. In 2002, large banks refused to lend more money to Vivendi, and Messier was forced out. His successor held a fire sale, unloading most of the company's assets and subsidiaries. The result was the greatest loss in French corporate history. One million stockholders lost their investments when the share price dropped more than 90%.

Vivendi Universal's collapse sparked investigations in the United States and France. The Securities and Exchange Commission fined Vivendi $50 million and Messier $1 million for inflating company profits. Messier also had to forfeit the $26-million severance package he received from the company and is barred from serving as a director of any publicly held U.S. corporation. France's stock market regulators also fined the company and Messier for misleading investors. Messier has not yet been convicted of a crime, however, and runs a small mergers and acquisition firm in New York City. The former Vivendi Universal CEO is unrepentant, blaming the French elite and U.S. executives for his company's failure. He describes his ouster as a blow to French capitalism.

Like Napoleon's, Messier's grandiose ambitions far outstripped his ability to bring them to reality. Unfortunately, he was able to persuade a great many investors, business owners, employees, financiers, government officials, and others to go along with his dreams. They paid a high price for Messier's self-centeredness and self-delusion.

DISCUSSION PROBES

1. What narcissistic qualities do you see in Messier?

2. How do we keep ourselves from developing narcissistic qualities?

3. Are narcissistic leaders doomed to failure, or can they succeed over the long term?

4. How do we protect ourselves from narcissistic leaders?

5. What leadership ethics lessons do you take from this case?

NOTE

1. Johnson, J., & Orange, M. (2003). *The man who tried to buy the world: Jean-Marie Messier and Vivendi Universal.* New York: Portfolio, p.146.

SOURCES

Biz Briefs. (2004, January 5). *Television Week.* Retrieved August 2, 2007, from LexisNexis Academic database.

The fallen. (2003, January 13). *Business Week.* Retrieved August 2, 2007, from LexisNexis Academic database.

Gumbel, P. (2004, July 5). Villain or fall guy? *Time Canada.* Retrieved August 2, 2007, from LexisNexis Academic database.

CASE STUDY 2.3

Chapter End Case:
The Ethical Saga of Salomon Inc.

Some companies can't seem to stay out of ethical trouble. For example, Firestone was forced to merge with Bridgestone of Japan due in part to financial losses caused by the recall of defective tires. Years later Bridgestone/Firestone was embroiled in another scandal, this time involving tires mounted on Ford Explorers. Salomon Inc. is another company with a troubled history. The firm survived one serious scandal only to be involved in another.

In the 1980s, giant brokerage house Salomon Inc. was one of the most influential players in the financial world. *Business Week* magazine proclaimed CEO John Gutfreund "The King of Wall Street." Salomon's ethical troubles began in the firm's government securities division. When the U.S. government issues treasury bonds to finance the national debt, it relies on a select group of dealers, including Salomon, to acquire and then resell the bonds to other dealers and private individuals. This arrangement worked well for many years until Salomon's government securities trader, Paul Mozer, began to corner a large share of the market. Concerned that Salomon's growing influence would reduce income from bond sales, the Treasury Department passed a regulation (called the Mozer law) preventing any one brokerage and its customers from bidding on more than 35% of the total bonds available at a given auction.

Mozer protested this "rash decision" by the Treasury department and, in February 1991, circumvented the new rule. He exceeded the 35% regulation by entering a bid from Salomon and one in the name of a customer (without that firm's knowledge or consent). Mozer later confessed to his boss, John Meriwether, but claimed that this was his first and only offense. Gutfreund and other company executives took no action against Mozer. On May 22, he once again submitted an illegal bid in the name of a customer. The firm investigated and found that Mozer had made a series of illegal bids dating back to the previous December, not just one. On August 8, some 3 months after first learning of Mozer's criminal behavior, Gutfreund finally revealed this information to the Treasury Department. Treasury then threatened to suspend Salomon's trading privileges. Soon Gutfreund resigned, and investor Warren Buffett assumed his role on a temporary basis. Buffett appointed himself chief legal compliance officer, ordered all Salomon officers to report every legal and moral violation (except parking tickets) directly to him, and spent hours answering the questions of federal investigators and the press.

Greed and jealousy motivated Mozer. He was paid based on his performance and was jealous of competing traders at other firms who received bigger bonuses. However, it is harder to explain the inaction of Mozer's superiors, particularly CEO Gutfreund. Why did he fail to punish the rogue trader (who had antagonized government officials), and why did he wait 3 months before reporting to the Treasury Department? The executive's style may account for part of his hesitation. Gutfreund admitted that he was an "indecisive" manager. He depended heavily on the firm's stars (such as Mozer) to produce profits. When the stars violated the rules, he was reluctant to rein them in.

Corporate culture also played a role in the scandal. Stock and bond trading is a high-stakes, high-risk business. Gutfreund sanctioned this "bet the company" atmosphere. His formula for success was to wake up every day "ready to bite the ass off a bear." Gutfreund once challenged Meriwether to a million-dollar game of Liar's Poker. Meriwether responded by raising the stakes to $10 million. In Liar's Poker, two or more players hold a dollar bill against their chests. They make statements, some true and some false, about the serial numbers on the bills. The winner is the person who correctly challenges the false claims of the other players. Gutfreund and Meriwether never played their winner-take-all game. However, their reckless example helped create a go-for-broke atmosphere that cost the company dearly.

Warren Buffett's single-minded devotion to restoring the firm's ethical image kept it from collapse, but the fallout was severe nevertheless. In addition to paying millions of dollars of fines, the company lost three-quarters of its stock underwriting business, was prevented from making $4 billion in bond trades, and saw its stock value plummet. Trader Mozer spent 4 months in jail, Gutfreund lost his pension and stock options, and several executives received limited or lifetime bans from the securities market. Salomon largely regained its financial health but was acquired by the Traveler's Group insurance company in 1997. A year later Travelers merged with Citicorp, and Salomon Smith Barney began to operate as the investment banking and brokerage arm of the new conglomerate.

Salomon's next ethical crisis came at the beginning of the new millennium. Salomon, Merrill Lynch, and other Wall Street firms were fined $1.4 billion for lying to investors. In some cases, brokers recommended stocks to clients that, in private, they referred to as "dogs" and "junk." Some of the most serious charges were leveled against Salomon's Jack Grubman, who, like Mozer a decade earlier, was a company star. Grubman was perhaps the top telecom research analyst in the world. His recommendations could make or break a phone company's stock price, and he was paid handsomely—$20 million a year—for his efforts.

After the telecom industry crashed in 2000, the New York Attorney General's office, the Securities and Exchange Commission, and investor groups began to question the objectivity of Grubman's advice. Grubman was an informal advisor to WorldCom and continued to tout its stock until it was too late for investors to bail out before the firm filed for bankruptcy. Salomon investment bankers also brought pressure to bear on Grubman. The company made huge profits handling the stock offerings of public firms such as WorldCom. Potential clients were much more likely to give their business to Salomon if they received a favorable rating from the firm. This pressure apparently played a part in Grubman's decision to issue a "buy" rating for Winstar Communications.

Grubman accepted a lifetime ban from the securities industry in 2003 and paid a $15-million fine. New federal guidelines have been instituted that clearly separate research and investment banking functions. The once proud Salomon name has been largely retired from Wall Street, reduced to a trademark under the Citicorp Global Markets umbrella.

DISCUSSION PROBES

1. Why do some firms continue to experience one scandal after another?

2. What shadow casters contributed to the ethical problems of Salomon, Inc.? Was any factor more important than the others? Why?

3. Should financial service companies be prevented from offering both research advice and investment banking services?

4. How can corporate image be restored after scandals such as those faced by Salomon?

5. What advice would you offer leaders supervising employee superstars such as Mozer and Grubman?

6. What steps can firms, particularly ones in high-pressure, high-stakes environments, take to prevent ethical abuses?

7. What leadership ethics lessons do you draw from this case?

SOURCES

Etzel, B. (2002, July 1). WorldCom's wrong number. *Investment Dealers' Digest,* pp. 9–12. Retrieved July 21, 2003, from LexisNexis Academic database.

Guyon, J. (2002, October 14). The king and I. *Fortune* (Europe), p. 38. Retrieved July 21, 2003, from LexisNexis Academic database.

Julavits, R. (2003, March 28). NASD's Grubman probe going up the ladder. *American Banker,* p. 20. Retrieved July 21, 2003, from LexisNexis Academic database.

Lewis, M. (1989). *Liar's poker.* New York: Norton.

Loomis, C. J., & Kahn, J. (1999, January 11). Citigroup: Scenes from a merger. *Fortune,* pp. 76–83. Retrieved July 21, 2003, from LexisNexis Academic database.

Sweeping up the street. (2003, May 12). *Business Week,* p. 114. Retrieved July 21, 2003, from LexisNexis Academic database.

Timmons, H., Cohn, L., McNamee, M., & Rossant, J. (2002, August 5). Citi's sleepless nights. *Business Week,* pp. 42–43. Retrieved July 21, 2003, from LexisNexis Academic database.

Useem, M. (1998). *The leadership moment: Nine stories of triumph and disaster and their lessons for us all.* New York: Times Business, Ch. 7.

Notes

1. Palmer, P. (1996). Leading from within. In L. C. Spears (Ed.), *Insights on leadership: Service, stewardship, spirit and servant-leadership* (pp. 197–208). New York: Wiley.

2. Bing, S. (2000). *What would Machiavelli do? The ends justify the meanness.* New York: HarperBusiness.

3. Palmer, p. 205.

4. Garvin, D. A. (1993, July–August). Building a learning organization. *Harvard Business Review,* pp. 78–91.

5. Nash, L. L. (1990). *Good intentions aside: A manager's guide to resolving ethical problems.* Boston: Harvard Business School Press.

6. Gold, J. (2005, December 22). Judge orders Lucent to pay $224 million to Winstar creditors. *Associated Press State & Local Wire.* Retrieved July 11, 2007, from LexisNexis Academic database.

7. Jennings, M. M. (2006). *The seven signs of ethical collapse.* New York: St. Martin's Press; Frosch, D. (2007, April 20). Ex-chief at Quest found guilty. *The New York Times,* p. C1.

8. Neumeister, L. (2006, January 6). U.S. appeals court upholds Martha Stewart's conviction. *Associated Press Worldstream.* Retrieved August 14, 2007, from LexisNexis Academic database.

9. Padilla, A., Hogan, R., & Kaiser, R. B. (2007). The toxic triangle: Destructive leaders, susceptible followers, and conducive environments. *The Leadership Quarterly, 18,* 176–194.

10. Milloy, R. E. (2000, June 21). 2 Sides give 2 versions of facts in Waco suit. *The New York Times,* p. A14; Johnston, D. (1995, April 25). Terror in Oklahoma: The overview. *The New York Times,* p. A1.

11. Messick, D. M., & Bazerman, M. H. (1996, Winter). Ethical leadership and the psychology of decision making. *Sloan Management Review, 37*(2), 9–23.

12. Verhovek, S. H. (1993, April 22). Death in Waco: F.B.I. saw the ego in Koresh, but not a willingness to die. *The New York Times,* p. A1.

13. Price, T. L. (2006). *Understanding ethical failures in leadership.* Cambridge, UK: Cambridge University Press.

14. Sternberg R. J. (2002). Smart people are not stupid, but they sure can be foolish. In R. Sternberg (Ed.), *Why smart people can be so stupid* (pp. 232–242). New Haven, CT: Yale University Press.

15. See Guroian, V. (1996). Awakening the moral imagination. *Intercollegiate Review, 32,* 3–13; Johnson, M. (1993). *Moral imagination: Implications of cognitive science for ethics.* Chicago: University of Chicago Press; Kekes, J. (1991). Moral imagination, freedom, and the humanities. *American Philosophical Quarterly, 28,* 101–111; Tivnan, E. (1995). *The moral imagination.* New York: Routledge, Chapman, and Hall.

16. Werhane, P. (1999). *Moral imagination and management decision-making.* New York: Oxford University Press, p. 93.

17. Useem, M. (1998). *The leadership moment: Nine stories of triumph and disaster and their lessons for us all.* New York: Times Books.

18. Gioia, D. A. (1992). Pinto fires and personal ethics: A script analysis of missed opportunities. *Journal of Business Ethics, 11,* 379–389.

19.   Kidder, R. M. (1995). *How good people make tough choices: Resolving the dilemmas of ethical living.* New York: Fireside.

20.   Janis, I. (1971, November). Groupthink: The problems of conformity. *Psychology Today,* pp. 271–279; Janis, I. (1982). *Groupthink* (2nd ed.). Boston: Houghton Mifflin; Janis, I. (1989). *Crucial decisions: Leadership in policymaking and crisis management.* New York: Free Press; Janis, I., & Mann, L. (1977). *Decision making.* New York: Free Press.

21.   Conrad, C., & Poole, M. S. (1998). *Strategic organizational communication: Into the twenty-first century* (4th ed.). Fort Worth, TX: Harcourt Brace, Ch. 12; Darley, J. M. (1996). How organizations socialize individuals into evildoing. In D. M. Messick & A. E. Tenbrunsel (Eds.), *Codes of conduct: Behavioral research into business ethics* (pp. 12–43). New York: Russell Sage Foundation.

22.   Anand, V., Ashforth, B. E., & Joshi, M. (2004). Business as usual: The acceptance and perpetuation of corruption in organizations. *Academy of Management Executive, 18,* 39–53.

23.   McCauley, C. D., & Van Velsor, E. (Eds.). (2004). *The Center for Creative Leadership handbook of leadership development* (2nd ed.). San Francisco: Jossey-Bass, p. 4.

24.   May, D. R., Chan, A. Y. L., Hodges, T. D., & Avolio, B. J. (2003). Developing the moral component of authentic leadership. *Organizational Dynamics, 32,* 247–260.

25.   Paine, L. S. (1996). Moral thinking in management: An essential capability. *Business Ethics Quarterly, 6,* 477–492.

26.   Johnson, C. E., & Hackman, M. Z. (2002). *Assessing ethical competence.* Paper presented at the National Communication Association convention, Atlanta, GA.

Part II

Looking Inward

The Leader's Character

The course of any society is largely determined by the quality of its moral leadership.

—Psychologists Anne Colby and William Damon

Virtue is not found at the end of a rational argument, but at the end of a quest—as also along the way.

—Boston College professor William Kirk Kilpatrick

What's Ahead

This chapter addresses the inner dimension of leadership ethics. To shed light rather than shadow, we need to develop strong, ethical character made up of positive traits or virtues. We promote our character development through direct interventions or indirectly by finding role models, telling and living collective stories, learning from hardship, establishing effective habits, determining a clear sense of direction, and examining our values.

Elements of Character

In football, the best defense is often a good offense. When faced with high-scoring opponents, coaches often design offensive game plans that run as much time as possible off the clock. If they're successful, they can rest their defensive players while keeping their opponent's offensive unit on the sidelines. Building strong, ethical character takes a similar proactive approach to dealing with our shadow sides. To keep from projecting our internal enemies and selfishness on others, we need to go on the offensive, replacing or managing our unhealthy motivations through the development of positive leadership traits or qualities called virtues. Interest in virtue ethics dates at least as far back as Plato, Aristotle, and Confucius. The premise of virtue ethics is simple: Good people (those of high moral character) make good moral choices. Despite its longevity, this approach has not always been popular among scholars. Only in recent years have modern philosophers turned back to it in significant numbers.[1] They've been joined by positive psychologists who argue that there is more value in identifying and promoting the strengths of individuals than in trying to repair their weaknesses (which is the approach of traditional psychologists).[2]

Character plays an important role in leadership. Former CEOs Jeffrey Skilling (Enron), Sam Nacchio (Quest), and Martha Stewart (Martha Stewart Living Omnimedia) cast shadows due to greed, arrogance, dishonesty, ruthlessness, and other character failings. Their lack of virtue stands in sharp contrast to the leaders of great companies described in the book *Good to Great*.[3] Jim Collins and his team of researchers identified 11 firms that sustained outstanding performance over 15 years (cumulative stock returns 6.9 times the general market average). Collins specifically told his investigators to downplay the role of top executives at these firms so they wouldn't fall into the trap of giving CEOs too much credit. But they couldn't. Team members soon discovered that leaders of great companies such as Abbott Laboratories, Kimberly Clark, and Wells Fargo combined humility with a strong will. These "Level 5 leaders," as Collins calls them, downplayed their role in their company's success, giving accolades to others. In fact, they were uncomfortable talking about themselves. For example, Darwin Smith of Kimberly Clark told researchers, "I never stopped trying to be qualified for the job." Another Level 5 leader stated that "there are a lot of people in this company who could do my job better than I do."

Level 5 leaders also lived modestly. Kent Iverson of Nucor was typical of the sample. He got his dogs from the pound and lived in a small house that had a carport instead of a garage. However, when it came to the collective success of their companies, Iverson and his fellow leaders set high standards and persevered in the face of difficult circumstances. They didn't hesitate to make tough choices such as removing family members from the business or to take major risks such as abandoning profitable product lines.

Proponents of virtue ethics start with the end in mind. They develop a description or portrait of the ideal person (in this case a leader) and identify the admirable qualities or tendencies that make up the character of this ethical role model. They then suggest ways in which others can acquire these virtues.

There are three important features of virtues. First, virtues are woven into the inner life of leaders. They are not easily developed or discarded but persist over time. Second, virtues shape the way leaders see and behave. Being virtuous makes them sensitive to ethical issues and encourages them to act morally. Third, virtues operate independently of the situation. A virtue may be expressed differently depending on the context (what's prudent in one situation may not be in the next). Yet a virtuous leader will not abandon his or her principles to please followers.[4] Important virtues for leaders include the following.

COURAGE

Courage is overcoming fear in order to do the right thing.[5] Courageous leaders acknowledge the dangers they face and their anxieties. Nonetheless, they move forward despite the risks and costs. The same is true for courageous followers (see Box 3.1). Courage is most often associated with acts of physical bravery and heroism such as saving a comrade in battle or running dangerous river rapids. For that reason, French philosopher Andre Comte-Sponville argues, "Of all the virtues, courage is no doubt the most universally admired."[6] However, most courageous acts involve other forms of danger, such as the school principal who faces the wrath of parents for suspending the basketball team's leading scorer before the state tournament or the manager who could lose his job for confronting the boss about unauthorized spending.[7]

People must have courage if they are to fulfill the two components of ethical leadership: acting morally and exerting moral influence. Ethical leaders recognize that moral action is risky but continue to model ethical behavior despite the danger. They refuse to set their values aside to go along with the group, to keep silent when customers may be hurt, or to lie to investors. They strive to create ethical environments even when faced with opposition from their superiors and subordinates.

INTEGRITY

Integrity is wholeness or completeness. Leaders possessing this trait are true to themselves, reflecting consistency between what they say publicly and how they think and act privately. In other words, they practice what they preach. They are also honest in their dealings with others.

Nothing undermines a leader's moral authority more quickly than lack of integrity. (The movie described in Box 3.2 describes a person who failed as an ethical leader because he lacked this virtue.) Followers watch the behavior of leaders closely. One untrustworthy act can undermine a pattern of credible behavior. Trust is broken, and cynicism spreads. In an organizational setting,

Box 3.1

Focus on Follower Ethics

COURAGEOUS FOLLOWERSHIP

Ira Chaleff, who acts as a management consultant to U.S. senators and representatives, believes that courage is the most important virtue for followers. Exhibiting courage is easier if followers recognize that their ultimate allegiance is to the purpose and values of the organization, not to the leader. Chaleff outlines five dimensions of courageous followership that equip subordinates to meet the challenges of their role.

The Courage to Assume Responsibility

Followers must be accountable both for themselves and for the organization as a whole. Courageous followers take stock of their skills and attitudes, consider how willing they are to support and challenge their leaders, manage themselves, seek feedback and personal growth, take care of themselves, and care passionately about the organization's goals. They take initiative to change organizational culture by challenging rules and mindsets and by improving processes.

The Courage to Serve

Courageous followers support their leaders through hard, often unglamorous work. This labor takes a variety of forms, such as helping leaders conserve their energies for their most significant tasks, organizing communication to and from the leader, controlling access to the leader, shaping a leader's public image, presenting options during decision making, preparing for crises, mediating conflicts between leaders, and promoting performance reviews for leaders.

The Courage to Challenge

Inappropriate behavior damages the relationship between leaders and followers and threatens the purpose of the organization. Leaders may break the law, scream at or use demeaning language with employees, display an arrogant attitude, engage in sexual harassment, abuse drugs and alcohol, and misuse funds. Courageous followers need to confront leaders acting in a destructive manner. In some situations, just asking questions about the wisdom of a policy decision is sufficient to bring about change. In more extreme cases, followers may need to disobey unethical orders.

The Courage to Participate in Transformation

Negative behavior, when unchecked, often results in a leader's destruction. Leaders may deny the need to change, or they may attempt to justify their behavior. They may claim that whatever they do for themselves (e.g., embezzling, enriching themselves at the expense of stockholders) ultimately benefits the organization.

Box 3.1 (Continued)

To succeed in modifying their behavior patterns, leaders must admit they have a problem and acknowledge that they should change. They need to take personal responsibility and visualize the outcomes of the transformation: better health, more productive employees, higher self-esteem, restored relationships. Followers can aid in the process of transformation by drawing attention to what needs to be changed; suggesting resources, including outside facilitators; creating a supportive environment; modeling openness to change and empathy; helping contain abusive behavior; and providing positive reinforcement for positive new behaviors.

The Courage to Leave

When leaders are unwilling to change, courageous followers may take principled action by resigning from the organization. Departure is justified when the leader's behaviors clash with the leader's self-proclaimed values or the values of the group, or when the leader degrades or endangers others. Sometimes leaving is not enough. In the event of serious ethical violations, followers must bring the leader's misbehavior to the attention of the public by going to the authorities or the press.

SOURCE: Chaleff, I. (2003). *The courageous follower: Standing up to & for our leaders* (2nd ed.). San Francisco: Berrett-Koehler.

---

common "trust busters" include inconsistent messages and behavior, inconsistent rules and procedures, blaming, dishonesty, secrecy, and unjust rewards.[8] Employees at United Airlines were particularly outraged by the bonuses given executives (see Chapter 1) because these officials had consistently promoted "shared sacrifice" during the bankruptcy. Performance suffers when trust is broken. Trust encourages teamwork, cooperation, and risk taking. Those who work in trusting environments are more productive and enjoy better working relationships.[9] (I'll have more to say about trust in Chapter 6.)

HUMILITY

The success of Level 5 leaders, described earlier, is one strong argument for encouraging leaders to be humble; the failure of many celebrity CEOs is another. In the 1990s, many business leaders, such as Carly Fiorina of Hewlett Packard (see Chapter 9), Revlon's Ron Perelman, Disney's Michael Eisner, WorldCom's Bernie Ebbers, and Tyco's Dennis Kozlowski seemed more like rock stars than corporate executives.[10] These charismatic figures became the public faces of their corporations, appearing on magazine covers and cable television shows and in company commercials. Within a few years, however, most of these celebrity leaders were gone because of scandal (some are in jail) or poor performance. Quiet leaders who shun the spotlight replaced them and, in many instances, produced superior results.

Management professors J. Andrew Morris, Celeste Brotheridge, and John Urbanski argue that true humility strikes a balance between having an overly low or high opinion of the self.[11] It does not consist of low self-esteem, as many people think, or of underestimating our abilities. Instead, humility is made up of three components. The first component is self-awareness. A humble leader can objectively assess her or his strengths and limitations. The second element is openness, which is a product of knowing one's weaknesses. Possessing humility means being open to new ideas and knowledge. The third component is transcendence. Humble leaders acknowledge that there is a power greater than the self. This prevents them from developing an inflated view of their importance while increasing their appreciation for the worth and contributions of others.

Humility has a powerful impact on ethical behavior. Humble leaders are less likely to be corrupted by power, claim excessive privileges, engage in fraud, abuse followers, and pursue selfish goals. They are more willing to serve others instead, putting the needs of followers first while acting as role models. Humility encourages leaders to build supportive relationships with followers that foster collaboration and trust. Because they know their limitations and are open to input, humble leaders are more willing to take advice that can keep them and their organizations out of trouble.

REVERENCE

University of Texas humanities professor Paul Woodruff argues that reverence, which was highly prized by the ancient Greeks and Chinese, is an important virtue for modern leaders.[12] Reverence has much in common with humility. It is the capacity to feel a sense of awe, respect, and even shame when appropriate. Awe, respect, and shame are all critical to ethical leadership, according to Woodruff. Ethical leaders serve higher causes or ideals. They are not concerned about power struggles or about winners or losers but with reaching common goals. They respect the input of others, rely on persuasion rather than force, and listen to followers' ideas. Ethical leaders also feel shame when they violate group ideals. Such shame can prompt them to self-sacrifice—accepting the consequences of telling the truth, for example, or supporting unpopular people or ideas.

OPTIMISM

Optimists expect positive outcomes in the future even if they are currently experiencing disappointments and difficulties.[13] They are more confident than

Box 3.2

Leadership Ethics at the Movies

THE LAST KING OF SCOTLAND

Key Cast Members: Forest Whitaker, James McAvoy, Kerry Washington, David Oyelowo, Gillian Anderson

Synopsis: Fresh out of medical school, Scottish doctor Nicholas Garrigan (McAvoy) volunteers to work at a rural medical clinic in Uganda in the 1970s. Soon he attracts the attention of the nation's dictator, Idi Amin (Whitaker), who makes Garrigan his personal physician. The power and perks of his new position corrupt the young Scot. Not only does he defend Amin (who is in the process of killing 300,000 Ugandan citizens), but he soon finds himself violating his medical oath to do no harm by becoming Amin's advisor. His rash decisions lead to the deaths of his supervisor and his lover. When he realizes the extent of his boss's crimes and his own, Garrigan must decide whether or not to betray Amin. Whitaker won an Oscar and a Golden Globe award for his portrayal of the brutal dictator who felt a special affinity for the Scottish people.

Rating: R for graphic violence and sexuality

Themes: corruption, lack of character, unhealthy motivations, the shadow side of leadership, moral decision making

pessimists, who expect that things will turn out poorly. People who are hopeful about the future are more likely to persist in the face of adversity. When faced with stress and defeat, optimists acknowledge the reality of the situation and take steps to improve. Their pessimistic colleagues, on the other hand, try to escape the problem through wishful thinking, distractions, and other means.

Optimism is an essential quality for leaders. As we'll see later in the chapter, nearly every leader experiences hardships. Those who learn and grow from these experiences will develop their character and go on to greater challenges. Those who ignore unpleasant realities stunt their ethical growth and may find their careers at an end. At the same time, leaders need to help followers deal constructively with setbacks, encouraging them to persist. Followers are more likely to rally behind optimists who appear confident and outline a positive image or vision of the group's future. (See Case Study 3.1 to see how one optimistic leader encouraged his followers to achieve extraordinary results.)

COMPASSION (KINDNESS, GENEROSITY, LOVE)

Compassion and related terms such as *concern, care, kindness, generosity,* and *love* all describe an orientation that puts others ahead of the self.[14] Those with compassion value others regardless of whether they get anything in return from them. Compassion is an important element of altruism, an ethical perspective we'll describe in more detail in Chapter 5. An orientation toward others rather than the self separates ethical leaders from their unethical colleagues.[15] Ethical leaders recognize that they serve the purposes of the group. They seek power and exercise influence on behalf of followers. Unethical leaders put their self-interests first. They are more likely to control and manipulate followers and subvert the goals of the collective. In extreme cases, this self-orientation can lead to widespread death and destruction.

JUSTICE

Justice has two components.[16] The first component is a sense of obligation to the common good. The second element is treating others as equally and fairly as possible. Just people feel a sense of duty and strive to do their part as a member of the team, whether that team is a small group, an organization, or society as a whole. They support equitable rules and laws. In addition, those driven by justice believe that everyone deserves the same rights even if they have different skills or status.

Although justice is a significant virtue for everyone, regardless of their role, it takes on added importance for leaders. To begin, leaders who don't carry out their duties put the group or organization at risk. Furthermore, leaders have a moral obligation to consider the needs and interests of the entire group and to take the needs of the larger community into account. The rules and regulations they implement should be fair and benefit everyone. Leaders also need to guarantee to followers the same rights they enjoy. Finally, they should set personal biases aside when making choices, judging others objectively and treating them accordingly.

Identifying important leadership virtues is only a start. We then need to blend desirable qualities together to form a strong, ethical character. This is far from easy, of course. At times, our personal demons will overcome even our best efforts to keep them at bay. We're likely to make progress in some areas while lagging in others. We may be courageous yet arrogant, reverent yet pessimistic, optimistic yet unjust. No wonder some prominent leaders reflect both moral strength and weakness. Martin Luther King, Jr., showed great courage and persistence in leading the civil rights movement but engaged in extramarital relationships. Franklin Roosevelt was revered by many of his contemporaries but had a long-standing affair with Lucy Mercer. In fact, Mercer (not Eleanor Roosevelt) was present when he died.

The poor personal behavior of political and business leaders has sparked debate about personal and public morality. One camp argues that the two cannot be separated. Another camp makes a clear distinction between the public and private arena. According to this second group, we can be disgusted by the private behavior of a politician such as Bill Clinton or Rudy Giuliani but vote for him anyway based on his performance in office.

I suspect that the truth lies somewhere between these extremes. We should expect contradictions in the character of leaders, not be surprised by them. Private lapses don't always lead to lapses in public judgment. On the other hand, it seems artificial to compartmentalize private and public ethics. Private tendencies can and do cross over into public decisions. Arizona State business ethics professor Marianne Jennings points out that many fallen corporate leaders (e.g., Richard Scrushy, Dennis Kowzlowski, Scott Sullivan, Bernie Ebbers) cheated on their wives or divorced them to marry much younger women.[17] She suggests that executives who are dishonest with the most important people in their lives—their spouses—are likely to be dishonest with others who aren't as significant: suppliers, customers, and stockholders. Furthermore, the energy devoted to an affair distracts a leader from his or her duties and provides a poor role model for followers. That's why the Boeing board fired CEO Harry Stonecipher when it discovered that he was having an affair with a high-ranking employee.[18]

In the political arena, Roosevelt tried to deceive the public as well as his wife and family. He proposed expanding the number of Supreme Court justices from 9 to 15, claiming that the justices were old and overworked. In reality, he was angry with the Court for overturning many New Deal programs and wanted to appoint new justices who would support him. Roosevelt's dishonest attempt to pack the Supreme Court cost him a good deal of his popularity. Bill Clinton's personal moral weaknesses overshadowed many of his political accomplishments.

Fostering character is a lifelong process requiring sustained emotional, mental, and even physical effort. Strategies for developing leadership virtues can be classified as direct or indirect. Direct approaches are specifically designed to promote virtues. For example, schools may display lists of the virtues in prominent places. However, deliberate moralizing (telling children how to behave) is less effective with older students. Psychological interventions appear to be much more successful. Therapists help clients become less egocentric (and therefore more humble) by encouraging them to develop a more realistic assessment of their strengths and weaknesses. Counselors suggest that their counselees convert pessimism into optimism by identifying their negative cognitions ("I am a failure") and then converting them into more positive thoughts ("I may have failed, but I can take steps to improve"). Psychologists have also found ways to help people deal with their fears (and build their courage). They first expose clients to low levels of threat. Once they've have mastered their initial fears, therapists then introduce clients to progressively greater dangers.[19]

Although direct methods can build character, more often than not virtues develop indirectly, as a byproduct of other activities. In the remainder of this chapter, I'll introduce a variety of indirect approaches or factors that encourage the development of leadership virtues. These include identifying role models, telling and living out shared stories, learning from hardship, cultivating good habits, creating a personal mission statement, and clarifying values.

CASE STUDY 3.1

The Hero as Optimist

Explorer Ernest Shackleton

The early 20th century has been called the Heroic Age of Polar Exploration. Teams of adventurers from Norway and Great Britain competed to see who would be first to reach the South Pole. Antarctic expeditions faced temperatures as low as –100° Fahrenheit and gale force winds up to 200 miles an hour. Britain's Captain Robert Scott tried unsuccessfully to claim Antarctica for the Crown in 1901. Ernest Shackleton, who had accompanied Scott on his first journey, came within 100 miles of the Pole in 1909 but had to turn back to save his party. Scott and his companions died during their second expedition, launched in 1911. Norwegian Roald Amundsen, who set out at the same time as Scott, succeeded in reaching the southernmost point on Earth in January 1912.

Undeterred by Amundsen's success, Shackleton decided to launch "one last great Polar journey" aimed at crossing the entire Antarctic continent. This adventure has been chronicled in a number of recent books and films. Author and museum curator Caroline Alexander provides one of the most detailed accounts in her book *The* Endurance: *Shackleton's Legendary Antarctic Expedition*. Shackleton and his crew of 27 men set sail on their wooden sailing ship, the *Endurance,* in August 1914, just days before World War I broke out. Soon the last great polar journey turned into one of the world's most incredible tales of survival.

The *Endurance* was trapped by pack ice at the end of January, stranding the party. When the ice melted the following October (springtime in the Southern Hemisphere), it crushed and sank the ship. The crew relocated to ice floes. At the end of April, 15 months after being marooned, the group abandoned camp on the shrinking ice packs and made it to an uninhabited island in three small dories.

Shackleton and five companions then set out in one of the small boats (only 22 feet long) to reach the nearest whaling station, on South Georgia Island, 800 miles away. This voyage was later ranked as one of the greatest sea journeys of all time. The odds were against the small party from the beginning. They were traveling in the dead of winter on one of the roughest oceans in the world. Darkness made navigation nearly impossible, and they survived a severe storm, one that sunk a much bigger tanker sailing at the same time in the same waters. The crew overcame these hurdles and, frostbitten and soaked to the skin, reached South Georgia Island. Even then, their suffering was far from over. Shackleton and two colleagues had to cross a series of ridges and glaciers before reaching the whaling camp. Alexander describes how the survivors looked when they finally reached help.

At three in the afternoon, they arrived at the outskirts of Stromness Station. They had traveled for thirty-six hours without rest. Their bearded faces were black with blubber smoke, and their matted hair, clotted with salt, hung almost to their shoulders. Their filthy clothes were in tatters. . . . Close to the station they encountered the first humans outside their own party they had set eyes on in nearly eighteen months—two small children, who ran from them in fright. (p. 164)

It was another 4 months before Shackleton could reach the rest of his crew stranded on the first island. Amazingly, not one member of the party died during the whole 22-month ordeal.

Many qualities made Shackleton an effective leader. He had great strength and physical stature that enabled him to endure extreme conditions and deal with rebellious followers. He understood the skills and limitations of each expedition member and made the most of each person's abilities. Shackleton was both accessible and firm. He mixed easily with his men but, at the same time, enforced discipline in a fair, even-handed manner. Whatever the setting, he quickly established a routine and made every effort to maintain the group's morale, planning song fests, lectures, dog races, and other activities for his men.

Alexander suggests that Shackleton's character was the key to his success. In 1909, Shackleton could have been the first to reach the South Pole, but he turned back to save the life of his companions. As the supply of food dwindled, he made expedition member Frank Wild (who would join him on the *Endurance* voyage) eat one of his (Shackleton's) daily ration of four biscuits. "I do not suppose that anyone else in the world can thoroughly realize how much generosity and sympathy was shown by this," the grateful Wild later wrote. "I DO by GOD I shall never forget it."

Shackleton continued to demonstrate concern and compassion for the needs of his followers on his Trans-Antarctic voyage. When the most unpopular crewmember was laid up with a bad back, the commander let him use his own cabin and brought him tea. He made sure that those of lower rank got the warmest clothes and sleeping bags. During the perilous trip to South Georgia Island, Shackleton kept an eye out for those who were growing weak but never embarrassed anyone by singling him out for special help. If one sailor appeared on the verge of collapse, he made sure that everyone got warm milk or food. Shackleton himself valued optimism above all other virtues. "Optimism," he said, "is true moral courage." Relentless optimism kept him going during the hard times, and he had little patience for those who were anxious about the future.

Alexander sums up the essential quality of Ernest Shackleton's leadership this way:

At the core of Shackleton's gift for leadership in crisis was an adamantine conviction that quite ordinary individuals were capable of heroic feats if the circumstances required; the weak and the strong could and *must* survive together. The mystique that Shackleton acquired as a leader may partly be attributed to the fact that he elicited from his men strength and endurance they had never imagined they possessed; he ennobled them. (p. 194)

DISCUSSION PROBES

1. What is the relationship between optimism and courage? Can we be optimistic without courage? Can we be courageous without being optimistic?

2. Generate a list of the virtues demonstrated by Shackleton on the *Endurance* voyage.

3. Do dangerous situations such as polar exploration put a premium on some aspects of character that would be less important in other, more routine contexts?

4. Who are our true, modern-day heroes? What character qualities do they possess?

5. What leadership ethics lessons can we draw from the life of Ernest Shackleton?

SOURCE: Alexander, C. (1999). *The* Endurance: *Shackleton's legendary Antarctic expedition.* New York: Alfred A. Knopf. (Also available as a PBS Nova documentary film.)

For more information on Shackleton and his expedition, see

Morrell, M., Capparell, S., & Shackleton, A. (2001). *Shackleton's way: Leadership lessons from the great Antarctic explorer.* New York: Viking.
Perkins, D. N. T. (2000). *Leading at the edge.* New York: AMACOM.
Shackleton, E. (1998). *South: A memoir of the* Endurance *voyage.* New York: Carroll & Graf.

Character Building

FINDING ROLE MODELS

Character appears to be more caught than taught. We often learn what it means to be virtuous by observing and imitating exemplary leaders. That makes role models crucial to developing high moral character.[20] Three such role models were selected as *Time* magazine's 2002 Persons of the Year. FBI agent Colleen Rowley testified before Congress about the agency's failure to take a terrorist warning seriously before 9/11. Cynthia Cooper, an auditor at WorldCom, blew the whistle on shady accounting practices to the company board's audit committee. Enron vice-president of development Sherron Watkins warned CEO Kenneth Lay of "an elaborate accounting hoax" that could mean disaster for the company.[21]

Government ethics expert David Hart argues that it is important to differentiate between different types of moral examples or exemplars.[22] Dramatic acts, such as rescuing a child from danger, capture our attention. However, if we're to develop worthy character we need examples of those who demonstrate virtue on a daily basis. Hart distinguishes between *moral episodes* and *moral processes.* Moral episodes are made up of *moral crises* and *moral confrontations.* Moral crises are dangerous, and Hart calls those who respond to them "moral heroes." Oskar Schindler, a German industrialist, was one such hero. He risked his life and fortune to save 1,000 Jewish workers during World War II. Moral confrontations aren't dangerous, but they do involve risk and call for "moral champions." Marie Ragghianti emerged as a moral champion when, as chair of the parole board in Tennessee, she discovered that the governor and his cronies were selling pardons and reported their illegal activities to the FBI.

Moral processes consist of *moral projects* and *moral work*. Moral projects are designed to improve ethical behavior during a limited amount of time and require "moral leaders." A moral leader sets out to reduce corruption in government, for example, or to improve the working conditions of migrant farm workers. In contrast to a moral project, moral work does not have a beginning or end but is ongoing. The "moral worker" strives for ethical consistency throughout life. This moral exemplar might be the motor vehicle department employee who tries to be courteous to everyone who comes to the office or the neighbor who volunteers to coach youth soccer.

Hart argues that the moral worker is the most important category of moral exemplar. He points out that most of life is lived in the daily valleys, not on the heroic mountain peaks. Because character is developed over time through a series of moral choices and actions, we need examples of those who live consistent moral lives. Those who engage in moral work are better able to handle moral crises. For instance, Andre and Magda Trocme committed themselves to a life of service and nonviolence as pastors in the French village of La Chambon. When the German occupiers arrived, the Trocmes didn't hesitate to protect the lives of Jewish children and encouraged their congregation to do the same. This small community became an island of refuge to those threatened by the Holocaust.[23] (Turn to Case Study 3.3 for a closer look at another outstanding moral exemplar.)

Anne Colby and William Damon studied 23 moral workers to determine what we can learn from their lives.[24] They found three common characteristics in their sample:

- *Certainty.* Moral exemplars are sure of what they believe and take responsibility for acting on their convictions.
- *Positivity.* Exemplars take a positive approach to life even in the face of hardship. They enjoy what they do and are optimistic about the future.
- *Unity of self and moral goals.* Exemplars don't distinguish between their personal identity and their ethical convictions. Morality is central to who they are. They believe they have no choice but to help others and consider themselves successful if they are pursuing their mission in life.

What sets exemplars apart from the rest of us is the extent of their engagement in moral issues. We make sure that our children get safely across the street. Moral exemplars, on the other hand, "drop everything not just to see their own children across the street but to feed the poor children of the world, to comfort the dying, to heal the ailing, or to campaign for human rights."[25]

Colby and Damon offer some clues about how we might develop broader moral commitments like the exemplars in their study. They note that moral capacity continues to develop well beyond childhood. Some in their sample didn't take on their life's work until their 40s and beyond. As a result, we should strive to develop our ethical capacity throughout our lives. The researchers also found that working with others on important ethical tasks or projects fosters moral growth by exposing participants to different points of view and new moral issues. We too can benefit by collaborating with others on significant causes such as working for better children's health care, building affordable housing, or fighting AIDS. The key is to view these tasks not as a burden but as an opportunity to act on what we believe. Adopting a joyful attitude will help us remain optimistic in the face of discouragement.

TELLING AND LIVING COLLECTIVE STORIES

Character building never takes place in a vacuum. Virtues are more likely to take root when nurtured by families, schools, governments, and religious bodies. These collectives impart values and encourage self-discipline, caring, and other virtues through the telling of narratives or stories. Shared narratives both explain and persuade. They provide a framework for understanding the world and, at the same time, challenge us to act in specified ways. For example, one of the most remarkable features of the American political system is the orderly transition of power between presidents.[26] George Washington set this precedent by voluntarily stepping down as the country's first leader. His story, told in classrooms, books, and films, helps explain why the current electoral system functions smoothly. Furthermore, modern presidents and presidential candidates follow Washington's example, as in the case of the 2000 election. Al Gore garnered more popular votes than George W. Bush but conceded defeat after the Supreme Court rejected his court challenge.

Character growth comes from living up to the roles we play in the story. According to virtue ethicist Alasdair MacIntyre, "I can only answer the question 'What am I to do?' if I can answer the prior question, 'Of what story or stories do I find myself a part?'"[27] Worthy narratives bring out the best in us, encouraging us to suppress our inner demons and to cast light instead shadow.

In the introduction to this text, I argued that we could learn about leadership ethics from fictional characters as well as from real-life ones. Ethics professor C. David Lisman offers several reasons why the ethical models contained in literature can provide a moral education that helps us to nurture our virtues.[28] Lisman focuses on literature, but his observations also apply to other forms of fiction (films, plays, television shows). In Lisman's estimation, fiction helps us understand our possibilities and limits. We can try to deny the reality of death, the fact that we're aging, and that there are factors outside our control. However, novels and short stories force us to confront these issues.

Literature explores many common human themes, such as freedom of choice, moral responsibility, conflict between individual and society, conflict between individual conscience and society's rules, and self-understanding. Fiction writers help us escape our old ways of thinking and acting. Their best works expand our emotional capacity, enabling us to better respond to the needs of others. They also provide us with an opportunity to practice moral reflection and judgment by evaluating the actions of important characters.[29] In sum, almost any story about leaders, whether real or fictional, can teach us something about ethical and unethical behavior. Moral exemplars can be found in novels, television series, and feature films as well as in news stories, biographies, documentaries, and historical records.

LEARNING FROM HARDSHIP

Hardship and suffering also play a role in developing character. The leaders we admire the most are often those who have endured the greatest hardships. Nelson Mandela, Václav Havel, and Aleksandr Solzhenitsyn served extended prison terms, for instance, and Moses endured 40 years in exile and 40 in the wilderness with his people.

Perhaps no other American leader has faced as much hardship as did Abraham Lincoln. He was defeated in several elections before winning the presidency. Because of death threats, he had to slip into Washington, D.C., to take office. He presided over the slaughter of many of his countrymen and women, lost a beloved son, and was ridiculed by northerners (some in his cabinet) and southerners alike. However, all these trials seemed to deepen both his commitment to the Union and his spirituality. His second inaugural address is considered to be one of the finest political and theological statements ever produced by a public official.

Trainers at the Center for Creative Leadership (CCL) have identified hardship as one of the factors contributing to leadership development. Leaders develop the fastest when they encounter situations that stretch or challenge them. Hardships, along with novelty, difficult goals, and conflict, challenge people. CCL staffers Russ Moxley and Mary Lynn Pulley believe that hardships differ from other challenging experiences because they're unplanned, are experienced in an intensely personal way, and involve loss.[30]

Research conducted by the CCL reveals that leaders experience five common categories of hardship events. Each type of hardship can drive home important lessons.

- *Business mistakes and failures.* Examples of this type of hardship event include losing an important client, failed products and programs, broken relationships, and bankruptcies. These experiences help leaders build stronger working relationships, recognize their limitations, and profit from their mistakes.

• *Career setbacks.* Missed promotions, unsatisfying jobs, demotions, and firings make up this hardship category. Leaders faced with these events lose control over their careers, their sense of self-efficacy or competence, and their professional identity. Career setbacks function as wake-up calls, providing feedback about weaknesses. They encourage leaders to take more responsibility for managing their careers and to identify the type of work that is most meaningful to them.

• *Personal trauma.* Examples of personal trauma include divorce, cancer, death, and difficult children. These experiences, which are a natural part of life, drive home the point that leaders (who are used to being in charge) can't control the world around them. As a result, they may strike a better balance between work and home responsibilities, learn how to accept help from others, and endure in the face of adversity.

• *Problem employees.* Troubled workers include those who steal, defraud, can't perform, or perform well only part of the time. In dealing with problem employees, leaders often lose the illusion that they can turn these people around. They may also learn how important it is to hold followers to consistently high standards and become more skilled at confronting subordinates.

• *Downsizing.* Downsizing has much in common with career setbacks, but in this type of hardship leaders lose their jobs through no fault of their own. Downsizing can help leaders develop coping skills and force them to take stock of their lives and careers. Those carrying out the layoffs can also learn from the experience by developing greater empathy for the feelings of followers.

Being exposed to a hardship is no guarantee that you'll learn from the experience. Some ambitious leaders never get over being passed over for a promotion, for instance, and become embittered and cynical. Benefiting from adversity takes what Warren Bennis and Robert Thomas call "adaptive capacity." Bennis and Thomas compared leaders who came of age between 1945 and 1954 (Geezers) and 1991 and 2000 (Geeks).[31] They found that, regardless of generation, effective leaders come through *crucible moments* that have a profound impact on their development. These intense experiences include failures such as losing an election but also encompass more positive events such as climbing a mountain or finding a mentor. Participants in their sample experienced just as many crises as everyone else but were able to learn important principles and skills from their struggles. This knowledge enabled them to move on to more complex challenges.

Successful Geeks and Geezers see hard times as positive high points of their lives. In contrast, less successful leaders are defeated and discouraged by similar events. To put it another way, effective leaders tell a different story than their ineffective counterparts. They identify hardships as stepping stones, not as insurmountable obstacles. We too can enlarge our adaptive capacity by paying close attention to our personal narratives, defining difficult moments in our lives as learning opportunities rather than as permanent obstacles.

DEVELOPING HABITS

One of the ways in which we build character is by doing well through the development of habits.[32] Habits are repeated routines or practices designed to foster virtuous behavior. Examples of good habits include working hard, telling the truth, giving to charity, standing up to peer pressure, and always turning in original work for school assignments. Every time we engage in one of these habits, it leaves a trace or residue. Over time, these residual effects become part of our personality and are integrated into our character. We also become more competent at demonstrating virtues. Take courage, for example. To develop the courage and skill to confront our bosses about their unethical behavior, we may first need to practice courage by expressing our opinions to them on less critical issues such as work policies and procedures.[33]

Business consultant Stephen Covey developed the most popular list of habits. Not only is he the author of the best-selling book *The Seven Habits of Highly Effective People,* but thousands of businesses, nonprofit groups, and government agencies have participated in workshops offered by the Covey Center.[34] Covey argues that effectiveness is based on such character principles as integrity, fairness, service, excellence, and growth. The habits are the tools that enable leaders and followers to develop these characteristics. Covey defines a habit as a combination of knowledge (what to do and why to do it), skill (how to do it), and motivation (wanting to do it). Leadership development is an "inside-out" process that starts within the leader and then moves outward to affect others. The seven habits of effective and ethical leaders are as follows:

> *Habit 1. Be Proactive.* Proactive leaders realize that they can choose how they respond to events. When faced with a career setback, they try to grow from the experience instead of feeling victimized by it. Proactive people also take the initiative by opting to attack problems instead of accepting defeat. Their language reflects their willingness to accept rather than avoid responsibility. A proactive leader makes such statements as "Let's examine our options" and "I can create a strategic plan." A reactive leader makes comments such as "The organization won't go along with that idea," "I'm too old to change," and "That's just who I am."
>
> *Habit 2. Begin With the End in Mind.* This habit is based on the notion that "all things are created twice." First we get a mental picture of what we want to

accomplish, and then we follow through on our plans. If we're unhappy with the current direction of our lives, we can generate new mental images and goals, a process Covey calls rescripting. Creating personal and organizational mission statements is one way to identify the results we want and thus control the type of life we create. (I'll talk more about how to create a mission statement in the next section.) Covey urges leaders to center their lives on inner principles such as fairness and human dignity rather than on such external factors as family, money, friends, or work.

Habit 3. Put First Things First. A leader's time should be organized around priorities. Too many leaders spend their days coping with emergencies, mistakenly believing that urgent means important. Meetings, deadlines, and interruptions place immediate demands on their time, but other less pressing activities, such as relationship building and planning, are more important in the long run. Effective leaders carve out time for significant activities by identifying their most important roles, selecting their goals, creating schedules that enable them to reach their objectives, and modifying plans when necessary. They also know how to delegate tasks and have the courage to say "no" to requests that don't fit their priorities.

Habit 4. Think Win–Win. Those with a win–win perspective take a cooperative approach to communication, convinced that the best solution benefits both parties. The win–win habit is based on these dimensions: character (integrity, maturity, and a belief that the needs of everyone can be met), trusting relationships committed to mutual benefit, performance or partnership agreements that spell out conditions and responsibilities, organizational systems that fairly distribute rewards, and principled negotiation processes in which both sides generate possible solutions and then select the one that works best.

Habit 5. Seek First to Understand, Then to Be Understood. Ethical leaders put aside their personal concerns to engage in empathetic listening. They seek to understand, not to evaluate, advise, or interpret. Empathetic listening is an excellent way to build a trusting relationship. Covey uses the metaphor of the emotional bank account to illustrate how trust develops. Principled leaders make deposits in the emotional bank account by showing kindness and courtesy, keeping commitments, paying attention to small details, and seeking to understand. These strong relational reserves help prevent misunderstandings and make it easier to resolve any problems that do arise.

Habit 6. Synergize. Synergy creates a solution that is greater than the sum of its parts and uses right brain thinking to generate a third, previously undiscovered alternative. Synergistic, creative solutions are generated in trusting relationships (those with high emotional bank accounts) where participants value their differences.

Habit 7. Sharpen the Saw. Sharpening the saw refers to continual renewal of the physical, mental, social or emotional, and spiritual dimensions of the self. Healthy leaders care for their bodies through exercise, good nutrition, and stress management. They encourage their mental development by reading good literature and writing thoughtful letters and journal entries. They create meaningful relationships with others and nurture their inner or spiritual values through study or meditation and time in Nature. Continual renewal, combined with the use of the first six habits, creates an upward spiral of character improvement.

DEVELOPING MISSION STATEMENTS

Developing a mission statement is the best way to keep the end or destination in mind. Leaders who cast light have a clear sense of what they hope to accomplish and seek to achieve worthwhile goals. For example, Abraham Lincoln was out to preserve the Union, Nelson Mandela wanted to abolish apartheid, and Mother Teresa devoted her whole life to reducing suffering.

Author and organizational consultant Laurie Beth Jones believes that useful mission statements are short (no more than a sentence long), easily understood and communicated, and committed to memory.[35] According to Jones, developing a personal mission statement begins with personal assessment. Take a close look at how your family has influenced your values and interests. Identify your strengths and determine what makes you unique (what Jones calls your "unique selling point"). Once you've isolated your gifts and unique features, examine your motivation. What situations make you excited or angry? Chances are, your mission will be related to the factors that arouse your passion or enthusiasm (teaching, writing, coaching or selling, for example).

Jones outlines a three-part formula for constructing a mission statement. Start with the phrase "My mission is to" and record three action verbs that best describe what you want to do (e.g., *accomplish, build, finance, give, discuss*). Next, plug in a principle, value, or purpose that you could commit the rest of your life to (joy, service, faith, creativity, justice). Finish by identifying the group or cause that most excites you (real estate, design, sports, women's issues). Your final statement ought to inspire you and should direct all your activities, both on and off the job.

Leadership consultant Juana Bordas offers an alternative method or path for discovering personal leadership purpose based on Native American culture. Native Americans discovered their life purposes while on vision quests. Vision cairns guided members of some tribes. These stone piles served both as directional markers and as a reminder that others had passed this way before. Bordas identifies nine cairns or markers for creating personal purpose.[36]

Cairn 1: Call Your Purpose; Listen for Guidance. All of us have to be silent in order to listen to our intuition. Periodically you will need to withdraw from the noise of everyday life and reflect on such questions as "What am I meant to do?" and "How can I best serve?"

Cairn 2: Find a Sacred Place. A sacred place is a quiet place for reflection. It can be officially designated as sacred (e.g., a church or meditation garden) or merely be a spot that encourages contemplation, such as a stream, park, or favorite chair.

Cairn 3: See Time as Continuous; Begin With the Child and Move With the Present. Our past has a great impact on where we'll head in the future. Patterns of behavior are likely to continue. Bordas suggests that you should examine the impact of your family composition, gender, geography, cultural background, and generational influences. A meaningful purpose will be anchored in the past but will remain responsive to current conditions such as diversity, globalization, and technological change.

Cairn 4: Identify Special Skills and Talents; Accept Imperfections. Take inventory by examining your major activities and jobs and evaluating your strengths. For example, how are your people skills? Technical knowledge? Communication abilities? Consider how you might further develop your aptitudes and abilities. Also take stock of your significant failures. What did they teach you about your limitations? What did you learn from them?

Cairn 5: Trust Your Intuition. Sometimes we need to act on our hunches and emotions. You may decide to turn down a job that doesn't feel right, for instance, in order to accept a position that seems to be a better fit.

Cairn 6: Open the Door When Opportunity Knocks. Be ready to respond to opportunities that are out of your control, such as a new job assignment or a request to speak or write. Ask yourself whether this possibility will better prepare you for leadership or fit in with what you're trying to do in life.

Cairn 7: Find Your Passion and Make It Happen. Passion energizes us for leadership and gives us stamina. Discover your passion by imagining the following scenarios: If you won the lottery, what would you still do? How would you spend your final 6 months on Earth? What would sustain you for a hundred more years?

Cairn 8: Write Your Life Story; Imagine a Great Leader. Turn your life into a story that combines elements of reality and fantasy. Imagine yourself as an effective leader and carry your story out into the future. What challenges did you overcome? What dreams did you fulfill? How did you reach your final destination?

Cairn 9: Honor Your Legacy, One Step at a Time. Your purpose is not static but will evolve and expand over time. If you're a new leader, you're likely to exert limited influence. That influence will expand as you develop your knowledge and skills. You may manage only a couple of people now, but in a few years you may be responsible for an entire department or division.

IDENTIFYING VALUES

If a mission statement identifies our final destination, then our values serve as a moral compass to guide us on our journey. Values provide a frame of reference, helping us to set priorities and to determine right or wrong. There are all sorts of values. For example, I value fuel economy (I like spending less on gas), so I drive a small, fuel-efficient pickup truck. However, ethical decision making is concerned primarily with identifying and implementing moral values. Moral values are directly related to judgments about what's appropriate or inappropriate behavior. I value honesty, for instance, so I choose not to lie. I value privacy, so I condemn

Internet retailers who gather personal information about me without my permission.

There are two ways to identify or clarify the values you hold. You can generate a list from scratch or rate a list of values supplied by someone else. If brainstorming a list of important values seems a daunting task, you might try the following exercise, developed by James Kousez and Barry Posner. The credo memo asks you to spell out the important values that underlie your philosophy of leadership.

> Imagine that your organization has afforded you the chance to take a six-month sabbatical, all expenses paid. You will be going to a beautiful island where the average temperature is about eighty degrees Fahrenheit during the day. The sun shines in a brilliant sky, with a few wisps of clouds. A gentle breeze cools the island down in the evening, and a light rain clears the air. You wake up in the morning to the smell of tropical flowers.
>
> You may not take any work along on this sabbatical. And you will not be permitted to communicate to anyone at your office or plant—not by letter, phone, fax, e-mail, or other means. There will be just you, a few good books, some music, and your family or a friend.
>
> But before you depart, those with whom you work need to know something. They need to know the principles that you believe should guide their actions in your absence. They need to understand the values and beliefs that you think should steer their decision making and action taking. You are permitted no long reports, however. Just a one-page memorandum.
>
> If given this opportunity, what would you write on your one-page credo memo? Take out one piece of paper and write that memo.[37]

Examples of values that have been included in credo memos include "Operate as a team," "listen to one another," "celebrate successes," "seize the initiative," "trust your judgment," and "strive for excellence." These values can be further clarified through dialogue with coworkers. Many discussions in organizations (e.g., how to select subcontractors, when to fire someone, how to balance the needs of various stakeholders) have an underlying value component. Listen for the principles that shape your opinions and the opinions of others.

Working with a list of values can also be useful. Psychologist Gordon Allport identified six major value types. People can be categorized based on how they organize their lives around each of the following value sets.[38] Prototypes are examples of occupations that fit best into a given value orientation.

- *Theoretical.* Theoretical people are intellectuals who seek to discover the truth and pride themselves on being objective and rational. Prototypes: research scientists, engineers.

- *Economic.* Usefulness is the most important criterion for those driven by economic values. They are interested in production, marketing, economics, and accumulating wealth. Prototype: small business owners.

- *Aesthetic.* Aesthetic thinkers value form and harmony. They enjoy each event as it unfolds, judging the experience based on its symmetry or harmony. Prototypes: artists, architects.

- *Social.* Love of others is the highest value for social leaders and followers. These "people persons" view others as ends, not means, and are kind and unselfish. Prototype: social workers.

- *Political.* Power drives political people. They want to accumulate and exercise power and enjoy the recognition that comes from being in positions of influence. Prototypes: senators, governors.

- *Religious.* Religious thinkers seek unity through understanding and relating to the cosmos as a whole. Prototypes: pastors, rabbis, Muslim clerics.

Identifying your primary value orientation is a good way to avoid situations that could cause you ethical discomfort. If you have an economic bent, you will want a job (often in a business setting) where you solve real-life problems. On the other hand, if you love people, you may be uncomfortable working for a business that puts profits first.

Milton Rokeach developed the most widely used value system.[39] He divided moral values into two subcategories. *Instrumental values* are a means to an end. For example, diligence and patience are valuable because they enable us to reach difficult goals such as completing a degree program or remodeling a house. *Terminal values* generally reflect our lifelong aspirations, such as becoming wise, experiencing happiness, or living comfortably. They stand by themselves. Rokeach's list of instrumental and terminal values is found in the self-assessment in Box 3.3. Take a moment and rank the items on both lists.

Comparing our responses with those of other individuals and groups opens the way for additional dialogue about priorities. We may discover that we don't fit in as well as we would like with the rest of the group and decide to leave or work for change. (We will take a closer look at the importance of shared organizational values in Chapter 9.) Researchers can also use a list of values to determine whether different classes of people have different priorities and how values change over time.[40]

Some well-meaning writers and consultants make values the end-all of ethical decision making. They assume that groups will prosper if they develop a set of lofty, mutually shared values. However, as we saw earlier, having worthy values doesn't mean that individuals, groups, or organizations will live by these principles. Other factors—time pressures, faulty assumptions, corrupt systems—undermine their influence. Values, though critical, have to be translated into action. Furthermore, our greatest struggles come from choosing between two good values. Many corporate leaders value both customer service and product

Box 3.3

Self-Assessment

INSTRUMENTAL AND TERMINAL VALUES

Instructions

Rank the values on each list from 1 (most important) to 18 (least important) to you. Rate the instrumental values first and then rank order the terminal values. You will end up with two lists. A low ranking doesn't mean that a value is insignificant; it means only that the item is less important to you than other, more highly rated values.

Terminal Values	Instrumental Values
Freedom (independence, free choice)	*Loving* (affection, tenderness)
Self-respect (self-esteem)	*Independent* (self-reliant, self-sufficient)
A sense of accomplishment (lasting contribution)	*Capable* (competent, effective)
Mature love (sexual and spiritual intimacy)	*Broad-minded* (open-minded)
An exciting life (activity)	*Intellectual* (intelligent, reflective)
A comfortable life (prosperity)	*Honest* (sincere, truthful)
Family security (taking care of loved ones)	*Responsible* (dependable, reliable)
True friendship (close companionship)	*Ambitious* (hardworking, aspiring)
Social recognition (respect, admiration)	*Imaginative* (daring, creative)
Wisdom (an understanding of life)	*Helpful* (working for the welfare of others)
Happiness (contentedness)	*Forgiving* (willing to pardon others)
Inner harmony (freedom from inner conflict)	*Self-controlled* (restrained, self-disciplined)
Equality (brotherhood, equal opportunity for all)	*Logical* (consistent, rational)
A world at peace (free of war and conflict)	*Courageous* (standing up for your own beliefs)
A world of beauty (beauty of nature and art)	*Cheerful* (lighthearted, joyful)
Pleasure (an enjoyable, leisurely life)	*Polite* (courteous, well-mannered)
National security (protection from attack)	*Obedient* (dutiful, respectful)
Salvation (saved, eternal life)	*Clean* (neat, tidy)

SOURCE: Reprinted with the permission of The Free Press, a division of Simon & Schuster, Inc., from *The nature of human values* (p. 28), by Milton Rokeach. Copyright © 1973 by The Free Press.

quality, but what do they do when reaching one of these goals means sacrificing the other? Pushing to get a product shipped to satisfy a customer may force the manufacturing division into cutting corners in order to meet the deadline. Resolving dilemmas such as these takes more than value clarification; we also need some standards for determining ethical priorities. With that in mind, I'll identify ethical decision-making principles in Chapters 5 and 6. But first we need to confront one final shadow caster—evil—in Chapter 4.

Implications and Applications

- Character is integral to effective leadership, often making the difference between success and failure.
- Virtues are positive leadership qualities or traits that help us manage our shadow sides.
- Important virtues to develop as a leader include courage (overcoming fear in order to do the right thing), integrity (wholeness, completeness, consistency), humility (self-awareness, openness, a sense of transcendence), reverence (a sense of awe, respect, and shame), optimism (expectation of positive outcomes in the future), compassion (kindness, generosity, love), and justice (obligation to the common good; treating others equally and fairly).
- Strive for consistency but don't be surprised by contradictions in your character or in the character of others. Become more tolerant of yourself and other leaders. At the same time, recognize that a leader's private behavior often influences his or her public decisions.
- Indirect approaches that build character include identifying role models, telling and living out shared stories, learning from hardship, cultivating habits, creating a personal mission statement, and clarifying values.
- Never underestimate the power of a good example. Be on the lookout for real and fictional ethical role models.
- Shared narratives nurture character development, encouraging you to live up to the role you play in the collective story.
- Hardships are inevitable part of life and leadership. The sense of loss associated with these events can provide important feedback, spur self-inspection, encourage the development of coping strategies, force you to reorder your priorities, and nurture your compassion. However, to benefit from them you must see challenges as learning opportunities that prepare you for future leadership responsibilities.
- Adopting habits can speed the development of character. Seek to be proactive, begin with the end in mind, organize around priorities, strive for cooperation, listen for understanding, develop synergistic solutions, and engage in continual self-renewal.
- Having an ultimate destination will encourage you to stay on your ethical track. Develop a personal mission statement that reflects your strengths and passions. Use your values as a moral compass to keep you from losing your way.

For Further Exploration, Challenge, and Self-Assessment

1. Which virtue is most important for leaders? Defend your choice.

2. Can the private and public morals of leaders be separated? Try to reach a consensus on this question in a group.

3. What steps can you take to develop a more positive outlook about future events?

4. Brainstorm a list of moral exemplars. What does it take to qualify for your list? How would you classify these role models according to the types described in the chapter?

5. Reflect on the ways in which a particular shared narrative has shaped your worldview and behavior. Write up your conclusions.

6. Examine the role that hardship has played in the life of a prominent leader. Summarize your findings in an oral presentation or research paper.

7. Interview a leader you admire. Determine his or her crucible moment and capacity to learn from that experience.

8. Rate yourself on each of the seven habits of effective people and develop a plan for addressing your weaknesses. Explore the habits further through reading and training seminars.

9. Develop a personal mission statement using the guidelines provided by Jones or Bordas.

10. What are your most important terminal and instrumental values? Are you comfortable with your rankings? Why or why not?

11. Complete the credo memo exercise on page 90 if you haven't already done so. Encourage others in your work group or organization to do the same and compare your statements. Use this as an opportunity to dialogue about values.

CASE STUDY 3.2

Chapter End Case: "Chainsaw" Al Dunlap and "Mensch" Aaron Feuerstein

In the 1990s, Al Dunlap may have been the most admired and the most hated CEO in America. Dunlap earned the name "Chainsaw" for aggressively cutting costs at troubled companies. He didn't shy away from tough decisions but would close plants, lay off employees, and sell assets in order to improve the bottom line. At the Lily-Tulip disposable cup and plate company, for example, he cut 20% of the staff and half the management team along with 40% of the firm's suppliers. At Scott Paper, Dunlap laid off more than 11,000 workers, deferred maintenance costs, slashed the research budget, and eliminated donations to charity. These cost reductions drove the stock price up 225% and made Scott Paper an attractive takeover candidate. When Kimberly-Clark bought the firm in 1995, Dunlap pocketed $100 million through the sale of his stock options. Dunlap then moved to the Sunbeam Corporation in 1996 and started another round of cutbacks. He hoped to once again reap millions by boosting the company's stock value and then selling out.

The media and Wall Street investors loved Al Dunlap. He was readily available to the press, and his forthright style made him a good interview. Chainsaw became the poster child of shareholder capitalism. Shareholder capitalists believe that publicly held corporations serve the interests of only one group: stockholders. Other constituencies, such as customers, employees, and local communities, don't matter. According to Dunlap, "Stakeholders are total rubbish. It's the shareholders who own the company" (Byrne, 1999, pp. xiv–xv). He made investors, particularly the large investors who sat on the boards of Scott and Sunbeam, lots of money.

Company insiders had an entirely different opinion of Dunlap. Those who lost their jobs despised him, and those who survived the cuts viewed him as a tyrant. Remaining employees had to work long hours to reach impossible production and sales goals. *Business Week* writer and author John Byrne offers this description of life under Dunlap:

> Working on the front lines of a company run by Albert Dunlap was like being at war. The pressure was brutal, the hours exhausting, and the casualties high. Dunlap and his consultants had imposed such unrealistic goals on the company that virtually everyone understood he was engaged in a short-term exercise to pretty up the business for a quick sale. . . .
>
> By sheer brutality, he began putting excruciating pressure on those who reported to him, who in turn passed that intimidation down the line. It went beyond the ordinary pressure to do well in a corporation. People were told, explicitly and implicitly, that

either they hit the number or another person would be found to do it for them. Their livelihood hung on making numbers that were not makeable.

At Sunbeam Dunlap created a culture of misery, an environment of moral ambiguity, indifferent to everything except the stock price. He did not lead by intellect or by vision, but by fear and intimidation. (pp. 153–154)

Dunlap's dream of selling Sunbeam and cashing in began to collapse when the firm's stock price went too high to interest corporate buyers. Shortly thereafter, the firm began falling short of its income projections. The company inflated 1997 sales figures by convincing dealers to sign up for merchandise that was then stored in Sunbeam warehouses. This maneuver allowed the corporation to count these "sales" as immediate income before customers had even paid for the products. By 1998, large accounts such as Wal-Mart and Costco were glutted with inventory, and this accounting trick no longer worked. Sunbeam couldn't reverse the slide because Dunlap had fired essential employees, eliminated profitable plants and product lines, and alienated vendors. Share prices then dropped dramatically, and Dunlap was forced out. After his ouster, the company defaulted on a major loan payment, and the Securities and Exchange Commission began to audit the company's books.

Chainsaw Al had few of the virtues we associate with high moral character. To his credit, he was decisive, hardworking, and loyal to a few business associates and subordinates. However, he was also bullying, angry, abusive (to family members as well as employees), egotistical, sensitive to the slightest criticism, vengeful, inconsistent, uncaring, and cowardly (he rarely fired anyone himself).

Working for Al could be hell on Earth. Why, then, was he so successful, and why did people continue to work for him? As I noted earlier, he appeared to get results (at least in the short term) and got lots of favorable attention in the press. If he hadn't fallen short of earnings projections, he probably would still be at Sunbeam despite his shabby treatment of employees and other stakeholder groups. High-level executives continued to work for Sunbeam out of fear and in hopes of getting rich. They would make millions from their stock options if the company succeeded and were afraid to stand up to the boss. Said one vice-president who had often considered quitting, "But it was like being in an abusive relationship. You just didn't know how to get out of it."

Summing up the career of Chainsaw Al, Byrne concludes,

At Sunbeam, he eluded all the safeguards of a public corporation: a well-meaning board of directors, independent, outside auditors, and an army of honest and talented executives. Every system depends on people, people who will say no even when faced with the threat of losing a job or a business. Dunlap worked so hard at creating fear, dependence, and guilt that no one dared to defy him—until it was too late. It is a lesson no one should ever forget. (p. 354)

While Al Dunlap was ransacking Sunbeam, Aaron Feuerstein, CEO of textile manufacturer Malden Mills, was setting a very different example. On December 11, 1995, the company's plant in Lawrence, Massachusetts, burned down in one of the largest fires in the state's history. Even while the ashes of the plant were still smoldering, Feuerstein pledged to continue to pay the salaries of his workers. Furthermore, he promised to rebuild in Lawrence rather than go out of business or move operations in order to reduce labor costs.

Feuerstein (69 at the time of the fire) was the latest in his family to run the privately held company, which was best known for producing Polartec fleece. He learned his business principles from his father and uncles. These principles included treating all employees fairly, encouraging loyalty, and being a responsible member of the community. Malden offered wages nearly 20% higher than the industry average, and its unionized workforce never went on strike.

CEO Feuerstein's decision to keep paying employees while rebuilding in the same location was based in large part on his values as an orthodox Jew. Feuerstein linked his choices to Hebrew scripture. In talking about the fire, he quoted the Jewish proverb, "When all is in moral chaos, this is the time to be a 'mensch.'" *Mensch* is the Yiddish word for a "man with a heart."

The Malden Mill executive exhibited the humility and modest lifestyle of the Level 5 leaders studied by Jim Collins. He could have taken the $300-million insurance settlement and retired, but as he told *60 Minutes* correspondent Morley Safer, he was not interested in moving to Florida to play golf. Mr. and Mrs. Feuerstein's idea of a good time was reading together in front of the fire at their five-room condominium.

Unfortunately, Feuerstein didn't enjoy the success of the Level 5 leaders in the Collins study. Malden Mills was forced to declare bankruptcy because of additional debt and reduced market share resulting from the fire. The company emerged from bankruptcy in 2003, and Feuerstein retired. For the first time in its history, Malden Mills was no longer owned and managed by the Feuerstein family. In 2007 the firm filed for bankruptcy again, citing financial problems left over from its first bankruptcy and foreign competition. Polartec (a company owned by a private equity firm) then acquired Malden Mills.

Once Feuerstein retired, Malden Mills seemed to lose its ethical way. Labor relations soured, and workers went on strike. Creditors accused the company of hiding its plans to file for bankruptcy a second time. The firm's board had to withdraw a plan to pay $1 million in bonuses to top executives while it owed millions to unsecured creditors.

DISCUSSION PROBES

1. What responsibility should followers share for the actions of Dunlap? How would you evaluate the character of those who decided to stay and work for him?

2. How much blame do you place on the company directors who hired Dunlap and were supposed to oversee his activities?

3. How can we prevent future Al Dunlaps from taking over companies and other organizations?

4. Was Feuerstein's decision to continue to pay workers foolish based on the firm's subsequent bankruptcies?

5. Could the CEO of a publicly held company make the same choice as Feuerstein? Why or why not?

6. What factors go into making a mensch?

7. What leadership ethics lessons do you glean from rise and fall of Chainsaw Al, from Feuerstein's example, and the fate of Malden Mills after Feuerstein retired?

SOURCES

Byrne, J. (1999). *The notorious career of Al Dunlap in the era of profit-at-any price.* New York: HarperCollins.

Kievra, B. (2007, January 12). Creditors challenge bankruptcy protection; Malden Mills accused of deceit, misconduct. *Worcester Telegram & Gazette,* p. E1. Retrieved July 12, 2007, from LexisNexis Academic database.

Malden Mills withdraws controversial plan for executive bonuses. (2007, February 6). *Associated Press State & Local Wire.* Retrieved July 12, 2007, from LexisNexis Academic database.

Malden Mills (Television series episode). (2002, March 24). *60 Minutes.* CBS Television.

Seeger, M. W., & Ulmer, R. R. (2001). Virtuous responses to organizational crisis: Aaron Feuerstein and Milt Cole. *Journal of Business Ethics, 31,* 369–376.

Ulmer, R. R., & Seeger, M. W. (2000). Communication ethics and the Malden Mills disaster. In G. L. Peterson (Ed.), *Communicating in organizations* (2nd ed., pp. 191–194). Boston: Allyn & Bacon.

CASE STUDY 3.3

Chapter End Case:
The Greatest Reformer in History

Finding a moral exemplar who has had more impact than English politician and philanthropist William Wilberforce (1759–1833) would be hard to do. The son of a wealthy merchant, Wilberforce spent his entire career as a member of the British parliament. There he labored tirelessly for the abolition of slavery and the reformation of British society. His efforts paid off. During his lifetime, Britain abolished slaveholding throughout the empire. Few in England tried to help the poor and suffering before Wilberforce. Under his direction, hundreds of groups sprung up to deal with social ills such as child labor, prisoner abuse, orphanhood, and cruelty to animals. (Wilberforce belonged to 69 such groups himself.) Great Britain developed a social conscience where none had existed before. Americans Thomas Jefferson, Abraham Lincoln, Harriet Beecher Stowe, Henry David Thoreau, and John Greenleaf looked to him for inspiration. In recognition of his impact, Wilberforce has been called the "greatest social reformer of the history of the world."[1]

Wilberforce was an unlikely candidate to become a reformer. His parents went to great lengths to keep him from the clutches of religion and encouraged him to adopt an extravagant lifestyle instead, one filled with trips to the theater, elegant balls, and card parties. He wasted much of his college career drinking and partying. When he first came to parliament, he focused solely on the interests of his district and was known to use his wit and sarcasm to belittle his opponents. Then Wilberforce underwent a gradual religious conversion he called "the Great Change." After this change, he wanted to drop out of politics but was dissuaded by close friend William Pitt, who was to become prime minister. At age 27, Wilberforce decided to take on the major missions or goals of his life: the abolition of the slave trade (and of slavery) and the "reformation of manners" (morals). He then put his superior intelligence and eloquence (he was considered one of the greatest orators of his day) to work in pursuit of these objectives.

Wilberforce had to overcome great odds to reach his goals, beginning with his physical condition. Short of stature (5-foot-3), he suffered ulcerative colitis throughout his life. This condition nearly killed him on several occasions, and he treated it with daily doses of morphine. Wilberforce's antislavery efforts met with stiff resistance from powerful merchants and politicians. He was mocked by opponents and in the popular press. Captains of slave ships threatened him with violence and death. Every year he introduced legislation to ban the slave trade, which cost the lives of hundreds of slaves who died on route to the West Indies. Every year he was defeated. It took 20 years to get the slave trade banned and another 26 years after that (within a few days of his death) to abolish slaveholding. Wilberforce's campaign to improve the lot of the poor had to overcome apathy on the part of the middle and upper classes, who felt no obligation to care for the less fortunate.

Wilberforce was sustained in his long battle for social justice by his religious faith and by his friends and fellow reformers. He took his inspiration from Christian scripture and regularly renewed his faith through private study and worship. (Wilberforce was also an avid reader of philosophy and almost any other literature he could get his hands on.) He had a large circle of friends who visited him regularly. Wilberforce and other like-minded people formed the Clapham Circle, a group that met together to share ideas and strategies for social change. Pastor Thomas Clarkson, politician Granville Sharp, John Newton (writer of the hymn "Amazing Grace"), and poet William Cowper worked with him in the campaign to abolish slavery.

By the end of his life, many of those who had opposed Wilberforce joined with him. His character won many over. Not only was he cheerful and compassionate, giving as much as one-fourth of his income away some years, he was also extremely humble. Wilberforce turned down the chance to become a British lord and was uncomfortable with celebrity and acclaim. When one friend praised him for his generosity, he replied, "With regard to myself, I have nothing whatsoever to urge, but the poor publican's plea, 'God be merciful to me a sinner.'"[2] Wilberforce was gentle in his dealings, choosing first to look for the good in others (even slave traders and owners) to see whether he could establish common ground. He tried to mix mercy with grace. For instance, he agreed to plans to reimburse slave owners in the West Indies even though other abolitionists believed that doing so could be seen as a reward for their bad behavior.

All the members of parliament, the Duke of Wellington, and huge crowds attended Wilberforce's funeral. Though a commoner, he was buried with royalty in Westminster Abbey. African freemen in the United States honored his memory by wearing a badge of mourning for 30 days. In a public eulogy for Wilberforce delivered in New York City, African American Benjamin Hughes described him as "the Philanthropist" and "the Hercules of Abolition."

DISCUSSION PROBES

1. What do you learn from the example of William Wilberforce?

2. What steps can you take to follow his example?

3. What does Wilberforce have in common with other moral exemplars?

4. Do you think Wilberforce was the "greatest social reformer in history"? Whom would you nominate for this honor?

5. What leadership ethics lessons do you take from this case?

NOTES

1. Metaxas, E. (2007). *Amazing grace: William Wilberforce and the heroic campaign to end slavery.* San Francisco: Harper San Francisco, p. xvii.
2. Metaxas, p. 273.

SOURCES

Belmonte, K. (2007). *William Wilberforce: A hero for humanity.* Grand Rapids, MI: Zondervan.
Metaxas, E. (2007). *Amazing grace: William Wilberforce and the heroic campaign to end slavery.* San Francisco: Harper San Francisco.

Notes

1. Johannesen, R. L. (2002). *Ethics in human communication* (5th ed.). Prospect Heights, IL: Waveland, Ch. 1.
2. Snyder, C. R., & Lopez, S. J. (2005). *Handbook of positive psychology.* Oxford, UK: Oxford University Press; Aspinwall, L. G., & Staudinger, U. M. (Eds.). (2002). *A psychology of human strengths: Fundamental questions about future directions for a positive psychology.* Washington, DC: American Psychological Association.
3. Collins, J. (2001). *Good to great.* New York: HarperBusiness; Collins, J. (2001, January). Level 5 leadership: The triumph of humility and fierce resolve. *Harvard Business Review,* pp. 67–76.
4. Johannsen, R. L. (1991). Virtue ethics, character, and political communication. In R. E. Denton (Ed.), *Ethical dimensions of political communication* (pp. 69–90). New York: Praeger.
5. Peterson, C., & Seligman, M. E. P. (2004). *Character strengths and virtues: A handbook and classification.* Oxford, UK: Oxford University Press.
6. Comte-Sponville, A. (2001). *A small treatise on the great virtues: The uses of philosophy in everyday life.* New York: Metropolitan, p. 44.
7. Kidder, R. M. (2005). *Moral courage.* New York: William Morrow.
8. See Bruhn, J. G. (2001). *Trust and the health of organizations.* New York: Kluwer/Plenum; Elangovan, A. R., & Shapiro, D. L. (1998). Betrayal of trust in organizations. *Academy of Management Review, 23,* 547–566.
9. See Dirks, K. T. (1999). The effects of interpersonal trust on work group performance. *Journal of Applied Psychology, 84,* 445–455; Kramer, R. M., & Tyler, T. L. (1996). *Trust in organizations: Frontiers of theory and research.* Thousand Oaks, CA: Sage.
10. Crosariol, B. (2005, November 21). The diminishing allure of rock-star executives. *Globe and Mail Update.* Retrieved June 5, 2007, from LexisNexis Academic database; Varachaver, N. (2004, November 11). Glamour! Fame! Org charts! *Fortune.* Retrieved June 5, 2007, from Academic Search Premier database.
11. Morris, J. A., Brotheridge, C. M., & Urbanski, J. C. (2005). Bringing humility to leadership: Antecedents and consequences of leader humility. *Human Relations,* pp. 1323–1350. See also Tangney, J. P. (2000). Humility: Theoretical perspectives,

empirical findings and directions for future research. *Journal of Social and Clinical Psychology, 19,* 70–82.

12. Woodruff, P. (2001). *Reverence: Renewing a forgotten virtue.* Oxford, UK: Oxford University Press.

13. Carver, C. S., & Scheier, M. F. (2005). Optimism. In C. R. Snyder & S. J. Lopez (Eds.), *Handbook of positive psychology* (pp. 231–243). Oxford, UK: Oxford University Press.

14. Peterson & Seligman.

15. Howell, J., & Avolio, B. J. (1992). The ethics of charismatic leadership: Submission or liberation? *Academy of Management Executive, 6,* 43–54.

16. Peterson & Seligman; Compte-Sponville; Smith, T. (1999). Justice as a personal virtue. *Social Theory & Practice, 25,* 361–384.

17. Jennings, M. M. (2006). *The seven signs of ethical collapse: How to spot moral meltdowns in companies . . . before it's too late.* New York: St. Martin's Press.

18. Wayne, L. (2005, March 8). Boeing chief is ousted after admitting affair. *The New York Times,* p. A1. Retrieved July 27, 2005, from LexisNexis Academic database.

19. Tangney; Carver & Scheier; Cavanagh, G. F., & Moberg, D. J. (1999). The virtue of courage within the organization. In M. L. Pava & P. Primeaux (Eds.), *Research in ethical issues in organizations* (Vol. 1, pp. 1–25). Stamford, CT: JAI Press.

20. MacIntyre, A. (1984). *After virtue: A study in moral theory* (2nd ed.). Notre Dame, IN: University of Notre Dame Press; Hauerwas, S. (1981). *A community of character.* Notre Dame, IN: University of Notre Dame Press.

21. Lacayo, R., & Ripley, A. (2002, December 30). Persons of the year. *Time,* pp. 30–60.

22. Hart, D. K. (1992). The moral exemplar in an organizational society. In T. L. Cooper & N. D. Wright (Eds.), *Exemplary public administrators: Character and leadership in government* (pp. 9–29). San Francisco: Jossey-Bass.

23. Haillie, P. (1979). *Lest innocent blood be shed: The story of the village of Le Chambon and how goodness happened there.* New York: Harper & Row.

24. Colby, A., & Damon, W. (1992). *Some do care: Contemporary lives of moral commitment.* New York: Free Press; Colby, A., & Damon, W. (1995). The development of extraordinary moral commitment. In M. Killen & D. Hart (Eds.), *Morality in everyday life: Developmental perspectives* (pp. 342–369). Cambridge, UK: Cambridge University Press.

25. Colby & Damon (1995), p. 363.

26. Burns, J. M. (2003). *Transforming leadership: A new pursuit of happiness.* New York: Atlantic Monthly Press, Ch. 5.

27. MacIntyre, p. 216.

28. Lisman, C. D. (1996). *The curricular integration of ethics: Theory and practice.* Westport, CT: Praeger.

29. Lisman's arguments are echoed by Goldberg, M. (1997). Doesn't anybody read the Bible anymo'? In O. F. Williams (Ed.), *The moral imagination: How literature and films can stimulate ethical reflection in the business world* (pp. 19–32). Notre Dame, IN: Notre Dame Press; Ellenwood, S. (2006). Revisiting character education: From McGuffey to narratives. *Journal of Education, 187,* 21–43.

30. Moxley, R. S., & Pulley, M. L. (2004). Hardships. In C. D. McCauley & E. Van Velsor (Eds.), *The Center for Creative Leadership handbook of leadership development* (2nd ed., pp. 183–203). San Francisco: Jossey-Bass.

31. Bennis, W. G., & Thomas, R. J. (2002). *Geeks and geezers: How era, values, and defining moments shape leaders.* Boston: Harvard Business School Press.

32. Aristotle. (350 B.C.E./1962). *Nichomachean ethics* (Martin Ostwald, Trans.). Indianapolis, IN: Bobbs-Merrill.

33. Cavanagh, G. F., & Moberg, D. J. (1999). The virtue of courage within the organization. In M. L. Pava & P. Primeaux (Eds.), *Research in ethical issues in organizations* (Vol. 1, pp. 1–25). Stamford, CT: JAI Press.

34. Covey, S. (1989). *The seven habits of highly effective people.* New York: Simon & Schuster.

35. Jones, L. B. (1996). *The path: Creating your mission statement for work and for life.* New York: Hyperion.

36. Bordas, J. (1995). Becoming a servant-leader: The personal development path. In L. Spears (Ed.), *Reflections on leadership* (pp. 149–160). New York: Wiley.

37. Kouzes, J. M., & Posner, B. Z. (2003). *Credibility: How leaders gain and lose it, why people demand it.* San Francisco: Jossey-Bass, pp. 62–63. Used by permission of the publisher.

38. Allport, G. (1961). *Pattern and growth in personality.* New York: Holt, Rinehart & Winston; Guth, W. D., & Tagiuri, R. (1965, September–October). Personal values and corporate strategy. *Harvard Business Review,* 123–132.

39. Rokeach, M. (1973). *The nature of human values.* New York: Free Press.

40. See Judge, W. Q. (1999). *The leader's shadow: Exploring and developing executive character.* Thousand Oaks, CA: Sage.

4 ~~

Combating Evil

Evil, in whatever intellectual framework, is by definition a monster.

—Essayist Lance Morrow

Without forgiveness there is no future.

—South African Archbishop Desmond Tutu

What's Ahead

In this chapter, we wrestle with the most dangerous of all unhealthy motivations: evil. The first section surveys some of the forms or faces of evil. The second section examines the role of forgiveness in breaking cycles of evil. The third section probes the relationship between spirituality and leadership, highlighting how spiritual practices can equip us to deal with evil and foster more ethical, productive workplaces.

The Faces of Evil

The terrorist attacks of September 11, 2001, reintroduced the word *evil* into the national vocabulary. No other term, it seemed, could adequately describe the death and destruction at the World Trade Center and the Pentagon. Ordinary citizens and commentators joined President Bush in condemning the hijackings as evil acts done by evildoers. The trauma of 9/11 and subsequent events, such as prisoner abuse at Abu Ghraib and genocide in Darfur (see the "Genocide in Slow Motion" chapter end case), heightened national and international awareness of the existence of evil, an important first step. However, we can't combat evil until we first understand our opponent. Contemporary Western definitions of evil emphasize its destructiveness.[1] Evil inflicts pain and suffering, deprives innocent people of their humanity, and creates feelings of hopelessness and despair. Evildoers do excessive harm, going well beyond what is needed to achieve their objectives. The ultimate product of evil is death. Evil destroys self-esteem, physical and emotional well-being, relationships, communities, and nations.

We can gain some important insights into the nature of evil by looking at the various forms or faces it displays. In this section, I'll introduce six perspectives on evil and then talk about how each approach can help us better deal with this powerful, destructive force.

EVIL AS DREADFUL PLEASURE

University of Maryland political science professor C. Fred Alford defines evil as a combination of dread and pleasure. Alford recruited 60 respondents from a variety of ages and backgrounds to talk about their experiences with evil. He discovered that people experience evil as a deep sense of uneasiness, "the dread of being human, vulnerable, alone in the universe and doomed to die."[2] They do evil when, instead of coming to grips with their inner darkness, they try to get rid of it by making others feel "dreadful." Inflicting this pain is enjoyable. Part of the pleasure comes from being in charge, of being the victimizer instead of the victim.

Evil can also be a product of chronic boredom.[3] Boredom arises when people lose their sense of meaning and purpose. They no longer enjoy life and try to fill the emptiness they feel inside. Ordinary distractions such as television, movies, surfing the Internet, shopping, and sports don't fill the void, so people turn to evil instead. Evil is an attractive alternative because it engages the full energy and attention of perpetrators. For example, a serial killer has to plan his crimes, locate victims, keep his actions secret, and outsmart law enforcement.

EVIL AS DECEPTION

Psychiatrist Scott Peck identifies evil as a form of narcissism or self-absorption.[4] Mentally healthy adults submit themselves to something beyond themselves, such as God or love or excellence. Submission to a greater power encourages them to obey their consciences. Evil people, on the other hand, refuse to submit and try to control others instead. They consider themselves above reproach and project their shortcomings, attacking anyone who threatens their self-concepts. Evil people are consumed with keeping up appearances. Peck calls them "the people of the lie" because they deceive themselves and others in hopes of projecting a righteous image. Peck believes that truly evil people are more likely to live in our neighborhoods than in our jails. They generally hide their true natures and appear to be normal and successful. Inmates, on the other hand, land in prison because they've been morally inconsistent or stupid.

EVIL AS BUREAUCRACY

The 20th century was the bloodiest period in history. More than 100 million people died as the direct or indirect result of wars, genocide, and other violence. According to public administration professors Guy Adams and Danny Balfour, the combination of science and technology made the 1900s so destructive.[5] Scientific and technological developments (tanks, airplanes, chemical warfare, nuclear weapons) made killing highly efficient. At the same time, belief in technological progress encouraged government officials to take a rational approach to problems. The integration of these factors produced administrative evil. In administrative evil, organizational members commit heinous crimes while carrying out their daily tasks. Balfour and Adams argue that the true nature of administrative evil is masked or hidden from participants. Officials are rarely asked to engage in evil; instead they inflict pain and suffering while fulfilling their job responsibilities.

The Holocaust provides the most vivid example of administrative evil in action. Extermination camps would not have been possible without the willing cooperation of thousands of civil servants engaged in such functions as collecting taxes, running municipal governments, and managing the country's social security system. These duties may seem morally neutral, but in carrying them out public officials condemned millions to death. Government authorities defined who was undesirable and then seized their assets. Administrators managed the ghettos, built concentration camp latrines, and employed slave labor. Even the railway authority did its part. The Gestapo had to pay for each prisoner shipped by rail to the death camps. Railroad officials billed the SS at third-class passenger rates (one way) for adult prisoners, with discounts for children. Guards were charged round-trip fares.

EVIL AS SANCTIONED DESTRUCTION

Social scientists Nevitt Sanford and Craig Comstock believe that widespread evil occurs when victimizers are given permission or sanction to attack groups that have been devalued or dehumanized.[6] Such permission opens the door for such crimes as mass murder and genocide. Sanctions can be overt (a direct statement or order) or disguised (a hint, praise for others engaging in aggressive behavior). Once given, sanctions open the door to oppression because targeted groups no longer enjoy the protections given to the rest of society. American history is filled with examples of devalued peoples. Native Americans were the targeted for extinction; African Americans were routinely lynched for, among other reasons, public entertainment; and Chinese laborers were denied citizenship. Recently the entire U.S. population has become the target of dehumanization. Some Muslims consider the United States to be the "Great Satan," populated by infidels. Such reasoning accounts for the spontaneous celebrations that broke out on the streets of some Islamic nations on news of the 9/11 attacks.

EVIL AS A CHOICE

Any discussion of good and evil must consider the role of human choice. Just how much freedom we have is a matter of debate, but a number of scholars argue that we become good or evil through a series of small, incremental decisions. In other words, we never remain neutral but are moving toward one pole or another. Medieval scholar C. S. Lewis draws on the image of a road to illustrate this point.[7] On a journey, we decide which direction to take every time we come to a fork in the road. We face a similar series of decisions throughout our lives. We can't correct poor decisions by continuing on but must go back to the fork and take the other path.

Psychologist Erich Fromm makes the same argument as Lewis. Only those who are very good or very bad have no choice; the rest of us do. However, each choice we make reduces our options.

> Each step in life which increases my self-confidence, my integrity, my courage, my conviction also increases my capacity to choose the desirable alternative, until eventually it becomes more difficult to choose the undesirable rather than the desirable action. On the other hand, each act of surrender and cowardice weakens me, opens the path for more acts of surrender, and eventually freedom is lost. Between the extreme when I can no longer do a wrong act and the other extreme when I have lost my freedom to right action, there are innumerable degrees of freedom of choice. In the practice of life the degree of freedom to choose is different at any given moment. If the degree of freedom to choose the good is great, it needs less effort to choose the good. If it is small, it takes a great effort, help from others, and favorable circumstances.[8]

Fromm uses the story of Israel's exodus from ancient Egypt to illustrate what happens when leaders make a series of evil choices. Moses repeatedly asks Pharaoh to let his people go, but the Egyptian ruler turns down every request. Eventually the king's heart is "hardened," and he and his army are destroyed.

EVIL AS ORDINARY

The evil as ordinary perspective focuses on the situational factors that cause otherwise ordinary or normal people to become evildoers. Although it is comforting to think that evildoers must be heartless psychopaths or deranged killers, in many cases perpetrators look and act a lot like the rest of us. Social philosopher Hannah Arendt pointed this out in her analysis of the trial of Adolf Eichmann in 1961.[9] Eichmann was responsible for deportation of millions of Jews to concentration and extermination camps. What struck Arendt was how ordinary Eichmann seemed. Half of a dozen psychiatrists examined him and certified him as "normal." Arendt used the term the "banality of evil" when describing Eichmann to point out that the sources of evil aren't mysterious or demonic but commonplace. If that is the case, then any one of us can commit heinous crimes.

Philip Zimbardo and other social psychologists have identified a number of situational factors that can turn otherwise "nice" people into torturers and murderers.[10] Zimbardo discovered first hand the power of the system to promote unethical behavior through his famous Stanford Prison Experiment. He created a mock prison in the basement of the psychology department and randomly assigned student volunteers to roles as prisoner and guards. It didn't take long for both groups to get caught up in their roles. Soon the prisoners revolted and the guards retaliated. The jailers strip searched prisoners, forced them into prolonged exercise, put them into solitary confinement, denied them bathroom privileges (they had to urinate and defecate in their cells), and made them clean toilets by hand. Two prisoners suffered significant emotional trauma and had to be immediately released from the experiment. Zimbardo, who served as the prison warden, also got caught up in the role-play. At one point, he tried to transfer the experiment to an empty cell at the local police station to ensure more security. He got angry when the police refused his request. Zimbardo ended the experiment early after a visitor (who would later become his wife) complained about the disgusting conditions at the "jail." Of the 50 outsiders who visited the experiment, she was the only person to object.

Zimbardo went on to analyze the role of situational variables in real-life cases of evil such as the widespread torture of political opponents in Brazil and prisoner abuse at Iraq's Abu Ghraib prison. According to Zimbardo, ordinary people, such as the military guards at Abu Ghraib, are motivated to do evil when they feel peer pressure to participate in such acts, obey authority, remain anonymous and are given permission to engage in antisocial behavior, and dehumanize others (treat them as less than fully human). Evil is likely to continue when others fail to intervene to stop it.

Facing Evil

"Your Honor, may I point out to the court that my client pleaded guilty to wrongdoing, but not evildoing."

Each of the perspectives just described provides insights into how we can come to grips with evil as leaders. The dreadful pleasure approach highlights both the origins of evil and the attraction of doing evil, forcing us to examine our motivations. We need to ask ourselves, "Am I projecting my insecurities onto others?" "Am I punishing a subordinate because of her or his poor performance or because exercising coercive power makes me feel strong?" "Am I making a legitimate request or merely demonstrating that I have the authority to control another person?" "Am I tempted to harm others just to fill the emptiness I feel inside?"

The evil-as-deception viewpoint makes it clear that people aren't always as they seem. On the surface, evil people appear to be successful and well adjusted. In reality, they exert tremendous energy keeping up appearances. (Turn to the "Covering Up Evil" chapter end case for an example of how one group of leaders tried to keep evil under wraps.) Deceit and defensiveness can serve as warning signs. If we routinely lie to protect our images, refuse constructive feedback, and always blame others, we may be engaged in evil. The same may be true of other leaders and followers who display these behaviors. Peck, like Parker Palmer, believes that to master our inner demons we must first name them. Once we've identified these tendencies, we can begin to deal with them by examining our will. We should determine whether we're willing to submit to a positive force (an ideal, authority) that is greater than we are. Peck urges us to respond to the destructive acts of others with love. Instead of attacking evildoers, we can react with goodness and thereby "absorb" the power of evil.

The administrative evil perspective introduces a new type of evil, one based on technology and logic. Modern evil has greater capacity for destruction. Its impact, once contained by distance and technological limitations, now extends to the entire world. Globalization and the miniaturization of nuclear and biochemical weapons mean that just one person can wreak as much havoc as infamous world leaders such as Caligula and Stalin did in the past.[11] Furthermore, the face of evil may be masked or hidden from those who participate in it. We need to be aware of how our activities contribute to good or evil. Claiming that we were "just following orders" is no excuse.

The evil-as-sanction approach should alert us to the danger of dehumanizing any segment of the population. Language is one of the evildoers' most powerful tools. It is much easier to persecute others who have been labeled as "nerds," "pigs," "scum," "Muslim extremists," or "tree huggers." We need to challenge and eliminate these labels (whether we use them or someone else does). Also, be alert to disguised sanctions. If you don't respond to racial slurs, for example, you legitimize these behaviors and encourage future attacks.

Evil as a choice puts the ethical burden squarely on our shoulders. Group and organizational pressures may contribute to our wrongdoing. However, we make the decision to participate in evil acts. Furthermore, the choices we make now will limit our options in the future. Every moral decision, no matter how insignificant it seems at the time, has lasting consequences.

The final perspective, evil as ordinary, is a sobering reminder that we all have the potential to become evildoers. Not only do we need to resist situational influences that can turn us into brutes as followers (see Box 4.1), but as leaders we should eliminate conditions that promote evil behavior in our subordinates. It is our ethical duty to intervene when we see evil behavior and to reward others who do the same.

Making a Case for Forgiveness

BREAKING THE CYCLE OF EVIL

Scott Peck is not alone in arguing that loving acts can overcome evil. A growing number of social scientists believe that forgiving instead of retaliating can prevent or break cycles of evil. In a cycle of evil, aggressive acts provoke retaliation followed by more aggression. When these destructive patterns characterize relations between ethnic groups (e.g., Turks vs. Armenians, Serbs vs. Croats), they can continue for hundreds of years. (The "Leadership Ethics at the Movies" case in Box 4.2 provides one example of the cycle of evil in action.) Courageous leaders can end retaliatory cycles through dramatic acts of reconciliation, however. Former Egyptian Prime Minister Anwar Sadat

Box 4.1

Focus on Follower Ethics

RESISTING SITUATIONAL PRESSURES
TO DO EVIL: A 10-STEP PROGRAM

Philip Zimbardo offers the following 10-step program designed to help followers resist situational forces that promote evildoing.

"I made a mistake!" Admit your mistakes. (Say "I'm sorry"; "I apologize"; "Forgive me.") Vow to learn from your errors and move on. Don't stay the course if you are engaged in an immoral activity.

"I am mindful." Don't rely on scripts from the past. They can blind you to the tactics of influencers and key elements of the situation. Instead, pay close attention to (be mindful of) the here and now. In addition, think critically. Ask for evidence, imagine future consequences, and reject simple solutions to complex problems. Encourage others to do the same.

"I am responsible." Maintaining personal accountability increases your resistance to conformity pressures. Take charge of your decisions and actions rather than spreading responsibility to your group, coworkers, or military unit. Remember that claiming "everyone else was doing it" is no defense in a court of law.

"I am me, the best I can be." Don't let others take away your individuality, making you anonymous. State your name, credentials, and unique features.

"I respect just authority but rebel against unjust authority." Distinguish between those in authority who deserve your respect and those who are leading others astray or promoting their own interests. Critically evaluate and disobey destructive leaders.

"I want group acceptance but value my independence." Group acceptance is a powerful force but shouldn't overpower our sense of right and wrong. Resist social pressure by stepping out of the group, getting other opinions, and finding new groups more in line with your values.

"I will be more frame-vigilant." Frames (words, pictures, slogans, logos) shape our attitudes toward issues and people, often without our being aware of their impact. For example, many politicians use the colors of the flag—red, white, and blue—on their campaign signs and other materials. Be vigilant, noting the way that the frame is designed to shape your thoughts and emotions.

"I will balance my time perspective." Living in the present increases the power of situational influences that promote evil. You are less likely to go along with abusive behavior if you consider the long-term consequences of such actions and remember the values and standards you developed in the past.

Box 4.1 (Continued)

"I will not sacrifice personal or civic freedoms for the illusion of security." Reject any offer that involves sacrificing even small freedoms for the promise of future security. Such sacrifices (e.g., loss of privacy, legal protections, and freedom of speech) are immediate and real, but the promised security is often a distant illusion.

"I can oppose unjust systems." Join with others to resist systems that promote evil. Try to bring about change, blow the whistle on corruption, get away from the group or organization, resist groupthink, draw on the resources of outsiders, and so on.

SOURCE: Adapted from Zimbardo, P. G. (2007). *The Lucifer effect: Understanding how good people turn evil.* New York: Random House, pp. 451–456.

Box 4.2

Leadership Ethics at the Movies

MUNICH

Key Cast Members: Eric Bana, Daniel Craig, Ciarán Hinds, Mathieu Kassovitz, Geoffrey Rush, Valerie Brumi-Tedeschi

Synopsis: Tells the story of the secret team assembled to execute the 11 Palestinians who planned the 1972 massacre of Israel's Munich Olympic Team. Team leader Avner (Bana) and his squad track down and eliminate their targets (and innocent bystanders) in Europe and the Middle East. The Palestinian group Black September retaliates by targeting squad members for assassination. As the death toll mounts, team members begin to doubt their mission, fearing that they are no more righteous than the men they pursue. After the group disbands, Avner must live with his nightmares and with the realization that he can no longer call Israel his home.

Rating: R for graphic violence, nudity, language, and strong subject matter

Themes: evil, revenge, cycle of evil, justice, loyalty, character

engaged in one such conciliatory gesture when he traveled to Jerusalem to further the peace process with Israel. Pope John Paul II went to the jail cell of his would-be assassin to offer forgiveness. Archbishop Desmond Tutu and Nelson Mandela prevented a bloodbath in South Africa by creating the Truth and Reconciliation Commission. This body, made up of both blacks and whites, investigated crimes committed during the apartheid era and allowed offenders to confess their guilt and ask for pardon. Similar commissions were created after widespread torture and murder in Argentina and Peru.

The concept of forgiving evildoers is controversial.[12] (See Case Study 4.1 for a closer look at some of the issues raised by forgiveness.) Skeptics worry that guilty parties will get off without acknowledging they have done wrong or paying for their crimes, that forgiveness is a sign of weakness, that forgiveness is impossible in some situations, that forgiveness can't be offered until after the offender asks for it, and that no leader has the right to offer forgiveness on behalf of other victims. Each of these concerns is valid. You will have to decide whether forgiveness is an appropriate response to evil deeds. However, before you make that determination, I want to describe the forgiveness process and identify some of the benefits that come from extending mercy to others.

CASE STUDY 4.1

To Forgive or Not to Forgive?

Like many other European Jews, Simon Wiesenthal endured unimaginable suffering at the hands of the Nazis. Eighty-nine of his relatives perished in the Holocaust, and Wiesenthal himself spent the war in a concentration camp. Hunger, torture, and death were his constant companions.

One day, a nurse called Wiesenthal away from his work detail, which was removing rubbish from a hospital, to hear the confession of an SS officer named Karl who had been severely wounded by an artillery shell. Blind and near death, Karl told how he had rejected his Catholic upbringing to join the Hitler Youth. Later, he volunteered for the SS. Posted to the Russian front, he participated in a massacre in a small town named Dnepropetrovsk. Jews from the area were crammed into a house that was set on fire. All who tried to escape, including small children, were shot. This incident haunted Karl, and now he wanted to confess his crime to Wiesenthal as a representative of the Jewish race. He begged for forgiveness so that he could die in peace. Wiesenthal pondered the request and then left without saying a word.

Prisoner Wiesenthal had mixed feelings about his decision, asking companions whether he had made the right choice. He went to Karl's home after the war ended and met Karl's mother, who still believed that her son was a "good boy." In order to protect Karl's reputation, Wiesenthal hid the fact that her son had become a murderer. Later Wiesenthal became the world's most famous Nazi hunter, bringing more than 1,100 war criminals to justice.

Wiesenthal describes his encounter with the SS soldier in a book titled *The Sunflower*. In the first half of the book, he recounts the story. In the second half, he asks 42 theologians, political leaders, writers, Holocaust survivors, and others what they would have done in his place. They wrestle with such questions as "Must we forgive when asked?" "Can we forgive on behalf of other people?" "Does forgiveness diminish the seriousness of the crime?" and "What does forgiveness do to the victim? To the perpetrator?"

As you might imagine, responses to this moral dilemma vary widely. Some respondents argue that forgiveness is a form of "cheap grace" that diminishes the enormity of the crime and the suffering of the victims. Even God can't forgive some atrocities, they argue. Others believe that only the offended can forgive the offenders; no one can offer mercy on their behalf. Still others claim that genuine remorse deserves forgiveness. They believe that mercy in the face of honest repentance is the way to break the cycle of retribution and to help victims regain control over their lives.

What would you have done had you been in Wiesenthal's place? Why?

THE FORGIVENESS PROCESS

There are many misconceptions about what it means to forgive another person or group of people. According to Robert Enright, professor of educational psychology and president of the International Forgiveness Institute at the University of Wisconsin, forgiveness is *not* the following:[13]

- Forgetting past wrongs to "move on"
- Excusing or condoning bad, damaging behavior
- Reconciliation or coming together again (forgiveness opens the way to reconciliation, but the other person must change or desire to reconcile)
- Reducing the severity of offenses
- Offering a legal pardon
- Pretending to forgive in order to wield power over another person
- Ignoring the offender
- Dropping our anger and becoming emotionally neutral

Enright and his colleagues define forgiveness as "a willingness to abandon one's right to resentment, negative judgment, and indifferent behavior toward one who unjustly injured us, while fostering the undeserved qualities of compassion, generosity, and even love toward him or her."[14] This definition recognizes that the wronged party has been unjustly treated (slandered, betrayed, imprisoned); the offended person willingly chooses forgiveness regardless of the offender's response; forgiving involves emotions, thoughts, and behavior; and forgiveness is a process that takes place over time. (To measure your likelihood to forgive others, complete the scale in Box 4.3.)

Enright and his fellow researchers offer a four-stage model to help people forgive. (A list of the psychological factors that go into each stage is found in Box 4.4.) In the first phase, *uncovering*, a victim may initially deny that a problem exists. However, when the person does acknowledge the hurt, he or she may experience intense feelings of anger, shame, and betrayal. The victim invests a lot of psychic energy in rehashing the offense and comparing his or her condition with that of the offender. Feeling permanently damaged, the person may believe that life is unfair.

During the second phase, *decision*, the injured party recognizes that he or she is paying a high price for dwelling on the injury, considers the possibility of forgiveness, and commits himself or herself to forgiving.

Forgiveness is accomplished in the third stage, *work*. The wronged party tries to understand (not condone) the victimizer's background and motivation. He or she may experience empathy and compassion for the offender. Absorbing pain is the key to this stage. The forgiver decides to endure suffering rather than pass it on, thereby breaking the cycle of evil. Viewed in this light, forgiveness is a gift of mercy to the wrongdoer.

Box 4.3

Self-Assessment

TENDENCY TO FORGIVE SCALE

Instructions: Respond to each of the following items on a scale of 1 (*strongly disagree*) to 7 (*strongly agree*).

1. "I tend to get over it quickly when someone hurts my feelings."
2. "If someone wrongs me, I often think about it a lot afterward."
3. "I have a tendency to harbor grudges."
4. "When people wrong me, my approach is just to forgive and forget."

Scoring:

Reverse your scores on items 2 and 3 and then add up your responses to all four statements. The higher the score (possible scores range from 4 to 28), the more likely you are to forgive others and the less likely you are to bring up offenses from the past.

SOURCE: Brown, R. P. (2003). Measuring individual differences in the tendency to forgive: Construct validity and links with depression. *Personality and Social Psychology Bulletin, 29*, p. 770. Used by permission.

The fourth and final phase, *deepening,* describes the outcomes of forgiving. A forgiver may find deeper meaning in suffering, realize his or her own need for forgiveness, and come to a greater appreciation for support groups (friends, congregations, classmates). In the end, the person offering forgiveness may develop a new purpose in life and find peace.

The four-stage model has been used successfully with a variety of audiences: survivors of incest, inmates, college students deprived of parental love, substance abusers, and elderly women suffering from depression. In each case, forgivers experienced significant healing. Enright emphasizes that personal benefits should be a byproduct, not the motivation, for forgiving. Nonetheless, a growing body of evidence suggests that forgiveness can pay significant psychological, physical, and relational dividends.[15] Those who forgive are released from resentments and experience less depression and anxiety. Overall, they enjoy a higher sense of well-being. By releasing their grudges, forgivers experience better physical health. Reducing anger, hostility, and hopelessness lowers the risks of heart attack and high blood pressure while increasing the

Box 4.4

Psychological Elements of Forgiveness

PSYCHOLOGICAL VARIABLES THAT MAY BE INVOLVED WHEN WE FORGIVE

Uncovering Phase

- Evaluation of psychological defenses.
- Confrontation of anger; the point is to release, not harbor, the anger.
- Admittance of shame, when this is appropriate.
- Awareness of cathexis.
- Awareness of cognitive rehearsal of the offense.
- Insight that the injured party may be comparing self with the injurer.
- Realization that one may be permanently and adversely changed by the injury.
- Insight into a possibly altered "just world" view.

Decision Phase

- A change of heart, conversion, new insights that old resolution strategies are not working.
- Willingness to consider forgiveness as an option.
- Commitment to forgive the offender.

Work Phase

- Reframing, through role taking, who the wrongdoer is by viewing him or her in context.
- Empathy toward the offender.
- Awareness of compassion, as it emerges, toward the offender.
- Acceptance and absorption of the pain.

Deepening Phase

- Finding meaning for self and others in the suffering and in the forgiveness process.
- Realization that self has needed others' forgiveness in the past.
- Insight that one is not alone (universality, support).
- Realization that self may have a new purpose in life because of the injury.
- Awareness of decreased negative affect and, perhaps, increased positive affect, if this begins to emerge, toward the injurer; awareness of internal, emotional release.

SOURCE: Enright, R. D., Freedman, S., & Rique, J. (1998). The psychology of interpersonal forgiveness. In R. D. Enright & J. North (Eds.), *Exploring forgiveness*. Madison: University of Wisconsin Press, p. 53. Used by permission.

body's resistance to disease. Acting mercifully toward transgressors also maintains relationships between friends and family members.

The social-scientific study of forgiveness is recent, but results so far are extremely encouraging. Forgiving does appear to absorb or defuse evil. If this is the case, then as leaders we should practice forgiveness when treated unjustly by followers, supervisors, peers, or outsiders. When we give offense ourselves, we will need to apologize and ask for mercy. At times, though, we will need to go further and follow the example of Anwar Sadat and Nelson Mandela by offering forgiveness on behalf of the group in hopes of reconciling with a long-standing enemy.

Donald Shriver uses the metaphor of a cable to explain how warring groups can overcome their mutual hatred and bind together to restore fractured relationships.[16] This cable is made up of four strands. The first strand is *moral truth*. Forgiveness starts with recalling the past and rendering a moral judgment. Both parties need to agree that one or both engaged in behavior that was wrong and unjust and caused injury. Refusal to admit the truth makes reconciliation impossible. That's why South Africa's Truth and Reconciliation Commission began the process of national healing after apartheid by publicly airing black victims' statements and requests for amnesty by white police officers.

The second strand of the cable is *forbearance*. Forbearance means rejecting revenge in favor of restraint. Moral indignation often fuels new crimes as offended parties take their vengeance. Forbearance breaks this pattern and may soften enemies who expect retaliation.

The third strand is *empathy* for the enemies' humanity. Empathy doesn't excuse wrongs but acknowledges that offender and offended share much in common. This recognition opens the way for both sides to live together in peace. Ulysses S. Grant demonstrated how to combine the judgment of wrong with empathy at Appomattox. When Southern troops surrendered to end the Civil War, Grant wrote the following in his journal. "I felt . . . sad and depressed at the downfall of a foe who had fought so long and valiantly, and had suffered so much for a cause, though that cause was, I believe, one of the worst for which a people ever fought."[17]

The fourth and final strand of the forgiveness cable is *commitment* to restore the broken relationship. Forgivers must be prepared to live and interact with their former enemies. At first, the two parties probably will coexist in a state of mutual toleration. Later, they may fully reconcile, as the United States and Germany have done since the end of World War II.

In sum, I believe that forgiveness is one of a leader's most powerful weapons in the fight against evil. Or, to return to the central metaphor of this text, forgiving is one of the ways in which leaders cast light rather than shadow. We must face our inner darkness, particularly our resentments and hostilities, in order to offer genuine forgiveness. By forgiving, we short circuit or break the shadowy, destructive cycles that poison groups, organizations, or societies. Offering forgiveness brightens our lives by reducing our anxiety levels and enhancing our sense of well-being.

Spirituality and Leadership

Coming to grips with evil is hard work. We must always be on the lookout for evil whatever form it takes, continually evaluate our motivations and choices, and make a conscious effort to forgive by reshaping our thoughts, emotions, and behaviors. A great number of leaders turn to spirituality to help equip themselves for these tasks. If spirituality seems to be a strange topic to discuss in a book about leadership ethics, consider the recent explosion of interest in spirituality in the workplace. More and more academics are studying the link between spiritual values and practices and organizational performance. One of the fastest-growing interest groups in the Academy of Management, for example, focuses on the connection between spirituality, religion, and managerial practice. A number of academic journals (*Journal of Managerial Psychology, Journal of Organizational Change Management, Journal of Management Education, Leadership Quarterly, Organization,* and *Journal of Managerial Inquiry*) have devoted special issues to the topic.

Popular interest in spirituality is also surging. Meditation rooms and reflective gardens are part of many company headquarters. Some organizations sponsor groups for spiritual seekers and send employees to business and spirituality workshops. An estimated 4,000 chaplains work in largely secular organizations.[18] Tom's of Maine, Toro, BioGenex, and Medtronic integrate spiritual values into their organizational cultures. David Whyte, James Autry, and Thomas Chappell are a few of the popular writers who encourage spiritual development at work.

The recent surge of interest in spirituality in the workplace has been fueled in large part by the growing importance of organizations. For better or worse, the organization has replaced other groups (family, church, social groups) as the dominant institution in society. Work takes up increasing amounts of our time and energy. As a result, we tend to develop more friendships with coworkers and fewer with people outside the organization. Many of us want a higher return on this investment of time and energy, seeking meaningful tasks and relationships that serve higher purposes. Organizations, in turn, hope to benefit from more connected members. Investigators have discovered that spirituality enhances the following:[19]

- Commitment to mission, core values, and ethical standards
- Organizational learning and creativity
- Morale
- Productivity and profitability

- Collaboration
- Loyalty
- Willingness to mentor others
- Job effort
- Job satisfaction
- Social support
- Sensitivity to ethical issues

Donde Asmos Plowman and Dennis Duchon define workplace spirituality as "the recognition that employees have an inner life that nourishes and is nourished by meaningful work that takes place in the context of community."[20] The *inner life* refers to the fact that employees have spiritual needs (their core identity and values) just as they have emotional, physical, and intellectual wants. *Meaningful work* describes the fact that workers typically are motivated by more than material rewards. They want their labor to be fulfilling and to serve the needs of society. *Community* refers to the fact that organization members desire connection to others. A sense of belonging fosters the inner life. It should be noted that religion and spirituality overlap but are not identical. Religious institutions encourage and structure spiritual experiences, but spiritual encounters can occur outside formal religious channels.[21]

Interest in spiritual leadership is an offshoot of the larger workplace spirituality movement. Many leaders report that spirituality has played an important role in their character development, giving them the courage to persist in the face of obstacles, remain optimistic, demonstrate compassion, learn from hardship, and clarify their values.[22] Spiritual leadership expert Laura Reave reviewed more than 150 studies and found that leaders who see their work as a calling demonstrate a higher degree of integrity (honesty) and humility, key virtues described in Chapter 3. These character traits, in turn, build trust with followers and foster honest communication.[23] Reave also found that leaders who engage in common spiritual practices are both more ethical and more effective. These behaviors, emphasized in a variety of belief systems, include the following:

- *Demonstrating respect for others' values.* Many spiritual traditions emphasize respect for the individual. Ethical leaders demonstrate their respect for followers by including them in important decisions. By doing so, they empower followers and bring individual, group, and organizational values into alignment. When values are aligned, an organization is more likely to enjoy long-term success.

- *Treating others fairly.* Fairness is a natural outcome of viewing others with respect. Employees are very concerned about how fairly they are treated, particularly when it comes to compensation. Followers are more likely to trust leaders who act justly. Subordinates who believe that their supervisors are fair also go beyond their job descriptions to help coworkers.

- *Expression of caring and concern.* Spirituality often takes the form of supportive behavior. Caring leaders typically have more satisfied and productive followers. Concerned leaders are also more likely to build positive relationships that are the key to their personal success. Furthermore, demonstrating care and concern for the community pays dividends. Employees working for firms known for their corporate philanthropy rate their work environments as excellent and ethical, get a greater sense of achievement from their work, and take more pride in their companies.

- *Listening responsively.* Listening and responding to the needs of others is another practice promoted in many spiritual paths. Good listeners are more likely to emerge as group leaders; organizational leaders who demonstrate better listening skills are rated as more effective. Ethical leaders also respond to what they hear by acting on feedback and suggestions.

- *Appreciating the contributions of others.* Most of the world's faith traditions encourage adherents to treat others as creations of God who are worthy of praise. Praise of God's creation, in turn, becomes an expression of gratitude to God. In the workplace, recognizing and praising employee contributions generates goodwill toward the organization, creates a sense of community, and fosters continuing commitment and contribution.

- *Engaging in reflective practice.* Spiritual practice doesn't end with demonstrating fairness, caring, and appreciation to others. It also incorporates individual self-examination or communication with God. Meditation, prayer, journaling, and spiritual reading not only deepen spirituality, they also pay practical dividends. (For a more complete list of reflective practices, see Box 4.5.) Leaders who engage in such activities are more effective because they experience less stress, enjoy improved mental and physical health, and develop stronger relationships with others. They are better equipped to rebound from crises and see a greater (transcendent) meaning in even the most stressful circumstances. Self-reflective leaders also manage their emotions more effectively and exercise greater self-discipline.

Spiritual values help leaders create ethical organizational climates. Spiritual leaders develop a vision that helps organization members experience a sense of calling, the belief that life has meaning and makes a difference.[24] This vision builds hope and faith in the future, which encourages group members to put forth their best efforts and to persevere. At the same time, spiritually focused leaders establish a culture based on altruistic love that fosters a sense of membership and connection. (I'll have more to say about altruism in Chapter 5.) Leaders and followers enjoy a sense of "ethical well-being" in which their behavior reflects their inner values. Members of such groups are more likely to help others in the community.

Box 4.5

Spiritual Disciplines

Practicing spiritual disciplines is one way to promote our spiritual progress. Richard Foster, director of the Renovare spiritual renewal movement, identifies 13 disciplines or practices that have been used for centuries by such spiritual seekers as Augustine, Madame Guyon, Brother Lawrence, George Fox, and Thomas Merton. Foster focuses on their use in the Judeo-Christian tradition, but adherents of other faiths also engage in these practices. Fasting plays an important role in Islam, for instance, and meditation is central to Zen Buddhism. Foster divides the spiritual disciplines into three categories: inward, outward, and corporate.

Inward Disciplines

The first group of disciplines encourages us to explore the inner dimension of spirituality. They tend to be "invisible" because they are practiced in private.

- *The discipline of meditation.* Meditation is quiet contemplation aimed at making a connection with God (Western tradition) or emptying the mind (Eastern religious tradition).
- *The discipline of prayer.* Prayer brings a different perspective. We begin to see the big picture, feel more compassion for those who have wronged us (see our earlier discussion of forgiveness), and become more patient.
- *The discipline of fasting.* Fasting is going without food for spiritual purposes. For example, we might fast to signal our spiritual commitment, to draw closer to our spiritual center, to increase our concentration on spiritual matters, or to provide more time for meditation and prayer.
- *The discipline of study.* Study is designed to change the way we think about reality. We can uncover important spiritual principles by reading spiritual classics, observing nature, analyzing relationships, and uncovering the underlying values of society.

Outward Disciplines

The outward disciplines are visible to others and have an impact on our relationships with others and society at large. The outward disciplines include the following:

- *The discipline of simplicity.* Simplicity means putting spiritual goals first by relegating material goods to a secondary position in our lives.
- *The discipline of solitude.* Setting aside time to be alone may seem selfish. However, after we've been silent, we listen more effectively to others and are more attentive to their needs.

(Continued)

Box 4.5 (Continued)

- *The discipline of submission.* Submission means putting aside our need to always have our way. With this attitude, we can decide to give up our rights for the benefit of other people.
- *The discipline of service.* True service is motivated by need, not mood. It is a lifestyle that quietly goes about caring for others on a regular basis. True service produces humility in the server. Ways to serve include protecting the reputation of coworkers, common courtesy, practicing hospitality, empathetic listening, and sharing spiritual insights.

Corporate Disciplines

The final set of disciplines recognizes that, for most of us, our spiritual formation takes place in the context of a larger community (church, synagogue, temple, worship group). Corporate disciplines are what believers do together to foster the spiritual growth of the entire group.

- *The discipline of confession.* Confession plays an important role in forgiveness (see our earlier discussion). An honest confession requires careful self-examination, genuine sorrow for the act, and a strong desire to not offend again.
- *The discipline of worship.* Worship occurs when seekers gather together for singing, praise, prayer, and teaching. Effective worship takes preparation. The inward disciplines are excellent preparation for the corporate expression of faith.
- *The discipline of guidance.* Wise leaders recognize the importance of receiving feedback from the larger group or mentors when making significant individual decisions. They're willing to delay or adjust their plans based on the feedback they receive.
- *The discipline of celebration.* Celebration is a central component of all the spiritual disciplines, according to Foster. A joyful spirit breathes life into the rest of the practices and is the product of a spiritually disciplined life. Joy encourages us to be disciplined, and spiritual development is something worth celebrating.

SOURCE: Foster, R. J. (1978). *Celebration of discipline: The path to spiritual growth.* New York: Harper & Row.

Carole L. Jurkiewicz and Robert Giacalone offer one framework for measuring the spiritual climate of a workplace.[25] You can use the following values or characteristics (which are the product of spiritual practices and spiritual leadership) to determine your organization's spiritual progress.

Benevolence: kindness toward others, desire to promote the happiness and prosperity of employees.

Generativity: long-term focus; concern about future consequences of actions for this and future generations.

Humanism: policies and practices that respect the dignity and worth of every employee; opportunity for personal growth when working toward organizational goals.

Integrity: adherence to a code of conduct; honesty; sincerity; candor.

Justice: even-handed treatment of employees; impartiality; unbiased rewards and punishments.

Mutuality: employees feel interconnected and mutually dependent, work together to complete projects and achieve goals.

Receptivity: flexible thinking; open mindedness; take calculated risks; reward creativity.

Respect: treat employees with esteem and value; show consideration and concern.

Responsibility: members independently follow through on goals despite obstacles; concerned with what is right.

Trust: member and outsiders have confidence in the character and truthfulness of the organization and its representatives.

Implications and Applications

- Evil takes a variety of forms or faces, including a sense of dreadful pleasure, deception, rational administration, sanctioned devaluation, a series of small but fateful decisions, and the product of situational forces that convert ordinary people into evildoers. Whatever face it displays, evil is a destructive force that inflicts pain and suffering and ends in death.
- Ultimately, the choice of whether to do or participate in evil is yours.
- Work to eliminate the situational factors—peer pressure, obedience to authority, anonymity, and dehumanization—that turn leaders and followers into evildoers. Intervene to stop evil behavior.
- Forgiveness is one way to defuse or absorb evil. As a leader, you need to seriously consider the role of forgiveness in your relations with followers, peers, supervisors, and outsiders.
- Forgiving does *not* mean forgetting or condoning evil. Instead, forgivers hold offenders accountable for their actions at the same time they offer mercy. Forgiving takes a conscious act of the will, unfolds over time, and replaces hostility and resentment with empathy and compassion.
- Forgiveness breaks cycles of evil and restores relationships. However, you may gain the most from extending mercy. Forgiving can heighten your sense of well-being, give you renewed energy, and improve your health.
- Warring groups can overcome their mutual hatred by facing and judging the past, rejecting revenge in favor of restraint, feeling empathy for their enemies' humanity, and being committed to restoring the broken relationship.

- Spiritual resources can equip you for the demanding work of confronting evil by contributing to your character development.
- Common spiritual practices that can make you more effective and ethical as a leader include (1) demonstrating respect for others' values, (2) treating others fairly, (3) expressing caring and concern, (4) listening responsively, (5) appreciating the contributions of others, and (6) engaging in reflective practice.
- You can foster an ethical organizational climate by acting as a spiritual leader who creates a vision that helps members experience a sense of calling and establishes a culture based on altruistic love.

For Further Exploration, Challenge, and Self-Assessment

1. Which of the perspectives on evil described in the chapter is most useful to you? How does it help you better understand and prevent evil?

2. Develop your own definition of forgiveness. Does your definition set boundaries that limit when forgiveness can be offered? What right do leaders have to offer or accept forgiveness on behalf of the group?

3. Consider a time when you forgave someone who treated you unjustly. Did you move through the stages identified by Enright and his colleagues? What benefits did you experience? Conversely, describe a time when you asked for and received forgiveness. What process did you go through? How did you and the relationship benefit?

4. Develop your own forgiveness case study based on the life of a leader who prevented or broke a cycle of evil through an act of mercy or reconciliation.

5. What should be the role of spirituality in leadership? Try to reach a consensus on this question in a group.

6. Define spiritual leadership. How does it differ from other forms of leadership?

7. Evaluate the spiritual climate of an organization using the values presented on page 123. Share your findings with the rest of the class.

CASE STUDY 4.2

Chapter End Case:
Genocide in Slow Motion

In 1994, the world stood by as 800,000 Tutsis were slaughtered by their Hutu neighbors. Some in the Western world claimed that they didn't know what was happening because the slaughter was over in a matter of weeks. The same excuse can't be used in the case of genocide in the Darfur region of Sudan. Arabs, with the support of the Sudanese government, have been murdering and displacing black villagers since 2003. This campaign of ethnic cleansing has gotten plenty of attention from the media, African political leaders, aid agencies, and the United Nations. As Canadian journalists Michael Petrou and Luiza Savage note, "This is genocide in slow motion, well documented and undeniable."[1]

Darfur is a barren, mountainous region in western Sudan, which is south of the Sahara Desert. Arabs (largely nomads) and black villagers (some of whom are also Muslim) generally lived in peace until non-Arab tribes joined together to rebel against the Sudanese government. Sudanese authorities retaliated by arming militias (the Janjaweed) and turning them loose to empty the region of African civilians. The Janjaweed, armed with machine guns and rocket-propelled grenades, overwhelm local patrols armed with bows and arrows and spears. They then engage in an orgy of rape, killing, and looting, leaving nothing but corpses and smoldering ashes in their wake. An estimated 200,000–250,000 people have died in the region, and 2.5 million have been displaced to refugee camps. The conflict has spread to eastern Chad, endangering another 2 million people. Relief workers are threatening to pull out of the region because of security concerns, and hundreds of thousands may starve as a result. The situation is getting increasingly chaotic as Arab militias have turned on each other now that the civilian population is largely gone.

There are several reasons for the Sudanese version of ethnic cleansing. One is a brand of Arab racist supremacism funded by Libya's Mu'ammar Gadhafi, which claims that "slaves" have ruled Darfur too long. Another is religious bigotry. Arab supremacists believe that they are superior because the Koran was revealed in the Arabic language. And then there is the constant competition for scarce resources as the Saharan Desert moves south because of global warming. Arab nomads compete for productive land with black farmers and herders.

The response of the world community to the crisis in Darfur has been weak and ineffectual. In 2004, the United States instituted economic sanctions against 100 Sudanese corporations and later expanded the number of companies on the list. However, the Sudanese government gets billions of dollars of support from the Chinese government in return for oil. The Chinese have consistently blocked UN attempts to enforce stricter sanctions. The African Union placed 7,000 peacekeeping troops in Sudan, but this force has done little to stem the violence. In 2006, the UN authorized the placement of 20,000 peacekeepers, but the

Sudanese government refused to let these troops enter the country. Projections are that the crisis could spread further in the region unless more pressure is brought to bear on the rebels, the Sudanese government, and Chinese officials.

There are signs of hope for Darfur. The UN secretary general has made ending the killing in Darfur his top priority. Additional peace talks are scheduled with plans for a larger, joint African Union–United Nations peacekeeping force. Prosecutors at the international criminal court have begun to charge Sudanese leaders with human rights violations. The Chinese government may change its stance as activist groups threaten to focus world attention on China's role in Darfur. However, even if conditions improve in the future, there is no doubt that the international community has been too slow to respond to Darfur's slow-motion genocide.

DISCUSSION PROBES

1. Which faces of evil are being reflected in the genocide in Darfur?

2. Why has the international community been so reluctant to respond to this crisis?

3. What steps should be taken to end the genocide? What obstacles must be overcome to implement these steps? How will they be overcome?

4. What can you do to help end the genocide in Darfur?

5. What leadership ethics lessons do you take from this case?

NOTE

1. Petrou, M., & Savage, L. (2006, December 11). Genocide in slow motion. *Macleans,* para. 15. Retrieved September 9, 2007, from LexisNexis Academic database.

SOURCES

Cooper, H. (2007, April 13). Darfur collides the Olympics, and China yields. *The New York Times,* p. A1. Retrieved September 7, 2007, from LexisNexis Academic database.

Gettleman, J. (2007, September 3). Chaos in Darfur on rise as Arabs fight with Arabs. *The New York Times,* p. A1. Retrieved September 8, 2007, from LexisNexis Academic database.

Hoge, W. (2007, September 6). U.N. chief sees protests and refugees in Sudan. *The New York Times,* p. A15. Retrieved September 7, 2007, from LexisNexis Academic database.

Hoge, W. (2007, September 7). Sudan officials and rebels to discuss peace in Darfur. *The New York Times,* p. 12. Retrieved September 7, 2007, from LexisNexis Academic database.

Perry, A. (2007, March 19). A war without end gets worse. *Time.* Retrieved September 3, 2007, from LexisNexis Academic database.

Perry, A. (2007, May 7). How to prevent the next Darfur. *Time.* Retrieved September 9, 2007, from LexisNexis Academic database.

Petrou, M., & Savage, L. (2006, December 11). Genocide in slow motion. *Macleans.* Retrieved September 3, 2007, from LexisNexis Academic database.

Reeves, E. (2007, Summer). Genocide without end?: The destruction of Darfur. *Dissent,* 9–13.

Simons, M. (2007, February 28). 2 face trials at The Hague over atrocities in Darfur. *The New York Times,* p. A3.

CASE STUDY 4.3

Chapter End Case:
Covering Up Evil

Sometimes evil shows up in the most unexpected places. That's the case with the child sexual abuse scandal involving hundreds of priests in the American Roman Catholic Church. Few could have anticipated that alarming numbers of these dedicated professionals would use their positions as spiritual advisors to victimize children in their care. And few could have anticipated the lengths to which church leaders would go to cover up their crimes.

The problem of priest sex abuse became the focus of national attention in January 2002 with a series of reports in *The Boston Globe*. *Globe* reporters found that child molestation was widespread in the Boston archdiocese, with 90 priests accused of abusing hundreds of victims over 40 years. They soon discovered that the problem was not limited to the Boston area. At least 1,500 U.S. priests from nearly every state have been charged with sexual misconduct with minors since the mid-1980s. According to one estimate, the U.S. Catholic Church spent $1.3 billion settling sexual assault claims during this time. Most cases involved parish priests who abused preteen boys. High-level church officials in the United States, Ireland, Poland, and Wales were also removed from office for sexual misconduct during this same period.

Faithful church members trusted these "servants of God" and welcomed them into their families. Often pedophiles targeted victims from needy, single-parent families whose mothers wanted their boys to develop relationships with godly men. Parents blame themselves for letting predators into their homes; victims blame themselves for being victimized. A great many of the abused have left the church or their faith. Others find it hard to trust others, hold jobs, build relationships, or enjoy sex. One victim summarized his feeling of betrayal this way: "A person who would wrap themselves in God and weave themselves into the very fabric of a family who came to know, love, and trust him for the purpose of molesting their children is the incarnation of evil."[1]

Public outrage at priest abusers has been magnified by the response of church leaders. Bishops and cardinals protected offenders rather than fire them and turn them over to the police. Boston cardinal Bernard Law's reaction to sex abuse allegations was all too typical. Law wrote a letter of recommendation to California church officials for alleged child rapist Paul Shanley after Shanley had been accused of sexual abuse. The cardinal later wrote a glowing retirement letter for Shanley after paying off Shanley's victims. He didn't object to Shanley's appointment to a position at a New York guest home that cared for children as well as adults. Law also protected Father John Geoghan, who was later killed in prison after being sentenced for child molestation. He periodically sent Geoghan to treatment and then reinstated him. The cardinal kept shuttling the predatory priest from one position to another. Law didn't inform new congregations about Geoghan's troubled history. Los Angeles cardinal Roger Mahony followed the same pattern, leaving 16 priests in ministry positions for periods up to 13 years after initial complaints about their inappropriate behavior with children. The archdiocese (the country's most populous) reached a $660-million settlement with 508 victims in 2007, the largest payout so far.

Catholic authorities who refused to confront the problem of priest abuse often acted out of ignorance and compassion. Relying on the advice of psychiatrists, they thought that pedophiles could be "cured." (In other cases, church leaders ignored the warnings of mental health professionals.) Well-meaning cardinals and bishops viewed sex abuse as a sin, not a crime. They wanted to restore offenders to ministry.

Church structure contributed to attempts to cover up the crimes. Catholicism is one of the world's most hierarchical faiths. Church officials wield great power with very little accountability to lay people or outside authorities. Those with lower status (church members, nuns, parish priests, victimized children) are reluctant to challenge the actions of superiors. In such an atmosphere, secrecy flourishes. Worst of all, Cardinal Law and others put loyalty to the image of the church and its staff above the needs of victims, their families, and their congregations. They did everything they could to protect the Catholic faith from scandal and to shelter their fellow priests. Congregation members, particularly the most vulnerable, paid the price. The cover-up itself became part of the evil. According to one prominent lay person hoping to reform the church, "The abusive priest, what he does is evil, but he could be mentally ill. The real evil are those who enable these priests."[2]

The U.S. Roman Catholic hierarchy has taken a number of steps to reform the way it handles sex abuse cases. Church officials have acknowledged the problem and apologized to victims and congregations. All reports of sexual allegations are immediately reported to prosecutors, and those accused are suspended pending investigation. Settlements with victims, which had been kept secret in the past, are now a matter of public record. Cardinal Law was replaced with a bishop noted for taking swift action against sexual offenders. Pope Benedict XVI has pledged that the church will actively work to prevent future abuse.

Dealing with the structural causes of the cover-up will be difficult. Despite pressure to give more power to lay people and women, the worldwide Catholic Church remains a male-dominated hierarchy.

DISCUSSION PROBES

1. Which leadership shadows were cast in this case? Why?

2. What additional steps can the church officials take to prevent future priest sexual abuse?

3. How can leaders restore trust in the Roman Catholic Church?

4. Should lay people have a greater voice in church operations? If so, what can they do to bring about change?

5. How do you maintain your faith in a secular cause or in a religious belief system when you lose your faith in its leaders?

6. What leadership ethics lessons do you draw from this case?

NOTES

1. Boston Globe Investigative Staff. (2002). *Betrayal: The crisis in the Catholic Church.* Boston: Little, Brown, p. 46.

2. Boston Globe Investigative Staff, p. 46.

SOURCES

Adler, J. (2002, December 23). A cardinal offense. *Newsweek,* p. 5.

Berry, J. (2007, July 18). A cardinal's shameless struggle for survival. *The Boston Globe,* p. A15. Retrieved September 23, 2007, from LexisNexis Academic database.

Burnett, J. (2002, April 22). James Burnett looks at how the Catholic Church might salvage its tainted reputation. *PR Week,* p. 17.

Cooperman, A. (2003, July 19). Catholic bishops look for leadership: Abuse scandal reshaping hierarchy. *The Washington Post,* p. A7.

Dreher, R. (2002, January 15). Boston travesty. *National Review* [Online]. Retrieved November 15, 2003, from LexisNexis Academic database.

Gilbert, N. (2003, August 22). Darkness in the Catholic confessional. *The New York Times Higher Education Supplement,* p. 18.

Higgins, M. W. (2003, May 13). A Canadian expert on the Vatican examines the sex abuse scandal. *Maclean's,* p. 48.

Miller, L., & France, D. (2003, March 4). Sins of the father. *Newsweek,* p. 42.

Mozingo, J., & Spano, J. (2007, July 15). $660 million in priest abuses. *Los Angeles Times,* p. A1. Retrieved September, 2007, from LexisNexis Academic database.

Paulson, M. (2003, July 1). Florida Bishop O'Malley seen choice to lead Boston diocese has strong record on abusive priests in 2 assignments. *The Boston Globe,* p. A1.

Paulson, M., & Farragher, T. (2003, August 24). Ex-priest Geoghan attacked, dies. *The Boston Globe,* p. A1.

Notes

1. Definitions of evil can be found in the following sources. Of course, a host of other definitions are offered by major religions and philosophical systems.

Hallie, P. (1997). *Tales of good and evil, help and harm.* New York: HarperCollins.

Katz, F. E. (1993). *Ordinary people and extraordinary evil: A report on the beguilings of evil.* Albany: State University of New York Press.

Kekes, J. (2005). *The roots of evil.* Ithaca, NY: Cornell University Press.

Peck, M. S. (1983). *People of the lie: The hope for healing human evil.* New York: Touchstone.

Sanford, N., & Comstock, C. (Eds.). (1971). *Sanctions for evil.* San Francisco: Jossey-Bass.

2. Alford, C. F. (1997). *What evil means to us.* Ithaca, NY: Cornell University Press, p. 3.

3. Kekes.

4. Peck.

5. Adams, G. B., & Balfour, D. L. (1998). *Unmasking administrative evil.* Thousand Oaks, CA: Sage.

6. Sanford & Comstock. For a closer look at the role of sanctions in genocide, see Staub, E. (1989). *The roots of evil: The origins of genocide and other group violence.* Cambridge, UK: Cambridge University Press.

7. Lewis, C. S. (1946). *The great divorce.* New York: Macmillan.

8. Fromm, E. (1964). *The heart of man: Its genius for good and evil.* New York: Harper & Row, p. 136.

9. Arendt, H. (1964). *Eichmann in Jerusalem: A report on the banality of evil.* New York: Viking.

10. Zimbardo, P. (2007). *The Lucifer effect: Understanding how good people turn evil.* New York: Random House. See also Waller, J. (2007). *Becoming evil: How ordinary people commit genocide and mass killing* (2nd ed.). Oxford, UK: Oxford University Press.

11. Morrow, L. (2003). *Evil: An investigation.* New York: Basic Books.

12. See the following:

Murphy, J. G. (2003). *Getting even: Forgiveness and its limits.* Oxford, UK: Oxford University Press.

Ransley, C., & Spy, T. (Eds.). (2004). *Forgiveness and the healing process: A central therapeutic concern.* New York: Brunner-Routledge.

13. Material on the definition and psychology of forgiveness is taken from the following:

Enright, R. D., Freedman, S., & Rique, J. (1998). The psychology of interpersonal forgiveness. In R. D. Enright & J. North (Eds.), *Exploring forgiveness* (pp. 46–62). Madison: University of Wisconsin Press.

Enright, R. D., & Gassin, E. A. (1992). Forgiveness: A developmental view. *Journal of Moral Education, 21,* 99–114.

Freedman, S., Enright, R. D., & Knutson, J. (2005). A progress report on the process model of forgiveness. In E. L. Worthington Jr. (Ed.), *Handbook of forgiveness* (pp. 393–406). New York: Routledge.

McCullough, M. E., Pargament, K. I., & Thoresen, C. E. (2000). The psychology of forgiveness: History, conceptual issues, and overview. In M. E. McCullough, K. I. Pargament, & C. E. Thoreson (Eds.), *Forgiveness: Theory, research, and practice* (pp. 1–14). New York: Guilford.

Thomas, G. (2000, January 10). The forgiveness factor. *Christianity Today,* pp. 38–43.

14. Enright et al.

15. For information on the byproducts of forgiveness, see the following:

Casarjian, R. (1992). *Forgiveness: A bold choice for a peaceful heart.* New York: Bantam.

Enright et al.

Freedman et al.

McCullough, M. E., Sandage, S. J., & Worthington, E. L. (1997). *To forgive is human: How to put your past in the past.* Downers Grove, IL: InterVarsity Press.

Thoresen, C. E., Harris, H. S., & Luskin, F. (2000). Forgiveness and health: An unanswered question. In M. E. McCullough, K. I. Pargament, & C. E. Thoresen (Eds.), *Forgiveness: Theory, research and practice* (pp. 254–280). New York: Guilford.

Worthington, E. L., Jr. (2005). Initial questions about the art and science of forgiving. In E. L. Worthington (Ed.), *Handbook of forgiveness* (pp. 1–13). New York: Routledge.

16. Shriver, D. W. (1995). *An ethic for enemies: Forgiveness in politics.* New York: Oxford University Press. See also Wilmot, W. W., & Hocker, J. L. (2001). *Interpersonal conflict* (6th ed.). New York: McGraw-Hill Higher Education, Ch. 1.

17. Shriver, p. 8.

18. Garcia-Zamor, J. C. (2003). Workplace spirituality and organizational performance. *Public Administration Review, 63,* 355–363.

19. Information on the benefits of workplace spirituality is taken from the following:

Craigie, F. C. (1999). The spirit and work: Observations about spirituality and organizational life. *Journal of Psychology and Christianity, 18,* 43–53.

Fairholm, G. W. (1996). Spiritual leadership: Fulfilling whole-self needs at work. *Leadership & Organization Development Journal, 17*(5), 11–17.

Garcia-Zamor.

Giacalone, R. A., & Jurkiewicz, C. L. (2003). Right from wrong: The influence of spirituality on perceptions of unethical business activities. *Journal of Business Ethics, 46,* 85–97.

Giacalone, R. A., & Jurkiewicz, C. L. (2003). Toward a science of workplace spirituality. In R. A. Giacalone & C. L. Jurkiewicz (Eds.), *Handbook of workplace spirituality and organizational performance* (pp. 3–28). Armonk, NY: M.E. Sharpe.

Jurkiewicz, C. L., & Giacalone, R. A. (2004). A values framework for measuring the impact of workplace spirituality on organizational performance. *Journal of Business Ethics, 49,* 129–142.

Mirvis, P. H. (1997). "Soul work" in organizations. *Organization Science, 8,* 193–206.

20. Ashmos, D. P., & Duchon, D. (2000). Spirituality at work: A conceptualization and measure. *Journal of Management Inquiry, 9,* 134–145, p. 137; see also Duchon, D., & Plowman, D. A. (2005). Nurturing the spirit at work: Impact on work unit performance. *Leadership Quarterly, 16,* 807–833.

21. See Zinnbauer, B. J., & Pargament, K. I. (2005). Religiousness and spirituality. In R. F. Paloutzian & C. L. Park (Eds.), *Handbook of the psychology of religion and spirituality* (pp. 21–42). New York: Guilford.

22. See Judge, W. Q. (1999). *The leader's shadow: Exploring and developing executive character.* Thousand Oaks, CA: Sage.

23. Reave, L. (2005). Spiritual values and practices related to leadership effectiveness. *Leadership Quarterly, 16,* 655–687.

24. Fry, L. W. (2003). Toward a theory of spiritual leadership. *Leadership Quarterly, 14,* 693–727; Fry, L. W., Vitucci, S., & Cedillo, M. (2005). Spiritual leadership and army transformation: Theory, measurement, and establishing a baseline. *Leadership Quarterly, 16,* 835–862.

25. Jurkiewicz & Giacalone.

Part III

Ethical Standards and Strategies

5

General Ethical Perspectives

Leaders are truly effective only when they are motivated by a concern for others.

—Rabindra Kanungo and Manuel Mendonca,
McGill University business professors

What's Ahead

This chapter surveys widely used ethical perspectives that can be applied to the leadership role. These approaches include utilitarianism, Kant's categorical imperative, Rawls's justice as fairness, communitarianism, and altruism. I provide a brief description of each perspective along with a balance sheet that identifies the theory's advantages and disadvantages.

L earning about well-established ethical systems can help dispel ethical ignorance and expand our ethical capacity. The ethical dilemmas we face as leaders may be unique. However, we can meet these challenges with the same tools that we apply to other ethical problems. I've labeled the ethical approaches or theories described in this chapter as "general" because they were developed for all kinds of moral choices. Yet as we'll see, they have much to say to those of us in leadership positions.

Utilitarianism: Do the Greatest
Good for the Greatest Number of People

Utilitarianism is based on the premise that ethical choices should be based on their consequences. People probably have always considered the likely outcomes of their decisions when determining what to do. However, this process wasn't formalized and given a name until the 18th and 19th centuries. English philosophers Jeremy Bentham (1748–1832) and John Stuart Mill (1806–1873) argued that the best decisions generate the most benefits as compared with their disadvantages and benefit the largest number of people.[1] In sum, utilitarianism is attempting to do the greatest good for the greatest number of people. Utility can be based on what is best in a specific case (act utilitarianism) or on what is generally best in most contexts (rule utilitarianism). For example, we can decide that telling a specific lie is justified in one situation (to protect someone's reputation) but, as a general rule, believe that lying is wrong because it causes more harm than good.

Leaders often take a utilitarian approach to ethical decision making. For instance, America's War on Terrorism has been guided by a series of utilitarian decisions. In response to the World Trade Center attacks on September 11, 2001, Congress passed the Patriot Act, which gave more power to law enforcement officials. Legislators determined that the benefits of preventing future attacks outweighed the costs: government intrusion, less privacy, and loss of legal protections. Administration and intelligence officials later argued that using harsh interrogation methods (e.g., sleep deprivation and simulated drowning) on terrorist suspects was justified because such tactics generate information that protects large numbers of U.S. citizens. (To see how followers must balance costs and benefits when making decisions, read Box 5.1.)

BALANCE SHEET

Advantages (+s)

- Is easy to understand

- Is frequently used

- Forces us to examine the outcomes of our decisions

Disadvantages (−s)

- Is difficult to identify and evaluate consequences

- May have unanticipated outcomes

- May result in decision makers reaching different conclusions

---

The notion of weighing outcomes is easy to understand and to apply. We create a series of mental balance sheets for all types of decisions, such as determining whether an item, car, or vacation package is worth the price; considering a job offer; or evaluating the merits of two political candidates. Focusing on outcomes encourages us to think through our decisions, and we're less likely to make rash, unreasoned choices, which is particularly important when it comes to ethical dilemmas. The ultimate goal of evaluating consequences is admirable: to maximize benefits to as many people as possible. Utilitarianism is probably the most defensible approach in emergency medical situations involving large numbers of injured victims. Top priority should go to those who are most likely to survive. It does little good to spend time with a terminal patient while another victim who would benefit from treatment dies. (The "Leadership Ethics at the Movies" case in Box 5.2 describes another group of leaders faced with life-and-death choices.)

Identifying possible consequences can be difficult, particularly for leaders who represent a variety of constituencies or stakeholders. Take the case of a college president who must decide what academic programs to cut in a budget crisis. Many different groups have a stake in this decision, and each probably will reach a different conclusion about potential costs and benefits. Every department believes that it makes a valuable contribution to the university and serves the mission of the school. Powerful alumni may be alienated by the elimination of their majors. Members of the local community might suffer if the education department is terminated and no longer supplies teachers to local schools or if plays and concerts end because of cutbacks in the theater and music departments. Unanticipated consequences further complicate the choice. If student enrollments increase, the president may have to restore programs that she eliminated earlier. Yet failing to make cuts can put the future of the school in jeopardy.

Even when consequences are clear, evaluating their relative merits can be daunting. As I noted in Chapter 2, we tend to favor ourselves when making decisions. Thus, we are likely to put more weight on consequences that most directly affect us. It's all too easy to confuse the "greatest good" with our selfish interests.

Based on the difficulty of identifying and evaluating potential costs and benefits, utilitarian decision makers sometimes reach different conclusions when faced with the same dilemma. Americans are still debating the merits of the War on Terrorism. Some argue that the costs of heightened security are justified because no further attacks have occurred. Others believe that officials have gone too far. They claim that the nation can be protected without the loss of important personal freedoms and legal rights. They object to what they consider to be the torture of terrorist suspects.

Box 5.1

Focus on Follower Ethics

BLOWING THE WHISTLE: ETHICAL TENSION POINTS

Deciding to go public with information about organizational misbehavior is serious business. Whistleblowers put their careers, health, and relationships at risk (see Chapter 2). At the same time, they put their leaders, coworkers, and the group as a whole in danger. Everyone suffers when the whistle blows. Employees lose their jobs, donations dry up, contracts are canceled, stock prices decline, and so on. Followers must engage in utilitarian reasoning, determining whether the benefits of going public (e.g., improving patient safety, protecting the public, eliminating waste and fraud) justify such wide-scale disruption. To make this determination, ethics professor J. Vernon Jensen argues that potential whistleblowers must respond to a series of questions or issues that he calls "ethical tension points." We can use these questions as a guide if we are faced with the choice of going public or keeping silent. Jensen identifies the following as key ethical tension points in whistleblowing:

What is our obligation to the organization? Do conditions warrant breaking contractual agreements, confidentiality, and loyalty to the group?

What are our moral obligations to colleagues in the organization? How will their lives be affected? How will they respond?

What are our ethical obligations to our profession? Does loyalty to the organization take precedence or do professional standards?

Will the act of whistleblowing adversely affect our families and others close to us? Is it fair to make them suffer? How much will they be hurt by our actions?

What moral obligation do we have to ourselves? Do the costs of going public outweigh the benefits of integrity and feelings of self-worth that come from doing so?

What is our ethical obligation toward the general public? How will outsiders respond to our message? Do the long-term benefits of speaking out outweigh any short-term costs (fear, anger, uneasiness)?

How will my action affect important values such as freedom of expression, truthfulness, courage, justice, cooperativeness, and loyalty? Will my coming forward strengthen these values or weaken them? What values (friendship, security) will have to take lower priority?

SOURCE: Jensen, J. V. (1996). Ethical tension points in whistleblowing. In J. A. Jaksa & M. S. Pritchard (Eds.), *Responsible communication: Ethical issues in business, industry, and the professions* (pp. 41–51). Cresskill, NJ: Hampton.

Box 5.2

Leadership Ethics at the Movies

THE GUARDIAN

Key Cast Members: Kevin Costner, Ashton Kutcher, Melissa Sagemiller, Sela Ward

Synopsis: Ben Randall (Costner) is a legendary Coast Guard rescue swimmer nearing the end of his career. Rescue swimmers dive into stormy seas from helicopters to save the crews of sinking vessels and others lost at sea. After losing his team (including his best friend) during a failed rescue attempt off the coast of Alaska, Randall takes charge of a grueling 18-week training program for new recruits. Prize pupil Jake Fisher (Kutcher) seems more interested in breaking Randall's swimming records than in saving lives or helping his fellow trainees. However, under Ben's guidance he commits himself to the Coast Guard's mission and later joins Randall as his swimming partner. Once on the job, Jake must face the reality that not everyone can be saved, including his mentor.

Rating: PG-13 for intense action sequences, strong language, and sexuality

Themes: altruism, utilitarianism, heroism, courage, duty, loyalty, ethical decision making, self-sacrifice, mentor–protégé relationships

---

Kant's Categorical Imperative:
Do What's Right No Matter What the Cost

In sharp contrast to the utilitarians, German philosopher Immanuel Kant (1724–1804) argued that people should do what is morally right no matter what the consequences.[2] (The term *categorical* means "without exception.") His approach to moral reasoning is the best-known example of deontological ethics. Deontological ethicists argue that we ought to make choices based on our duty (*deon* is the Greek word for duty) to follow universal truths that are imprinted on our consciences. Guilt is an indication that we have violated these moral laws.

According to Kant, what is right for one is right for all. We need to ask ourselves one question: "Would I want everyone else to make the decision I did?" If the answer is yes, the choice is justified. If the answer is no, the decision is wrong. Based on this reasoning, certain behaviors such as truth telling and helping the poor are always right. Other acts, such as lying, cheating, and murder, are always wrong. Testing and grading would be impossible if everyone cheated, for example, and cooperation would be impossible if no one could be trusted to tell the truth.

Kant lived well before the advent of the automobile, but violations of his decision-making rule could explain why law enforcement officials have to crack down on motorists who run red lights. So many Americans regularly disobey traffic signals (endangering pedestrians and other drivers) that some communities have installed cameras at intersections to catch violators. Drivers have failed to recognize one simple fact: They may save time by running lights, but they shouldn't do so because the system breaks down when large numbers of people ignore traffic signals.

Kant also emphasized the importance of treating humanity as an end. That is, although others can help us reach our goals, they should never be considered solely as tools. Instead, we should respect and encourage the capacity of others to think and choose for themselves. Under this standard, it is wrong for companies to expose neighbors living near manufacturing facilities to dangerous pollutants without their knowledge or consent. Coercion and violence are immoral because such tactics violate freedom of choice. Failing to help a neighbor is unethical because ignoring this person's need limits his or her options.

BALANCE SHEET

Advantages (+s)

- Promotes persistence and consistency

- Is highly motivational

- Demonstrates respect for others

Disadvantages (−s)

- Exceptions exist to nearly every "universal" law

- Actors may have warped consciences

- Is demonstrated through unrealistic examples

- Is hard to apply, particularly under stress

Emphasis on duty encourages persistence and consistent behavior. Those driven by the conviction that certain behaviors are either right or wrong no matter what the situation are less likely to compromise their personal ethical standards. They are apt to "stay the course" despite group pressures and opposition and to follow through on their choices. Transcendent principles serve as powerful motivational tools. Seeking justice, truth, and mercy is more inspiring than pursuing selfish concerns. Respecting the right of others to choose is an important guideline to keep in mind when making moral choices. This standard promotes the sharing of information and concern for others while condemning deception, coercion, and violence.

Most attacks on Kant's system of reasoning center on his assertion that there are universal principles that should be followed in every situation. In almost every case, we can think of exceptions. For instance, many of us believe that lying is wrong yet would lie or withhold the truth to save the life of a friend. Countries regularly justify homicide during war. Then, too, how do we account for those who seem to have warped or dead consciences, such as serial killers Jeffrey Dahmer and Ted Bundy? They didn't appear to be bothered by guilt. Psychological factors and elements of the environment, such as being born to an alcoholic mother or to abusive parents, can blunt the force of conscience.

Despite the significant differences between the categorical and utilitarian approaches, both theories involve the application of universal rules or principles to specific situations. Dissatisfaction with rule-based approaches is widespread.[3] Some contemporary philosophers complain that these ethical guidelines are applied to extreme situations, not the types of decisions we typically make. Few of us will be faced with the extraordinary scenarios (stealing to save a life or lying to the secret police to protect a fugitive) that are often used to illustrate principled decision making. Our dilemmas are less dramatic. We have to determine whether to confront a coworker about a sexist joke or tell someone the truth at the risk of hurting his or her feelings. We also face time pressures and uncertainty. In a crisis, we don't always have time to carefully weigh consequences or to determine which abstract principle to follow.

Justice as Fairness: Guaranteeing Equal Rights and Opportunities Behind the Veil of Ignorance

Many disputes in democratic societies center on questions of justice or fairness. Is it just to give more tax breaks to the rich than to the poor? What is equitable compensation for executives? Should a certain percentage of federal contracts be reserved for minority contractors? Is it fair that Native Americans are granted special fishing rights? Why should young workers have to contribute to the Social Security system that may not be around when they retire?

In the last third of the 20th century, Harvard philosopher John Rawls addressed questions such as these in two books and a series of articles.[4] He set out to identify principles that would foster cooperation in a society made up of free and equal citizens who, at the same time, must deal with inequalities (e.g., status and economic differences, varying levels of talent and abilities).

Rawls rejected utilitarian principles because generating the greatest number of benefits for society as a whole can seriously disadvantage certain groups and individuals. Consider the impact of cutting corporate taxes, for example. This policy may spur a region's overall economic growth, but most of the benefits of this policy go to the owners of companies. Other citizens have to pay higher taxes to make up for the lost revenue. Those making minimum wage, who can barely pay for rent and food, are particularly hard hit. They end up subsidizing wealthy corporate executives and stockholders.

Instead of basing decisions on cost–benefit analyses, Rawls argues that we should follow these principles of justice and build them into our social institutions:

> *Principle 1:* Each person has an equal right to the same basic liberties that are compatible with similar liberties for all.

> *Principle 2:* Social and economic inequalities are to satisfy two conditions: (A) They are to be attached to offices and positions open to all under conditions of fair equality of opportunity. (B) They are to provide the greatest benefit to the least advantaged members of society.

The first principle, the "principle of equal liberty," has priority. It states that certain rights, such as the right to vote and freedom of speech, are protected and must be equal to what others have. Attempts to deny voting rights to minorities would be unethical according to this standard. Principle 2A asserts that everyone should have an equal opportunity to qualify for offices and jobs. Discrimination based on race, gender, or ethnic origin is forbidden. Furthermore, everyone in society ought to have access to the training and education needed to prepare for these roles. Principle 2B, "the difference principle," recognizes that inequalities exist but that priority should be given to meeting the needs of the poor, immigrants, minorities, and other marginalized groups.

Rawls introduces the "veil of ignorance" to back up his claim that his principles provide a solid foundation for a democratic society such as the United States. Imagine, he says, a group of people who are asked to come up with a set of principles that will govern society. These group members are ignorant of their characteristics or societal position. Standing behind this veil of ignorance, these people would choose (a) equal liberty, because they would want the maximum amount of freedom to pursue their interests; (b) equal opportunity, because if they turned out to be the most talented members of society, they would probably land the best jobs and elected offices; and (c) the difference principle, because they would want to be sure they were cared for if they ended up disadvantaged.

BALANCE SHEET

Advantages (+s)

- Nurtures both individual freedom and the good of the community

- Highlights important democratic values and concern for the less fortunate

- Encourages leaders to treat followers fairly

- Provides a useful decision-making guide

Disadvantages (–s)

- Principles can be applied only to democratic societies

- Groups disagree about the meaning of justice and fairness

- Lack of consensus about the most important rights

Rawls offers a system for dealing with inequalities that encompasses both individual freedom and the common good. More talented, skilled, or fortunate people are free to pursue their goals, but the fruits of their labor must also benefit their less fortunate neighbors. His principles also uphold important democratic values such as equal opportunity, freedom of thought and speech, and the right to own and sell property. Following Rawls's guidelines would ensure that everyone receives adequate health care, decent housing, and a high-quality education. At the same time, the glaring gap between the haves and have-nots would shrink. Using such principles in the organizational setting could help resolve disputes over how to allocate limited organizational resources such as bonuses, corner offices, computers, and departmental budgets and ensure more equitable treatment of employees. (Complete the self-assessment in Box 5.3 to assess your perceptions of justice at your workplace.)

The justice-as-fairness approach is particularly relevant to leaders who, as we noted in Chapter 1, cast shadows by acting inconsistently. Inconsistent leaders violate commonly held standards of fairness, arbitrarily giving preferential treatment to some followers while denying the same benefits to others who are equally deserving (or more so). Rawls encourages leaders to be fair. They have a responsibility to guarantee basic rights to all followers; to ensure that followers have equal access to promotion, training, and other benefits; and to make special efforts to help followers who have special needs.

Box 5.3

Self-Assessment

ORGANIZATIONAL JUSTICE SCALE

This scale measures employee perceptions of justice in the workplace. The first four items assess whether you believe you have input and involvement in decisions (procedural justice). The last three items assess whether you believe that organizational rewards and recognition are distributed fairly (distributive justice). In addition to completing the instrument yourself, you can also share it with coworkers and subordinates.

1 = strongly disagree, 5 = strongly agree

1. People involved in implementing decisions have a say in making the decisions.

   1   2   3   4   5

2. Members of my work unit are involved in making decisions that directly affect their work.

   1   2   3   4   5

3. Decisions are made on the basis of research, data, and technical criteria, as opposed to political concerns.

   1   2   3   4   5

4. People with the most knowledge are involved in the resolution of problems.

   1   2   3   4   5

5. If a work unit performs well, there is appropriate recognition and rewards for all.

   1   2   3   4   5

6. If one performs well, there is appropriate recognition and reward.

   1   2   3   4   5

7. If one performs well, there is sufficient recognition and rewards.

   1   2   3   4   5

SOURCE: Parker, C. P., Baltes, B. B., & Christiansen, N. D. (1997). Support for affirmative action, justice perceptions, and work attitudes: A study of gender and racial-ethnic group differences. *Journal of Applied Psychology, 82*(3), 376–389, Table 1, p. 381. Copyright 1997 by the American Psychological Association. Reprinted with permission.

Stepping behind a veil of ignorance is a useful technique to use when making moral choices. Behind the veil, wealth, education, gender, and race disappear. The least advantaged usually benefit when social class differences are excluded from the decision-making process. Our judicial system is one example of an institution that should treat disputants fairly. Unfortunately, economic and racial considerations influence the selection of juries, the determination of guilt and innocence, the length of sentences (and where they are served), and nearly every other aspect of the judicial process (see Case Study 5.1).

Rawls's theory of justice as fairness has come under sharp attack. Rawls himself acknowledged that his model applies only to liberal democratic societies. It would not work in cultures governed by royal families or religious leaders (Saudi Arabia, Iran, Nepal) who are given special powers and privileges denied to everyone else. In fact, the more diverse democratic nations become, the more difficult it is for groups to agree on common values and principles.[5]

Rawls's critics note that definitions of justice and fairness vary widely, a fact that undermines the usefulness of his principles. What seems fair to one group or individual often appears grossly unjust to others. Evidence of this fact is found in disputes over college admission criteria. Minorities claim that they should be favored in admission decisions to redress past discrimination and to achieve equal footing with whites. Caucasians, on the other hand, feel that such standards are unfair because they deny equal opportunity and ignore legitimate differences in abilities.

Some philosophers point out that there is no guarantee that parties who step behind the veil of ignorance would come up with the same set of principles as Rawls. Rather than emphasize fairness, these people might decide to make decisions based on utilitarian criteria or to emphasize certain rights. For example, libertarians hold that freedom from coercion is the most important human right. Every person should be able to produce and sell as he or she chooses regardless of impact on the poor. Capitalist theorists believe that benefits should be distributed based on the contributions each person makes to the group. They argue that helping out the less advantaged rewards laziness while discouraging productive people from doing their best. Because decision makers may reach different conclusions behind the veil, skeptics contend that Rawls's guidelines lack moral force. Other approaches to managing society's inequities are just as valid as the notion of fairness.

CASE STUDY 5.1
Equal Justice for All? The Jena Six

Racial tension in the central Louisiana town of Jena (pronounced "Gee-nuh") has raised questions about the equality of justice in the South. Trouble started when a black student at Jena high school defied tradition by sitting under a tree that was unofficially reserved for whites. The next day three nooses appeared on the tree. The school principal expelled three white students for hanging the nooses, but the school board, which called the incident "a childish prank," overruled him and briefly suspended the trio instead. Three months later six black schoolmates beat up a white student outside the school gymnasium. The victim was taken to the hospital but was released later that day. The six students were charged not with assault but with attempted murder. After public pressure, the charges were scaled back to aggravated battery and conspiracy, though conviction on these charges could bring 15- to 20-year sentences. An all-white jury convicted Mychal Bell, who jumped the white classmate from behind, of battery and conspiracy in adult court. These convictions were reversed on appeal when a judge ruled that the teen should have been tried as a juvenile. Bell (who has a previous criminal record for violent offenses) remained in jail for 10 months before being released on bail. School authorities cut down the "White Tree."

College students, particularly those from historically black colleges, took up the cause of the Jena Six. Ten thousand demonstrators marched through the town to protest racial bias in the criminal justice system. According to one marcher, "If you can figure out how to make a school yard fight into an attempted murder charge, I'm sure you can figure out how to make stringing nooses into a hate crime."[1] (The local district attorney claims that he could find no hate crime statute that would apply in this case.) President George Bush assigned the Justice Department and FBI to monitor the case, and Congress scheduled hearings on the matter.

Local reaction to events in Jena (which is 85% white) didn't always divide along racial lines. Some white residents agreed that the teens should have been tried as juveniles. Some black townspeople agreed that the six deserved punishment if they committed a crime (though in juvenile, not adult court).

DISCUSSION PROBES

1. Do you think the hanging of the nooses was a prank, a hate crime, or something else?

2. What would be a just punishment for the white students who hung the nooses? Why?

3. What would be a just punishment for the Jena Six? Why?

4. What steps can school authorities take to reduce racial tensions at Jena High School?

5. What can legal authorities do to prevent racial bias in the justice system as a whole? How can local prosecutors restore the faith of minorities in the courts of central Louisiana?

6. What leadership ethics lessons do you take from this case?

NOTE

1. Jones, R. G. (2007, September 20). Protest in Louisiana case echoes the civil rights era. *The New York Times,* p. A15. Retrieved September 21, 2007, from LexisNexis Academic database.

SOURCES

Jarvie, J. (2007, September 20). In La., thousands to rally for "Jena Six." *Los Angeles Times,* p. A12. Retrieved September 21, 2007, from LexisNexis Academic database.

Jones, R. G. (2007, September 19). In Louisiana, a tree, a fight and a question of justice. *The New York Times,* p. A14. Retrieved September 21, 2007, from LexisNexis Academic database.

Jones, R. G. (2007, September 20). Protest in Louisiana case echoes the civil rights era. *The New York Times,* p. A15. Retrieved September 21, 2007, from LexisNexis Academic database.

Race, justice and Jena: Black leadership in America. (2007, September 29). *The Economist.* Retrieved October 1, 2007, from LexisNexis Academic database.

Red, C., & Kennedy, H. (2007, September 28). Jena suspect freed. *Daily News.* Retrieved October 1, 2007, from LexisNexis Academic database.

Walters, R. (2007, September 26). Justice in Jena. *The New York Times,* p. A27. Retrieved October 1, 2007, from LexisNexis Academic database.

Communitarianism: Shoulder Your Responsibilities and Seek the Common Good

The modern communitarian movement began in 1990 when a group of 15 ethicists, social scientists, and philosophers led by sociologist Amitai Etzioni met in Washington, D.C., to express their concerns about the state of American society. Members of this gathering took the name *communitarian* to highlight their desire to shift the focus of citizens from individual rights to communal responsibilities. The next year the group started a journal and organized a teach-in that produced the communitarian platform. In 1993, Etzioni published the communitarian agenda in a book titled *The Spirit of Community: The Reinvention of American Society.*[6] Etzioni suggests a moratorium on the generation of new individual rights; recognition that citizenship means accepting civic responsibilities (serving on a jury) along with rights and privileges (the right to a trial by jury); acknowledgment that certain duties may not bring any immediate payoffs; and reinterpretation of some legal rights in order to improve public safety and health. For example, sobriety checkpoints mean less personal freedom but are justified because they can significantly reduce traffic deaths.

Many communitarians resemble evangelists more than philosophers. They are out to recruit followers to their movement that promotes moral revival. American society is fragmenting and in a state of moral decline, they proclaim. Evidence of this decay is all around us in the form of high divorce and crime rates, campaign attack ads, and the growing influence of special interest groups in politics. The United States needs renewal that can come only through the creation of healthy local, regional, and national communities. Healthy or responsive communities are made up of the following:[7]

- *Wholeness incorporating diversity.* The existence of community depends on sharing some vision of a common good or purpose that makes it possible for people to live and work together. Yet at the same time, segments of the system are free to pursue their diverse and often competing interests.
- *A reasonable set of shared values.* Responsive communities agree on a set of core values that are reflected in written rules and laws, unwritten customs, a shared view of the future, and so on. Important ideals include justice, equality, freedom, the dignity of the individual, and the release of human talent and energy.
- *Caring, trust, and teamwork.* Healthy communities foster cooperation and connection at the same time they respect individual differences. Citizens feel a sense of belonging as well as a sense of responsibility. They recognize the rights of minorities, engage in effective conflict resolution, and work together on shared tasks.
- *Participation.* To function effectively, large, complex communities depend on the efforts of leaders dispersed throughout every segment of society.
- *Affirmation.* Healthy collectives sustain a sense of community through continuous reaffirmation of the history, symbols, and identity of the group.
- *Institutional arrangements for community maintenance.* Responsive communities ensure their survival through such structures as city and regional governments, boards of directors, and committees.

Creation of the kinds of communities envisioned by Gardner and others requires citizens to shoulder a number of collective responsibilities. Communitarian citizens should stay informed about public issues and become active in community affairs. They must serve on juries, work with others on common projects, care for the less fortunate, clean up corruption, provide guidance to children, and so forth. These tasks are often accomplished through voluntary associations such as environmental groups, churches, neighborhood patrols, youth sports leagues, and service organizations.

Concern for the common good may be the most important ethical principle to come out of the communitarian movement. Considering the needs of the broader community discourages selfish, unethical behavior. Lying, polluting, or manufacturing dangerous products may serve the needs of a leader or an organization, but such actions are unethical because they rarely benefit society as a whole. Furthermore, if each group looks out only for its own welfare, the larger community suffers. Communitarians address the problems posed by competing interests by urging leaders and followers to put the needs of the whole above the needs of any one individual, group, or organization. By promoting the common good, the communitarian movement encourages dialogue and discussion within and between groups. Consensus about ethical choices may come out of these discussions.

BALANCE SHEET

Advantages (+s)

- Discourages selfish individualism

- Fosters dispersed leadership and ethical dialogue

- Encourages collaborative leadership strategies

- Promotes character development

Disadvantages (−s)

- Evangelistic fervor of its proponents

- Promotes one set of values in a pluralistic society

- May erode individual rights

- Fails to resolve competing community standards

Communitarianism is a promising approach to moral reasoning, particularly for leaders. First, communitarianism addresses selfishness head on, encouraging us to put responsibilities above rights and to seek the common good. We're less tempted to abuse power or to accumulate leadership perks, for example, if we remember that we have obligations both to our immediate followers and to the entire communities in which we live.

Second, communitarianism promotes the benefits of dispersed leadership and ethical dialogue. Healthy nations are energized networks of leaders operating in every segment of society: business, politics, health care, unions, social service, religion, and education. Leaders in these countries create a framework (characterized by equality, openness, and honesty) that encourages discussion of moral questions.

Third, communitarianism encourages collaborative leadership, a new way of solving public problems based on partnership.[8] Collaborative leaders bring together representatives of diverse groups to tackle civic problems such as failing schools, substandard housing, economic blight, and uncontrolled development. They focus on the decision-making process rather than promote a particular solution. Collaborative leaders have little formal power but function as "first among equals," convening discussions, providing information, finding resources, helping the group reach agreement, and seeing that the solution is implemented. Collaborative efforts have produced concrete, tangible results in cities both large (Phoenix, Denver, Baltimore) and small (Missoula, Montana; Sitka, Alaska). Perhaps just as important, these efforts change the way in which communities do business. Trust is created, new communication networks form, the focus shifts from serving special interests to serving a common vision, and citizens are more likely to collaborate again in the future.

Fourth, the rise of communitarianism coincides with renewed interest in virtue ethics, which was our focus in Chapter 3. Both are concerned with the development of moral character. The communitarian movement fosters the development of the virtues by supporting strong families, schools, religious congregations, and governments. A "virtue cycle" is created. Virtuous citizens build moral communities that, in turn, encourage further character formation.

The communitarian movement has its share of detractors. Some critics are uncomfortable with the fact that its founders are out to make converts. Others worry about promoting one set of values in a pluralistic society. For example, who decides which values are taught in the public schools? Christians want the Ten Commandments displayed in courtrooms, but Buddhists, Muslims, and other religious groups object. Still other critics fear that focusing on the needs of the community will erode individual rights.

Competing community standards may pose the greatest threat to communitarianism. Communities often have conflicting moral guidelines. For example, the National Collegiate Athletic Association (NCAA) has banned Indian nicknames, mascots, or logos from championship competition and refuses to award championship events to schools who keep these symbols. The organization calls Indian mascots at 18 schools "hostile and abusive." Many fans and alumni oppose the ban, claiming that their mascots are an integral part of school tradition and honor Native Americans, not defame them. On the other hand, many tribal leaders support the NCAA, arguing that these symbols degrade native peoples and reinforce racist stereotypes. The University of Illinois retired its 81-year-old Indian mascot, Chief Illiniwek, in response to the NCAA pressure.[9]

Communitarians turn first to community agreement when resolving conflicts such as these.[10] Local values should be respected because they reflect the unique history of the group. Community standards can be oppressive, however. After all, Native Americans have been the continuing victims of discrimination since whites first arrived on the continent. Communitarian thinkers turn next to societal values in such cases. Local preferences must be accountable to the larger society. Based on this reasoning, Native American mascots should be retired because they undermine such national principles as equality, tolerance, respect, and diversity.

Applying societal norms does not always resolve intercommunity moral conflicts. This is the case with Oregon's "Death With Dignity Act," which sanctions physician-assisted suicide. Twice state voters approved this measure despite strong opposition from medical and religious groups. The U.S. attorney general tried to outlaw the use of painkillers for medically assisted suicide under the federal Controlled Substances Act. However, he was prevented from doing so by a federal court ruling.[11] Both sides in the dispute claim that their positions are based on widely shared societal principles. Proponents of death with dignity believe that suicide is justified by such values as compassion, quality of life, free will, and self-determination. Opponents give more priority to the sanctity of life and argue that extending life is more compassionate than prematurely ending it.

Altruism: Love Your Neighbor

Advocates of altruism argue that love of neighbor is the ultimate ethical standard. People are never a means to an end; they *are* the ends. Our actions should be designed to help others whatever the personal cost. The altruistic approach to moral reasoning, like communitarianism, shares much in common with virtue ethics. Many of the virtues that characterize people of high moral character, such as compassion, hospitality, empathy, and generosity, reflect concern for other people. Clearly, virtuous leaders are other-centered, not self-centered.

Altruism appears to be a universal value, one promoted in cultures from every region of the world. The Dalai Lama urges followers to practice an ethic of compassion, for instance, and Western thought has been greatly influenced by the altruistic emphasis of Judaism and Christianity. The command to love God and to love others as we love ourselves is our most important obligation in Judeo-Christian ethics. Because humans are made in the image of God and God is love, we have an obligation to love others no matter who they are and no matter what their relationship to us. Jesus drove home this point in the parable of the Good Samaritan.

> A man was going down from Jerusalem to Jericho when he fell into the hands of robbers. They stripped him of his clothes, beat him, and went away, leaving him half dead. A priest happened to be going down the same road, and when he saw the man, he passed by on the other side. So too, a Levite, when he came to the place and saw him, passed by on the other side. But a Samaritan, as he traveled, came where the man was; and when he saw him, he took pity on him. He went to

him and bandaged his wounds, pouring on oil and wine. Then he put the man on his own donkey, took him to an inn, and took care of him. The next day he took out two silver coins and gave them to the innkeeper. "Look after him," he said, "and when I return, I will reimburse you for any extra expense you may have." Which of these three do you think was a neighbor to the man who fell into the hands of robbers? The expert replied, "The one who had mercy on him." Jesus told him, "Go and do likewise." (Luke 1:3–35, New International Version)

Hospice volunteers provide a modern-day example of the unconditional love portrayed in the story of the Good Samaritan. They meet the needs of the dying regardless of a person's social or religious background, providing help at significant personal cost without expecting anything in return.

Concern for others promotes healthy social relationships. Society as a whole functions more effectively when people help one another in their daily interactions. Researchers from social psychology, economics, political science, and other fields have discovered that altruistic behavior is more often than not the norm, not the exception.[12] Every day we help others by pitching in to help finish a project, shoveling the driveway of an elderly neighbor, listening a roommate's problems, and so on. Altruism is the driving force behind all kinds of movements and organizations designed to help the less fortunate and to eliminate social problems. Name almost any nonprofit group, ranging from a hospital or medical relief team to a youth club or crisis hotline, and you'll find that it was launched by someone with an altruistic motive. (See the "Curing One Patient at a Time" chapter end case, for example.) In addition, when we compare good to evil, altruistic acts generally come to mind. Moral heroes and moral champions shine so brightly because they ignore personal risks to battle evil forces.

From this discussion, it's easy to see why altruism is a significant ethical consideration for all types of citizens. However, management professors Rabindra Kanungo and Manuel Mendonca believe that concern for others is even more important for leaders than it is for followers.[13] By definition, leaders exercise influence on behalf of others. They can't understand or articulate the needs of followers unless they focus on the concerns of constituents. To succeed, leaders may have to take risks and sacrifice personal gain. According to Kanungo and Mendonca, leaders intent on benefiting followers will pursue organizational goals, rely on referent and expert power bases, and give power away. Leaders intent on benefiting themselves will focus on personal achievements; rely on legitimate, coercive, and reward power bases; and try to control followers.

Followers prefer selfless leaders to selfish ones.[14] Self-focused leaders destroy loyalty and trust and are more likely to lead their communities into disaster. On the other hand, leaders who sacrifice on behalf of the group demonstrate their commitment to its mission. They set a powerful example that encourages followers to do the same. Higher performance often results. (Turn to Box 5.4 for examples of altruistic behavior that can boost organizational performance.)

Box 5.4

Organizational Altruistic Behaviors

Directed to Benefit Individuals

Consideration of others' needs

Technical assistance on the job

Job orientation in new jobs

Buddy system of induction for new employees

Training to acquire new skills

Empowerment practices including mentoring and modeling for others to gain competence

Directed to Benefit Groups

Team building

Participative group decision making

Protecting people from sexual harassment

Minority promotion and advancement programs

Counseling programs

Educational support programs

Interdepartmental cooperation

Directed to Benefit the Organization

Organizational commitment and loyalty

Work dedication

Equitable compensation programs

Whistleblowing to maintain organizational integrity

Protecting and conserving organizational resources

Presenting a positive image of the organization to outsiders

Sharing of organizational wealth through profit-sharing programs

Directed to Benefit Society

Contributions to social welfare and community needs in the areas of health, education, the arts, and culture

Lobbying for public interest legislation

Affirmative action programs for minorities

Training and employment for handicapped and the hard-core unemployed

Environmental pollution control

Economic sanctions against oppressive social control

Ensuring product safety and customer satisfaction

SOURCE: Kanungo, R. N., & Conger, J. A. (1990). The quest for altruism in organizations. In S. Srivastra & D. L. Cooperrider (Eds.), *Appreciative management and leadership* (pp. 248–249). San Francisco: Jossey-Bass. Used by permission.

BALANCE SHEET

Advantages (+s)

- Ancient yet contemporary

- Important to society and leaders

- Powerful and inspiring

Disadvantages (−s)

- Failure of many who profess to love their neighbor to act as if they do

- Many different, sometimes conflicting forms

Altruism is an attractive ethical perspective for several reasons. First, concern for others is an ancient yet contemporary principle. Two thousand years have passed since Jesus told the story of the Good Samaritan. However, we're still faced with the same type of dilemma as the characters in the story. Should we stop to help a stranded motorist or drive on? Should we give our spare change to the homeless person on the street or ignore him? Do we help a fallen runner in a marathon race or keep running? Second, as I noted earlier, altruism is essential to the health of society in general and leaders in particular. Third, altruism is both powerful and inspiring. Acting selflessly counteracts the effects of evil and inspires others to do the same.

Although attractive, love of neighbor is not an easy principle to put into practice. Far too many people who claim to follow the Christian ethic fail miserably, for instance. They come across as less, not more, caring than those who don't claim to follow this approach. Some of the bitterest wars are religious ones, fought by believers who seemingly ignore the altruistic values of their faiths. There's also disagreement about what constitutes loving behavior. For example, committed religious leaders disagree about the legitimacy of war. Some view military service as an act of love, one designed to defend their families and friends. Others oppose the military, believing that nonviolence is the only way to express compassion for others.

Ethical Pluralism

I've presented these five ethical perspectives as separate and sometimes conflicting approaches to moral reasoning. In so doing, I may have given you the impression that you should select one theory and ignore the others. That would be a mistake. Often you'll need to combine perspectives (practice *ethical pluralism*) in order to resolve an ethical problem. I suggest that you apply all five approaches to the same problem and see what insights you gain from each one. You might find that a particular perspective is more suited to some kinds of ethical dilemmas than others. For example, when discussing the "Battle Over the Cervical Cancer Vaccine" case at the end of the chapter, you may conclude that communitarianism is less helpful than utilitarianism or the categorical imperative.

Implications and Applications

- Well-established ethical systems can help you set your ethical priorities as a leader.
- Utilitarianism weighs the possible costs and benefits of moral choices. Seek to do the greatest good for the greatest number of people.
- The categorical imperative urges you to do what's right no matter what the consequences. By this standard, some actions (lying, cheating, murder) are always wrong. Respect the right of followers to choose for themselves.
- The justice-as-fairness approach guarantees the same basic rights and opportunities to everyone in a democratic society. When these basic requirements are met, your responsibility as a leader is to give special consideration to the least advantaged.
- Communitarians focus attention on responsibility to the larger community and the need to make decisions that support the common good.
- Altruism encourages you to put others first, no matter what the personal cost.
- Don't expect perfection from any ethical perspective. Ethical approaches, like leaders themselves, have their strengths and weaknesses.
- Two well-meaning leaders can use the same ethical theory and reach different conclusions.
- Whenever possible, you should practice ethical pluralism by applying more than one perspective to the same problem.

For Further Exploration, Challenge, and Assessment

1. Can you think of any absolute moral laws or duties that must be obeyed without exception?

2. Reflect on one of your recent ethical decisions. What ethical system(s) did you follow? Were you satisfied with your choice?

3. What items can you add to each of the balance sheets in this chapter?

4. Given that inequalities will always exist, what is the best way to allocate wealth, education, health care, and other benefits in a democratic society? In organizations?

5. In a group, create a list of the characteristics of healthy and unhealthy communities. Then evaluate a town or city of your choice based on your list. Overall, how would you rate the health of this community?

6. Create your own ethics case based on your personal experience or on current or historical events. Describe the key ethical issues raised in the case and evaluate the characters in the story according to each of the five ethical standards.

7. Apply each of the five perspectives to the "Battle Over the Cervical Cancer Vaccine" case at the end of the chapter to determine whether you would support a mandatory cervical vaccine program. Write up your conclusions.

CASE STUDY 5.2

Chapter End Case: The Battle Over the Cervical Cancer Vaccine

Cervical cancer, the second most common cancer among women, claims the lives of 250,000 people worldwide every year. The disease is spread through sexually transmitted human papillomaviruses (HPVs). Up to 80% of younger women in the United States are infected 5 years after they become sexually active, although most of those who come in contact with the virus successfully fight it off. Men are also infected, though only a few develop genital warts and other symptoms. The only way to completely avoid HPV is to abstain from sex before marriage and then stay monogamous for life.

The Food and Drug Administration approved the sale of a vaccine that prevents cervical cancer in 2006. Gardasil (developed by Merck) was the first cancer vaccine ever. In clinical trials the vaccine prevented infection of the two types of HPV that account for 70% of cervical cancer and the two strains that cause 90% of genital warts. Very few negative side effects were discovered. Approximately a year later Glaxo released a similar vaccine, Cervarix. Although Gardasil and Cervarix prevent the most common types of cervical cancer, they don't eliminate the need for routine cancer screening examinations. The vaccine is most effective if it is given to girls before they become sexually active.

Public health officials hailed the release of the vaccine. "This is a huge breakthrough for public health, for prevention and for cancer prevention," proclaimed the director of the Centers for Disease Control and Prevention's National Center for Immunization and Respiratory Diseases.[1] Shortly after the vaccine was approved, Texas governor Rick Perry ordered mandatory vaccination for girls in his state. He compared vaccinating for cervical cancer to requiring vaccinations for polio. South Dakota and New Hampshire began to offer the vaccine for free. The District of Columbia, New York, Maryland, California, Minnesota, and other states considered proposals to encourage or to require cervical vaccinations for fifth and sixth graders. Provinces in Canada also started to make the vaccine available to schoolgirls.

Efforts to promote mandatory cervical vaccine programs soon ran into stiff resistance. Opponents, and even some supporters of the vaccine, raised a variety of concerns, including the following:

High cost. When first released, the three-shot Gardasil treatment cost $360–400. Public health funds devoted to vaccinations could go toward more urgent health needs such as curing breast cancer. In addition, Gardasil and Cervarix don't prevent all types of cervical cancer or eliminate the need for regular checkups.

Limited benefits. Although cervical cancer may be the second leading cause of cancer deaths among women, only 3,900 U.S. residents die from the disease annually. Current health programs, which promote regular cancer screenings, have already dramatically reduced cervical cancer rates.

Limited access. Cervical cancer is a much greater problem in the developing world, where women don't have access to cancer screening. The Gates Foundation and other groups are working to make the cancer vaccines available in poorer nations. However, it is likely that only a small portion of those who would benefit from the vaccines will have access to them.

Rush to judgment. States rushed to require vaccinations instead of first educating the public about the benefits of the treatment. Other vaccines, such as the one for chicken pox, were used on a limited basis for years before being mandated. Gardasil and Cervarix may yet be found to produce serious side effects.

Suspicions about motives. Merck, which stands to make billions from Gardasil, lobbied hard at first for mandatory vaccine programs. It contributed money to pro-vaccine candidates and campaigns and funded Women in Government, the association of female state legislators that spearheaded the vaccine effort nationally. The company later suspended its lobbying efforts in response to public criticism.

Conservative values. Religious conservatives argue that vaccinating girls sends "the wrong message" by encouraging premarital sex, not abstinence. They fear that the government would overrule the rights of parents who didn't want their daughters to be treated, although many proposed vaccine programs would allow families to opt out.

Distaste. Many parents are squeamish about vaccinating their daughters against a sexually transmitted disease when they are as young as 10 years old. Few fathers and mothers want to believe that their children will become sexually active when they enter puberty.

Equity issues. Men carry HPV and also respond to the vaccine. So far girls, not boys, have been singled out for treatment.

Based on these concerns, momentum for mandatory cervical vaccine programs has slowed. However, the battle is far from over. The next months and years will determine whether cervical cancer vaccinations become as common as those for measles and tetanus.

DISCUSSION PROBES

1. Was it ethical for Merck executives to lobby for vaccination programs?

2. Do the benefits of the vaccine outweigh its costs?

3. Should boys also be vaccinated?

4. Does vaccinating girls encourage sex outside marriage?

5. What values are in conflict in this case? Is there any way that they can be reconciled? If not, how will you determine which ones should take priority?

6. If you were a state legislator or governor, would you support a mandatory cervical vaccine program for girls in your state? A voluntary program? What ethical theory would you base your decision on?

7. What leadership ethics lessons do you take from this case?

NOTE

1. Austin Peterson, L. (2007, January 30). Merck lobbies to require cervical-cancer vaccine for school girls. *The Associated Press State & Local Wire.* Retrieved March 13, 2007, from LexisNexis Academic database, para. 19.

SOURCES

Anderssen, E., & Aphonso, C. (2007, September 15). Should our daughter get the needle? *The Globe and Mail,* p. A1+. Retrieved October 8, 2007, from LexisNexis Academic database.

Arias, D. C. (2006, August). New vaccine for cervical cancer virus raises access questions. *Nation's Health,* pp. 1, 41. Retrieved October 8, 2007, from LexisNexis Academic database.

Austin Peterson, L. (2007, January 30). Merck lobbies to require cervical-cancer vaccine for school girls. *The Associated Press State & Local Wire.* Retrieved March 13, 2007, from LexisNexis Academic database.

Brokaw, C. (2007, January 9). S. Dakota plans to provide free cervical cancer vaccine. *The Associated Press State & Local Wire.* Retrieved March 13, 2007, from LexisNexis Academic database.

Cancer vaccines. (2007, April 13). *Drug Week.* Retrieved October 8, 2007, from LexisNexis Academic database.

Grady, D. (2007, March 6). A vital discussion, clouded. *The New York Times,* p. F5. Retrieved October 8, 2007, from LexisNexis Academic database.

Guyon, J. (2005, October 31). The coming storm over a cancer vaccine. *Fortune,* pp. 123–130. Retrieved March 13, 2007, from LexisNexis Academic database.

Henderson, D. (2006, May 19). Federal advisers back cervical cancer vaccine. *The Boston Globe.* Retrieved March 13, 2007, from Newspaper Source database.

Johnston, J. (2007, April 16). Our very modern dilemma. *Daily Mail.* Retrieved March 13, 2007, from Newspaper Source database.

Levine, S., & Hamil, H. (2007, January 12). Wave of support for HPV vaccination of girls. *The Washington Post.* Retrieved March 13, 2007, from Newspaper Source database.

Pollack, A., & Saul, S. (2007, February 21). Lobbying for vaccine to be halted. *The New York Times,* p. C1. Retrieved March 13, 2007, from LexisNexis Academic database.

Ricks, D. (2007, February 11). Push for mandatory cervical cancer vaccine. *Newsday.* Retrieved March 13, 2007, from Newspaper Source database.

Saul, S., & Pollack, A. (2007, February 17). Furor on rush to require cervical cancer vaccine. *The New York Times,* p. A1. Retrieved March 13, 2007, from LexisNexis Academic database.

CASE STUDY 5.3

Chapter End Case:
Curing One Patient at a Time

When asked to name someone who exemplifies service to others, most people think immediately of Mother Teresa. Yet Mother Teresa is only one example of altruism in action. There are many other leaders who help the less fortunate at great cost to themselves. Pulitzer Prize–winning journalist Tracy Kidder profiled the life of one such modern hero, Dr. Paul Farmer, in a book titled *Mountains Beyond Mountains*. The publication of the book has inspired college students from around the United States to enter careers in international health.

Paul Farmer is both a medical doctor and an anthropologist who teaches at Harvard medical school. He is a past recipient of a MacArthur Foundation "genius" grant and an international authority on infectious diseases. With credentials like these, Farmer could enjoy the lifestyle of a wealthy doctor. Farmer runs a clinic in the impoverished highlands of Haiti instead. He splits his time between Boston and his work among the desperately poor peasants who flock to his Zanmi Lasante medical complex to be treated for everything from malnutrition and gangrene to meningitis and cancer. The organization he co-founded to support his work in Haiti, Partners in Health (PIH), also oversees efforts to eradicate drug-resistant tuberculosis in the prisons and slums of Peru and Russia; projects in Boston, Mexico, and Guatemala; and clinics in the African countries of Rwanda and Lesotho.

Farmer is consumed with bringing health care to the poor, one patient at a time. Dokte Paul, as the Haitians call him, never turns away a sick person. He and his staff go to extraordinary lengths to make sure their clients follow through on treatment plans. (Failure to ensure that patients take their medications often undermines medical projects in developing nations.) According to Farmer, "The only noncompliant people are physicians. If the patient doesn't get better, it's your own fault. Fix it."[1] Farmer walks for hours over mountain paths to visit his patients in their huts to make sure that they are taking their medicines. Along the way, he stops frequently to talk with former patients and recruits new clients for the clinic. On his frequent trips back to the United States, he shops on behalf of his patients, returning with watches, Bibles, radios, and nail clippers.

Not satisfied just to treat disease, Dokte Paul established a public health system to root out the causes of illness. Zanmi Lasante administers a variety of educational and health programs, including schools, sanitation systems, vaccination and feeding programs, and literacy campaigns. These efforts have paid off. Malnutrition and infant mortality rates in the clinic's service area have dropped dramatically. The mother-to-baby HIV transmission rate is half that of the United States; deaths from tuberculosis are rare.

Farmer's medical successes have come at significant personal cost. He works constantly, sleeping only a few hours a night in a small house on clinic grounds. His teaching salary and book royalties go largely toward supporting the clinic. When Farmer does have personal funds, he may give the money to a needy patient. Expansion of PIH has increased his already demanding travel schedule. He can spend weeks on the road, traveling between project sites, speaking at international conferences, and stopping in at PIH headquarters in Boston. He rarely sees his wife and daughter.

Some would like to call Dokte Paul a saint for his self-sacrifice, but he resists this designation. Farmer believes that sacrifice for the poor should be the norm rather than the exception. He is convinced that God has special concern for the less fortunate. They are in misery because the wealthy have refused to share: "God gives us humans everything we need to flourish, but he's not the one who's supposed to divvy up the loot. That charge was laid upon us."[2]

Although most admire his efforts, Farmer does have his critics. The majority of international health decisions are made on a cost–benefit basis, with money going where it can help the most people. Farmer ignores utilitarian considerations by spending what it takes to meet the needs of a particular patient. As a result, a few could benefit at the expense of the many. Many donors focus their contributions on one narrowly defined cause, hoping to have a major impact on one disease, such as malaria or tuberculosis. Farmer rejects this "vertical funding" approach. He believes that treating a disease such as AIDS can be the gateway to solving poverty-related problems such as women's health, high unemployment (PIH hires many local workers), and deforestation (higher employment means that fewer people need to cut trees to earn a living). Some medical experts argue that distributing free vaccines as Farmer does creates dependency and can't be sustained in the long term. Dokte Paul feels that curing the patient at hand comes first.

Even sympathetic observers argue that Farmer is wasting his time by making rural house calls when he should be addressing global health issues. Not many others will follow his example, they say. Even if they do, only a handful of the sick will be cured. However, these "journeys to the sick" keep Farmer going by helping him connect as a doctor to his patients. Failing to hike to isolated families would mean that their lives matter less than the lives of others. Farmer refuses to make this distinction. Such treks also reflect his philosophy, which is taken from the Haitian proverb that serves as the inspiration for the title of Kidder's biography of Farmer. Haitians say, "Beyond mountains there are mountains." When you cross one mountain range (solve one problem), another mountain or problem will appear. So you travel on to solve that problem as well.

DISCUSSION PROBES

1. What are the advantages and disadvantages of Farmer's methods?

2. Is Farmer wasting his time by investing so much in individual patients?

3. Do leaders have an obligation to give special consideration to the poor, as Farmer believes? Why or why not?

4. Do you think that Dokte Paul will experience burnout from sacrificing so much for others? Should he expect that others would follow his example?

5. Should altruism or utilitarianism be the basis for making medical decisions in poor regions?

6. If you could sit down and talk to Dr. Farmer, what would you ask him or say to him?

7. What leadership ethics lessons do you draw from this case?

NOTES

1. Kidder, T. (2003). *Mountains beyond mountains*. New York: Random House, p. 36.
2. Kidder, p. 79.

SOURCES

Farmer, P. (2007, September 4). Commentary. *Forbes.com*. Retrieved October 3, 2007, from LexisNexis Academic database.
Kidder, T. (2003). *Mountains beyond mountains*. New York: Random House.
Narell, M. (2007, May 16). Dr. Paul Farmer and philanthropy for global health. *On Philanthropy*. Retrieved October 3, 2007, from http://www.onphilanthropy.com

Notes

1. See the following:
Barry, V. (1978). *Personal and social ethics: Moral problems with integrated theory*. Belmont, CA: Wadsworth.
Bentham, J. (1948). *An introduction to the principles of morals and legislation*. New York: Hafner.
De George, R. T. (1995). *Business ethics* (4th ed.). Englewood Cliffs, NJ: Prentice Hall, Ch. 3.
Gorovitz, S. (Ed.). (1971). *Utilitarianism: Text and critical essays*. Indianapolis, IN: Bobbs-Merrill.
2. Kant, I. (1964). *Groundwork of the metaphysics of morals* (H. J. Ryan, Trans.). New York: Harper & Row; Christians, C. G., Rotzell, K. B., & Fackler, M. (1999). *Media ethics* (3rd ed.). New York: Longman; Leslie, L. Z. (2000). *Mass communication ethics: Decision-making in postmodern culture*. Boston: Houghton Mifflin; Velasquez, M. G. (1992). *Business ethics: Concepts and cases* (3rd ed.). Englewood Cliffs, NJ: Prentice Hall, Ch. 2.
3. Meilander, G. (1986). Virtue in contemporary religious thought. In R. J. Nehaus (Ed.), *Virtue: Public and private* (pp. 7–30). Grand Rapids, MI: Eerdmans;

Alderman, H. (1997). *By virtue of a virtue.* In D. Statman (Ed.), *Virtue ethics* (pp. 145–164). Washington, DC: Georgetown University Press.

4. Material on Rawls's theory of justice and criticism of his approach are taken from Rawls, J. (1971). *A theory of justice.* Cambridge, MA: Belknap. See also the following:

Rawls, J. (1993). Distributive justice. In T. Donaldson & P. H. Werhane (Eds.), *Ethical issues in business: A philosophical approach* (pp. 274–285). Englewood Cliffs, NJ: Prentice Hall.

Rawls, J. (2001). *Justice as fairness: A restatement* (E. Kelly, Ed.). Cambridge, MA: Belknap.

Velasquez.

Warnke, G. (1993). *Justice and interpretation.* Cambridge: MIT Press, Ch. 3.

5. Rawls, J. (1993). *Political liberalism.* New York: Columbia University Press.

6. Etzioni, A. (1993). *The spirit of community: The reinvention of American society.* New York: Touchstone. See also the following:

Bellah, N., Madsen, R., Sullivan, W. M., Swidler, A., & Tipton, S. M. (1991). *The good society.* New York: Vintage.

Eberly, D. E. (1994). *Building a community of citizens: Civil society in the 21st century.* Lanham, MD: University Press of America.

Etzioni, A. (Ed.). (1995). *New communitarian thinking: Persons, virtues, institutions, and communities.* Charlottesville: University Press of Virginia.

Etzioni, A. (Ed.). (1995). *Rights and the common good: A communitarian perspective.* New York: St. Martin's, pp. 271–276.

Johnson, C. E. (2000). Emerging perspectives in leadership ethics. *Proceedings of the International Leadership Association, USA,* pp. 48–54.

7. Gardner, J. (1995). Building a responsive community. In A. Etzioni (Ed.), *Rights and the common good: The communitarian perspective* (pp. 167–178). New York: St. Martin's.

8. Chrislip, D. D., & Larson, C. E. (1994). *Collaborative leadership: How citizens and civic leaders can make a difference.* San Francisco: Jossey-Bass; Chrislip, D. D. (2002). *The collaborative leadership fieldbook.* San Francisco: Jossey-Bass.

9. Illinois yields to NCAA, will retire mascot. *The Washington Post,* p. E02. Retrieved September 29, 2007, from LexisNexis Academic database.

10. Etzioni, A. (1996). *The new golden rule: Community and morality in a democratic society.* New York: Basic Books.

11. Liptak, A. (2002, April 18). Judge blocks U.S. bid to ban suicide law. *The New York Times,* p. A16.

12. Piliavin, J. A., & Chang, H. W. (1990). Altruism: A review of recent theory and research. *American Sociological Review, 16,* 27–65; Batson, C. D., Van Lange, P. A. M., Ahmad, N., & Lishner, D. A. (2003). Altruism and helping behavior. In M. A. Hogg & J. Cooper (Eds.), *The Sage handbook of social psychology* (pp. 279–295). London: Sage.

13. Kanungo, R. N., & Mendonca, M. (1996). *Ethical dimensions of leadership.* Thousand Oaks, CA: Sage.

14. Avolio, B. J., & Locke, E. E. (2002). Contrasting different philosophies of leader motivation: Altruism versus egoism. *Leadership Quarterly, 13,* 169–191.

6

Normative Leadership Theories

The Presidency is . . . preeminently a place of moral leadership.

—Franklin D. Roosevelt

What's Ahead

In this chapter, we continue to look at ethical perspectives but narrow our focus to approaches that directly address the behavior of leaders and followers. These include transformational leadership, servant leadership, authentic leadership, and Taoism. As in the last chapter, I'll describe each theory and then offer a balance sheet outlining some of its advantages and disadvantages.

In Chapter 5, we looked at well-established ethical systems or theories. I referred to them as general perspectives because they can be applied to any situation or role in which we find ourselves. In this chapter, we'll examine what philosopher and ethicist Joanne Ciulla of the University of Richmond calls "normative leadership theories."[1] Normative leadership theories tell leaders how they ought to act. They are built on moral principles or norms, but unlike general ethical perspectives, they specifically address leader behavior.

Transformational Leadership: Raising the Ethical Bar

Social scientists offered a series of explanations for leadership behavior over the course of the 20th century. Until the 1940s, researchers believed that leaders were born, not made. Only people who inherited the necessary mental and physical characteristics or traits (intelligent, extroverted, tall, good looking) could be leaders. When investigators had trouble isolating one set of traits common to all leaders, this model was largely (but not completely) abandoned. The next group of scholars assumed that, in order to be effective, leaders had to adapt to elements of the situation, such as the nature of the task, the emotional, motivational, and skill level of followers, and the quality of the leader–follower relationship. New workers need more direction than experienced ones, for example. These situational or contingency theories are still popular but suffer from two major shortcomings. First, they are hard to apply. It's not easy to decide what leadership style to use because so many factors must be taken into consideration. Second, contingency theories give too much weight to contextual factors. Elements of the situation are important, but there are strategies that can be effective in a variety of settings.

The transformational approach addressed the limitations of both the traits and situational perspectives by isolating sets of behaviors (which are learned, not inherited) that can produce positive results in many different contexts. Interest in transformational leadership began in 1978 with the publication of the book titled *Leadership* by James McGregor Burns, a former presidential adviser, political scientist, and historian.[2]

Burns contrasted traditional forms of leadership, which he called "transactional," with a more powerful form of leadership he called "transforming." Transactional leaders appeal to lower-level needs of followers, that is, the need for food, shelter, and acceptance. They exchange money, benefits, recognition, and other rewards in return for the obedience and labor of followers; the underlying system remains unchanged. In contrast, transformational leaders speak to higher-level needs, such as esteem, competency, self-fulfillment, and self-actualization. In so doing, they change the very nature of the groups, organizations, or societies they guide. Burns points to Franklin Roosevelt and Mahatma Gandhi as examples of leaders who transformed the lives of followers and their cultures as a whole. (A lesser-known transformational leader is profiled in the movie described in Box 6.1.) In his most recent work, *Transforming Leadership,* Burns argues that the greatest task facing transformational leaders is defeating global poverty, which keeps the world's poorest people from meeting their basic needs for food, medicine, education, and shelter.[3]

Moral commitments are at the heart of Burns's definition of transforming leadership. "Such leadership," states Burns, "occurs when one or more persons *engage* with others in such a way that leaders and followers raise one another to higher levels of motivation and morality."[4] Transformational leaders focus on terminal values such as liberty, equality, and justice. These values mobilize and energize followers, create an agenda for action, and appeal to larger audiences.[5] In contrast, transactional leaders emphasize instrumental values, such as responsibility, fairness, and honesty, that make routine interactions go smoothly.

Box 6.1

Leadership Ethics at the Movies

COACH CARTER

Starring: Samuel L. Jackson, Rob Brown, Robert Ri'chard, Rick Gonzalez, Nana Gbewonyo, Ashanti

Rating: PG-13 for language and sexuality

Synopsis: Based on the real-life story of Ken Carter (Jackson), a former basketball star at Richmond, California, High School who returns to his alma mater as coach. Coach Carter wants to win games but, more importantly, wants his players to succeed academically in a community where most young men end up on the street or in jail. Carter uses strict discipline and respect for self and others to transform a discouraged, undisciplined squad into one of the best teams in the region. However, in a move that draws national media coverage, he locks the team out of the gym until his players pass all their classes. The school board overrules Carter, but team members decide to stay with their studies until everyone earns passing marks. Although the Richmond High School basketball team doesn't win the state championship, several team members do go on to college.

Themes: transformational leadership, followership, power, empowerment, persistence, overcoming hardship

---

In a series of studies, leadership experts Bernard Bass, Bruce Avolio, and their colleagues identified the factors that characterize transactional and transformational forms of leadership.[6] They found that transactional leadership has both active and passive elements. Active transactional leaders engage in *contingent reward* and *management-by-exception.* They provide rewards and recognition contingent on followers' carrying out their roles and reaching their objectives. After specifying standards and the elements of acceptable performance, active transactional leaders then discipline followers when they fall short. *Passive–avoidant* or *laissez-faire* leaders wait for problems to arise before taking action, or they avoid taking any action at all. These leaders fail to provide goals and standards or to clarify expectations.

According to Bass and Avolio, transformational leadership is characterized by the following:

- *Idealized influence.* Transformational leaders become role models for followers who admire, respect, and trust them. They put followers' needs above their own, and their behavior is consistent with the values and principles of the group.

• *Inspirational motivation.* Transformational leaders motivate by providing meaning and challenge to the tasks of followers. They arouse team spirit, are enthusiastic and optimistic, and help followers develop desirable visions for the future.

• *Intellectual stimulation.* Transformational leaders stimulate innovation and creativity. They do so by encouraging followers to question assumptions, reframe situations, and approach old problems from new perspectives. Transforming leaders don't criticize mistakes but instead solicit solutions from followers.

• *Individualized consideration.* Transformational leaders act as coaches or mentors who foster personal development. They provide learning opportunities and a supportive climate for growth. Their coaching and mentoring are tailored to the individual needs and desires of each follower.

Burns believed that leaders display either transactional or transformational characteristics, but Bass found otherwise. Transforming leadership uses both transactional and transformational elements. Explains Bass, "Many of the great transformational leaders, including Abraham Lincoln, Franklin Delano Roosevelt, and John F. Kennedy, did not shy away from being transactional. They were able to move the nation as well as play petty politics."[7] The transformational leader uses the active elements of the transactional approach (contingent reward and management-by-exception) along with idealized influence, inspirational motivation, intellectual stimulation, and individualized consideration.[8]

The popularity of the transformational approach probably has more to do with practical considerations than with ethical ones. Evidence from more than 100 empirical studies establishes that transforming leaders are more successful than their transactional counterparts.[9] Their followers are more committed, form stronger bonds with colleagues, work harder, and persist in the face of obstacles. As a result, organizations led by transforming figures often achieve extraordinary results: higher quality, greater profits, improved service, military victories, and better win–loss records. James Kouzes, Barry Posner, Tom Peters, Warren Bennis, and Burt Nanus are just some of the popular scholars, consultants, and authors who promote the benefits of transformational leadership.[10]

Burns originally believed that the transforming leader is a moral leader because the ultimate product of transformational leadership is higher ethical standards and performance. However, his definition didn't account for the fact that some leaders can use transformational strategies to reach immoral ends. A leader can act as a role model, provide intellectual stimulation, and be passionate about a cause. Yet the end product of her or his efforts can be evil. Hitler was a charismatic figure who had a clear vision for Germany but left a trail of unprecedented death and destruction.

Acknowledging the difference between ethical and unethical transformational leaders, Bass adopted the terms *authentic* and *pseudotransformational* to distinguish between the two categories.[11] Authentic transformational leaders are motivated by altruism and marked by integrity. (See Box 6.2 for one measure of leader integrity.) They don't impose ethical norms but allow followers free choice, hoping that constituents will voluntarily commit themselves to moral principles. Followers are viewed as ends in themselves, not as a means to some other end. Pseudotransformational leaders are self-centered. They manipulate followers in order to reach their personal goals. Envy, greed, anger, and deception mark the groups they lead. Mahatma Gandhi and Martin Luther King Jr. deserve to be classified as transformational because they promoted universal brotherhood. Iran's President Mahmoud Ahmadinejad appears to be pseudotransformational because he encourages followers to reject those who hold different beliefs. A list of the products of transformational and pseudotransformational leadership is found in Box 6.3.

BALANCE SHEET

Advantages (+s)

- Strives for higher morality

- Reflects higher-level ethical reasoning

- Is highly effective

- Is inspirational

- Recognizes that leaders are made, not born

- Not bound by the context or culture

Disadvantages (−s)

- Practitioners often overlook moral principles

- Is leader-centric

- Creates dependency

Transformational leadership rests on a clear ethical foundation. The goal of a transforming leader is to raise the level of morality in a group or organization. Pursuit of this goal will increase the ethical capacity of followers, create a more moral climate, foster independent action, and serve the larger

Box 6.2

Self-Assessment

PERCEIVED LEADER INTEGRITY SCALE

You can use this scale to measure the integrity of your immediate supervisor or, as an alternative, ask a follower to rate you. The higher the score (maximum 124), the lower the integrity of the leader rated.

The following items concern your immediate supervisor. You should consider your immediate supervisor to be the person who has the most control over your daily work activities. Circle responses to indicate how well each item describes your immediate supervisor.

Response choices: 1 = Not at all; 2 = Somewhat; 3 = Very much; 4 = Exactly

1. Would use my mistakes to attack me personally

2. Always gets even

3. Gives special favors to certain "pet" employees but not to me

4. Would lie to me

5. Would risk me to protect himself or herself in work matters

6. Deliberately fuels conflict among employees

7. Is evil

8. Would use my performance appraisal to criticize me as a person

9. Has it in for me

10. Would allow me to be blamed for his or her mistake

11. Would falsify records if it would help his or her work reputation

12. Lacks high morals

13. Makes fun of my mistakes instead of coaching me as to how to do my job better

14. Would deliberately exaggerate my mistakes to make me look bad when describing my performance to his or her superiors

15. Is vindictive

16. Would blame me for his or her own mistake

17. Avoids coaching me because she or he wants me to fail

Box 6.2 (Continued)

18. Would treat me better if I belonged to a different ethnic group

19. Would deliberately distort what I say

20. Deliberately makes employees angry at each other

21. Is a hypocrite

22. Would limit my training opportunities to prevent me from advancing

23. Would blackmail an employee if she or he could get away with it

24. Enjoys turning down my requests

25. Would make trouble for me if I got on his or her bad side

26. Would take credit for my ideas

27. Would steal from the organization

28. Would risk me to get back at someone else

29. Would engage in sabotage against the organization

30. Would fire people just because she or he doesn't like them if she or he could get away with it

31. Would do things which violate organizational policy and then expect subordinates to cover for him or her

Total Score _____

SOURCE: Bartholomew, C. S., & Gustafson, S. B. (1998). Perceived leader integrity scale: An instrument for assessing employee perceptions of leader integrity. *Leadership Quarterly, 9,* 143–144. Used by permission.

good. Indeed, there is evidence that those exhibiting transformational leadership behaviors demonstrate higher levels of moral reasoning.[12] Transformational leaders also get results. Identify a successful corporation, team, or military unit, many experts say, and you'll find the guiding hand of a transformational leader. This combination of morality and pragmatism makes transformational leadership very attractive. After all, who wouldn't want to be an extraordinary leader who is both good and effective?

The transformational approach holds promise for those wanting to become better, more ethical leaders. If transforming leadership consists of a set of practices, then anyone can function as a transformational leader by adopting

---

Box 6.3

Products of Transformational and Pseudotransformational Leadership

Transformational Leaders

Raise awareness of moral standards

Highlight important priorities

Increase followers' need for achievement

Foster higher moral maturity in followers

Create an ethical climate (shared values, high ethical standards)

Encourage followers to look beyond self-interests to the common good

Promote cooperation and harmony

Use authentic, consistent means

Use persuasive appeals based on reason

Provide individual coaching and mentoring

Appeal to the ideals of followers

Allow followers freedom of choice

Pseudotransformational Leaders

Promote special interests at the expense of the common good

Encourage dependency of followers and may privately despise them

Foster competitiveness

Pursue personal goals

Foment greed, envy, hate, and deception

Engage in conflict rather than cooperation

Use inconsistent, irresponsible means

Use persuasive appeals based on emotion and false logic

Keep their distance from followers and expect blind obedience

Seek to become idols for followers

Manipulate followers

SOURCES: Bass, B. M. (1995). The ethics of transformational leadership. In J. B. Ciulla (Ed.), *Ethics: The heart of leadership* (pp. 169–192). Westport, CT: Praeger; Bass, B. M., & Steidlmeier, P. (1999). Ethics, character, and authentic transformational leadership behavior. *Leadership Quarterly, 1,* 181–217.

these behaviors. The same set of practices works in every context, ranging from small informal groups and military units to large complex organizations. No longer do leaders have to balance a host of situational factors when making decisions. Instead, they display the same set of characteristics that they adapt to their particular context. Furthermore, transforming leadership appears to be effective in a variety of cultures. Researchers at the Global Leadership and Organizational Behavior Effectiveness (GLOBE) Research Project asked managers in 62 cultures to identify the characteristics of successful leaders. Nine charismatic and transformational attributes were universally associated with outstanding leadership: motive arouser, foresight, encouraging, communicative, trustworthy, dynamic, positive, confidence builder, and motivational.[13]

Unfortunately, the ethical assumptions underlying transformational leadership have often been overlooked in the pursuit of greater results. Many writers and researchers appear more interested in what works than in what is right. To them, transformational leadership is another name for successful or effective leadership; leaders are transforming because they achieve extra-ordinary, tangible results, such as rescuing failing corporations or winning battles. These theorists are less concerned with whether leaders foster higher moral standards or whether transforming tactics serve ethical ends.

Writers who fail to distinguish between pseudotransformational and transformational leadership engage in blind hero worship. There are true leadership heroes, but let's not confuse them with the villains. Remember, too, that all leaders suffer from the uneven character development we described in Chapter 3. No leader is perfect but is a mix of virtues and vices.

Some scholars label transformational theorists as "leader-centric" for paying too much attention to leaders while downplaying the contributions of followers. These skeptics have reason for concern. Burns, Bass, and other proponents of transformative leadership argue that leaders play the most important role in determining group morality and performance. Leaders craft the vision, challenge the status quo, and inspire. At times, they may decide to transform the organization in spite of, not because of, followers, as in the case of the CEO who overrules his staff in order to bring about change. Critics of transformational leadership argue that stakeholders are just as important to the success of a group as leaders, if not more so. After all, followers do most of the work. Worse yet, transforming leaders can silence dissent and encourage followers to sacrifice their legitimate self-interests in order to meet the needs of the group.[14]

So much focus on the leader can create dependency and undermine such values as shared decision making and consensus. Followers won't act indepen-dently if they continually look to the leader for guidance. Leaders may also get an inflated sense of their own importance, tempting them to cast shadows. Bass believes that the distinction between pseudotransformational and authentic transformational leadership addresses these concerns. Transforming leaders are much less prone to ethical abuses, he asserts, because they put the needs of others first, treat followers with respect, and seek worthy objectives. You'll need to decide for yourself whether transformational theorists have adequately responded to the dangers posed by their perspective.

Servant Leadership: Put the Needs of Followers First

Servant leadership has roots in both Western and Eastern thought. Jesus told his disciples that "whoever wants to become great among you must be your servant, and whoever wants to be first must be slave of all" (Mark 1:43–44, New International Version). As we'll see in the final section of this chapter, Chinese philosophers encouraged leaders to be humble valleys. Robert Greenleaf sparked contemporary interest in leaders as servants. Greenleaf, who spent 40 years in research, development, and education at AT&T and 25 years as an organizational consultant, coined the term "servant leader" in the 1970s to describe a leadership model that puts the concerns of followers first.[15] Later he founded a center to promote servant leadership. A number of businesses (The Container Store, AFLAC), nonprofit organizations, and community leadership programs have adopted his model.[16] Margaret Wheatley, Peter Block, Max DePree, and James Autry have joined Greenleaf in urging leaders to act like servants.

The basic premise of servant leadership is simple yet profound. Leaders should put the needs of followers before their own needs. In fact, what happens in the lives of followers should be the standard by which leaders are judged. According to Greenleaf, when evaluating a leader we ought to ask, "Do those served grow as persons? Do they, while being served, become healthier, wiser, freer, more autonomous, more likely themselves to become servants?"[17]

By continually reflecting on what would be best for their constituents, servant leaders are less likely to cast shadows by taking advantage of the trust of followers, acting inconsistently, or accumulating money and power. Four related concepts are central to servant leadership:

1. *Stewardship.* Being a servant leader means acting on behalf of others.[18] Leaders function as the agents of followers, who entrust them with special duties and opportunities for a limited time. (See the "Betraying the Student Borrower" chapter end case for a description of one group of leaders who failed to carry out their stewardship responsibilities.) Servant leaders are charged with protecting and nurturing their groups and organizations while making sure that these collectives serve the common good. Stewardship implies accountability for results. However, stewards reach their objectives through collaboration and persuasion rather than through coercion and control.

2. *Obligation.* Servant leaders take their obligations or responsibilities seriously. Max DePree, former CEO of Herman Miller, a major office furniture manufacturer, offers one list of what leaders owe their followers and institutions.[19]

- *Assets.* Leaders need to ensure financial stability as well as the relationships and reputation that will ensure future prosperity. Leaders must also provide followers with adequate tools, equipment, and facilities.
- *A legacy.* When they depart, leaders ought to leave behind people who find more meaning, challenge, and joy in their work.
- *Clear institutional values.* Servant leaders articulate principles that shape both individual and organizational behavior.
- *Future leadership.* Current leaders are obligated to identify and then develop their successors.
- *Healthy institutional culture.* Servant leaders are responsible for fostering such organizational characteristics as quality, openness to change, and tolerance of diverse opinions.
- *Covenants.* Covenants are voluntary agreements that serve as reference points for organization members, providing them with direction. Leaders and followers who enter into a covenant are bound together in pursuit of a common goal.
- *Maturity.* Followers expect a certain level of maturity from their leaders. Mature leaders have a clear sense of self-worth, belonging, responsibility, accountability, and equality.
- *Rationality.* Leaders supply the reason and understanding that help followers make sense of organizational programs and relationships. A rational environment builds trust, allows followers to reach their full potential, and encourages ongoing organizational learning.
- *Space.* Space is a sense of freedom that allows followers and leaders to be and express themselves. Leaders who create adequate space allow for the giving and receiving of such gifts as new ideas, healing, dignity, and inclusion.
- *Momentum.* Servant leaders help create the feeling that the group is moving forward and achieving its goals. Momentum arises out of a clear vision and strategy supported by productive research, operations, financial, and marketing departments.
- *Effectiveness.* Effectiveness comes from enabling followers to reach their personal and institutional potential. Servant leaders allow followers to assume leadership roles when conditions warrant.
- *Civility and values.* A civilized institution is marked by good manners, respect for others, and service. Wise leaders can distinguish between what is healthy for the organization (dignity of work, hope, simplicity) and what is superficial and unhealthy (consumption, instant gratification, affluence).

3. *Partnership.* Servant leaders view followers as partners, not subordinates. As a consequence, they strive for equity or justice in the distribution of power. Strategies for empowering followers include sharing information, delegating authority to carry out important tasks, and encouraging constituents to develop and exercise their talents. Concern for equity extends to the distribution of rewards as well. For example, both employees and executives receive bonuses when the company does well.

4. *Elevating purpose.* In addition to serving followers, servant leaders also serve worthy missions, ideas, and causes. Seeking to fulfill a high moral purpose and understanding the role one plays in the process make work more meaningful to leaders and followers alike. Consider the example of three bricklayers at work in the English countryside. When asked by a traveler to describe what they were doing, the first replied, "I am laying bricks." The second said, "I am feeding my family by laying bricks." The third bricklayer, who had a clearer sense of the purpose for his labor, declared, "Through my work of laying bricks, I am constructing a cathedral, and thereby giving honor and praise to God."

BALANCE SHEET

Advantages (+s)

- – Is altruistic

- – Incorporates simplicity

- – Promotes self-awareness

- – Incorporates moral sensitivity

Disadvantages (–s)

- – Seems unrealistic

- – May not work in every context

- – Poses the danger of serving the wrong cause or offering unwise service

- – Carries a negative connotation in the term *servant*

Altruism is the first strength of servant leadership. Concern for others, in this case followers, comes before concern for self. We can serve only if we commit ourselves to the principle that others should come first.

Simplicity is the second strength of servant leadership. We are far less likely to cast shadows if we approach our leadership roles with one goal in mind: the desire to serve. A great number of ethical abuses, as we emphasized in Chapter 2, stem from leaders putting their personal interests first. Instead, servant leaders act out of a sense of stewardship and obligation, promoting the growth of followers and the interests of the larger community. They share, rather than hoard, power, privilege, and information.

Self-awareness is the third strength of servant leadership. Servant leaders listen to themselves as well as to others, take time for reflection, and recognize the importance of spiritual resources.

Moral sensitivity is the fourth strength of servant leadership. Servant leaders are acutely aware of the importance of pursuing ethical purposes that bring meaning and fulfillment to work. Serving a transcendent goal means that every act of leadership has a moral dimension.

Despite its strengths, servant leadership has not met with universal approval. Cynicism is often the first response when this model is presented. "Sounds good in principle," listeners respond, "but it would never work at my company, in my family, at my condominium association meeting, or _____" (fill in the blank). Skeptics report that they have been "walked on" whenever they've tried to be nice to poor performers at work, rebellious teenagers, or nasty neighbors. Others equate a servant attitude with passivity.

Skepticism about servant leadership may stem in part from a misunderstanding that equates service with weakness. Servant leaders need to be tough. Sometimes the best way to serve someone is to reprimand or fire that person. Nevertheless, there may be situations in which servant leadership is extremely difficult, if not impossible, to implement, such as in prisons, military boot camps, and emergencies.

Misplaced goals are problems for servant leaders and followers alike. The butler in the novel *Remains of the Day*, by Kazuo Ishiguro, illustrates the danger of misspent service. He devotes his entire life to being the perfect servant who meets the needs of his English employer. Sadly, his sacrifice is wasted because the lord of the manor turns out to be a Nazi sympathizer. The desire to serve must be combined with careful reasoning and value clarification. We need to carefully examine who and what we serve, asking ourselves questions such as the following: Is this group, individual, or organization worthy of our service? What values are we promoting? What is the product of our service: light or darkness? (For a closer look at outstanding followership, see Box 6.4.)

We are also charged with giving wise service. Lots of well-intentioned efforts to help others are wasted when leaders fail to do their homework. After the devastation of Hurricane Mitch in Honduras, for example, one well-known humanitarian organization built a large housing development miles from the nearest town or city. Years later nearly all the homes stand empty because the neighborhood is too far from jobs, schools, and shopping.

Finally, members of some minority groups, particularly African Americans, associate the word *servant* with a history of slavery, oppression, and discrimination. The negative connotations surrounding the word may keep you from embracing the idea of servant leadership. You may want to abandon this term and focus instead on related concepts such as altruism and the virtues of concern and compassion.

Box 6.4

Focus on Follower Ethics

SERVANT FOLLOWERSHIP

Consultant and author Robert Kelley believes that servant followership is more important than servant leadership. He points out that most people spend most of their time in follower roles and that followers contribute the most to organizational success. From an ethical perspective, seeking to be a follower rather than a leader reduces the destructive competition and conflict that occur when people fight each other for leadership positions. Servant followers are more likely to build trust and keep the focus on organizational goals. They avoid the temptation to adopt authoritarian, self-centered styles when they do land in leader roles.

Kelley uses the term *exemplary* to describe ideal servant followers. The best followers score high in two dimensions: independent, critical thinking and active engagement. They think for themselves and, at the same time, take initiative. Outstanding followers contribute innovative ideas and go beyond what is required. Leaders can count on them to take on new challenges, follow through on projects without much supervision, disagree constructively, and think through the implications of their actions.

Kelley outlines five behavior patterns for those who hope to become exemplary followers.

• *Leading yourself.* Excellent followers know how to lead themselves. They step up to their responsibilities and view their work as equal in importance to leaders because they recognize that implementation is critical to success.

• *Commit and focus.* Exemplary followers are committed to ideas and causes bigger than themselves. They look beyond their personal careers and needs to serve an elevating purpose such as fighting illness or protecting the environment. Because they're committed to a broad principle, exemplary followers feel less need for status or titles.

• *Develop competence and credibility.* Exemplary followers set high personal standards that are more strenuous than those set by the leader or the organization as a whole. They are proactive, taking advantage of continuing education and performance development opportunities. Outstanding followers also know their weaknesses and take steps to compensate by either acquiring the necessary skills or stepping aside to let others complete the task.

• *Use your courageous conscience.* Exemplary followers are very concerned about the ethics of their actions even if their leaders are not. Such followers serve as ethical watchdogs. They refuse to abandon personal principles but challenge immoral directives instead.

• *Disagree agreeably.* Servant followers work cooperatively with their leaders, recognizing that their responsibility is to make the job of the leader easier, not harder. However, when conflicts arise and decisions must be challenged, outstanding followers gather the facts, seek the advice of others, build coalitions, and work within established guidelines whenever possible (although they have the courage to go to higher authorities if absolutely necessary).

SOURCE: Kelley, R. (1998). Followership in a leadership world. In L. C. Spears (Ed.), *Insights on leadership: Service, stewardship, spirit and servant-leadership* (pp. 170–184). New York: Wiley. See also Johnson, C. E. (2007). *Ethics in the workplace: Tools and tactics for organizational transformation.* Thousand Oaks, CA: Sage, Ch. 7.

Authentic Leadership:
Know Yourself and To Your Own Self Be True

Ancient Greek and Roman philosophers prized authenticity. "Know thyself" was inscribed on the frieze above the oracle of Delphi and appears in the writings of Cicero and Ovid.[20] Greek thinkers also exhorted listeners "to thine own self be true." Modern scholars have rediscovered the importance of this quality. Proponents of Authentic Leadership Theory (ALT) identify authenticity as the "root construct" or principle underlying all forms of positive leadership. The practice of authentic leadership leads to sustainable (long-term) and veritable (ethically sound) organizational performance.[21]

Authenticity has four components: awareness, unbiased (balanced) processing, action, and relational orientation.[22] *Awareness* means being conscious of and trusting in our motives, desires, feelings, and self-concept. Self-aware people know their strengths and weaknesses, personal traits, and emotional patterns, and they are able to use this knowledge when interacting with others and their environments. *Unbiased (balanced) processing* describes remaining objective when receiving information from internal or external sources. Inauthentic responses involve denying, distorting, or ignoring feedback we don't want to acknowledge. We may have to accept the fact that we aren't very good at certain activities (accounting, writing, playing basketball) or that we have problems managing our anger. *Action* is acting in harmony with what we believe and not changing our behavior to please others or to earn rewards or avoid punishment. *Relational orientation* means seeking openness and truthfulness in close relationships, which includes letting others see the good and bad aspects of who we really are.

According to Bruce Avolio, Fred Luthans, and their colleagues at the Gallup Leadership Institute at the University of Nebraska at Lincoln, authentic leadership has a strong moral component. They make ethics a starting point for their theory, just as Burns did for transforming leadership. This moral element is reflected in their definition of authentic leaders as "those who are deeply aware of how they think and behave and are perceived by others as being aware of their own and others' values/moral perspectives, knowledge, and strengths; aware of the context in which they operate; and who are confident, hopeful, optimistic, resilient, and of high moral character."[23] Such leaders acknowledge the ethical responsibilities of their roles, can recognize and evaluate ethical issues, and take moral actions that are thoroughly grounded in their beliefs and values. In order to carry out these tasks, they draw on their courage and resilience—the ability to adapt when confronted with significant risk or adversity.[24]

Because authenticity is so critical to positive leadership performance, Avolio, Luthans, and others are interested in how leaders develop this quality. They report that critical incidents called *trigger events* play an important role in the development of moral component of authentic leadership.[25] These events, like the crucible moments described in Chapter 3, can be positive or negative and promote introspection and reflection. Trigger experiences are often dramatic (facing racial hatred, visiting a third-world village) but can also be more mundane, such as reading a significant book. Sometimes a series of small events, such as several minor successes or failures, can have a cumulative effect, triggering significant thought. Leaders develop a clearer sense of who they are, including their standards of right and wrong, through these experiences. They build a store of moral knowledge that they can draw on to make better choices when facing future ethical dilemmas.

Authenticity can also be fostered through training and education. For example, trainers and educators can help leaders develop their moral capacity by (1) encouraging them to think about the possible consequences of their leadership decisions, (2) enhancing their perspective taking through discussion and training, (3) exposing them to common moral dilemmas to help them recognize the ethical issues they will face in their jobs, (4) building their belief in their ability to follow through on choices, (5) helping them develop strategies for adapting and coping with new ethical challenges, and (6) pairing them with moral leaders so they can observe authentic behavior first hand.[26]

Authentic leadership produces a number of positive ethical effects in followers. Followers are likely to emulate the example of authentic leaders who set a high ethical standard. They feel empowered to make ethical choices on their own without the input of the leader. They align themselves with the values of the organization and become authentic moral agents themselves. Authentic followers, for their part, provide feedback that reinforces the authentic behavior of leaders and increases the leaders' self-knowledge. They also reward their leaders by giving them more latitude to make difficult, unpopular choices. Authentic leadership and followership are more likely develop in organizational climates that provide the information and other resources that employees need to get their work done, encourage learning, treat members fairly, and set clear goals and performance standards.[27]

Proponents of ALT argue that authenticity pays practical as well as ethical dividends. They believe authenticity multiplies the effectiveness of leaders. Because authentic leaders are more predictable, followers have to waste less time and energy figuring out what their leaders will do next. Authentic leaders engender more trust, and trust, in turn, has been linked to higher organizational productivity and performance. Those who work in a trusting environment are more productive because they have high job satisfaction, enjoy better relationships, stay focused on their tasks, feel committed to the group, sacrifice for the greater organizational good, and are willing to go beyond their job descriptions to help out fellow employees.[28] Authenticity also releases positive emotions that build self-efficacy.[29] Followers who believe in their abilities are more likely to take initiative and achieve more, even in the face of difficult circumstances. (Read Case Study 6.1 to learn how one authentic leader has helped her followers believe in themselves.)

CASE STUDY 6.1

The Airline Executive as "Mom in Chief"

The career of Southwest Airlines executive Colleen Barrett demonstrates the power that comes from knowing yourself and living in harmony with your strengths and values. Barrett started work as a legal secretary for San Antonio attorney Herb Kelleher. When Kelleher founded Southwest Airlines in the early 1970s, she became his alter ego. Kelleher was the visionary; Barrett brought his visions to reality. According to Barrett, "Herb could have a dream in the middle of the night and say, 'Okay, this is what I want to do.' But he wouldn't have a clue, God love him, what steps have to be taken to get there. I'm not the most brilliant person in the whole world, but I can see systematically from A to Z, and I know what has to be done."[1]

Barrett's role at Southwest expanded as the company grew. She started as the secretary of the corporation, became vice president of administration, then became executive vice president of customers, and assumed the role of CEO and president in 2001 after Kelleher stepped aside. (She dropped her CEO duties in 2004.) During this period, Southwest went from a small startup serving three cities in Texas to the largest domestic air carrier in the United States, with 32,000 employees. The company went 34 years without losing money at the same time many of its competitors went into bankruptcy or out of business. In 2008, she stepped down as company president to work exclusively on customer relations.

Barrett is credited with being the architect of Southwest's culture, which emphasizes customer service, concern for employees, empowerment, and fun ("We take the competition seriously, but we don't take ourselves seriously."). She considers employees to be her "family," and they, in turn, consider her to be the company "mom." When she served as president (as "Mom in Chief"), for example, Barrett encouraged employees to put pictures of their families and pets on the walls. Over her years at the company she has handed out plenty of hugs and words of encouragement. Kelleher called her the "Heroine of Hearts."

Southwest's former president exemplifies authentic leadership. To begin, she gives the impression that she is much the same person now as she was when she worked in Kelleher's law practice. Barrett never aspired to become a top airline executive because she knew that her strengths were caring for people, not finance. (Besides, she loved being a legal secretary.) During her tenure as president, she dressed casually, in comfortable shoes, with her gray hair pulled back in a ponytail. Observers noted that she looked more like a neighborly grandmother than the most powerful woman in the airline industry and one of the 50 most powerful women in American business. She never used e-mail and didn't own a car.

Whatever her role at Southwest, Colleen Barrett has consistently lived out her respect for others, love, and forgiveness. The most vivid demonstration of her commitment to her values may have come after the events of September 11, 2001. Southwest was the only domestic air carrier not to lay off employees and paid workers for the days the airline was grounded. Barrett encourages her employees to express their individuality and gives them the power to make decisions that benefit the customer. Her decision to step down as company president was a reflection of her belief in her followers, allowing others to take the lead as she stepped back. "I have always thought," Barrett said, "that one of the best traits of a leader is to know when to follow."[2]

DISCUSSION PROBES

1. Would you like to work for Colleen Barrett? Why or why not?

2. Do you think Barrett's leadership style would work in other companies? Why or why not?

3. Do you agree that authenticity is the key to Barrett's effectiveness as a leader? What other factors might have contributed to her success?

4. Based on your experience with Southwest Airlines, does the culture of the company reflect Barrett's values?

5. Is one of the best traits of a leader knowing when to follow?

6. What leadership ethics lessons do you take from this case?

NOTES

1. Booker, K. (2001, May 28). The chairman of the board looks back. *Fortune,* p. 76.
2. Fisher, S. (2007, September). Flying off into the sunset. *Costco Connection,* p. 17.

SOURCES

Booker, K. (2001, May 28). The chairman of the board looks back. *Fortune,* pp. 63–76.
Clark, K. (2001, December 31). Nothing but the plane truth. *U.S. News & World Report.* Retrieved October 3, 2007, from Business Source Complete database.
Fisher, S. (2007, September). Flying off into the sunset. *Costco Connection,* pp. 17–19.
Fitzpatrick, D. (2005, May 12). "Aw-shucks" president embodies Southwest style. *Pittsburgh Post-Gazette.* Retrieved October 3, 2007, from Newspaper Source database.
Stewart, D. R. (2006, June 1). Southwest staff "family": The airline's corporate culture is tied to its success. *Tulsa World.* Retrieved October 3, 2007, from Newspaper Source database.

BALANCE SHEET

Advantages (+s)

- Strong moral emphasis

- Developmental focus

- Is highly effective

- Incorporates followers and organizational climate

Disadvantages (–s)

- In the early stages of development

- Not clearly differentiated from related theories

- Overstates the importance of authenticity

- Equates authenticity with morality

- Differing interpretations of authentic behavior

Authentic leadership has much to offer, beginning with its strong moral emphasis. Its leading proponents incorporate values, moral perspectives, virtues, and character in their definition of the authentic leadership. They have a worthy objective: to promote positive leadership behavior that makes a fundamental difference in the lives of organizations and their members. Their ultimate goal is not just to understand authenticity but also to help leaders become more authentic. ALT theorists make practical suggestions for helping leaders develop this strength. Furthermore, authentic leadership is effective as well as ethical. Authenticity multiplies the impact of leaders and lays the foundation for long-term organizational success. Finally, the theory acknowledges the role that followers and organizational culture and climate play in developing authentic leadership.

ALT is still in the development stage. Most of the articles and chapters on authentic leadership offer propositions about ALT that have yet to be supported by empirical research. For example, there is no widely used measure of authentic leadership. Then, too, there is confusion about the distinction between authentic leadership and transformational and servant leadership.[30] All three theories encourage concern for others and promote the growth of followers, for example, and self-awareness is critical to both servant and authentic leadership.

Further theory and research may address the disadvantages described here. Of greater concern is the theory's underlying premise that authenticity is the source of all positive forms of leadership. There may be some other as yet undiscovered source instead. Or there may be multiple sources of ethical leadership. ALT theorists also seem to equate self-awareness with morality. The clearer we are about the self-concept, they claim, the more likely we are to act ethically. Yet the core values of some leaders promote self-seeking, destructive behavior. Then, too, expressing our "true" selves can produce undesirable consequences. Take the case of the boss who fails to temper his criticism to a subordinate. By accurately reflecting what he feels at that moment, he may do lasting damage to the self-concept of his employee. The critical boss believes he is acting authentically; the unfortunate employee and observers probably will conclude that he is callous instead. This suggests that there will be differing interpretations of just what constitutes authentic behavior.

Taoism: Lead Nature's Way

Taoism (pronounced "Dowism") is one of the world's oldest philosophies, dating back to ancient China (600–300 B.C.). The nation had enjoyed peace and prosperity under a series of imperial dynasties but had become a patchwork of warring city-states. Groups of philosophers traveled from one fiefdom to another offering leaders advice for restoring harmony. The Taoists were one of these "100 Schools of Thought."[31]

The *Tao Te Ching* (usually translated as *The Classic of the Way and Its Power and Virtue*) is Taoism's major text. According to popular tradition, a royal librarian named Lao-tzu authored this book as he departed China for self-imposed exile. However, most scholars believe that this short volume (5,000 words) is a collection of the teachings of several wise men or sages.

Taoism divided into religious and philosophical branches by A.D. 200. Religious Taoists sought to extend their lives through diet and exercise and developed a priesthood that presided over elaborate temple rituals. Today Taoist religious practices are popular in both the East and the West, but those interested in Taoist leadership principles generally draw from the movement's philosophical roots. These principles are described for Western audiences in such books as *The Tao of Leadership, The Tao of Personal Leadership,* and *Real Power: Business Lessons From the Tao Te Ching.*

Understanding the "Way" or Tao is the key to understanding Taoist ethical principles. The Tao is the shapeless, nameless force or "Non-Being" that brings all things into existence, or being, and then sustains them. The Tao takes form in nature and reveals itself through natural principles. These principles then become the standards for ethical behavior. Ethical leaders and followers develop *te,* or character, by acting in harmony with the Tao, not by following rules and commandments. Laws reflect a distrust of human nature and create a new class of citizens—lawbreakers—instead of encouraging right behavior. Efforts to reduce crime, for example, seem to increase it instead:

> Throw away holiness and wisdom,
>
> And people will be a hundred times happier.
>
> Throw away morality and justice,
>
> And people will do the right thing.
>
> Throw away industry and profit, and there won't be any thieves.[32]

"Leave well enough alone" seems to capture the essence of Taoist ethics. Consistent with their hands-off approach, Taoist sages argue that he or she governs best who governs least. Leading is like cooking a small fish: Don't overdo it. The ideal Taoist leader maintains a low profile, leading mostly by example and letting followers take ownership.

> When the Master governs, the people
>
> Are hardly aware that he exists.
>
> Next best is a leader who is loved.
>
> Next, one who is feared.
>
> The worst is one who is despised.
>
> If you don't trust the people,
>
> You make them untrustworthy.
>
> The Master doesn't talk, he acts.
>
> When his work is done,
>
> The people say, "Amazing:
>
> We did it, all by ourselves!"[33]

Taoists rely on images or metaphors drawn from nature and daily life to illustrate the characteristics of model leaders. The first image is that of an uncarved block. An uncarved block of stone or wood is nameless and shapeless, like the Tao itself. Leaders should also be blocklike, avoiding wealth, status, and glory while they leave followers alone.

The second image is the child. Children serve as another reminder that wise leaders don't get caught up in the pursuit of power and privilege but remain humble. Mahatma Gandhi demonstrated childlike character. He dressed simply in clothes he made himself, owned almost nothing, and did not seek political office. Yet he emerged as one of history's most influential leaders.

The third image is water. Water provides an important insight into how leaders ought to influence others by illustrating that there is great strength in weakness. Water cuts through the hardest rock given enough time. In the same way, the weak often overcome the powerful.[34] Authoritarian governments in Soviet Russia, Argentina, and the Philippines were overthrown not by military means but through the efforts of ordinary citizens. Leaders who use "soft" tactics (listening, empowering, and collaborating) rather than "hard" ones, such as threats and force, are more likely to overcome resistance to change. Flexibility or pliability is an important attribute of water as well. Water seeks new paths when it meets resistance; leaders should do the same.

The fourth image is the valley. To the Taoists, the universe is made up of two forces: the yin (negative, dark, cool, female, shadows) and the yang (positive, bright, warm, male, sun). Creation operates as it should when these forces are in balance. Although both the yin and yang are important, Taoists highlight the importance of the yin, or feminine side of leadership, which is represented by the valley metaphor. Leaders should seek to be valleys (which reflect the yin) rather than prominent peaks (which reflect the yang).

The fifth image is the clay pot, which celebrates emptiness by elevating nothing to higher status than something. The most useful part of a pot is the emptiness within. Similarly, the most useful part of a room is the empty space between the walls. Leaders ought to empty themselves, putting aside empty words, superficial thinking, technology, and selfishness. By being empty, leaders can use silence, contemplation, and observation to better understand the workings of the Tao and its ethical principles.

BALANCE SHEET

Advantages (+s)

- Provides an alternative to Western approaches

- Is suited to the modern work environment

- Parallels trends in leadership studies

- Emphasizes inner peace, silence, contemplation, and service

- Focuses on character

- Addresses the leader's use of power and privilege and his or her relationship to nature

Disadvantages (−s)

- — Denies reason

- — Rejects codes and laws

- — Is ambiguous about many moral issues

- — Promotes ethical pragmatism and ethical relativism

- — Does not adequately explain evil

Nearly all the concepts presented in the typical Western leadership or ethics text are drawn from the United States, Great Britain, and Europe. Taoism is one of the few non-Western approaches to attract much attention. It's easy to see why Taoist thought is catching on with leaders and scholars alike. Taoist principles provide an ethical framework for such important trends or themes in leadership studies as empowerment, innovation, teamwork, spirituality, and collaboration. Taoist philosophy seems particularly well suited to leaders working in fast-paced, rapidly changing, and decentralized work environments. Taoist thinkers encourage us to be flexible and to use "soft" tactics such as listening and negotiation that facilitate teamwork in leaner, flatter organizations. They urge us to embrace silence and contemplation, to develop a sense of inner peace, to reject ambition, and to serve. Focusing on being rather than doing (being blocklike and childlike) encourages leaders to develop character, our focus in Chapter 3.

Taoism speaks most directly to the leader's use of power and privilege. The authors of the *Tao Te Ching* reject the use of force except as a last resort. They criticize the feudal lords of their day for living in splendor while their people sink into poverty and starvation. It is difficult to imagine that Taoist sages would approve of the vast difference in pay between American executives and employees, for example, or give their blessing to such perks as company jets, private chauffeurs, and executive dining rooms.

The Taoist perspective also addresses environmental issues. According to Taoists, we need to work with nature instead of controlling or managing it. The natural world seems to renew itself when left alone. When cows are kept out of streams, for instance, vegetation returns to the riverbank, providing shade that cools the water and encourages the return of native fish. On the other hand, attempts to manage the environment often end in disaster. Consider our attempts to suppress forest fires. Putting out wildfires allows tinder to build up over a period of years. When a blaze does take hold, it is much more likely to burn out of control. In addition, Taoists encourage us to look to nature for insights about leadership. Contemporary authors have begun to follow their lead, identifying leadership lessons that can be drawn from the natural world.[35]

There are some serious disadvantages to Taoist ethics. In their attempt to follow nature, Taoists encourage leaders to empty themselves of, among other things, reason. Intuition has its place, but we need to learn how to make more reasoned decisions, not to abandon logic. Taoists are rightly skeptical about the effectiveness of moral codes and laws. Nevertheless, laws can change society for the better. For example, civil rights legislation played a significant role in reducing racial discrimination and changing cultural norms. In organizations, reasonable rules, professional guidelines, and codes of conduct can and do play a role in improving ethical climate. (See Chapter 9.)

Although Taoism has much to say about the shadow of power and our relationship to the world around us, it is silent on many common ethical dilemmas, such as the case of the manager asked to keep information about an upcoming merger to herself (see Chapter 1). What does it mean to follow nature's example when faced with this decision? Perhaps the manager should keep quiet to keep from intruding into the lives of followers. Nonetheless, withholding information would put her in the position of a mountain instead of a valley, giving her an advantage.

Basing moral decision making on conformity to principles manifested in the natural world promotes ethical pragmatism and relativism. The Taoist is pragmatic, believing that the ethical action is the one that blends with natural rhythms to produce the desired outcome. In other words, what works is what is right. This pragmatic approach seems to ignore the fact that what may "work" (generate profits, create pleasure, ensure job security, earn a raise) may be unethical (result in an unsafe product, destroy public trust, exploit workers). The follower of the Tao also practices ethical relativism. Natural conditions are always changing: Seasons shift, plants and animals grow and die. The flexible leader adapts to shifting circumstances. However, this makes it impossible to come to any definite conclusion about right or wrong. What is the right moral choice in one context may be wrong in another.

One final concern should be noted: Taoism's firm conviction that humans, in their natural state, will act morally seems to deny the power of evil. My thesis has been that leaders and followers can and do act destructively, driven by their shadow sides.

Implications and Applications

- Many popular leadership theories are built on moral principles. Try to understand a perspective's underlying values and standards before you adopt it as your blueprint for leadership.
- Contrary to popular belief, being ethical makes us more, not less, successful. Being a good leader means being both ethical *and* effective.

- Seek to be a transforming leader who raises the level of morality in a group or organization. Transformational leaders speak to higher-level needs and bring about profound changes. They are motivated by altruism and marked by personal integrity.
- Putting the needs of followers first reduces the likelihood that you'll cast ethical shadows. Servant leaders are stewards who have significant obligations to both their followers and their institutions, practice partnership, and serve worthy purposes.
- Be careful who and what you serve. Make sure your efforts support worthy people and goals and are carefully thought out.
- Authentic leaders have an in-depth knowledge of themselves and act in ways that reflect their core values and beliefs. Authenticity, which has a strong moral component, multiplies the effectiveness of leaders and promotes ethical behavior in followers.
- Taoists argue that nature and elements of everyday life serve as a source of leadership lessons. You can learn from uncarved blocks, children, water, valleys, and clay pots.

For Further Exploration, Challenge, and Self-Assessment

1. What additional advantages and disadvantages can you add for each approach described in the chapter? Which perspective do you find most useful? Why?

2. Brainstorm a list of pseudotransformational and transformational leaders. What factors distinguish between the two types of leaders? How do your characteristics compare with those presented in the chapter?

3. Discuss the following proposition in a group: "The most successful leaders are also the most ethical leaders." Do you agree? Why or why not?

4. Make a diligent effort to serve your followers for a week. At the end of this period, reflect on your experience. Did focusing on the needs of followers change your behavior? What did you do differently? What would happen if you made this your leadership philosophy?

5. Write a case study based on someone you consider to be an authentic leader. How does this person demonstrate authenticity? What impact has this person had on followers and her or his organization? What can we learn from this leader's example?

6. Which image from nature or daily life from Taoism do you find most interesting and helpful? Why? Can you think of additional natural metaphors that would be useful to leaders?

7. Read a popular book on transformational leadership or on a transformational leader. Write a review. Summarize the contents for those who have not read it. Next, evaluate the book. What are its strengths and weaknesses from an ethical point of view? Would you recommend it to others? Why or why not?

CASE STUDY 6.2

Chapter End Case:
Transforming Clear Lake College

Clear Lake College was in serious trouble in 1992. Enrollment at the Midwestern school had dropped from 650 to 600 undergraduates. Because it had no emergency endowment fund, Clear Lake counted on tuition revenue to pay its bills. The loss of so many students threatened to close the 90-year-old school. The college's president, who seemed unable to respond to the crisis, resigned.

The school's board of directors appointed Samuel (Sam) Thomas as the next president. Thomas had a PhD in higher education but came to Clear Lake directly out of a marketing position in business. Unlike his predecessor, Thomas didn't hesitate to make bold, sometimes risky decisions. He hired a new admission staff, convinced faculty to agree to a salary and benefit freeze, and spent several hundred thousand dollars to launch the college's first graduate degree program.

The 1994 school year saw a surge in new students. The graduate program was a big success, and Sam used his marketing background to improve the college's visibility. An entrepreneur at heart, he encouraged faculty and staff to develop additional programs for new markets. In the next 10 years, enrollment grew to nearly 2,000 students. The college added more graduate degrees and several new undergraduate majors. Clear Lake College earned a national listing as "one of America's hidden educational gems."

Thomas had many admirable leadership qualities. To begin, he was a "people person" who enjoyed mixing with donors, students, faculty, and administrators at other schools. No one would think of calling him "Dr. Thomas." He was "Sam" to everyone. Second, he was more than willing to tackle tough problems and fire those who weren't performing up to standards. Third, he kept his word to faculty and staff. When the financial picture of the school improved, he raised faculty salaries dramatically. Fourth, he had an uncanny ability to sense new educational markets. He never made a major miscalculation when it came to proposing additional programs.

Yet all was not well under Sam's leadership. His friendly exterior masked an explosive temper. He dressed down faculty and other employees in public meetings and made personnel decisions on his own, based on his instincts rather than on hard data. A number of employees were let go without warning, and many of his hires lasted less than a year. In several instances, the college had to offer generous severance packages to dismissed employees in order to avoid costly lawsuits. Sam's autocratic style wasn't limited strictly to personnel decisions. He would change the school's governance structure without consulting faculty, who expected to participate in these choices. In addition, Sam engaged in micromanagement. He read minutes from every department meeting held on campus, for example, and didn't hesitate to send scathing memos if he disagreed with the group's conclusions.

Sam received lots of accolades for his success at Clear Lake College. He was credited for the school's turnaround and was named as the area's outstanding citizen one year. He was popular with other university presidents, serving on national collegiate boards and commissions. The board of the college was eager to renew his contract despite the concerns of the faculty. Unfortunately, Sam's successes made him less, not more, flexible. Frustrated by faculty criticism, he made even fewer efforts to consult them when making decisions. He began to call students who had offended him into his office to berate them.

By the late 1990s, it looked as if the college had "outgrown" Sam's leadership style. After all, the school was much bigger and more complex than it had been when he took over. Sam had no intention of stepping down, however. He referred to Clear Lake as "my college" and continued to be involved in every detail of college life. In fact, Sam had to be forced to resign when he contracted Parkinson's disease in 1999. The college has continued to grow under the leadership of a new president who, while maintaining a good deal of decision-making power, relies heavily on his vice presidents and has very little input in the day-to-day operations of most departments.

DISCUSSION PROBES

1. What elements of transactional and transforming leadership did Sam exhibit?

2. Was Sam a transformational or a pseudotransformational leader?

3. Have you ever had to confront a leader about her or his behavior? What did you say or do? What was the outcome of the encounter? Would you do anything differently next time?

4. Does success make leaders more dangerous, more likely to cast shadows?

5. How do you determine when to remove a leader, particularly one who has a proven track record of success?

6. What leadership ethics lessons do you draw from this case?

CASE STUDY 6.3

Chapter End Case:
Betraying the Student Borrower

Students generally trust their colleges and universities to have their best inter-ests in mind. That certainly is the case when it comes to student loans. Those who don't borrow directly from the federal government generally turn to finan-cial aid administrators for advice about which private lenders to use. Approximately 90% of all students referred to university "preferred lender" lists borrow from the companies on the lists.

Recently many students discovered that, when it comes to loans, their colleges can't be trusted. New York State attorney General Andrew Cuomo (and later the news media) uncovered a variety of unethical practices in the student loan industry involving colleges and universities around the country. In each case, college aid officials put their needs, the needs of their institutions, and the interests of lenders above the needs of students. The unethical and illegal practices included the following:

- *Payoffs.* Universities received kickbacks from lenders for putting them on their "preferred lender" lists. The greater the volume of loans, the more money the schools got back.
- *Consulting fees and travel expenses.* Lenders such as Citibank and Sallie Mae treated administrators to lavish vacations and paid them consulting fees, sometimes for sitting on their advisory boards. A Johns Hopkins financial aid director received more than $60,000 in such fees and sup-port for her doctoral work.
- *Stock deals.* Financial aid officials at the University of Southern California, Columbia University, and the University of Texas at Austin all held stock in the parent companies of lenders who appeared on their "preferred lender" lists.
- *Deceptive advice.* Students at some colleges were referred for loan advice to call centers staffed by loan company employees. In some instances, those who answered the phones falsely identified themselves as employ-ees of the financial aid office. At Loyola Marymount, lenders conducted exit counseling for seniors, which was supposed to tell them how to pay off their loans. Instead, this session gave lenders another chance to sell financial products to students.

Citibank, Sallie Mae, JP Morgan, Bank of America, and Education Finance Partners paid millions in fines for their role in the student loan scandal. Syracuse University, Fordham University, the University of Pennsylvania, New York University, and Long Island University agreed to reimburse students for inflated loan prices caused by kickbacks. Attorney General Cuomo and Congress introduced a series of reforms designed to clean up the student loan business. Cuomo's College Code of Conduct prohibits lenders from making gifts to colleges and their employees in return for preferential treatment, prevents university staff from serving on lender advisory boards, and bars lender employees from posing as college and university employees. The Senate is considering legislation that would require schools to supply preferred lender lists with at least three lenders and to ensure that students max out federally guaranteed loans before turning to private lenders.

Even with these reforms, some students may never regain their trust in their alma maters. After all, the very people and institutions they counted on to serve their needs took advantage of them instead.

DISCUSSION PROBES

1. Where did you turn for advice when seeking student loans? Do you think the advice you received was in your best interest?

2. Has your college or university been accused of any of the ethical abuses described in the case? How has it responded?

3. Do the proposed reforms go far enough? Will they prevent future abuses?

4. What principles of servant leadership were violated by financial aid officers accused of unethical behavior?

5. What leadership ethics lessons do you draw from this case?

SOURCES

Block, S., Chu, K., & Edelman, A. (2007, April 25). How students borrow for college could soon change. *USA Today,* p. 1B. Retrieved October 8, 2007, from LexisNexis Academic database.

Johnson, M. (2007, April 11). Nation's largest student-loan provider settles in loan scandal. *The Associated Press State & Local Wire.* Retrieved October 8, 2007, from LexisNexis Academic database.

Kinsley, M. (2007, September 15). The wacky world of student loans. *The Washington Post,* p. A17. Retrieved October 8, 2007, from LexisNexis Academic database.

Pappano, L. (2007, July 29). Lessons from the loan scandal. *The New York Times,* Education Life Supplement, p. 16. Retrieved October 8, 2007, from LexisNexis Academic database.

Pringle, P. (2007, April 24). Probe into student lending spotlights dual role of U.S. *Los Angeles Times,* p. B1. Retrieved October 8, 2007, from LexisNexis Academic database.

Shady practices taint college loan business. (2007, April 24). *USA Today,* p. 10A. Retrieved October 8, 2007, from LexisNexis Academic database.

Zuckerbrod, N. (2007, April 19). Student loan probe moves Congress to act. *Associated Press Online.* Retrieved October 8, 2007, from LexisNexis Academic database.

Notes

1. Ciulla, J. B. (2004). Leadership ethics: Mapping the territory. In J. B. Ciulla (Ed.), *Ethics: The heart of leadership* (pp. 3–24). Westport, CT: Praeger.

2. Burns J. M. (1978). *Leadership.* New York: Harper & Row.

3. Burns, J. M. (2003). *Transforming leadership: A new pursuit of happiness.* New York: Atlantic Monthly Press.

4. Burns (1978), p. 2.

5. Burns (2003), Ch. 12.

6. See the following:

> Bass, B. M. (1996). *A new paradigm of leadership: An inquiry into transformational leadership.* Alexandria, VA: U.S. Army Research Institute for the Behavioral and Social Sciences.

> Bass, B. M., Avolio, B. J., Jung, D. I., & Berson, Y. (2003). Predicting unit performance by assessing transformational and transactional leadership. *Journal of Applied Psychology, 88,* 207–218.

7. Bass, B. M. (1990). *Bass & Stogdill's handbook of leadership* (3rd ed.). New York: Free Press, p. 53.

8. See the following:

> Bass, B. M., & Avolio, B. J. (1993). Transformational leadership: A response to critiques. In M. M. Chemers & R. Ayman (Eds.), *Leadership theory and research: Perspectives and directions* (pp. 49–60). San Diego: Academic Press.

> Waldman, D. A., Bass, B. M., & Yammarino, F. J. (1990). Adding to contingent-reward behavior: The augmenting effect of charismatic leadership. *Group and Organizational Studies, 15,* 381–394.

9. For evidence of the effectiveness of transformational leadership, see Bass et al. (2003) and the following:

> DeGroot, T., Kiker, D. S., & Cross, T. C. (2000). A meta-analysis to review organizational outcomes related to charismatic leadership. *Canadian Journal of Administrative Sciences, 17,* 356–371.

> Fiol, C. M., Harris, D., & House, R. J. (1999). Charismatic leadership: Strategies for effecting social change. *Leadership Quarterly, 1,* 449–482.

> Lowe, K. B., & Kroeck, K. G. (1996). Effectiveness correlates of transformational and transactional leadership: A meta-analytic review. *Leadership Quarterly, 7,* 385–425.

10. A few examples of popular leadership sources based on a transformational approach include the following:

> Bennis, W., & Nanus, B. (2003). *Leaders: Strategies for taking charge.* New York: Harper Business Essentials.

> Kotter, J. P. (1990). *A force for change: How leadership differs from management.* New York: Free Press.

> Kouzes, J. M., & Posner, B. (2007). *The leadership challenge* (4th ed.). San Francisco: Jossey-Bass.

> Nanus, B. (1992). *Visionary leadership.* San Francisco: Jossey-Bass.

> Peters, T. (1992). *Liberation management.* New York: Ballantine.

11. Bass, B. M. (1995). The ethics of transformational leadership. In J. Ciulla (Ed.), *Ethics: The heart of leadership* (pp. 169–192). Westport, CT: Praeger.

12. Turner, N., Barling, J., Epitropaki, O., Butcher, V., & Milner, C. (2002, April). Transformational leadership and moral reasoning. *Journal of Applied Psychology, 87,* 304–311.

13. Den Hartog, D. N., House, R. J., Hanges, P. U., Ruiz-Quintanilla, S. A., & Dorfman, P. W. (1999). Culture-specific and cross-culturally generalizable implicit leadership theories: Are attributes of charismatic/transformational leadership universally endorsed? *Leadership Quarterly, 10,* 219–257.

14. Criticisms of transformational leadership can be found in the following: Kelley, R. (1992). *The power of followership.* New York: Doubleday/Currency.
Tourish, D., & Pinnington, A. (2002). Transformational leadership, corporate cultism and the spirituality paradigm: An unholy trinity in the workplace? *Human Relations, 55*(2), 147–172.

15. Greenleaf, R. K. (1977). *Servant leadership.* New York: Paulist Press.

16. Spears, L. (1998). Introduction: Tracing the growing impact of servant-leadership. In L. C. Spears (Ed.), *Insights on leadership* (pp. 1–12). New York: Wiley; Ruschman, N. L. (2002). Servant-leadership and the best companies to work for in America. In L. C. Spears & M. Lawrence (Eds.), *Focus on leadership: Servant-leadership for the twenty-first century* (pp. 123–139). New York: Wiley.

17. Greenleaf, pp. 13–14.

18. Block, P. (1996). *Stewardship: Choosing service over self-interest.* San Francisco: Berrett-Koehler; DePree, M. (2003). Servant-leadership: Three things necessary. In L. C. Spears & M. Lawrence (Eds.), *Focus on leadership: Servant-leadership for the 21st century.* New York: Wiley.

19. DePree, M. (1989). *Leadership is an art.* New York: Doubleday.

20. Klenke, K. (2005). The internal theater of the authentic leader: Integrating cognitive, affective, conative and spiritual facets of authentic leadership. In W. L. Gardner, B. J. Avolio, & F. O. Walumbwa (Eds.), *Authentic leadership theory and practice: Origins, effects and development* (pp. 43–81). Amsterdam: Elsevier.

21. Avolio, B. J., & Gardner, W. L. (2005). Authentic leadership development: Getting to the root of positive forms of leadership. *Leadership Quarterly, 16,* 315–340; Chan, A., Hannah, S. T., & Gardner, W. L. (2005). Veritable authentic leadership: Emergence, functioning, and impacts. In W. L. Gardner, B. J. Avolio, & F. O. Walumbwa (Eds.), *Authentic leadership theory and practice: Origins, effects and development* (pp. 3–41). Amsterdam: Elsevier.

22. Kernis, M. H. (2003). Toward a conceptualization of optimal self-esteem. *Psychological Inquiry, 14,* 1–26.

23. Avolio & Gardner, p. 321.

24. May, D. R., Chan, A. Y. L., Hodges, T. D., & Avolio, B. J. (2003). Developing the moral component of authentic leadership. *Organizational Dynamics, 32,* 247–260; Hanna, S. T., Lester, P. B., & Vgelgesang, G. R. (2005). Moral leadership: Explicating the moral component of authentic leadership. In W. L. Gardner, B. J. Avolio, & F. O. Walumbwa (Eds.), *Authentic leadership theory and practice: Origins, effects and development* (pp. 43–81). Amsterdam: Elsevier.

25. Gardner, W. L., Avolio, B. J., Luthans, F., May, D. R., & Walumbwa, F. O. (2005). "Can you see the real me?" A self-based model of authentic leader and follower development. *Leadership Quarterly, 16,* 343–372.

26. May et al.; Ilies, R., Morgeson, F. P., & Nahrgang, J. D. (2005). Authentic leadership and eudemonic well-being: Understanding leader–follower outcomes. *Leadership Quarterly, 16,* 373–394.

27. Gardner et al. (2005); Harvey, P., Martinko, M. J., & Gardner, W. L. (2006). Promoting authentic behavior in organizations: An attributional perspective. *Journal of Leadership and Organizational Studies, 12,* 1–11; Zhu, W., May, D. R., & Avolio, B. J. (2004). The impact of ethical leadership behavior on employee outcomes: The roles of psychological empowerment and authenticity. *Journal of Leadership and Organizational Studies, 11,* 16–26; Avolio, B. J., Gardner, W. L., Walumbwa, F. O., Luthans, F., & May, D. R. (2004). Unlocking the mask: A look at the process by which authentic leaders impact follower attitudes and behaviors. *Leadership Quarterly, 15,* 801–823.

28. See the following:

> Bruhn, J. G. (2001). *Trust and the health of organizations.* New York: Kluwer/ Plenum.
>
> Dirks, K. T. (1999). The effects of interpersonal trust on work group performance. *Journal of Applied Psychology, 84,* 445–455.
>
> Driscoll, J. W. (1978). Trust and participation in organizational decision making as predictors of satisfaction. *Academy of Management Journal, 21,* 44–56.
>
> Gilbert, J. A., & Tang, T. L (1998). An examination of organizational trust antecedents. *Public Personnel Management, 27,* 321–338.
>
> Kramer, R. M., & Tyler, T. R. (1996). *Trust in organizations: Frontiers of theory and research.* Thousand Oaks, CA: Sage.
>
> Mayer, R. C., & Gavin, M. B. (2005). Trust in management and performance: Who minds the shop while the employees watch the boss? *Academy of Management Journal, 48,* 874–888.
>
> Shockley-Zalabak, P., Ellis, K. & Winograd, G. (2000). Organizational trust: What it means, why it matters. *Organization Development Journal, 18,* 35–47.

29. Hanna et al.

30. Cooper, C. D., Scandura, T. A., & Schriesheim, C. A. (2005). Looking forward but learning from our past: Potential challenges to developing authentic leadership theory and authentic leaders. *Leadership Quarterly, 16,* 475–493; Avolio & Gardner.

31. Material on key components of Taoist thought is adopted from:

> Johnson, C. E. (1997, Spring). A leadership journey to the East. *Journal of Leadership Studies, 4,* 82–88.
>
> Johnson, C. E. (2000). Emerging perspectives in leadership ethics. *Proceedings of the International Leadership Association,* pp. 48–54.
>
> Johnson, C. E. (2000). Taoist leadership ethics. *Journal of Leadership Studies, 7,* 82–91.
>
> For an alternative perspective on the origins of Taoism, see Kirkland, R. (2002). Self-fulfillment through selflessness: The moral teachings of the Daode Jing. In M. Barnhart (Ed.), *Varieties of ethical reflection: New directions for ethics in a global context* (pp. 21–48). Lanham, MA: Lexington.

32. Mitchell, S. (1988). *Tao te ching.* New York: Harper Perennial, p. 19.

33. Mitchell, p. 17.

34. Chan, W. (1963). *The way of Lao Tzu.* Indianapolis: Bobbs-Merrill, p. 236.

35. See the following:

> Kiuchi, T., & Shireman, B. (2002). *What we learned in the rainforest: Business lessons from nature.* San Francisco: Berrett-Koehler.
>
> White, B. J., & Prywes, Y. (2007). *The nature of leadership: Reptiles, mammals, and the challenge of becoming a great leader.* New York: AMACOM.

7

Ethical Decision Making and Behavior

As we practice resolving dilemmas we find ethics to be less a goal than a pathway, less a destination than a trip, less an inoculation than a process.

—Ethicist Rushworth Kidder

What's Ahead

This chapter surveys the components of ethical behavior—moral sensitivity, moral judgment, moral motivation, and moral character—and introduces systematic approaches to ethical problem solving. We'll take a look at four decision-making formats: Kidder's ethical checkpoints, Rush's 12 questions, the SAD formula, and the case study method. After presenting each approach, I'll discuss its relative advantages and disadvantages.

Understanding how we make and follow through on ethical decisions is the first step to making better choices; taking a systematic approach is the second. We'll explore both of these steps in this chapter. After examining the ethical decision-making process, we'll see how guidelines or formats can guide our ethical deliberations.

Components of Moral Action

There are a number of models of ethical decision making and action. For example, business ethics educators Charles Powers and David Vogel identify six factors or elements that underlie moral reasoning and behavior and that are particularly relevant in organizational settings.[1] The first is *moral imagination,* the recognition that even routine choices and relationships have an ethical dimension. The second is *moral identification and ordering,* which, as the name suggests, refers to the ability to identify important issues, determine priorities, and sort out competing values. The third factor is *moral evaluation,* or using analytical skills to evaluate options. The fourth element is *tolerating moral disagreement and ambiguity,* which arises when managers disagree about values and courses of action. The fifth is the ability to *integrate managerial competence with moral competence.* This integration involves anticipating possible ethical dilemmas, leading others in ethical decision making, and making sure any decision becomes part of an organization's systems and procedures. The sixth and final element is a sense of *moral obligation,* which serves as a motivating force to engage in moral judgment and to implement decisions.

James Rest of the University of Minnesota and his colleagues developed what may be the most widely used model of moral behavior. Rest built his four-component model by working backwards. He started with the end product—moral action—and then determined the steps that produce such behavior. He concluded that ethical action is the result of four psychological subprocesses: (1) moral sensitivity (recognition), (2) moral judgment or reasoning, (3) moral motivation, and (4) moral character.[2]

COMPONENT 1: MORAL SENSITIVITY (RECOGNITION)

Moral sensitivity (recognizing the presence of an ethical issue) is the first step in ethical decision making because we can't solve a moral problem unless we first know that one exists. A great many moral failures stem from ethical insensitivity. The safety committee at Ford Motor decided not to fix the defective gas tank on the Pinto automobile (see Chapter 2) because members saw no problem with saving money rather than human lives. Apple computer has been slow to address the problem of e-waste generated when consumers dispose of their iBooks, iPods, and iPhones.[3] Many students, focused on finishing their degrees, see no problem with cheating (see the "Cutting Corners at the University" case in Chapter 9).

According to Rest, problem recognition requires that we consider how our behavior affects others, identify possible courses of action, and determine the consequences of each potential strategy. Empathy and perspective skills are essential to this component of moral action. If we understand how others might feel or react, we are more sensitive to potential negative effects of our choices and can better predict the likely outcomes of each option.

A number of factors prevent us from recognizing ethical issues. We may not factor ethical considerations into our typical ways of thinking or mental models.[4] We may be reluctant to use moral terminology (*values, justice, right, wrong*) to describe our decisions because we want to avoid controversy or believe that keeping silent will make us appear strong and capable.[5] We may even deceive ourselves into thinking that we are acting morally when we are clearly not, a process called *ethical fading*. The moral aspects of a decision fade into the background if we use euphemisms to disguise unethical behavior, numb our consciences through repeated misbehavior, blame others, and claim that only we know the "truth."[6]

Fortunately, we can take steps to enhance our ethical sensitivity (and the sensitivity of our fellow leaders and followers) through:

- Active listening and role playing
- Imagining other perspectives
- Stepping back from a situation to determine whether it has moral implications
- Using moral terminology to discuss problems and issues
- Avoiding euphemisms
- Refusing to excuse misbehavior
- Accepting personal responsibility
- Practicing humility and openness to other points of view

In addition to these steps, we can also increase ethical sensitivity by making an issue more salient. The greater the moral intensity of an issue, more likely it is that decision makers will take note of it and respond ethically.[7] We can build moral intensity by

- Illustrating that the situation can cause significant harm or benefit to many people (magnitude of consequences)
- Establishing that there is social consensus or agreement that a behavior is moral or immoral (e.g., legal or illegal, approved or forbidden by a professional association)
- Demonstrating probability of effect, that the act will happen and will cause harm or benefit
- Showing that the consequences will happen soon (temporal immediacy)
- Emphasizing social, psychological, physical, or psychological closeness (proximity) with those affected by our actions
- Proving that one person or a group will greatly suffer due to a decision (concentration of effect)

COMPONENT 2: MORAL JUDGMENT

Once an ethical problem is identified, decision makers select a course of action from the options generated in Component 1. In other words, they make judgments about what is the right or wrong thing to do in this situation.

Moral judgment has generated more research than the other components of Rest's model. Investigators have been particularly interested in cognitive moral development, the process by which people develop their moral reasoning abilities over time. Harvard psychologist Lawrence Kohlberg argued that individuals progress through a series of moral stages just as they do physical ones.[8] Each stage is more advanced than the one before. Not only do people engage in more complex reasoning as they progress up the stages, but they also become less self-centered and develop broader definitions of morality.

Kohlberg identified three levels of moral development, each divided into two stages. Level I, *preconventional thinking,* is the most primitive and focuses on consequences. This form of moral reasoning is common among children who choose to obey to avoid punishment (Stage 1) or follow the rules in order to meet their interests (Stage 2). Stage 2 thinkers are interested in getting a fair deal: You help me and I'll help you.

Level II, *conventional* thinkers look to others for guidance when deciding how to act. Stage 3 people want to live up to the expectations of those they respect, such as parents, siblings, and friends, and value concern for others and respect. Stage 4 individuals take a somewhat broader perspective, looking to society as a whole for direction. They believe in following rules at work, for example, and the law. Kohlberg found that most adults are Level II thinkers.

Level III, *postconceptual* or *principled* reasoning, is the most advanced type of ethical thinking. Stage 5 people are guided by utilitarian principles. They are concerned for the needs of the entire group and want to make sure that rules and laws serve the greatest good for the greatest number. Stage 6 people operate according to internalized, universal principles such as justice, equality, and human dignity. These principles consistently guide their behavior and take precedence over the laws of any particular society. According to Kohlberg, less than 20% of American adults ever reach Stage 5, and almost no one reaches Stage 6.

Critics take issue with both the philosophical foundation of Kohlberg's model and its reliance on concrete stages of moral development.[9] They contend that Kohlberg based his postconventional stage on Rawls's justice-as-fairness theory and made deontological ethics superior to other ethical approaches. They note that the model applies more to societal issues than to individual ethical decisions. A great many psychologists challenge the notion that people go through a rigid or "hard" series of moral stages, leaving one stage completely behind before moving to the next. They argue instead that a person can engage in many ways of thinking about a problem, regardless of age.

Rest (who studied under Kohlberg) and his colleagues responded to the critics by replacing the hard stages with a staircase of developmental schemas.[10] Schemas are networks of knowledge organized around life events. We use schemas when encountering new situations or information. You are able to master information in new classes, for instance, by using strategies you developed in previous courses. According to this "neo-Kohlbergian" approach, decision makers develop more sophisticated moral schemas as they develop. The least sophisticated schema is based on personal interest. People at this level are concerned only with what they may gain or lose in an ethical dilemma. No consideration is given to the needs of broader society. Those who reason at the next level, the maintaining norms schema, believe they have a moral obligation to maintain social order. They are concerned with following rules and laws and making sure that regulations apply to everyone. These thinkers believe that there is a clear hierarchy with carefully defined roles (e.g., bosses–subordinates, teachers–students, officers–enlisted personnel). The postconventional schema is the most advanced level of moral reasoning. Thinking at this level is not limited to one ethical approach, as Kohlberg argued, but encompasses many different philosophical traditions. Postconventional individuals believe that moral obligations are to be based on shared ideals, should not favor some people at the expense of others, and are open to scrutiny (testing and examination). Such thinkers reason like moral philosophers, looking behind societal norms to determine whether they serve moral purposes. (Refer to the "Leadership Ethics at the Movies" case in Box 7.1 for an example of a leader who shifts to a higher level of moral reasoning.)

Rest developed the Defining Issues Test (DIT) to measure moral development. Subjects taking the DIT (and its successor, the DIT-2) respond to six ethical scenarios and then choose statements that best reflect the reasoning they used to come up with their choices. These statements, which correspond to the three levels of moral reasoning, are then scored. In the best-known dilemma, Heinz's wife is dying of cancer and needs a drug he cannot afford to buy. He must decide whether to steal the drug to save her life.

Hundreds of studies using the DIT reveal that moral reasoning generally increases with age and education.[11] Undergraduate and graduate students benefit from their educational experiences in general and ethical coursework in particular. When education stops, moral development stops. In addition, moral development is a universal concept, crossing cultural boundaries. Principled leaders can boost the moral judgment of a group by encouraging members to adopt more sophisticated ethical schemas.[12]

Models of cognitive development provide important insights into the process of ethical decision making. First, contextual variables play an important role in shaping ethical behavior. Most people look to others as well

---

Box 7.1

Leadership Ethics at the Movies

THE LIVES OF OTHERS

Key Cast Members: Martina Gedeck, Ulrich Mühe, Sebastian Koch, Ulrich Tuker

Synopsis: Set in communist East Germany 5 years before the fall of the Berlin Wall. The country's secret police (Stasi) make it their job to know everything about everyone. When the minister of culture falls for the girlfriend of socialist playwright Georg Dreyman (Koch), Stasi captain Gerd Weisler (Mühe) bugs Dreyman's apartment to gather incriminating evidence that the minister can use against his rival. Weisler has dedicated his life to the socialist cause, following orders and wringing confessions from enemies of the state. However, he soon finds himself protecting Dreyman and his fellow dissident artists instead of turning them in to his superiors. He loses his career as a result but earns Dreyman's gratitude after East and West Germany reunite. Winner of an Oscar for Best Foreign Language Film.

Rating: R for sexuality, nudity

Themes: conventional and postconventional moral reasoning, courage, deceit, betrayal, moral motivation, and character

---

as rules and regulations when making ethical determinations. They are more likely to make wise moral judgments if coworkers and supervisors encourage and model ethical behavior. As leaders, we need to build ethical environments. (We'll take a closer look at the formation of ethical groups and organizations in Chapters 9 and 10.) Second, education fosters moral reasoning. Pursuing a bachelor's, master's, or doctorate degree can promote your moral development. As part of your education, focus as much attention as you can on ethics (i.e., take ethics courses, discuss ethical issues in groups and classes, reflect on the ethical challenges you experience in internships). Third, a broader perspective is better. Consider the needs and perspectives of others outside your immediate group or organization; determine what is good for the local area, the larger society, and the global community. Fourth, moral principles produce superior solutions. The best ethical thinkers base their choices on widely accepted ethical guidelines. Do the same by drawing on important ethical approaches such as utilitarianism, the categorical imperative, altruism, communitarianism, and justice-as-fairness theory.

COMPONENT 3: MORAL MOTIVATION

After concluding what course of action is best, decision makers must be motivated to follow through on their choices. Moral values often conflict with other significant values. For instance, an accounting supervisor who wants to blow the whistle on illegal accounting practices at her firm must balance her desire to do the right thing against her desire to keep her job, provide income for her family, and maintain relationships with her fellow workers. She will report the accounting abuses to outside authorities only if moral considerations take precedence over these competing priorities.

Rewards play an important role in ethical follow-through. People are more likely to give ethical values top priority when rewarded through raises, promotions, public recognition, and other means for doing so. Conversely, moral motivation drops when the reward system reinforces unethical behavior.[13] Unfortunately, misplaced rewards are all too common. The housing market collapsed in 2007, in part because lending officers were rewarded based on the number of mortgages they sold. Some offered loans to applicants who had no chance of ever paying them back. Thousands of borrowers lost their homes when interest rates rose. Several large lenders went bankrupt.

Emotions also play a part in moral motivation.[14] Positive emotions such as joy and happiness make people more optimistic and more likely to live out their moral choices and to help others. Depression lowers motivation, and powerful negative emotions such as jealousy, rage, and envy contribute to lying, revenge, stealing, and other antisocial behaviors.

Empathy is critical to moral motivation, just as it is to moral sensitivity. When we experience empathy, we have feelings that reflect another person's situation rather than our own. The distress we feel about their situation (they may be in danger or being treated unjustly, for instance) encourages us to help them. Empathy is a powerful motivator, helping us set aside concern for our own comfort and safety to follow through on our choices. However, according to moral development expert Martin Hoffman, empathy by itself may not be enough to guarantee intervention.[15] We can decide to offer empathy only to those close to us, become too distressed to help, or shift our focus from the other's person plight to imagining how we would feel in the same situation. Hoffman advocates bonding empathy with moral principles. Moral principles (e.g., caring, justice) are activated by empathy but transcend the immediate situation. They keep us from getting too distressed and sustain action over the long term. For example, our empathy for a neighbor hurt by unjust treatment may later become a lifelong concern that all members of society be treated fairly.

To increase your moral motivation and the moral motivation of followers, seek out and create ethically rewarding environments. Make sure the reward system of an organization supports ethical behavior before joining it as an employee or volunteer. Work to align rewards with desired behavior in your current organization. Be concerned about how goals are reached. If all else fails, reward yourself. Take pride in following through on your choices and to living up to your self-image as a person of integrity. Regulate your emotions, making a conscious effort to control negative feelings and to put yourself in a positive frame of mind. Focus on the needs of others rather than your own, and tie your feelings of empathy to principles you hold to be important, such as social justice and protecting the dignity of others.

COMPONENT 4: MORAL CHARACTER

Executing the plan of action takes character. Moral agents have to overcome opposition, resist distractions, cope with fatigue, and develop tactics and strategies for reaching their goals. This helps explain why there is only a moderate correlation between moral judgment and moral behavior. Many times deciding does not lead to doing.

The positive character traits described in Chapter 3 contribute to ethical follow-through. Courage helps leaders implement their plans despite the risks and costs of doing so. Integrity encourages leaders to be true to themselves and their choices. Humility forces leaders to address limitations that might prevent them from taking action. Reverence promotes self-sacrifice. Optimism equips leaders to persist in the face of obstacles and difficulties. Compassion and justice focus the attention of leaders on the needs of others rather than on personal priorities.

In addition to virtues, other personal characteristics contribute to moral action.[16] Those with a strong will, as well as confidence in themselves and their abilities, are more likely to persist. The same is true for those with an internal locus of control. Internally oriented people (internals) believe that they have control over their lives and can determine what happens to them. Externally oriented people (externals) believe that life events are beyond their control and are the product of fate or luck instead. Because they have personal responsibility for their actions, internals are more motivated to do what is right. Externals are more susceptible to situational pressures and therefore less likely to persist in ethical tasks.

Successful implementation also requires competence. For instance, modifying the organizational reward system may entail researching, organizing, arguing, networking, and relationship building skills. These skills are put to maximum use when actors have an in-depth understanding of the organizational context: important policies, the group's history and culture, informal leaders, and so on.

Following the character building guidelines presented in Chapter 3 will go a long way to helping you build the virtues you need to put your moral choices into action. You may also want to look at your past performance to see why you succeeded or failed. Believe that you can have an impact. Otherwise, you are probably not going to carry through when obstacles surface. Develop your skills so that you can better put your moral choice into action and master the context in which you operate.

Decision-Making Formats

Decision-making guidelines or formats can help us make better ethical choices. Taking a systematic approach encourages teams and individuals to carefully define the problem, gather information, apply ethical standards and values, identify and evaluate alternative courses of action, and follow through on their choices. They're also better equipped to defend their decisions. Four ethical decision-making formats are described in the pages to come. All four approaches are useful. You may want to use just one or a combination of all of them. The particular format you use is not as important as using a systematic approach to moral reasoning. You can practice these guidelines by applying them to the scenarios described at the end of the chapter.

KIDDER'S ETHICAL CHECKPOINTS

Ethicist Rushworth Kidder suggests that nine steps or checkpoints can help bring order to otherwise confusing ethical issues.[17]

1. *Recognize that there is a problem.* This step is critically important because it forces us to acknowledge that there is an issue that deserves our attention and helps us separate moral questions from disagreements about manners and social conventions. For example, being late for a party may be bad manners and violate cultural expectations. However, this act does not translate into a moral problem involving right or wrong. On the other hand, deciding whether to accept a kickback from a supplier is an ethical dilemma.

2. *Determine the actor.* Once we've determined that there is an ethical issue, we then need to decide who is responsible for addressing the problem. I may be concerned that the owner of a local business treats his employees poorly. Nonetheless, unless I work for the company or buy its products, there is little I can do to address this situation.

3. *Gather the relevant facts.* Adequate, accurate, and current information is important for making effective decisions of all kinds, including ethical ones. Details do make a difference. In deciding whether it is just to suspend a student for fighting, for instance, a school principal will want to hear from teachers, classmates, and the offender to determine the seriousness of the offense, the student's reason for fighting, and the outcome of the altercation. The administrator will probably be more lenient if this is the offender's first offense and he was defending himself.

4. *Test for right-versus-wrong issues.* A choice is generally a poor one if it gives you a negative, gut-level reaction (the stench test), would make you uncomfortable if it appeared on the front page of tomorrow's newspaper (the front-page test), or would violate the moral code of someone that you care a lot about (the Mom test). If your decision violates any of these criteria, you had better reconsider.

5. *Test for right-versus-right values.* Many ethical dilemmas pit two core values against each other. Determine whether two good or right values are in conflict with one another in this situation. Right-versus-right value clashes include the following:

   – Truth telling versus loyalty to others and institutions. Telling the truth may threaten our allegiance to another person or to an organization, such as when leaders and followers are faced the decision of whether to blow the whistle on organizational misbehavior (see Chapter 5).
   – Personal needs versus the needs of the community. Our desire to serve our immediate group or ourselves can run counter to the needs of the larger group or community.
   – Short-term benefits versus long-term negative consequences. Sometimes satisfying the immediate needs of the group (giving a hefty pay raise to employees, for example) can lead to long-term negative consequences (endangering the future of the business).
   – Justice versus mercy. Being fair and even-handed may conflict with our desire to show love and compassion.

   Kidder believes that truth versus loyalty is the most common type of conflict involving two deeply held values. This tension is at the heart of the follower dilemma described in Box 7.2.

6. *Apply the ethical standards and perspectives.* Apply the ethical principle that is most relevant and useful to this specific issue. Is it communitarianism? Utilitarianism? Kant's categorical imperative? A combination of perspectives?

7. *Look for a third way.* Sometimes seemingly irreconcilable values can be resolved through compromise or the development of a creative solution. Negotiators often seek a third way to bring competing factions together. Such was the case in the deliberations that produced the Camp David peace accord. Egypt demanded that Israel return land on the West Bank seized in the 1967 War. Israel resisted because it wanted a buffer zone to protect its security. The dispute was settled when Egypt pledged that it would not attack Israel again. Assured of safety, the Israelis agreed to return the territory to Egypt.[18]

8. *Make the decision.* At some point we need to step up and make the decision. This seems a given (after all, the point of the whole process is to reach a conclusion). However, we may be mentally exhausted from wrestling with the problem, get caught up in the act of analysis, or lack the necessary courage to come to a decision. In Kidder's words,

Box 7.2

Focus on Follower Ethics

THE GOALKEEPER'S OUTBURST

Want to know what your favorite sports hero really thinks? Chances are you'll never find out. Players have been taught to keep many of their opinions to themselves. They know better than to point out the weaknesses of opponents for fear that such comments will be used as motivational tools by opposing coaches. More importantly, they refrain from criticizing their coaches and teammates in public. Those who go on record with their critiques could be cut from the team, see their playing time reduced, face hostility from teammates, and become the targets of criticism themselves.

Reaction to the candid comments of U.S. national soccer team goalkeeper Hope Solo vividly demonstrates the price that athletes can pay for speaking out. Solo was the starting goalie during the opening rounds of the Women's World Cup in 2007. She went 300 minutes without giving up a goal. Before the team's semifinal match with Brazil, however, coach Greg Ryan pulled Solo in favor of Brianna Scurry, who had been goalie during the team's Olympic gold medal victory against Brazil in 2004.

The result of the goalie switch was disastrous. Scurry was rusty after a long layoff and failed to stop two goals that Solo probably could have prevented. The team suffered the worst loss in its history, 4–0. Soccer experts and fans criticized Ryan for his decision.

In a brief statement after the loss, Solo said,

It was the wrong decision, and I think anybody that knows anything about the game knows that. There's no doubt in my mind that I would have made those saves. And the fact of the matter is it's not 2004 anymore. . . . It's 2007, and I think you have to live in the present. And you can't live by big names. You can't live in the past. It doesn't matter what somebody did in an Olympic gold-medal game in the Olympics three years ago. Now is what matters, and that's what I think.[1]

Team reaction to Solo's outburst was swift and strong. Coach Ryan benched Solo for the final medal game against Norway for violating the team's code of support for other players. She did not go to the stadium for the Norway match. Ryan hinted that Solo's future on the team was in doubt. Other players ostracized the goalkeeper for criticizing her replacement, refusing to eat with her.

Solo later claimed that her intent wasn't to criticize Scurry but to express her reaction to Ryan's decision to bench her. Within a month, U.S. Soccer announced that it wasn't going to renew Coach Ryan's contract. The goalkeeper controversy and loss to Brazil apparently played a major role in the decision to fire Ryan. The president of the soccer federation made it clear that Solo was not suspended from the team and would be invited to training camp the next year.

Were Solo's comments justified? How would you evaluate the response of her coach and teammates?

Box 7.2 (Continued)

Note

1. Hersh, P. (2007, September 30). Women's team facing turmoil. *Los Angeles Times,* p. D1. Retrieved October 25, 2007, from LexisNexis Academic database.

Sources

Goff, S. (2007, May 30). Solo apologizes, but won't play for U.S. vs. Norway. *The Washington Post,* p. D05. Retrieved October 25, 2007, from LexisNexis Academic database.

Grahame, L. J. (2007, October 23). Ryan out as coach of U.S. women. *Los Angeles Times,* p. D6. Retrieved October 25, 2007, from LexisNexis Academic database.

Hersh, P. (2007, September 30). Women's team facing turmoil. *Los Angeles Times,* p. D1. Retrieved October 25, 2007, from LexisNexis Academic database.

Longman, J. (2007, October 23). After haunting loss, U.S. fires women's coach. *The New York Times,* p. D6. Retrieved October 25, 2007, from LexisNexis Academic database.

Ruibal, S., & Steeg, J. L. (2007, October 1). Solo's outburst draws strong reaction; U.S. teammates shun goalkeeper. *USA Today,* p. 8C. Retrieved October 25, 2007, from LexisNexis Academic database.

At this point in the process, there's little to do but decide. That requires moral courage—an attribute essential to leadership and one that, along with reason, distinguishes humanity most sharply from the animal world. Little wonder, then, that the exercise of ethical decision-making is often seen as the highest fulfillment of the human condition.[19]

9. *Revisit and reflect on the decision.* Learn from your choices. Once you've moved on to other issues, stop and reflect. What lessons emerged from this case that you can apply to future decisions? What ethical issues did it raise?

BALANCE SHEET

Advantages (+s)

– Thorough

– Considers problem ownership

– Emphasizes the importance of getting the facts straight

- Recognizes that dilemmas can involve right–right as well as right–wrong choices

- Encourages the search for creative solutions

- Sees ethical decision making as a learning process

Weaknesses (–s)

- Not easy to determine who has the responsibility to solve a problem

- The facts are not always available, or there may not be enough time to gather them

- Decisions don't always lead to action

There is a lot to be said for Kidder's approach to ethical decision making. For one thing, he seems to cover all the bases, beginning with defining the issue all the way through to learning from the situation after the dust has settled. He acknowledges that there are some problems that we can't do much about and that we need to pay particular attention to gathering as much information as possible. The ethicist recognizes that some decisions involve deciding between two "goods" and leaves the door open for creative solutions. Making a choice can be an act of courage, as Kidder points out, and we can apply lessons learned in one dilemma to future problems.

On the flip side, some of the strengths of Kidder's model can also be seen as weaknesses. As we'll see in Chapter 10, determining responsibility or ownership of a problem is getting harder in an increasingly interdependent world. Who is responsible for poor labor conditions in third-world countries, for instance? The manufacturer? The subcontractor? The store that sells the products made in sweatshops? Those who buy the items? Kidder also seems to assume that leaders will have the time to gather necessary information. Unfortunately, in crisis situations like that described in Case Study 7.1, time is in short supply. Finally, the model seems to equate deciding with doing. As we saw in our earlier discussion of moral action, we can decide on a course of action but not follow through. Kidder is right to say that making ethical choices takes courage. However, it takes even more courage to put the choice into effect.

What seem like compelling reasons for a decision may not seem so important months or years later. Consider the U.S. decision to invade Iraq, for instance. American intelligence experts and political leaders tied Saddam Hussein to terrorist groups and claimed that he was hiding weapons of mass destruction. After the invasion, no solid links between Iraqis and international terrorists or weapons of mass destruction were discovered. Our decision to wage this war doesn't appear as justified now as it did in the months leading up to the conflict.

10. *Could you disclose without qualm your decision or action to your boss, your CEO, the board of directors, your family, or society as a whole?* No ethical decision is too trivial to escape the disclosure test. If you or your group would not want to disclose this action, then you'd better reevaluate your choice.

11. *What is the symbolic potential of your action if understood? Misunderstood?* What you intend may not be what the public perceives (see questions 5 and 6). If your company is a notorious polluter, contributions to local arts groups may be seen as an attempt to divert attention from your firm's poor environmental record, not as a generous civic gesture.

12. *Under what conditions would you allow exceptions to your stand?* Moral consistency is critical, but is there any basis for making an exception? Dorm rules might require that visiting hours end at midnight on weekdays. Yet, as a resident assistant, is there any time when you would be willing to overlook violations? During finals week? On the evening before classes start? When dorm residents and visitors are working on class projects?

BALANCE SHEET

Advantages (+s)

- Highlights the importance of gathering facts

- Encourages perspective taking

- Forecasts results and consequences over time

Disadvantages (−s)

- Extremely time consuming

- May not always reach a conclusion

- Ignores implementation

Like the ethical checkpoints, the 12 questions highlight the importance of problem identification and information gathering. They go a step further, however, by encouraging us to engage in perspective taking. We need to see the problem from the other party's point of view, consider the possible injury we might cause, invite others to give us feedback, and consider how our actions will be perceived. We also need to envision results and take a long-term perspective, imagining how our decisions will stand the test of time. Stepping back can keep us from making choices we might regret later. For example, the decision to test nuclear weapons on U.S. soil without warning citizens may have seemed justified to officials waging the Cold War. However, now even the federal government admits that these tests were immoral. Test your perspective taking skills by analyzing the case described in the self-assessment in Box 7.3.

Box. 7.3

Self-Assessment

THE GIFT

Instructions: Determine your ability to take other perspectives into account by reading the following case and answering the questions that follow.

Alfredo Ruiz is director of development at a small liberal arts college in the South. He supervises a small staff that raises funds for the school. Every 3 or 4 years his office organizes capital campaigns to complete new buildings on campus. In between capital campaigns, Ruiz and his colleagues spend most of their time raising money for the college's annual fund. The annual fund covers shortfalls in projected revenue and underwrites small remodeling projects. The development office also works with donors on an ongoing basis to establish student scholarships.

Recently a donor died and left the university with an estate gift of $400,000. The will does not state a specific designation or use for the money. However, Alfredo knows that during the donor's lifetime she gave $10,000 a year to fund student scholarships. At the same time, this year's annual fund drive is falling seriously short of projections. Ruiz will be called on to explain the shortfall and his use of the $400,000 gift at the upcoming Board of Trustees meeting.

Alfredo is very tempted to use the gift to meet the college's annual fund goal instead of establishing an endowed scholarship in the donor's name. However, before making this choice, he comes to you for advice about how others will respond if he applies the money to the annual fund drive.

How do you think the donor's family would view such a choice? Other donors? Students? The public? The board of trustees? What would be the long-term consequences of such a decision? After considering these various viewpoints, do you think that Alfredo should use the money for the annual fund?

SOURCE: Dana Miller, George Fox University.

I suspect that some groups will be frustrated by the amount of time it takes to answer the 12 questions. Not only is the model detailed, but discussing the problem with affected parties could take a series of meetings over a period of weeks and months. Complex issues such as determining who should clean up river pollution involve a variety of constituencies with very different agendas (government agencies, company representatives, citizens' groups, conservation clubs). Some decision makers may also be put off by the model's ambiguity. Nash admits that experts may define problems differently, that there may be exceptions to the decision, and that groups may use the procedure and never reach a conclusion. Finally, none of the questions use the ethical standards we identified in Chapter 5 or address the problem of implementing the choice once it is made.

THE SAD FORMULA

Media ethicist Louis Alvin Day of Louisiana State University developed the SAD formula in order to build important elements of critical thinking into moral reasoning. Critical thinking is a rational approach to decision making that emphasizes careful analysis and evaluation. It begins with an understanding of the subject to be evaluated, moves to identifying the issues, information, and assumptions surrounding the problem, and then concludes with evaluating alternatives and reaching a conclusion.[21]

Each stage of the SAD formula—situation definition, analysis of the situation, decision—addresses a component of critical thinking. (See Box 7.4.) To demonstrate this model, I'll use a conflict involving a school board and a teacher.

Situation Definition

Shirley Katz, a high school English teacher in Medford, Oregon, sued the school district when officials refused to let her bring a concealed pistol to class.[22] She wanted to protect herself against her ex-husband, whom she claimed had previously violated restraining orders and threatened to kill her. Police were stationed in the school, but Ms. Katz thought they were too far away to intervene in time if her ex-husband, an approved substitute teacher for the district, came to her classroom. The ex-husband denied Katz's accusations and claimed that he was no longer working for the district. According to state law, the teacher, who holds a gun permit, can carry her weapon onto most public properties, including schools. However, the lawyer representing the Medford schools argued that the gun ban was a condition of employment and that the district has a right to regulate the conduct of teachers to ensure a safe environment for students and staff. Most other districts in the state also ban teachers from carrying guns on school property. Proponents of gun rights paid the legal costs of Katz's suit, whereas the superintendent of public instruction came out in support of the district.

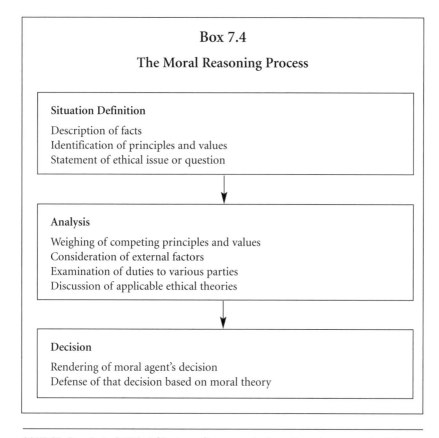

Box 7.4

The Moral Reasoning Process

Situation Definition

Description of facts
Identification of principles and values
Statement of ethical issue or question

Analysis

Weighing of competing principles and values
Consideration of external factors
Examination of duties to various parties
Discussion of applicable ethical theories

Decision

Rendering of moral agent's decision
Defense of that decision based on moral theory

SOURCE: Day. L. A. (2003). *Ethics in media communications: Cases & controversies*. Belmont, CA: Wadsworth/Thompson, p. 67. Used by permission.

Competing principles and values come into play in this situation. Katz is motivated by concern for her safety. Her backers put high value on the legal right to bear arms and argue that schools would be safer places if teachers carried weapons. Opponents give more weight to the safety of the students than the teacher, arguing that an entire classroom could be endangered in an armed confrontation. If the suit succeeds, parents and other visitors could bring guns to school as well. The superintendent of public instruction and some legislators believe that school boards should be given the authority to make schools gun free.

Day says that the ethical question to be addressed in his model should be as narrow as possible. In our example, we will seek to answer the following query: Is the Medford School Board ethically justified in preventing Katz from carrying her concealed weapon to school?

Analysis

Evaluation of Values and Principles. In the gun scenario, both sides can claim moral justification for their positions. Katz is justified in wanting to protect herself from a very real danger. She is following the law and the right to bear arms is protected by state and federal statutes. The school district is to be commended for putting the needs of children first and for trying to foster a safe environment for students and staff.

External Factors. The massacre at Virginia Tech and school shootings in Philadelphia, Wisconsin, and elsewhere have heightened concerns about student safety. Both sides contend that their position will guarantee greater security for students. Another important external factor is the strength of the pro-gun lobby. To date, supporters of gun rights have been able to prevent districts from banning firearms from school property.

Moral Duties or Loyalties. Professor Day borrows from theologian Ralph Potter for this part of his model. Potter believes that we need to take into account important duties or loyalties when making ethical choices.[23] In this case, the following duties have to be kept in mind:

- Loyalty to self
- Loyalty to students at the school
- Loyalty to fellow teachers and other colleagues
- Loyalty to others in the same profession
- Loyalty to the law

Teacher Katz is concerned primarily for her personal safety. This may be a natural reaction, but she seems to overlook her loyalty to others. Students could be endangered if the weapon was stolen or if the teacher shot at her ex-husband. (Law enforcement officers receive training on how to use their weapons in confrontations, but concealed weapon permit holders do not.) Parents might be less trustful of schools if they knew that large numbers of teachers were armed in the classroom. Katz's supporters claim that they are defending the law and, to a lesser degree, students. School district officials claim that their primary loyalty lies with students while recognizing that if the district wins the case, it will be protecting other school boards that have similar regulations.

Moral Theories. Each of the ethical perspectives outlined in Chapter 5 can be applied to this dilemma. From a utilitarian perspective, the immediate benefit to Katz of arming herself has to be weighed again the potential long-term danger of putting more guns in schools. Based on Kant's categorical imperative, Katz has an obligation to carry through on her lawsuit regardless of the consequences, such as negative publicity and criticism. However, it's not clear that we would want all teachers to bring guns to class because of the dangers they pose. Rawls's theory of justice could be applied to say that the Medford teacher has the same right to bear arms and to defend herself as anyone else. Communitarianism seems to support the board's position. School officials put the emphasis on responsibility to children, the community, and other districts. Katz and her supporters seem to be emphasizing individual rights rather than duties. Both sides can claim altruistic motives: to increase school safety. Nonetheless, opponents of the gun ban appear to put more priority on protecting the rights of individuals to bear arms than on protecting children.

Decision

Decisions often emerge out of careful definition and analysis of the problem. It may be clear which course of action is best after external constraints, principles, duties, and moral theories are identified and evaluated. In our example, however, observers can reach and defend different conclusions. To many, the handgun ban is morally justified. This restriction puts loyalty to students and staff first, considers the needs of the community and other districts, and generates the most long-term benefits. This option also seems to be best supported by moral theory. Nonetheless, opponents of the ban can claim that allowing Katz to carry a gun to class can save her life and perhaps the lives of students. Overturning the gun ban also protects a valuable right granted to U.S. citizens.

BALANCE SHEET

Advantages (+s)

- Encourages orderly, systematic reasoning

- Incorporates situation definition, duties, and moral theories

Disadvantages (−s)

- Failure to reach consensus

- Limits creativity

- Ignores implementation

The SAD formula does encourage careful reasoning by building in key elements of the critical thinking process. Following the formula keeps decision makers from reaching hasty decisions. Instead of jumping immediately to solutions, they must carefully identify elements of the situation, examine and evaluate ethical alternatives, and then reach a conclusion.

Three elements of the SAD formula are particularly praiseworthy. First, the formula recognizes that the keys to solving a problem often lie in clearly identifying and describing it. Groups are far less likely to go astray when members clearly outline the question they are to answer. Second, Day's formula highlights duties or loyalties. In the case of the concealed weapon dispute, prioritizing loyalties is key to supporting or opposing the gun ban. Third, the formula incorporates moral theories directly into the decision-making process.

The strengths of the SAD model must be balanced against some troubling weaknesses. Day implies that a clear choice will emerge after the problem is defined and analyzed. Nevertheless, our example demonstrates that this is not always the case. Both sides in the concealed weapons debate argue that their position will make schools safer. Focusing on a narrowly defined question may exclude creative options and make it hard to apply principles from one decision to other settings. Finally, because it was developed for use in discussing cases in classroom settings, the formula leaves out the important implementation stage.

THE CASE STUDY METHOD

The case study method is widely used for making medical diagnoses. At many hospitals, groups made up of doctors, nurses, and other staff meet regularly to talk about particularly troublesome cases. They may be unable to determine the exact nature of the illness or how to best treat a patient. Many of these deliberations involve ethical issues such as whether to keep a terminally ill person on life support or how to respond to patients who demand unnecessary tests and procedures. The group solicits a variety of viewpoints and gathers as much information as possible. Members engage in analogical reasoning, comparing the specifics of a particular case with similar cases by describing the patient, her illness, and relationships with her family. Instead of focusing on how universal principles and standards can be applied in this situation, hospital personnel are more concerned with the details of the case itself. Participants balance competing perspectives and values, reach tentative conclusions, and look for similarities between the current case and earlier ones.

Medical ethicist and communication scholar David H. Smith argues that the case-based approach is a powerful technique because it is based on narrative or story.[24] When decision makers describe cases, they are telling stories. These narratives say as much about the storyteller as they do about the reality of the case. "Facts" are not objective truth but rather are reflections of what the narrator thinks is true and important. Stories knit these perceptions into a coherent whole.

When discussing the fate of patients, it is not enough to know medical data. Hospital personnel need to learn about the patient's history, the costs and benefits of various treatment options, and other factors such as the wishes of relatives and legal issues. Smith outlines the following steps for case-based decision making.

1. *Foster storytelling.* Alert participants to the fact that they will be sharing their story about the problem. Framing the discussion as a storytelling session invokes a different set of evaluation criteria than is generally used in decision making. We judge evidence based on such factors as the quality of sources and logical consistency (see the discussion of argumentation in Chapter 8). We judge stories by how believable they seem to be, how well the elements of the story fit together and mesh with what we know of the world, and the values reflected in the narrative.[25]

2. *Encourage elaboration of essential events and characters.* Details are essential to the case study method. Additional details make it easier to draw comparisons with other examples.

3. *Encourage the sharing of stories by everyone with an interest in the problem.* Bringing more perspectives to bear on the problem reveals more details. In the end, a better, shared story emerges. Consider the case of an elderly man refusing a heart operation that could extend his life. Finding out why he is rejecting the surgery is an important first step to solving this ethical dilemma. As nurses, social workers, and doctors share information, they may discover that the patient is suffering from depression or feels cut off from his family. Addressing these problems may encourage the patient to agree to the operation and thus resolve the moral issue.

4. *Offer alternative meanings.* Change the interpretation of the story by
   - Providing additional expert information and pointing out where the facts of the story do not fit with other facts. The first diagnosis may not be correct. Press on when needed. In the case of our patient, claims that he is alienated from his family would be rejected if his children and grandchildren visit him daily.
   - Focusing attention on the characters in the story (the patient) rather than on some overarching ethical principle such as utilitarianism or the categorical imperative.
   - Examining analogies critically to make sure they really hold. Don't assume that the reasons one patient turns down treatment are the same as those of other patients, for example.
   - Offering alternative futures that might come to pass depending on decisions made by the group. In our case, what will be the likely outcome if treatment is delayed or never given? How much will the patient improve if he has the heart operation? Will attempts to persuade him backfire, locking him into his current position? What might happen if the hospital enlists his family to force him into compliance?

BALANCE SHEET

Advantages (+s)

- – Unique

- – Harnesses the power of narrative and analogical reasoning

- – Avoids ethical polarization; allows for ethical middle ground

Disadvantages (−s)

- – Downplays the importance of objective reality

- – Details are not always available to decision makers

- – Consensus on the right course of action is not always possible

The case study method is significantly different from the others presented in this chapter. These other models outline a linear, step-by-step process for resolving ethical dilemmas that call for the application of universal ethical principles or standards. The case study approach is not linear but circular, calling on participants to share a variety of perspectives. Decision makers keep ethical principles in mind but don't try to invoke them to provide the resolution to a problem. They use them as general guides instead and focus on the case itself. Though unique, the case study method still requires decision makers to meet, systematically share information and analyze the problem, evaluate options, and reach a conclusion.

Many of us like to think that we are rational thinkers who decide based on the facts. In reality we often make choices based on stories. A good narrative is more persuasive than statistical evidence, for instance, and we often use the type of analogical reasoning reflected in the case study approach.[26] For instance, when faced with an ethical decision about whether to tell your current employer about a job offer from another firm, you probably would consider the following: (1) the details of the situation (your relationship to your immediate supervisor, how hard it will be to replace you, your loyalty to the organization); (2) similar situations or cases in your past (what happened when you revealed this information before leaving your last job); and (3) what your friends did when facing similar circumstances. The case study method takes advantage of our natural tendency to reason through story and analogy.

As I noted in the discussion of character ethics in Chapter 3, universal principles can be difficult to apply to specific situations. There always seem to be

4. Brainstorm a list of possible ethical dilemmas faced by a college student. How many of these problems involve a clash between two important values (right versus right)? Identify which values are in conflict in each situation.

5. Apply each of the formats to one of the chapter end scenarios. Do you reach different conclusions depending on the system you follow? To enhance the experience, first reach your own conclusions and then discuss the situations in a group. See whether you can reach a consensus. Make note of the important factors dividing or uniting group members.

6. Use a format from the chapter to analyze an ethical decision facing society (e.g., gay marriage or ordination, illegal music file sharing, illegal immigration). Write up your analysis and conclusions.

CASE STUDY 7.2

Chapter End Case:
Ethical Scenarios for Analysis

SCENARIO A: CLOTHING THE CAMP COUNSELORS

You are a first-year counselor at a camp for needy children, which is subsidized through contributions from individuals and local businesses. Yours is the only camp experience that these disadvantaged kids will ever have. One afternoon, a few hours before the next batch of children is due to arrive, a semi truck stops by with a donated shipment of new shoes, shirts, and shorts for your campers. Immediately the other counselors (all of whom have more experience than you do) begin selecting items for personal use. They encourage you to do the same. When questioned, they argue that there is plenty to go around for both kids and counselors and that the clothes are a "fringe benefit" for underpaid camp staff.

Would you take any shoes or clothing to wear?

SOURCE: Kristina Findley, George Fox University.

SCENARIO B: SCHOOL BUS ADVERTISING

You are the business manager for a suburban school district. Residents of the community have repeatedly refused to raise property taxes or to pass bond issues, leaving your school district in a financial crisis. It is up to you to come up with new ways to raise revenue. You are investigating the option of school bus advertising. Placing full-length ads on the sides of district buses could eventually raise hundreds of thousands of dollars a year. School bus advertising programs are in use in a number of other states, including Colorado, Arizona, and Massachusetts. Bus ads are controversial, however. Consumer groups and some parent groups contend that students are already bombarded with ads and shouldn't be used for commercial purposes. Even supporters of bus advertising acknowledge that certain types of ads are inappropriate, such as those for alcohol, tobacco, and gambling. At least one district won't accept ads for sugary snacks or fast food that could promote childhood obesity. You don't have the final decision on whether the district will adopt a bus-advertising program. Although the school board will make that determination, board members won't consider this funding option unless you propose it.

Will you propose a school bus advertising program to the school board?

SOURCE: Bazar, E. (2005, December 27). Advertisers catch the school bus: Signs generate cash, criticism for local districts. *USA Today*, p. 3A.

SCENARIO C: PENALIZING TIMELY PAYMENTS

You are the manager at a regional center that processes credit card payments. Company profits are down because of increased competition from other card issuers that charge lower interest rates. To boost income, the firm raised its penalties for late payments and reduced the length of the billing cycle. These changes were announced to cardholders. However, at the same time, company officials made an unofficial policy change. They instructed you and managers at the other processing centers to apply late penalties when checks arrive right before the due date. In these cases it will be difficult for cardholders to prove that their payments arrived on time. Some of your colleagues at other processing centers around the country have already begun this practice, knowing that failure to do so could cost them their jobs.

Will you institute this new policy at your processing center?

SCENARIO D: THE FAULTY SALES CONTRACT

You are the sales manager for a high-tech firm that makes engineering software for the design of circuit boards, monitors, and other electronic components. One of your salespeople has just landed a contract with a major computer manufacturer. This contract will be the largest in your firm's 10-year history. Because of the importance of the account, you go with the lucky salesperson to the final meeting where the sales documents will be signed.

As you are waiting for all the parties to arrive, the company's buying manager begins to talk excitedly about all the features of your product. The only trouble is, your software package doesn't contain a number of the features she is describing. Either the buying manager has confused your product with a competitor's, or your salesperson (who is out of the room for the moment) has lied in order to make the sale.

Would you go ahead and sign the contract?

SOURCE: Mark Reed, High Ground Partners, Lake Oswego, Oregon.

Notes

1. Powers, C. W., & Vogel, D. (1980). *Ethics in the education of business managers.* Hasting-on-Hudson, NY: Institute of Society, Ethics and the Life Sciences.

2. Rest, J. (1986). *Moral development: Advances in research and theory.* New York: Praeger; Rest, J. R. (1993). Research on moral judgment in college students. In A. Garrod (Ed.), *Approaches to moral development* (pp. 201–211). New York: Teachers College Press; Rest, J. R. (1994). Background: Theory and research. In J. R. Rest & D. Narvaez (Eds.), *Moral development in the professions: Psychology and applied ethics* (pp. 1–25). Hillsdale, NJ: Erlbaum.

3. How green is your Apple? (2006, August 26). *Economist.* Retrieved March 15, 2007, from Business Source Premier database.

4. Werhane, P. (1999). *Moral imagination and management decision-making.* New York: Oxford University Press.

5. Bird, F. B. (1996). *The muted conscience: Moral silence and the practice of ethics in business.* Westport, CT: Quorum.

6. Tenbrunsel, A. E., & Messick, D. M. (2004). Ethical fading: The role of self-deception in unethical behavior. *Social Justice Research, 17,* 223–236.

7. Jones, T. M. (1991). Ethical decision making by individuals in organizations: An issue-contingent model. *Academy of Management Review, 15,* 366–395.

8. Kohlberg, L. A. (1984). *The psychology of moral development: The nature and validity of moral stages* (Vol. 2). San Francisco: Harper & Row; Kohlberg, L. A. (1986). A current statement on some theoretical issues. In S. Modgil & C. Modgil (Eds.), *Lawrence Kohlberg: Consensus and controversy* (pp. 485–546). Philadelphia: Palmer.

9. Rest, J., Narvaez, D., Bebeau, M. J., & Thoma, S. J. (1999). *Postconventional moral thinking: A neo-Kohlbergian approach.* Mahwah, NJ: Erlbaum; Trevino, L. K., & Weaver, G. R. (2003). *Managing ethics in business organizations: Social scientific perspectives.* Stanford, CA: Stanford University Press.

10. Rest, Narvaez, Bebeau, & Thoma; Thoma, S. J. (2006). Research on the defining issues test. In M. Killen & J. G. Smetana (Eds.), *Handbook of moral development* (pp. 67–91). Mahwah, NJ: Erlbaum.

11. See the following:

> Rest, J. R., & Narvaez, D. (1991). The college experience and moral development. In W. M. Kurtines & J. L. Gewirtz (Eds.), *Handbook of moral behavior and development. Vol. 2: Research* (pp. 229–245). Hillsdale, NJ: Erlbaum.
>
> Rest (1993).
>
> Thoma.

12. Trevino & Weaver.

13. James, H. S. (2000). Reinforcing ethical decision-making through organizational structure. *Journal of Business Ethics, 28*(1), 43–58; Werhane.

14. See the following:

> Connelly, S., Helton-Fauth, W., & Mumford, M. D. (2004). A managerial in-basket study of the impact of trait emotions on ethical choice. *Journal of Business Ethics, 51,* 245–267.
>
> Eisenberg, N. (2000). Emotion, regulation, and moral development. *Annual Review of Psychology, 51,* 665–697.
>
> Gaudine, A., & Thorne, L. (2001). Emotion and ethical decision-making in organizations. *Journal of Business Ethics, 31,* 175–187.
>
> Griffin, R. W., & O'Leary-Kelly, A. M. (Eds.). (2004). *The dark side of organizational behavior.* San Francisco: Jossey-Bass.

15. Hoffman, M. (2000). *Empathy and moral development: Implications for caring and justice.* Cambridge, UK: Cambridge University Press.

16. Trevino & Weaver.

17. Kidder, R. M. (1995). *How good people make tough choices: Resolving the dilemmas of ethical living.* New York: Fireside.

18. Fisher, R., & Ury, W. (1991). *Getting to yes* (2nd ed.). New York: Penguin.

19. Kidder, p. 186.

20. Nash, L. L. (1989). Ethics without the sermon. In K. R. Andrews (Ed.), *Ethics in practice: Managing the moral corporation* (pp. 243–257). Boston: Harvard Business School Press.

21. Day, L. A. (2003). *Ethics in media communications: Cases & controversies* (4th ed.). Belmont, CA: Wadsworth/Thomson Learning, Ch. 3.

22. Burdick, G. (2007, September 16). Armed teachers? Just think about the scenarios. *The Oregonian,* p. D5; Carson, T. (2007, September 20). Pistol-packing teacher sues. *Herald Sun,* p. 41. Retrieved October 27, 2007, from LexisNexis Academic database. Larson, L. (2007, October 16). Disarming only amplifies the likelihood of violence. *The Oregonian,* p. D5. Sleeth, P. (2007, October 3). Teacher goes public in fight to pack pistol. *The Oregonian.* Retrieved October 27, 2007, from Newspaper Source database.

23. Potter, R. B. (1972). The logic of moral argument. In P. Deats (Ed.), *Toward a discipline of social ethics* (pp. 93–114). Boston: Boston University Press.

24. Smith, D. H. (1993). Stories, values, and patient care decisions. In C. Conrad (Ed.), *The ethical nexus* (pp. 123–148). Norwood, NJ: Ablex. For a history of the case study method, see: Jonsen, A. R., & Toulmin, S. (1988). *The abuse of casuistry: A history of moral reasoning.* Berkeley: University of California Press.

25. Fisher, W. (1987). *Human communication as narration: Toward a philosophy of reason, value, and action.* Columbia: University of South Carolina Press.

26. Martin, J., & Powers, M. E. (1983). Truth or corporate propaganda: The value of a good story. In L. R. Pondy, P. J. Frost, G. Morgan, & T. C. Dandridge (Eds.), *Organizational symbolism* (pp. 93–107). Greenwich, CT: JAI Press.

Part IV

Shaping Ethical Contexts

8

Building an Effective, Ethical Small Group

A monologue is not a decision.

—Clement Attlee, former British prime minister

Truth springs from argument amongst friends.

—Philosopher David Hume

What's Ahead

This chapter examines ethical leadership in the small-group context. Groups are often charged with making ethical decisions because they have the potential to make better choices than individuals. To make the most of the small-group advantage, however, leaders must foster ethical accountability, resist groupthink, and initiate productive (enlightening) communication patterns rooted in the pursuit of dialogue.

In his metaphor of the leader's light or shadow, Parker Palmer emphasizes that leaders shape the settings or contexts around them. According to Palmer, leaders are people who have "an unusual degree of power to create the conditions under which other people must live and move and have their being, conditions that can either be as illuminating as heaven or as shadowy as hell."[1]

In this final section of the text, I'll describe some of the ways we can create conditions that illuminate the lives of followers in small-group, organizational, and diverse settings. Shedding light means both resisting and exerting influence. We must fend off pressures to engage in unethical behavior while actively seeking to create healthier moral environments.

The Leader and the Small Group

Leaders spend a great deal of their time in small groups, either chairing or participating in meetings. You can expect to devote more of your workday to meetings with every step up the organizational hierarchy. Some top-level executives spend as much as 21 weeks a year working in committees, task forces, and other small-group settings.[2] Meeting expert John Tropman points out that high-quality management is the product of high-quality meetings that render high-quality decisions. Meetings aren't distractions from our work, he argues, they *are* the work. Successful meetings are "absolutely central to the achievement of organizational goals."[3]

Groups meet for many different purposes: to coordinate activities, to pass along important information, to clarify misunderstandings, and to build relationships. In this chapter, however, I'll focus on the role of groups in making ethical decisions. Examples of ethical group dilemmas include the following:

- A congressional subcommittee debating the morality of the inheritance tax
- Court justices determining the legal rights of terrorist suspects
- The board of the local United Way responding to a funding request from an abortion clinic or a Boy Scout troop that doesn't allow gay men to be leaders
- Foreign aid officials deciding whether their agency should send food to a drought-stricken nation ruled by a dictator
- Student officers disciplining a campus organization that has violated university and student government policies
- Corporate executives devising a plan to dispose of toxic waste

Groups have significant advantages over lone decision makers when it comes to solving ethical problems such as those described above as well as the dilemma presented in Case Study 8.1. In a group, members can pool their information, divide up assignments, draw from a variety of perspectives, and challenge questionable assumptions. They are more likely to render carefully reasoned, defensible decisions as a result.[4] Of course, groups don't always make good moral choices, as in the case of executives who decide to hide product defects from the public or city officials who bypass regulations and award construction contracts to friends. Our task as leaders is to create the conditions that ensure that teams make the most of the small-group advantage. In particular, we must encourage members to take their ethical responsibilities seriously, prevent the problems of groupthink, and promote productive or "enlightening" communication patterns.

CASE STUDY 8.1

Tougher Safety Standards
for All-Terrain Vehicles?

A mericans love their all-terrain vehicles (ATVs). Sales of these low-profile, four-wheel, off-road vehicles have soared to more than 1 million units a year. Buyers use them for work and play. Ranchers ride ATVs instead of horses, for instance, to check their fences and herd their livestock. Entire families ride together while on weekend trips to the mountains or the beach. Sadly, the rate of deaths and injuries due to ATV accidents appears to be rising as fast as ATV sales. Between 1995 and 2005, the number of ATV-related emergency room visits more than doubled, from 52,000 to 135,700. More than 700 riders die in ATV accidents every year; one quarter of these victims are under age 16. The number of children hospitalized after ATV crashes rose 67% between 2000 and 2004.

The Consumer Product Safety Commission (CPSC) is the federal agency charged with regulating ATV safety along with the safety of a host of other products ranging from toys to televisions. In 1988, the CPSC forced ATV manufacturers to stop building three-wheel models and implemented stability standards. Manufacturers also agreed to a set of guidelines, which include the use of warning stickers, free training programs, and a ban on advertising to children younger than 16. The companies volunteered to continue to follow these manufacturing standards and safety regulations even though they expired in 1998.

The voluntary guidelines don't seem to be working. Stability continues to be a problem. ATV rollovers account for many injuries and deaths; riders are thrown from their seats or are crushed by the 400- to 600-pound machines. Many parents and kids do not take the training designed to help them ride safely on uneven terrain. Cheaper Chinese imports, which are not subject to the voluntary guidelines, are grabbing a larger market share.

Critics complain that the CPSC has abdicated its responsibility to the U.S. public when it comes to ATV safety. The chair of the American Academy of Pediatrics committee on injury prevention describes injuries and deaths to child ATV riders as a "national epidemic." He wants legislation preventing children under 16 from using ATVs. Others call for mandatory safety training. Domestic manufacturers such as Honda, Arctic Cat, Yamaha Motor U.S.A., and American Suzuki want the safety commission to recall Chinese imports that fall short of current voluntary standards. For their part, CPSC commissioners claim that it would be impossible to enforce a ban on children riding ATVs. Furthermore, the agency doesn't have the staff it needs to take manufacturers to court to enforce stricter standards. The CPSC has issued a safety warning, but not a recall, for one Chinese model.

Representatives of domestic ATV manufacturers blame riders, not current standards, for most injuries and deaths. Eighty percent of fatal crashes involve riders who violate one or more safety warnings by drinking and driving, riding without a helmet, carrying a passenger, and operating an adult machine while under age 16. ATV users have joined manufacturers in decrying stricter safety standards. Many recreational riders oppose any effort to regulate what they view as an enjoyable family activity. Rural ATV users resent what appears to be yet another attempt by big government to restrict their lifestyle.

Imagine that you are a member of the CPSC meeting to decide whether to require stricter regulations for the manufacture, sale, and use of ATVs. You should come out of your discussions with a ruling (including which, if any, new standards you would propose) and a list of reasons for your decision.

SOURCES

Lipton, E. (2007, September 3). Safety agency failing consumers? *The International Herald Tribune*, p. 15. Retrieved November 5, 2007, from LexisNexis Academic database.

Manning, J. (2007, May 16). Riders throttle safety legislation. *The Oregonian*. Retrieved November 5, 2007, from NewsBank database.

Manning, J., Walth, B., & Goldsmith, S. (2007, May 17). Deceptively dangerous: Why ATVs keep killing. *The Oregonian*. Retrieved November 5, 2007, from NewsBank database.

Scelfo, J. (2007, May 14). Accidents will happen. *Newsweek*, p. 59. Retrieved November 5, 2007, from LexisNexis Academic database.

Shinn, A. (2007, October 28). ATV "non-recall" reveals Consumer Safety Board's constraints. *The Washington Post*, p. A01. Retrieved November 5, 2007, from LexisNexis Academic database.

Skrzycki, C. (2007, July 10). ATV industry plays the China card. *The Washington Post*, p. D02. Retrieved November 5, 2007, from LexisNexis Academic database.

Fostering Ethical Accountability

A group's success or failure is highly dependent on the behaviors of its individual members. Destructive behavior by just one person can be enough to derail the group process. Every team member has an ethical responsibility to take her or his duties seriously. The job of the leader, then, is to foster ethical accountability, to encourage followers to live up to their moral responsibilities to the rest of the group (see Box 8.2). A critical moral duty of group members is to pursue shared goals—to cooperate. Although this might seem like a basic requirement for joining a team, far too many people act selfishly or competitively when working with others. Those pursuing individual goals ignore the needs of teammates. For example, some athletes care more about individual statistics such as points and goals than team victories. Competitive individuals seek to advance at the expense of others. For instance, the ambitious salesperson hopes to beat out the rest of the sales group to earn the largest bonus.

Cooperative groups are more productive than those with an individualistic or competitive focus. Cooperative groups[5]

- Are more willing to take on difficult tasks and persist in the face of difficulties
- Retain more information
- Engage in higher-level reasoning and more critical thinking
- Generate more creative ideas, tactics, and solutions
- Transfer more learning from the group to individual members
- Are more positive about the task
- Spend more time working on tasks

In addition to being more effective, cooperative groups foster more positive relationships and cohesion between members. This cohesion reduces absenteeism and turnover while producing higher commitment and satisfaction. Members of cooperative groups also enjoy better psychological health (i.e., emotional maturity, autonomy, self-confidence) and learn important social and communication skills.[6] (I'll have more to say about group communication skills later in the chapter.)

As a leader, you can focus attention on shared goals by (1) emphasizing the moral responsibility members have to cooperate with one another, (2) structuring the task so that no one person succeeds unless the group as a whole succeeds, and (3) ensuring that all group members are fairly rewarded (don't reward one person for a group achievement, for example).[7]

Creating a cooperative climate is difficult when group members fail to do their fair share of the work. Social psychologists use the term *social loafing* to describe the fact that individuals often reduce their efforts when placed in groups.[8] Social loafing has been found in teams charged with all kinds of tasks ranging from shouting and rope pulling, to generating ideas and rating poems, to writing songs and evaluating job candidates. Gender, nationality, and age don't seem to have much impact on the rate of social loafing, although women and people from Eastern cultures are less likely to reduce their efforts.

A number of explanations have been offered for social loafing. When people work in a group, they may feel that their efforts will have little impact on the final result. Responsibility for the collective product is shared or diffused throughout the team. It is difficult to identify and evaluate the input of individual participants. The Collective Effort Model, developed by Steven Karau and Kipling Williams, is an attempt to integrate the various explanations for social loafing into one framework. Karau and Williams believe that "individuals will be willing to exert effort on a collective task only to the degree that they expect their efforts to be instrumental in obtaining outcomes that they value personally."[9] According to this definition, the motivation of group members depends on three factors: *expectancy,* or how much a person expects that her or his effort will lead to high group performance; *instrumentality,* the belief that one's personal contribution and the group's collective effort will bring about the desired result; and *valence,* how desirable the outcome is for individual group members.[10] Motivation drops if any of these factors are low. Consider the typical class project group, for example. Team members often slack off because they believe that the group will succeed in completing the project and getting a passing grade even if they do little (low expectancy). Participants may also be convinced that the group won't get an "A" no matter how hard they and others try (low instrumentality). Or some on the team may have other priorities and don't think that doing well on the project is all that important (low valence).

Social loafers take advantage of others in the group and violate norms for fairness or justice. Those being victimized are less likely to cooperate and may slack off for fear of being seen as "suckers." The small-group advantage can be lost because members aren't giving their best effort. Leaders need to take steps to minimize social loafing. According to the Collective Effort Model, they can do so by

- Evaluating the inputs of individual members
- Keeping the size of work groups small
- Making sure that each person makes a unique and important contribution to the task
- Providing meaningful tasks that are intrinsically interesting and personally involving
- Emphasizing the collective group identity
- Offering performance incentives
- Fostering a sense of belonging

Resisting Groupthink

In addition to encouraging accountability on the part of individual members of the group, leaders must also help the group as a whole resist the destructive force of groupthink.

Social psychologist Irving Janis believed that cohesion is the greatest obstacle faced by groups charged with making effective, ethical decisions. He developed the label *groupthink* to describe groups that put unanimous agreement ahead of reasoned problem solving. Groups suffering from this symptom are both ineffective and unethical.[11] They fail to (a) consider all the alternatives, (b) gather additional information, (c) reexamine a course of action when it's not working, (d) carefully weigh risks, (e) work out contingency plans, or (f) discuss important moral issues. Janis first noted faulty thinking in small groups of ordinary citizens (such as an antismoking support group that decided that quitting was impossible). He captured the attention of fellow scholars and the public through his analysis of major U.S. policy disasters such as the failure to anticipate the attack on Pearl Harbor, the invasion of North Korea, the Bay of Pigs fiasco, and the escalation of the Vietnam War. In each of these incidents, some of the brightest (and presumably most ethically minded) political and military leaders in our nation's history made terrible choices. (See the NASA chapter end case for a contemporary example of the tragic consequences of groupthink.)

Janis identified the following as symptoms of groupthink. The greater the number of these characteristics displayed by a group, the greater the likelihood that members have made cohesiveness their top priority.

SIGNS OF OVERCONFIDENCE

- *Illusion of invulnerability.* Members are overly optimistic and prone to take extraordinary risks.

- *Belief in the inherent morality of the group.* Participants ignore the ethical consequences of their actions and decisions.

SIGNS OF CLOSED-MINDEDNESS

- *Collective rationalization.* Group members invent rationalizations to protect themselves from any feedback that would challenge their operating assumptions.

- *Stereotypes of outside groups.* Group members underestimate the capabilities of other groups (armies, citizens, teams), thinking that people in these groups are weak or stupid.

SIGNS OF GROUP PRESSURE

- *Pressure on dissenters.* Dissenters are coerced to go along with the prevailing opinion in the group.

- *Self-censorship.* Individuals keep their doubts about group decisions to themselves.

- *Illusion of unanimity.* Because members keep quiet, the group mistakenly assumes that everyone agrees on a course of action.

- *Self-appointed mindguards.* Certain members take it on themselves to protect the leader and others from dissenting opinions that might disrupt the group's consensus.

The risk of groupthink increases when teams made up of members from similar backgrounds are isolated from contact with other groups. The risks increase still further when group members are under stress (due to recent failure, for instance) and follow a leader who pushes one particular solution.

Resisting groupthink is more important than ever before because more firms are using self-directed work teams (SDWTs). An SDWT is made up of 6 to 10 employees from a variety of departments who manage themselves and their tasks. SDWTs operate much like small businesses within the larger organization, overseeing the development of a service or product from start to finish. SDWTs have been credited with improving everything from attendance and morale to productivity and product quality. Unfortunately, SDWTs are particularly vulnerable to groupthink. Members, working under strict time limits, are often isolated and undertrained. They may fail at first, and the need to function as a cohesive unit may blind them to ethical dilemmas.[12]

Irving Janis made several suggestions for reducing groupthink. If you're appointed as the group's leader, avoid expressing a preference for a particular solution. Divide regularly into subgroups and then bring the entire group back together to negotiate differences. Bring in outsiders—experts or colleagues—to challenge the group's ideas. Avoid isolation, keeping in contact with other groups. Role-play the reactions of other groups and organizations to reduce the effects of stereotyping and rationalization. Once the decision has been made, give group members one last chance to express any remaining doubts about the decision. Janis points to the ancient Persians as an example of how to revisit decisions. The Persians made every major decision twice—once while sober and again while under the influence of wine!

Interest in the causes and prevention of groupthink remains high.[13] Researchers have discovered that a group is in greatest danger when the leader actively promotes his or her agenda and when it doesn't have any procedures in place (like those described in the last chapter) for solving problems. With this in mind, don't offer your opinions as a leader but solicit ideas from group members instead. Make sure that the group adopts a decision-making format before discussing an ethical problem. (See Box 8.1, "Focus on Follower Ethics," for an alternative explanation of group moral failure.)

Management professor Charles Manz and his colleagues believe that self-managing work teams should replace groupthink with "teamthink." In teamthink, groups encourage divergent views, combining the open expression of concerns and doubts with a healthy respect for their limitations. The teamthink process is an extension of *thought self-leadership*.[14] In thought self-leadership, individuals improve their performance (lead themselves) by adopting constructive thought patterns. They visualize a successful performance (mental imagery), eliminate critical and destructive self-talk, such as "I can't do it," and challenge unrealistic assumptions. For example, the mental statement,

Box 8.1

Focus on Follower Ethics

AVOIDING FALSE AGREEMENT: THE ABILENE PARADOX

George Washington University management professor Jerry Harvey believes that blaming group pressure is just an excuse for our individual shortcomings. He calls this the *Gunsmoke* myth. In this myth, the lone Western sheriff (Matt Dillon in the radio and television series) stands down a mob of armed townsfolk out to lynch his prisoner. If group tyranny is really at work, Harvey argues, Dillon stands no chance. After all, he is outnumbered 100 to 1 and could be felled with a single bullet from one rioter. The mob disbands because its members really didn't want to lynch the prisoner in the first place. Harvey contends that falling prey to the *Gunsmoke* myth is immoral because as long as we can blame our peers, we don't have to accept personal responsibility as group members. In reality, we always have a choice as to how to respond.

Professor Harvey introduces the Abilene paradox as an alternative to the *Gunsmoke* myth. He describes a time when his family decided to drive (without air conditioning) 100 miles across the desert from their home in Coleman, Texas, to Abilene to eat dinner. After returning home, family members discovered that no one had really wanted to make the trip. Each agreed to go to Abilene based on the assumption that everyone else in the group was enthusiastic about eating out. Harvey believes that organizations and small groups, like his family, also take needless "trips." An example of the Abilene paradox would be teams who carry out illegal activities that everyone in the group is uneasy about. Five psychological factors account for the paradox:

- *Action anxiety.* Group members know what should be done but are too anxious to speak up.
- *Negative fantasies.* Action anxiety is driven in part by the negative fantasies members have about what will happen if they voice their opinions. These fantasies ("I'll be fired or branded as disloyal") serve as an excuse for not attacking the problem.
- *Real risk.* There are risks to expressing dissent: getting fired, losing income, damaging relationships. However, most of the time the danger is not as great as we think.
- *Fear of separation.* Alienation and loneliness constitute the most powerful force behind the paradox. Group members fear being cut off or separated from others. To escape this fate, they cheat, lie, break the law, and so forth.
- *Psychological reversal of risk and certainty.* Being trapped in the Abilene paradox means confusing fantasy with real risk. This confusion produces a self-fulfilling prophecy. Caught up in the fantasy that something bad may happen, decision makers act in a way that fulfills the fantasy. For instance, group members may support a project with no chances of success because they are afraid they will be fired or demoted if they don't. Ironically, they are likely to be fired or demoted anyway when the flawed project fails.

Box 8.1 (Continued)

Breaking out of the paradox begins with diagnosing its symptoms in your group or organization. If the group is headed in the wrong direction, call a meeting where you own up to your true feelings and invite feedback and encourage others to do the same. (Of course, you must confront your fear of being separated from the rest of the group to take this step.) The team may immediately come up with a better approach or engage in extended conflict that generates a more creative solution. You might suffer for your honesty, but you could be rewarded for saying what everyone else was thinking. In any case, you'll feel better about yourself for speaking up.

SOURCE: Harvey, J. (1988). *The Abilene paradox and other meditations on management.* New York: Simon & Schuster. See also Harvey, J. B. (1999). *How come every time I get stabbed in the back my fingerprints are on the knife?* San Francisco: Jossey-Bass.

"I must succeed at everything or I'm a failure," is irrational because it sets an impossibly high standard. This destructive thought can be restated as, "I can't succeed at everything, but I'm going to try to give my best effort no matter what the task."

Teamthink, like thought self-leadership, is a combination of mental imagery, self-dialogue, and realistic thinking. Members of successful groups use mental imagery to visualize how they will complete a project and jointly establish a common vision ("to provide better housing to the homeless," "to develop the best new software package for the company"). When talking with each other (self-dialogue), leaders and followers are particularly careful not to put pressure on deviant members, and at the same time, they encourage divergent views.

Teamthink members challenge three forms of faulty reasoning that are common to small groups. The first is all-or-nothing thinking. If a risk doesn't seem threatening, too many groups dismiss it and proceed without a backup plan. In contrast, teamthink groups realistically assess the dangers and anticipate possible setbacks. The second common form of faulty group thinking, described earlier, is the assumption that the team is inherently moral. Groups under the grip of this misconception think that anything they do (including lying and sabotaging the work of other groups) is justified. Ethically insensitive, they don't stop to consider the moral implications of their decisions. Teamthink groups avoid this trap, questioning their motivations and raising ethical issues. The third faulty group assumption is the conviction that the task is too difficult, that the obstacles are too great to overcome. Effective, ethical groups instead view obstacles as opportunities and focus their efforts on reaching and implementing the decision.

Promoting Enlightening Communication

Communication is the key to both the relationships between group members and the quality of their ethical choices. Shadowy groups are marked by ineffective, destructive communication patterns that generate negative emotions while derailing the moral reasoning process. Healthier groups engage in productive or *enlightened* communication strategies that enable members to establish positive bonds and make wise ethical choices. Another responsibility of the leader, then, is to promote positive interaction between group members. Enlightening communication skills and tactics arise out of the pursuit of dialogue and include comprehensive, critical listening; supportive communication; productive conflict management; and argumentation.

SEEKING DIALOGUE

The attitude we have toward other group members largely determines whether our interactions with them are destructive or productive. There are two primary human attitudes or relationships, according to philosopher Martin Buber: I–It and I–Thou.[15] Communicators in I–It relationships treat others as objects and engage in monologue. At its best, monologue is impersonal interaction focused on gathering and understanding information about the other party. At its worst, monologue manipulates others for selfish gain and is characterized by deception, exploitation, and coercion. Participants in I–Thou (You) relationships, in contrast, treat others as unique human beings and engage in dialogue. Dialogue occurs between equal partners who focus on understanding rather than on being understood. Communication experts Kenneth Cissna and Robert Anderson identify the following characteristics of dialogue:[16]

- *Presence.* Participants in dialogue are less interested in a specific outcome than in working with others to come up with a solution. Their interactions are unscripted and unrehearsed.
- *Emergent unanticipated consequences.* Dialogue produces unpredictable results that are not controlled by any one person in the group.
- *Recognition of "strange otherness."* If dialogue is to flourish, discussants must refuse to believe that they already understand the thoughts, feelings, or intentions of others in the group, even people they know well. They are tentative instead, continually testing their understanding of the perspectives of other group members and revising their conclusions when needed.
- *Collaborative orientation.* Dialogue demands a dual focus on self and others. Participants don't hesitate to take and defend a position. At the same time, they care about the point of view of their conversational partners and about maintaining relationships. They focus on coming up with a shared, joint solution, not on winning or losing.

- *Vulnerability.* Dialogue is risky because discussants open their thoughts to others and may be influenced by the encounter. They must be willing to change their minds.
- *Mutual implication.* Speakers engaged in dialogue always keep listeners in mind when speaking. In so doing, they may discover more about themselves as well.
- *Temporal flow.* Dialogue takes time and emerges over the course of a group discussion. It is a process that can't be cut into segments and analyzed.
- *Genuineness and authenticity.* Participants in dialogue give each other the benefit of the doubt, assuming that the other person is being honest and sharing from personal experience. Although speakers don't share all their thoughts, they don't deliberately hide thoughts and feelings that are relevant to the topic and to the relationship.

By its nature, "pure" dialogue is difficult to achieve. Focusing on the needs and positions of others is hard work. Nonetheless, as leaders we should identify dialogue as the ethical ideal or standard for group interactions. Striving for dialogue acknowledges the intrinsic value of every group member and lays the groundwork for the enlightening communication strategies that follow. As leaders and followers we are much more likely to listen and to support others when we treat them as equals whose experiences and opinions are just as valid as our own. Dialogue encourages healthy argument and conflict as well. Buber argued that the best example of the I–Thou relationship comes not when friends or intimates interact but when acquaintances profoundly disagree and yet remain in dialogue.[17] Confrontation tempts us to treat others like obstacles that need to be overcome so that we can win. Dialogue empowers us to remain genuinely present to fellow group members while holding fast to our own positions.

COMPREHENSIVE, CRITICAL LISTENING

We spend much more time listening than speaking in small groups. If you belong to a team with 10 members, you can expect to devote approximately 10% of your time to talking and 90% to listening to what others have to say. All listening involves receiving, paying attention to, interpreting, and then remembering messages. However, our motives for listening vary.[18] *Discriminative listening* processes the verbal and nonverbal components of a message. It serves as the foundation for the other forms of listening because we can't accurately process or interpret messages unless we first understand what is being said and how the message is being delivered. Tom and Ray Magliozzi of National Public Radio's *Car Talk* demonstrate the importance of discriminative listening on their weekly call-in program. They frequently ask callers to repeat the sounds made by their vehicles. A "clunk" sound can signal one type of engine problem; a "chunk" noise might indicate that something else is wrong.

Comprehensive listening is motivated by the need to understand and retain messages. We engage in this type of listening when we attend lectures, receive job instructions, attend oral briefings, and watch the evening weather report. *Therapeutic or empathetic listening* is aimed at helping the speaker resolve an issue by encouraging him or her to talk about the problem. Those in helping professions such as social work and psychiatry routinely engage in this listening process. All of us act as empathetic listeners, however, when friends and family come to us for help. *Critical listening* leads to evaluation. Critical listeners pay careful attention to message content, logic, language, and other elements of persuasive attempts so that they can identify strengths and weaknesses and render a judgment. *Appreciative listening* is prompted by the desire for relaxation and entertainment. We act as appreciative listeners when we enjoy a CD, live concert, or play.

Group members engage in all five types of listening during meetings, but comprehensive and critical listening are essential to ethical problem solving. Coming up with a high-quality decision is nearly impossible unless group members first understand and remember what others have said. Participants also have to critically analyze the arguments of other group members in order to identify errors (see the discussion of conflict and argumentation that follows).

There are several barriers to comprehensive, critical listening in the group context. In one-to-one conversations, we know that we must respond to the speaker, so we tend to pay closer attention. In a group, we don't have to carry as much of the conversational load, so we're tempted to lose focus or to talk to the person sitting next to us. The content of the discussion can also make listening difficult. Ethical issues can generate strong emotional reactions because they involve deeply held values and beliefs. The natural tendency is to dismiss the speaker ("What does he know?" "He's got it all wrong!") and become absorbed in our own emotions instead of concentrating on the message.[19] Reaching an agreement then becomes more difficult because we don't understand the other person's position but are more committed than ever to our point of view.

Listening experts Larry Barker, Patrice Johnson, and Kittie Watson make these suggestions for improving listening performance in a group setting. Our responsibility as leaders is to model these behaviors and encourage other participants to follow our example.[20]

- *Avoid interruptions.* Give the speaker a chance to finish before you respond or ask questions. The speaker may address your concerns before he or she finishes, and you can't properly evaluate a message until you've first understood it.

- *Seek areas of agreement.* Take a positive approach by searching for common ground. What do you and the speaker have in common? Commitment to solving the problem? Similar values and background?

- *Search for meanings and avoid arguing about specific words.* Discussions of terms can keep the group from addressing the real issue. Stay focused on what speakers mean; don't be distracted if they use different terms than you do.

- *Ask questions and request clarification.* When you don't understand, don't be afraid to ask for clarification. Chances are others in the group are also confused and will appreciate more information. However, asking too many questions can give the impression that you're trying to control the speaker.

- *Be patient.* We can process information faster than speakers can deliver it. Use the extra time to reflect on the message instead of focusing on your own reactions or daydreaming.

- *Compensate for attitudinal biases.* All of us have biases based on such factors as personal appearance, age differences, and irritating mannerisms. Among my pet peeves? Men with Elvis hairdos, grown women with little girl voices, and nearly anyone who clutters his or her speech with "ums" and "uhs." I have to suppress my urge to dismiss these kinds of speakers and concentrate on listening carefully. (Sadly, I don't always succeed.)

- *Listen for principles, concepts, and feelings.* Try to understand how individual facts fit into the bigger picture. Don't overlook nonverbal cues such as tone of voice and posture that reveal emotions and, at times, can contradict verbal statements. If a speaker's words and nonverbal behaviors don't seem to match (as in expression of support uttered with a sigh of resignation), probe further to make sure you clearly understand the person's position.

- *Compensate for emotion-arousing words and ideas.* Certain words and concepts such as *fundamentalist, euthanasia, gay pride, terrorist,* and *feminist* spark strong emotional responses. We need to overcome our knee-jerk reactions to these labels and strive instead to remain objective.

- *Be flexible.* Acknowledge that other views may have merit, even though you may not completely agree with them.

- *Listen, even if the message is boring or tough to follow.* Not all messages are exciting and simple to digest, but we need to try to understand them anyway. A boring comment made early in a group discussion may later turn out to be critical to the team's success.

DEFENSIVE VERSUS SUPPORTIVE COMMUNICATION

Defensiveness is a major threat to accurate listening. When group members feel threatened, they divert their attention from the task to defending themselves. As their anxiety levels increase, they think less about how to solve the problem and more about how they are coming across to others, about winning, and about protecting themselves. Listening suffers because participants distort the messages they receive, misinterpreting the motives, values, and emotions of senders. On the other hand, supportive messages increase accuracy because group members devote more energy to interpreting the content and emotional states of sources. Psychologist Jack Gibb identified the following six pairs of behaviors that promote either a defensive or supportive group atmosphere.[21] Our job as the group's leader is to engage in supportive communication, which contributes to a positive emotional climate and accurate understanding. At the same time, we need to challenge comments that spark defensive reactions and lead to poor ethical choices.

Evaluation Versus Description. Evaluative messages are judgmental. They can be sent through statements ("What a lousy idea!") or through such nonverbal cues as a sarcastic tone of voice or a raised eyebrow. Those being evaluated are likely to respond by placing blame and making judgments of their own ("Your proposal is no better than mine"). Supportive messages ("I think I see where you're coming from," attentive posture, eye contact) create a more positive environment.

Control Versus Problem Orientation. Controlling messages imply that the recipient is inadequate (i.e., uninformed, immature, stubborn, overly emotional) and needs to change. Control, like evaluation, can be communicated both verbally (issuing orders, threats) and nonverbally (stares, threatening body posture). Problem-centered messages reflect a willingness to collaborate, to work together to resolve the issue. Examples of problem-oriented statements might include "What do you think we ought to do?" and "I believe we can work this out if we sit down and identify the issues."

Strategy Versus Spontaneity. Strategic communicators are seen as manipulators who try to hide their true motivations. They say they want to work with others yet withhold information and appear to be listening when they're not. This "false spontaneity" angers the rest of the group. On the other hand, behavior that is truly spontaneous and honest reduces defensiveness.

Neutrality Versus Empathy. Neutral messages such as "You'll get over it" and "Don't take it so seriously" imply that the listener doesn't care. Empathetic statements, such as "I can see why you would be depressed" and "I'll be thinking about you when you have that appointment with your boss," communicate reassurance and acceptance. Those who receive them enjoy a boost in self-esteem.

Superiority Versus Equality. Attempts at one-upmanship generally provoke immediate defensive responses. The comment "I got an A in my ethics class" is likely to be met with this kind of reply: "Well, you may have a lot of book learning, but I had to deal with a lot of real-world ethical problems when I worked at the advertising agency." Superiority can be based on a number of factors, including wealth, social class, organizational position, and power. All groups contain members who differ in their social standing and abilities. However, these differences are less disruptive if participants indicate that they want to work with others on an equal basis.

Certainty Versus Provisionalism. Dogmatic group members (those who are inflexible and claim to have all the answers) are unwilling to change or consider other points of view. As a consequence, they appear more interested in being right than in solving the problem. Listeners often perceive certainty as a mask for feelings of inferiority. In contrast to dogmatic individuals, provisional discussants signal that they are willing to work with the rest of the team in order to investigate issues and come up with a sound ethical decision.

PRODUCTIVE CONFLICT

In healthy groups, members examine and debate the merits of the proposal before the group, a process that experts call *substantive conflict*.[22] Substantive conflicts produce a number of positive outcomes, including these:

- Accurate understanding of the arguments and positions of others in the group
- Higher-level moral reasoning
- Thorough problem analysis
- Improved self-understanding and self-improvement
- Stronger, deeper relationships
- Creativity and change
- Greater motivation to solve the problem
- Improved mastery and retention of information
- Deeper commitment to the outcome of the discussion
- Increased group cohesion and cooperation
- Improved ability to deal with future conflicts
- High-quality solutions that integrate the perspective of all members

It is important to differentiate between substantive conflict and *affective conflict*, which is centered on the personal relationships between group members. Those caught in personality-based conflicts find themselves either trying to avoid the problem or, when the conflict can't be ignored, escalating hostilities through name calling, sarcasm, threats, and other means. In this poisoned environment, members aren't as committed to the group process, sacrifice in-depth discussion of the problem in order to get done as soon as possible, and distance themselves from the decision. The end result? A decline in moral reasoning that produces an unpopular, low-quality solution. (Turn to the "Leadership Ethics at the Movies" case in Box 8.2 for one example of a team that shifted from affective to substantive conflict.)

Box 8.2

Leadership Ethics at the Movies

A FEW GOOD MEN

Starring: Tom Cruise, Jack Nicholson, Demi Moore, Kevin Pollak, Kevin Bacon

Rating: R for language

Synopsis: Tom Cruise, Demi Moore, and Kevin Pollak play three military lawyers assigned to defend two Marines charged with murder. Top Navy officials hope that lead attorney Lt. Daniel Kaffee (Cruise) will enter a plea bargain on behalf of his clients and that the case will be quickly forgotten. Instead, Kaffee decides to take the case to court at the urging of co-counsel Lt. Commander Joanne Galloway (Moore). Kaffee, Galloway, and the third member of the team, Lt. Weinberg (Pollak), must overcome their differences in order to assemble their case. Along the way they reveal a cover-up, overcome the loss of a key witness, and challenge one of the Marines' most popular officers, Colonel Nathan Jessup (Nicholson). During the climactic courtroom scene Nicholson utters one of the most famous lines in recent movie history: "The truth? You can't handle the truth!"

Themes: destructive and productive conflict, argumentation, social loafing, supportive versus defensive communication, group roles, loyalty, altruism

---

There are a number of ways in which you as a leader can encourage substantive conflict. Begin by paying attention to the membership of the group. Encourage the emergence of minority opinion by forming teams made up of people with significantly different backgrounds. Groups concerned with medical ethics, for example, generally include members from both inside the medical profession (nurses, surgeons, hospital administrators) and outside (theologians, ethicists, government officials). Individuals and subgroups that disagree with the majority cast doubt on the prevailing opinion and stimulate further thought. In the end, the majority generally comes up with a better solution because members have examined their assumptions and considered more viewpoints and possible solutions.[23]

Next, lay down some procedural ground rules—a conflict covenant—before discussion begins. Come up with a list of conflict guideposts as a group. "Absolutely no name-calling or threats." "No idea is a dumb idea." "Direct all critical comments toward the problem, not the person." "You must repeat the message of the previous speaker—to that person's satisfaction—before you can add your comments." Highlight the fact that conflict about ideas is an integral part of group discussion and caution against hasty decisions. Encourage individuals to stand firm instead of capitulating. If need be, appoint someone to play the role of devil's advocate with the responsibility to cast doubt on the group's proposals.

During the discussion, make sure that members follow their conflict covenant and don't engage in conflict avoidance or escalation. Stop to revisit the ground rules when needed. Be prepared to support your position. Challenge and analyze the arguments of others as you encourage them to do the same. If members get stuck in a battle of wills, reframe the discussion by asking such questions as "What kind of information would help you change your mind?" "Why shouldn't we pursue other options?" "What would you do if you were in my position?"[24] You can also ask participants to develop new ways to describe their ideas (in graphs, as numbers, as bulleted lists) and ask them to step back and revisit their initial assumptions in order to find common ground.

After the decision is made, ensure that the team and its members will continue to develop their conflict management skills. Debrief the decision-making process to determine whether the group achieved its goals, work on repairing relationships that might have been bruised during the discussion, and celebrate or remember stories of outstanding conflict management.[25]

ENGAGING IN EFFECTIVE ARGUMENT

Making arguments is the best way to influence others when the group is faced with a controversial decision. That's why argumentative people are more likely to emerge as leaders.[26] An argument is an assertion or claim that is supported by evidence and reasons. In the argumentation process, group members interact with each other using claims, evidence, and reasoning in hopes of reaching the best decision. They avoid personal attacks that characterize affective conflicts.

Argumentation in a small group is not as formal and sophisticated as a legal brief or a debate at a college forensics tournament. In more formal settings, there are strict limits on such things as how long arguers can speak, what evidence they can introduce, how they should address the audience, and how the argument should be constructed. Argumentation in a group is much less structured. No one enforces time limits for individual speakers, and members may interrupt each other and get off track. Nonetheless, when leading a group, you'll have to make sure the group carries out the same basic tasks as the members of a university debate team.[27] (Complete the self-assessment in Box 8.3 to determine how likely you are to engage in arguments.)

The first task is to identify just what the controversy is about. All too often teams waste their time debating the wrong issues and end up solving the wrong problem. In Case Study 8.1, "Tougher Safety Standards for All-Terrain Vehicles?," the controversy surrounds strengthening safety rules. The decision is not a referendum on the role of the federal government in society (although some critics want it to be). The Consumer Product Safety Commission must determine its response to the following assertion: "Stricter standards should be put in place to improve ATV safety."

Once the controversy is clearly identified, you need to assemble and present your arguments. As I noted earlier, arguments consist of a claim supported by evidence and reasons. Back up your claim with examples, personal experience, testimonials from others, and statistics. Also, supply reasons or logic for your position. The most common patterns of logic include *analogical* (drawing similarities between one case and another, as we saw in Chapter 7), *causal* (one event leads to another), *inductive* (generalizing from one or a few cases to many), and *deductive* (moving from a larger category or grouping to a smaller one).

You could use all four types of reasoning if you believe that safety standards for ATVs ought to be strengthened. You might note that ATVs are as dangerous as motorcycles, which are more closely regulated (analogical reasoning). You could argue that the increasing popularity of ATVs will lead to greater numbers of injuries and deaths if nothing is done (causal reasoning). You could illustrate the likely benefits of stronger national regulations by pointing to reduced accident rates in states that have adopted stricter safety standards (inductive reasoning). You might point out that the push for stronger ATV standards is just the latest evidence of increased public concern about product safety (deductive reasoning).

While you formulate your position, you need to identify and attack the weaknesses in the positions of other participants. This process is often neglected in group discussions. Group communication experts Dennis Gouran and Randy Hirokawa found that undetected errors are the primary cause of poor-quality decisions.[28] These errors include incomplete data, accepting bad information as fact, selecting only the information that supports a flawed choice, rejecting valid evidence, poor reasoning, and making unreasonable inferences from the facts. Be on the lookout for the common errors in evidence and reasoning found in Box 8.4. According to Gouran and Hirokawa, all groups make mistakes, but members of successful groups catch their errors and get the group back on track through corrective communication called *counteractive influence.*

Implications and Applications

- As a leader, you will do much of your work in committees, boards, task forces, and other small groups. Making ethical choices is one of a team's most

Box 8.3

Self-Assessment

ARGUMENTATIVENESS SCALE

Instructions: This questionnaire contains statements about arguing controversial issues. Indicate how often each statement is true for you personally by placing the appropriate number in the blank to the left of the statement.

Never true = 1, Rarely true = 2, Occasionally true = 3, Often true = 4, Almost always true = 5

____ 1. While in an argument, I worry that the person with whom I am arguing will form a negative impression of me.

____ 2. Arguing over controversial issues improves my intelligence.

____ 3. I enjoy avoiding arguments.

____ 4. I am energetic and enthusiastic when I argue.

____ 5. Once I finish an argument, I promise myself that I will not get into another.

____ 6. Arguing with a person creates more problems for me than it solves.

____ 7. I have a pleasant, good feeling when I win a point in an argument.

____ 8. When I finish arguing with someone, I feel nervous and upset.

____ 9. I enjoy a good argument over a controversial issue.

____ 10. I get an unpleasant feeling when I realize I am about to get into an argument.

____ 11. I enjoy defending my point of view on an issue.

____ 12. I am happy when I keep an argument from happening.

____ 13. I do not like to miss the opportunity to argue a controversial issue.

____ 14. I prefer being with people who rarely disagree with me.

____ 15. I consider an argument an exciting intellectual challenge.

____ 16. I find myself unable to think of effective points during an argument.

____ 17. I feel refreshed and satisfied after an argument on a controversial issue.

____ 18. I have the ability to do well in an argument.

____ 19. I try to avoid getting into arguments.

____ 20. I feel excitement when I expect that a conversation I am in is leading to an argument.

Argumentativeness Scoring

1. Add your scores on items 2, 4, 7, 9, 11, 13, 15, 17, 18, 20.

2. Add 6 to the sum obtained in Step 1.

3. Add your scores on items 1, 3, 5, 6, 8, 10, 12, 14, 16, 19.

4. To compute your argumentativeness score, subtract the total obtained in Step 3 from the total obtained in Step 2.

Interpretation

73–100 = High in argumentativeness
56–72 = Moderate in argumentativeness
2–55 = Low in argumentativeness

SOURCE: Infante, D. A., & Rancer, A. S. (1982). A conceptualization and measure of argumentativeness. *Journal of Personality Assessment, 46,* 72–78. Used by permission.

Box 8.4

Common Fallacies

Faulty Evidence

Unreliable and biased sources

Source lacking proper knowledge and background

Inconsistency (disagrees with other sources, source contradicts himself or herself)

Outdated evidence

Evidence appears to support a claim but does not

Information gathered from second-hand observers

Uncritical acceptance of statistical data

Inaccurate or incomplete citation of sources and quotations

Plagiarism (using the ideas or words of others without proper attribution)

Faulty Reasoning

Comparing two things that are not alike (false analogy)

Drawing conclusions based on too few examples or examples that aren't typical of the population as a whole (hasty generalization)

Believing that the event that happens first always causes the event that happens second (false cause)

Arguing that complicated problems have only one cause (single cause)

Assuming without evidence that one event will inevitably lead to a bad result (slippery slope)

Using the argument to support the argument (begging the question)

Failing to offer evidence that supports the position (non sequitur)

Attacking the person instead of the argument (ad hominem)

Appealing to the crowd or popular opinion (ad populum)

Resisting change based on past practices (appeal to tradition)

Attacking a weakened version of an opponent's argument (straw argument)

SOURCE: Inch, E. S., Warnick, B., & Endres, D. (2006). *Critical thinking and communication: The use of reason in argument* (5th ed.). Boston: Pearson.

important responsibilities. Your task is to foster the conditions that promote effective, ethical decisions.

- Because destructive behavior on the part of just one member can derail the group process, encourage participants to take their ethical responsibilities seriously. Promote commitment to shared goals and take steps to minimize social loafing.

- An overemphasis on group cohesion is a significant threat to ethical decision making. Be alert for the symptoms of groupthink. These include signs of overconfidence (illusion of invulnerability, belief in the inherent morality of the group), signs of closed-mindedness (collective rationalization, stereotypes of outside groups), signs of group pressure (pressure on dissenters, self-censorship, illusion of unanimity, and self-appointed mindguards).

- Adopting teamthink strategies is one way to resist the temptation to put agreement ahead of reasoned problem solving. Encourage your group to visualize successful outcomes, avoid pressure tactics, and challenge faulty assumptions.

- A dialogic approach to communication, one that treats others as humans rather than as objects, lays the groundwork for productive group interaction.

- If you want a healthy group that makes effective ethical decisions, engage productive or enlightened communication patterns and help followers to do the same. Enlightening communication skills and tactics include comprehensive, critical listening; supportive messages; productive conflict management; and effective argumentation.

For Further Exploration, Challenge, and Self-Assessment

1. Interview a leader at your school or in another organization to develop a "meeting profile" for this person. Find out how much time this person spends in meetings during an average week and whether this is typical of other leaders in the same organization. Identify the types of meetings she or he attends and her or his role. Determine whether ethical issues are part of these discussions. As part of your profile, record your reactions. Are you surprised by your findings? Has this assignment changed your understanding of what leaders do?

2. Brainstorm strategies for encouraging commitment to shared goals in a group that you lead or belong to. What steps can you take to implement these strategies?

3. Evaluate the level of social loafing in your group. What factors encourage members to reduce their efforts? What can you as a leader do to raise the motivation level of participants?

4. Have you ever been part of a group that was victimized by groupthink? Which symptoms were present? How did they affect the group's ethical decisions and actions? Does the Abilene paradox described in Box 8.1 offer a better explanation for what happened?

5. Evaluate a recent ethical decision made by one of your groups. Was it a high-quality decision? Why or why not? What factors contributed to the group's success or failure? Which of the keys to effective ethical problem solving were present? Absent? How did the leader (you or someone else) shape the outcome, for better or worse? How would you evaluate your performance as a leader or team member? Write up your analysis.

6. Develop a plan for becoming a better listener in a group. Implement your plan and then evaluate your progress.

7. Pair off with a partner and discuss your argumentativeness scores. What experiences and attitudes contribute to your willingness or unwillingness to argue? Are you more willing to argue in some situations than in others? How could you increase your argumentativeness score? As an alternative, share your responses in an ongoing group. Determine how the group as a whole can engage in more productive argument.

8. Identify forms of faulty evidence and reasoning in an argument about an ethical issue. Draw from talk shows, newspaper editorials, speeches, interviews, debates, congressional hearings, and other sources. Possible topics might include national health care, the wars in Iraq and Afghanistan, stem cell research, illegal immigration, and cloning.

9. With other team members, develop a conflict covenant. Determine how you will enforce this code.

10. Fishbowl discussion: In a fishbowl discussion, one group discusses a problem while the rest of the class looks on and then provides feedback. Assign a group to Case 8.1 at the beginning of this chapter or the "Incentives for Organ Donations" chapter end case. Make sure that each discussant has one or more observers who specifically note his or her behavior. When the discussion is over, observers should meet with their "fish." Then the class as a whole should give its impressions of the overall performance of the team. Draw on chapter concepts when evaluating the work of individual participants and the group.

CASE STUDY 8.2

Chapter End Case:
Incentives for Organ Donations

Each year more than 6,000 Americans die while waiting for an organ transplant. More than half of those who need transplants die before they get the kidneys, livers, or other organs they need. And the problem is only going to get worse as the population ages. Estimates are that 40,000 join the list each year but only 20,000 are matched with donors.

While the demand for organ transplants is rising, the rate of donated organs has remained much the same. Less than half of the organs that could be salvaged from cadavers are recovered. Living donors are filling part of the need, but the growing gap between organ supply and demand has prompted doctors, patients, politicians, ethicists, and others to consider offering incentives in order to increase the organ supply. Paying living donors for their organs is one option. For instance, two doctors from Yale University argue that people should have the right to control what happens to their bodies. They suggest that donors charge $40,000, with a federal agency regulating costs and marketing. A booming international market in organ harvesting already exists, with residents of poorer countries such as Brazil, China, and Bulgaria selling their organs to people from richer nations such as Canada, Britain, Australia, and the United States. Some patients become "transplant tourists," traveling to other countries to have their operations done. However, critics claim that selling organs favors the rich at the expense of the poor and can lead to serious abuses. For example, the Chinese government was accused of executing prisoners in order to harvest their organs for sale. Federal legislation in the United States currently forbids selling organs, but states can offer tax deductions for nonmedical expenses such as travel, lodging, and lost wages related to giving an organ.

An association called LifeSharers offers a different incentive. Members, who agree to donate, specify that their organs should go first to someone else in the group. Some observers argue that this approach ought to be expanded to all citizens. Unless a person had been a registered donor for at least 2 years, they argue, he or she could not receive a transplant. This system would replace the current one, which allocates organs based on such criteria as medical urgency, length of time on the waiting list, and the physical match between organ and recipient.

A great many ethicists are troubled by the thought of offering nonfinancial incentives for organs. Incentives replace altruistic motives with selfish ones. Those who receive donations under incentive programs might not be the people who need them most. Giving first priority to those who agree to donate might discriminate against people who didn't hear about this requirement or simply never considered being a donor. According to the director of Ethics, Trade, Human Rights and Health Law at the World Health Organization, signing up to be a donor shouldn't be the criterion for receiving an organ: "It's like saying unless you're a volunteer fireman, you shouldn't expect anyone to come when your house is burning down."[1]

DISCUSSION PROBES

1. What ethical principles can be applied when deciding whether or not to offer incentives to organ donors?

2. What values are in conflict in this case?

3. Should donors be allowed to sell their organs? Why or why not?

4. Should those who have signed up to be donors get top priority for transplants? Why or why not?

5. How should organs be allocated?

6. Would you become a transplant tourist if you needed a new organ and couldn't get one?

7. What leadership ethics lessons do you draw from this case?

NOTE

1. Reid, C. (2007, April 29). Organ donation group spurs debate. *The State* (Columbia, SC). Retrieved January 7, 2008, from Newspaper Source database, para. 9.

SOURCES

Cohen, L. R., & Undis, D. J. (2006, March/April). New solution to the organ shortage. *Saturday Evening Post.* Retrieved January 7, 2008, from Academic Source Premier database.

Lister, S. (2006, February 16). Let people sell their kidneys for transplant, say doctors. *The Times (London)*, p. 31. Retrieved January 7, 2008, from Academic Source Premier database.

Not for sale at any price. (2006, April 8). *The Lancet,* p. 1118. Retrieved January 7, 2008, from Academic Source Premier database.

Reid, C. (2007, April 29). Organ donation group spurs debate. *The State* (Columbia, SC). Retrieved January 7, 2008, from Newspaper Source database.

Robertson, C. (2005, Spring). Organ advertising: Desperate patients solicit volunteers. *The Journal of Law, Medicine & Ethics*, pp. 170–174. Retrieved January 7, 2008, from Academic Source Premier database.

Turner, L. (2007, July 18). China's deadly scheme to harvest organs. *The Globe and Mail* (Canada), p. A23. Retrieved January 7, 2008, from Academic Source Premier database.

CASE STUDY 8.3

Chapter End Case: Responding to Groupthink and Faulty Reasoning at NASA

On January 31, 2003, America's space program suffered its second shuttle disaster when the *Columbia* disintegrated on reentry into the earth's atmosphere. All seven aboard died in the explosion. The accident occurred nearly 17 years to the day after the *Challenger* explosion. That disaster also took the lives of seven astronauts, including the first teacher headed into space.

Space shuttle *Columbia*'s troubles began when a piece of foam the size of a flat-screen television broke off the propellant tank and hit the spacecraft 82 seconds after liftoff. The debris struck with a ton of force and probably caused a 6- to 10-inch hole. This opening allowed superheated gas to enter the craft when it came back to Earth.

The day after the launch, NASA officials reviewed tracking videos. This footage showed the debris strike but didn't reveal any damage because the pictures couldn't pick up details smaller than 2 feet. Five days after launch, the mission control team in charge of the *Columbia* flight first discussed the possibility that a piece of insulating foam might have damaged the shuttle's left wing. Mission project leader Linda Ham downplayed the likelihood that the shuttle had been seriously compromised. She pointed out that the group had earlier concluded that foam, which routinely comes off during shuttle launches, wouldn't do any significant damage. Foam damage was considered a minor maintenance problem that could be taken care of between trips.

Other engineers and managers at NASA were not convinced that the foam strike was insignificant. Bryan O'Connor, NASA's top safety official, ordered a hazard assessment. Those carrying out the assessment requested permission to ask for additional satellite images from the Pentagon to determine whether there was damage to the orbiting ship. Ham denied their request in part because the shuttle would have to slow in order to position the wing for a photograph. This maneuver would disrupt the mission. The hazard assessment group was then forced to depend on the conclusions of a team of Boeing engineers. These experts used a computer program that determined there was potential for "significant tile damage" but not a complete "burn-through." However, their analysis was flawed. The group's software was not designed for use in making in-flight decisions. Also, Boeing engineers assumed that the reinforced carbon material around the strike area was as damage resistant as the glassy tiles on the rest of the ship. It was not.

During the same period, a group of low-level NASA engineers launched their own independent investigation. Their requests for photos were denied because they didn't come through proper channels. Senior structural engineer Rodney Rocha then drafted an e-mail pointing out the "grave hazards" caused by the foam. Sadly, he never sent the message to Ham, claiming, "I was too low down here in the organization, and she's way up here. I just couldn't do it."[1]

Meanwhile, members of the mission control team continued to express concern about possible damage to the shuttle but backed down when pressured by Ham. Dissenters lacked hard data to establish that the shuttle had been damaged. When the group met for the final time, engineers did not even discuss possible dangers to the shuttle. Instead, they talked about how eager they were to review the astronauts' launch day photos after the shuttle landed to determine exactly where the foam had come off the tank. Mission control informed the astronauts that debris had hit their craft. However, controllers said that the problem was "not even worth mentioning" except that a reporter might ask them about it.

After the explosion, the Columbia Accident Investigation Board, chaired by Admiral Harold Gehman (USN, retired), wrote a scathing report that placed much of the blame on NASA's culture. Board members accused the agency of becoming overconfident after years of flying safely. Safety, which was elevated to top priority after the first disaster, became less important as years passed and space budgets were cut. NASA administrator Sean O'Keefe and other top managers were more interested in keeping the shuttles flying in order to complete the space station by February 2004. Engineers also lost sight of the fact that a space shuttle is a highly risky experimental craft. Communication between teams, departments, and organizational levels broke down. Nobody, including the leaders of NASA, seemed clear about the agency's mission after the success of the manned moon landing and the unmanned Mars probes.

Although flawed culture drew most of the headlines describing the Columbia board's final report, groupthink and faulty reasoning were just as much to blame. Mission control team members displayed many groupthink symptoms. They rationalized that shredding foam was only a routine problem, and team leader Ham pressured dissenters. Individuals eventually kept their doubts to themselves and thus gave the appearance that everyone in the group solidly backed its conclusions. The hazard assessment task force and Boeing engineers fell prey to shaky logic. These groups relied on a flawed computer model and assumed that all materials covering the spacecraft were equally durable.

There is no guarantee that the Columbia crew could have been rescued even if NASA officials had recognized the danger. Shuttle astronauts had a limited amount of food, water, and air and couldn't go to the space station for repairs. Any attempt to launch a rescue shuttle would have endangered another crew, because the second shuttle would face the same risk of a fatal foam strike as the first. Nonetheless, by falling victim to both groupthink and faulty assumptions, leaders at NASA eliminated any chance that the Columbia crew would make it back to Earth safely.

NASA grounded the space shuttle fleet after the Columbia disaster and spent more than $1 billion trying to fix insulation problems. Foam damage continues to be a problem despite these efforts. Discovery shed several pieces of foam during the first shuttle flight after the Columbia crash, and its 2006 mission was nearly delayed after a small piece of foam fell off before launch. Endeavor's heat shield was damaged during a 2007 liftoff.

Although foam damage remains a concern, the way in which NASA responds to this and other safety issues has changed dramatically. No longer are safety concerns routinely dismissed as they were before *Columbia*; engineers don't have to prove that a part will fail in order to be heard. Instead, the shuttle program manager and other leaders encourage detailed discussion of safety problems and listen carefully. For example, when the shuttle *Endeavour* was gashed, the crew deliberately flipped the ship over as it orbited the space station, allowing the station crew to identify the location and size of the gouge. The *Endeavour* astronauts also used a laser scanner attached to a robotic arm to inspect the damage. On the ground, more than 100 people worked on the analysis of the *Endeavour* gash. One team of engineers conducted computer simulations to predict what would happen upon reentry, and another group of engineers from a different research center double-checked the first team's work. During mission management meetings, they reviewed the data and agreed that the gouge was not a threat. As a final precaution, engineers determined what would happen if they were wrong and some of the aluminum structure above the gash was lost. They decided that the *Endeavor* would still return safely. And it did.

DISCUSSION PROBES

1. How much blame do you assign to those who questioned the safety of the *Columbia* mission but either kept their doubts to themselves or failed to communicate them to NASA's top management?

2. What advice would you give to group members (such as those on the mission control team) who have doubts but lack the evidence to support their position?

3. If you were the head of NASA, would you have launched a rescue shuttle if you had identified the damage to the *Columbia*? Why or why not?

4. Evaluate the steps NASA has taken to change its culture and to resist groupthink. Can you suggest any additional strategies to make the agency less susceptible to future disasters?

5. What leadership ethics lessons do you draw from this case?

NOTE

1. Sawyer, K. (2003, August 24). Shuttle's "smoking gun" took time to register. *The Washington Post*, p. A1.

SOURCES

Barrett, J. (2003, July 18). Q&A: Clearly there is a problem here. *Newsweek* (Web exclusive). Retrieved September 2, 2003, from LexisNexis Academic database.

Chang, K. (2007, August 20). Caution over damage to *Endeavour* illustrates changes at space agency. *The New York Times*, p. A12. Retrieved November 22, 2007, from LexisNexis Academic database.

Glanz, W. (2003, August 27). NASA ignored dangers to shuttle, panel says. *The Washington Times,* p. A1. Retrieved September 2, 2003, from LexisNexis Academic database.

Grose, T. K. (2003, September 1). Can the manned space program find a new, revitalizing mission in the wake of the *Columbia* tragedy? *U.S. News & World Report,* p. 36.

Hilzenrath, D. S. (2003, September 2). Rescue of *Columbia* a hindsight dream. *The Washington Post,* p. A8.

Johnson, J. (2007). Dinged up *Endeavour* returns. *Los Angeles Times,* p. A10. Retrieved November 22, 2007, from LexisNexis Academic database.

Leary, W. E., & Schwartz, J. (2006, July 4). Shuttle launching set for today despite broken foam. *The New York Times,* p. A11. Retrieved November 22, 2007, from LexisNexis Academic database.

Mishra, R. (2003, August 27). Probe hits NASA in crash of shuttle. *The Boston Globe.* Retrieved September 2, 2003, from LexisNexis Academic database.

Sawyer, K. (2003, August 24). Shuttle's "smoking gun" took time to register. *The Washington Post,* p. A1.

Notes

1. Palmer, P. (1996). Leading from within. In L. C. Spears (Ed.), *Insights on leadership: Service, stewardship, spirit, and servant-leadership* (pp. 197–208). New York: Wiley, p. 2.

2. Rothwell, J. D. (1998). *In mixed company: Small group communication* (3rd ed.). Fort Worth, TX: Harcourt Brace, p. 2.

3. Tropman, J. (2003). *Making meetings work: Achieving high quality group decisions* (2nd ed.). Thousand Oaks, CA: Sage, p. 196.

4. Dukerich, J. M., Nichols, M. L., Elm, D. R., & Voltrath, D. A. (1990). Moral reasoning in groups: Leaders make a difference. *Human Relations, 43,* 473–493; Nichols, M. L., & Day, V. E. (1982). A comparison of moral reasoning of groups and individuals on the "defining issues test." *Academy of Management Journal, 24,* 21–28.

5. Johnson, D. W., Maruyama, G., Johnson, R., Nelson, D., & Skon, L. (1981). Effects of cooperative, competitive, and individualistic goal structures on achievement: A meta-analysis. *Psychological Bulletin, 82,* 47–62; Johnson, D. W., & Johnson, R. (1989). *Cooperation and competition: Theory and research.* Edina, MN: Interaction Book Company; Johnson, D. W., & Johnson, F. P. (2000). *Joining together: Group theory and group skills* (7th ed.). Boston: Allyn & Bacon.

6. Johnson, D. W., & Johnson, R. T. (2005). Training for cooperative group work. In M. A. West, D. Tjosvold, & K. G. Smith (Eds.), *The essentials of teamworking: International perspectives* (pp. 131–147). West Sussex, UK: Wiley.

7. Johnson & Johnson (2000).

8. Amichai-Hamburger, Y. (2003). Understanding social loafing. In A. Sagie, S. Stashevsky, & M. Koslowsky (Eds.), *Misbehaviour and dysfunctional attitudes in organizations* (pp. 79–102). New York: Palgrave Macmillan.

9. Karau, S. J., & Williams, K. D. (2001). Understanding individual motivation in groups: The Collective Effort Model. In M. E. Turner (Ed.), *Groups at work: Theory and research* (pp. 113–141). Mahwah, NJ: Erlbaum, p. 119.

10. Karau, S. J., & Williams, K. D. (1995). Social loafing: Research findings, implications, and future directions. *Current Directions in Psychological Science, 4,* 134–140; Williams, K. D., Harkins, S. G., & Karau, S. J. (2003). Social performance. In M. A. Hogg & J. Cooper (Eds.), *The Sage handbook of social psychology* (pp. 327–346). London: Sage.

11. Janis, I. (1971, November). Groupthink: The problems of conformity. *Psychology Today,* 271–279; Janis, I. (1982). *Groupthink* (2nd ed.). Boston: Houghton Mifflin; Janis, I. (1989). *Crucial decisions: Leadership in policymaking and crisis management.* New York: Free Press.

12. Moorhead, G., Neck, C. P., & West, M. S. (1998). The tendency toward defective decision making within self-managing teams: The relevance of groupthink for the 21st century. *Organizational Behavior and Human Decision Processes, 73,* 327–351.

13. See the following:

Chen, A., Lawson, R. B., Gordon, L. R., & McIntosh, B. (1996). Groupthink: Deciding with the leader and the devil. *Psychological Record, 46,* 581–590.

Esser, J. K. (1998). Alive and well after 25 years: A review of groupthink research. *Organizational Behavior and Human Decision Processes, 73,* 116–141.

Flippen, A. R. (1999). Understanding groupthink from a self-regulatory perspective. *Small Group Research, 3,* 139–165.

Jones, P. E., & Roelofsma, P. H. M. P. (2000). The potential for social contextual and group biases in team decision-making: Biases, conditions and psychological mechanisms. *Ergonomics, 43,* 1129–1152.

Street, M. D. (1997). Groupthink: An examination of theoretical issues, implications, and future research suggestions. *Small Group Research, 28,* 72–93.

14. Manz, C. C., & Neck, C. P. (1995). Teamthink: Beyond the groupthink syndrome in self-managing work teams. *Journal of Managerial Psychology, 1*(1), 7–15; Manz, C. C., & Sims, H. P. (1989). *Superleadership: Leading others to lead themselves.* Upper Saddle River, NJ: Prentice Hall.

15. Buber, M. (1970). *I and thou.* (R. G. Smith, Trans.). New York: Charles Scribner's Sons; Johannesen, R. L. (2002). *Ethics in human communication* (5th ed.). Prospect Heights, IL: Waveland, Ch. 4.

16. Cissna, K. N., & Anderson, R. (1994). Communication and the ground of dialogue. In R. Anderson, K. N. Cissna, & R. C. Arnett (Eds.), *The reach of dialogue: Confirmation, voice, and community* (pp. 9–3). Cresskill, NJ: Hampton.

17. Czubaroff, J. (2000). Dialogical rhetoric: An application of Martin Buber's philosophy of dialogue. *Quarterly Journal of Speech, 2,* 168–189.

18. Wolvin, A. D., & Coakley, G. C. (1993). A listening taxonomy. In A. D. Wolvin & C. G. Coakley (Eds.), *Perspectives in listening* (pp. 15–22). Norwood, NJ: Ablex.

19. Johnson, J. (1993). Functions and processes of inner speech in listening. In D. Wolvin & C. G. Coakley (Eds.), *Perspectives in listening* (pp. 170–184). Norwood, NJ: Ablex.

20. Barker, L., Johnson, P., & Watson, K. (1991). The role of listening in managing interpersonal and group conflict. In D. Borisoff & M. Purdy (Eds.), *Listening in everyday life: A personal and professional approach* (pp. 139–157). Lanham, MD: University Press of America.

21. Gibb, J. R. (1961). Defensive communication. *Journal of Communication, 11–12,* 141–148.

22. See the following:

Bell, M. A. (1974). The effects of substantive and affective conflict in problem-solving groups. *Speech Monographs, 41,* 19–23.

Bell, M. A. (1979). The effects of substantive and affective verbal conflict on the quality of decisions of small problem-solving groups. *Central States Speech Journal, 3,* 75–82.

Johnson, D. W., & Tjosvold, D. (1983). *Productive conflict management.* New York: Irvington.

23. Moscovici, S., Mugny, G., & Van Avermaet, E. (Eds.). (1985). *Perspectives on minority influence.* Cambridge, UK: Cambridge University Press; Maas, A., & Clark, R. D. (1984). Hidden impact of minorities: Fifteen years of minority influence research. *Psychological Bulletin, 95,* 428–445; Nemeth, C., & Chiles, C. (1986). Modeling courage: The role of dissent in fostering independence. *European Journal of Social Psychology, 18,* 275–280.

24. Roberto, M. A. (2005). *Why great leaders don't take yes for an answer.* Upper Saddle River, NJ: Wharton School Publishing.

25. Roberto.

26. Schultz, B. (1982). Argumentativeness: Its effect in group decision-making and its role in leadership perception. *Communication Quarterly, 3,* 368–375.

27. Infante, D., & Rancer, A. (1996). Argumentativeness and verbal aggressiveness: A review of recent theory and research. In B. Burleson (Ed.), *Communication yearbook 19* (pp. 319–351). Thousand Oaks, CA: Sage; Infante, D. (1988). *Arguing constructively.* Prospect Heights, IL: Waveland.

28. Gouran, D. S., Hirokawa, R. Y., Julian, K. M., & Leatham, G. B. (1993). The evolution and current status of the functional perspective on communication in decision-making and problem-solving groups. *Communication Yearbook, 16,* 573–576; Gouran, D. S., & Hirokawa, R. Y. (1986). Counteractive functions of communication in effective group decision making. In R. Y. Hirokawa & M. S. Poole (Eds.), *Communication and group decision making* (pp. 81–89). Beverly Hills, CA: Sage.

9

Creating an Ethical Organizational Climate

Bad ethics is bad business.

—Anonymous

What's Ahead

Leaders act as ethics officers for their organizations, exercising influence through the process of social learning and by building positive ethical climates. Healthy ethical climates are marked by zero tolerance for destructive behaviors, integrity (ethical soundness, wholeness, and consistency), concern for process as well as product, structural reinforcement, and social responsibility. Important tools for building an ethical organizational climate include shared values, codes of ethics, and continuous ethical improvement.

The Leader as Ethics Officer

In the introduction to this text, I argued that ethics is at the heart of leadership. When we become leaders, we assume the ethical responsibilities that come with that role. Nowhere is this more apparent than in the organizational context. Examine nearly any corporate scandal—AIG Insurance, Arthur Andersen, Enron, HealthSouth, Sotheby's auction house, Fannie Mae, Hollinger International, Marsh & McLennan, Quest—and you'll find leaders who engaged in immoral behavior and encouraged their followers to do the same. The same pattern can be found in the nonprofit sector (e.g., the Baptist Foundation of Arizona, New Era Philanthropy, United Way). On a more positive note, leaders are largely responsible for creating the organizations we admire for their ethical behavior.

Leaders are the ethics officers of their organizations, casting light or shadow in large part through the example they set. Michael Brown and Linda Trevino draw on social learning theory to explain why and how ethical organizational leaders influence followers.[1] Social learning theory is based on the premise that people learn by observing and then emulating the values, attitudes, and behaviors of people they find legitimate, attractive, and credible. When it comes to ethics, followers look to their leaders as role models and act accordingly. Leaders are generally seen as legitimate, credible, and attractive because they occupy positions of authority with power and status. Ethical leaders build on this foundation. They increase their legitimacy by treating employees fairly and boost their attractiveness by expressing care and concern for followers. They enhance their credibility (particularly perceptions of their trustworthiness) by living up to the values they espouse. Such leaders are open and honest and set clear, high standards that they follow themselves.

Moral leaders make sure that ethics messages aren't drowned out by other messages about tasks and profits. They focus attention on ethics through frequent communication about values, mission, corporate standards, and the importance of ethical behavior. They reinforce follower learning by using rewards and punishments to regulate behavior, which makes it clear which actions are acceptable and which are not.

Trevino, Brown, and their colleagues distinguish between ethical leaders and those who are unethical, hypocritical, or ethically neutral.[2] The *unethical leader*, like Al Dunlap, falls short as both a moral person and a moral influence agent. This person casts one or more of the shadows described in Chapter 1 by bullying others, deceiving investors, acting irresponsibility, and so on. At the same time, the unethical leader clearly communicates that ethics don't matter, just results. The *hypocritical leader* talks a lot about ethical values but doesn't live up to the rhetoric. Prominent pastor Ted Haggard is an example of a hypocritical leader. As leader of the National Association of Evangelicals, he led public efforts to condemn homosexuality while he was carrying on an affair with a male prostitute. (Another hypocritical leader is the subject of the "Leadership Ethics at the Movies" case in Box 9.1.) The *ethically neutral leader* is not clearly seen as either ethical or unethical. This person doesn't send out strong messages about ethics and leaves followers unsure about where he or she stands on moral issues. Ethically neutral leaders appear to be self-centered and focus exclusively on the bottom line. Sandy Weill, former Citigroup CEO, typifies the ethically neutral leader. Weill stayed on the sidelines when it came to ethics, rewarding his managers according to their results. It was during his tenure that Salomon analyst Jack Grubman continued to promote Winstar Communications even as it was heading for bankruptcy. The chapter end case, "The High Cost of Ethical Neutrality," is another case in which a leader focused more on financial performance than on ethics.

From their analysis of the four categories of ethical leadership, Trevino and her colleagues conclude that acting ethically is not enough. Executives must also ensure that employees know that they care (aren't just neutral) about ethics. Otherwise, followers will continue to focus on financial results without concern for ethics. Ethical leaders make ethical considerations a top organizational priority. They create positive ethical climates that promote moral behavior by leaders and followers alike. Identifying the characteristics of healthy ethical climates is the subject of the next section.

Ethical Climates

Ethical climate is best understood as part of an organization's culture. From the cultural vantage point, an organization is a tribe. As tribal members gather, they develop their own language, stories, beliefs, assumptions, ceremonies, and power structures. These elements combine to form a unique perspective on the world called the organization's culture.[3] How an organization responds to

---

Box 9.1

Leadership Ethics at the Movies

BREACH

Key Cast Members: Chris Cooper, Ryan Phillippe, Laura Linney

Synopsis: Based on the true story of FBI operative Robert Hanssen, the source of the greatest security breach in U.S. history. A devoted church member and grandparent, Hanssen sold classified information to the Soviets that caused billions of dollars worth of damage and resulted in the executions of American agents. Young Eric O'Neill (Phillippe) is assigned to work for Hanssen (Cooper) in order to gather enough information to convict him. O'Neill struggles to maintain his integrity and marriage while he betrays Hanssen.

Rating: PG-13 for violence, sexual content, and language

Themes: hypocritical and unethical leadership, courageous followership, deception, loyalty, character, unhealthy motivations

ethical issues is a part of this culture. Every organization faces a special set of ethical challenges, creates its own set of values and norms, develops guidelines for enforcing its ethical standards, honors particular ethical heroes, and so on. Ethical climate, in turn, determines what members believe is right or wrong and shapes their ethical decision making and behavior.

Management professors Bart Victor and John Cullen argue that ethical climates can be classified according to the criteria members use to make moral choices and the groups members refer to when making ethical determinations.[4] Victor and Cullen identify five primary climate types. *Instrumental* climates follow the principle of ethical egotism. Ethical egotists make decisions based on selfish interests that serve the individual and his or her immediate group and organization. *Caring* climates emphasize concern or care for others. *Law and order* climates are driven by external criteria such as professional codes of conduct. *Rules* climates are governed by the policies, rules, and procedures developed in the organization. *Independence* climates give members wide latitude to make their own decisions.

Leaders would do well to know the particular ethical orientation of their organizations. To begin, each of the five climate types poses unique ethical challenges. Members of instrumental organizations often ignore the needs of others, whereas those driven by a care ethic are tempted to overlook the rules to help out friends and colleagues. Leaders and followers in law and order cultures may be blind to the needs of coworkers because they rely on outside standards for guidance. On the other hand, those who play by organizational rules may be blinded to societal norms. Independence produces the best results when members have the knowledge and skills they need to make good decisions.

Follow-up studies using the Victor and Cullen climate types suggest that self-interest poses the greatest threat to ethical performance.[5] Rates of immoral behavior are highest in work units and organizations with instrumental climates. Members of these groups are also less committed to their organizations. Rules and law and code climates encourage ethical behavior; caring (benevolent) climates promote employee loyalty. Employees are more satisfied when their personal ethical preferences match those of their organizations.

Signs of Healthy Ethical Climates

There is no one-size-fits-all approach to creating an ethical climate. Rather, we need to identify principles and practices that characterize positive ethical climates. Then we have to adapt these elements to our particular organizational setting. Key markers of highly ethical organizations include zero tolerance for destructive behaviors, integrity, a focus on process, and structural reinforcement. (For a list of the signs of unhealthy climates, see Box 9.2.)

Box 9.2

Focus on Follower Ethics

THE SEVEN SIGNS OF ETHICAL COLLAPSE

Arizona State University business ethics professor Marianne Jennings identifies seven signs that a company is in deep ethical trouble. Identifying these signs can keep us from joining a questionable organization, help us recognize whether our current organization is in danger, and encourage us to take steps as followers to stop the decline.

Sign 1: Pressure to Maintain Numbers

The first sign of ethical trouble is obsession with meeting quantifiable goals. Driven by numbers, companies overstate sales, hide expenses, make bad loans, and ship defective products. Nonprofits also feel the pressure to reach their goal numbers. Universities want to be ranked highly by *U.S. News and World Report* and other publications, so they may lie about graduation and placement rates. Charities, driven to achieve their fund-raising objectives, may make false claims about how many people they serve (see Case Study 9.1).

Sign 2: Fear and Silence

In every moral meltdown, there are indications that something is seriously amiss. For example, employees at Enron circulated a top 10 list titled "Top Ten Reasons Enron Restructures So Frequently." Item 7 on the list said, "To keep the outside investment analysts so confused that they will not be able to figure out that we don't know what we're doing." However, few challenge the status quo because those who do so are publicly shamed, demoted, or dismissed. Others don't want to believe that the organization is in trouble; still others are bribed into silence through generous salaries and loan packages.

Sign 3: Young 'Uns and a Bigger-Than-Life CEO

Some CEOs become icons who are adored by the community and the media (though often not by employees). Outsiders are loath to criticize the legendary CEO when everyone is singing his or her praises. The iconic CEO also surrounds him- or herself with loyal supporters who are often young and inexperienced. For example, CEOs brought in their sons and daughters to help them run AIG Insurance, Archer Daniels Midland, and Adelphia, all companies that ran afoul of the law.

Sign 4: Weak Board

The boards of companies on the verge of moral collapse are weak for a variety of reasons. They may have inexperienced members, be made up of friends of the CEO, or be reluctant to reign in a legendary CEO. Members may fail to attend meetings or devote the necessary time to their board roles. The board of HealthSouth is a case in point. HealthSouth (which engaged in Medicare and accounting fraud) was made up of company officers and outsiders who had contracts and other financial relationships with CEO Richard Scrushy and the firm. The HealthSouth board ignored lawsuits and federal investigations that indicated that the company was in trouble.

Box 9.2 (Continued)

Sign 5: Conflicts

Conflicts of interest arise when an individual plays two roles and the interests of one role are at odds with those of the other role. Officers of the company are then tempted to profit at the expense of stockholders, employees, and others. That was the case with CFO Andrew Fastow of Enron, who made millions from the entities he designed to hide company debt.

Sign 6: Innovation Like No Other

Highly successful companies often believe that they can defy economic and business reality. They might have been the first in a new industry or be headed by an entrepreneurial leader who succeeded against all odds. Their arrogance convinces them that they can continually innovate themselves out of any tight spot. Instead, these groups and their leaders innovate themselves into moral trouble by inventing illegal accounting practices, tax evasion schemes, and faulty business models. Finova Group grew rapidly by making loans to small businesses and time-share properties turned down by other financial institutions. The firm could charge higher interest, generating greater margins. However, Finova soon had a portfolio full of bad loans. Rather than write these loans off, the company used creative accounting to hide these losses. In some cases, company officers even counted the poor loans as assets.

Sign 7: Goodness in Some Areas Atones for Evil in Others

A good many fallen organizations and leaders try to atone for their sins in one area by doing good in others. Tyco and Dennis Kozlowski, WorldCom and Bernie Ebbers, and Adelphia and John Rigas were all known for their charitable acts, giving to universities and local communities, contributing to disaster relief, encouraging employees to volunteer for service projects, and so on. In the case of endangered organizations, the motive for philanthropy isn't serving the common good but soothing the conscience of those involved in fraud, insider trading, accounting tricks, and other misdeeds.

SOURCE: Jennings, M. M. (2006). *The seven signs of ethical collapse: How to spot moral meltdowns in companies . . . before it's too late.* New York: St. Martin's Press.

ZERO TOLERANCE FOR DESTRUCTIVE BEHAVIORS

Researchers report that organizations, like individuals, have their "dark sides." Some organizations, such as humanitarian relief agencies and socially responsible businesses, shine brightly. Others, such as corrupt police departments and authoritarian political regimes, are cloaked in darkness. Few of us will experience the oppression of truly dark organizations. However, most of us will experience the shadows cast by dark side behaviors. These are destructive or antisocial actions that deliberately attempt to harm others or the organization.[6] Those who engage in such unethical behaviors are driven to meet their own needs at the expense of coworkers and the group as a whole. Common categories of misbehaviors include incivility, aggression, sexual harassment, and discrimination.

Incivility consists of rude or discourteous actions that disregard others and violate norms for respect.[7] Such actions can be intentional or unintentional; they include leaving a mess for the maintenance staff to pick up, sending a "flaming" e-mail, claiming credit for someone else's work, making fun of a peer, or inadvertently ignoring a team member on the way into the office. Incivility reduces employee job satisfaction, task performance, motivation, loyalty, performance, creativity, and willingness to cooperate.

Aggression refers to consciously trying to hurt others or the organization itself.[8] Aggressive behaviors can take a variety of forms, ranging from refusing to answer e-mails to swearing at coworkers to murder. Such behaviors can be categorized along three dimensions. They can be physical–verbal (destructive words or deeds), active–passive (doing harm by acting or failing to act), or direct–indirect (doing harm directly to the other person or indirectly through an intermediary and attacking something that the target values). Aggression does extensive damage to individuals and organizations. Victims may be hurt; experience more stress, which leads to poor health; become fearful, depressed, or angry; lose the ability to concentrate; and feel less committed to their jobs. Observers of aggressive incidents also experience more anxiety and have a lower sense of well-being and commitment. Performance at the organizational level drops as a product of the aggressive actions of employees. Workplace aggression reduces productivity while increasing absenteeism and turnover. Organizations become the targets of lawsuits and negative publicity.

Sexual harassment is a form of aggression directed largely at women.[9] Quid pro quo harassment occurs when targets are coerced into providing sexual favors in return for keeping their jobs or getting promoted. Hostile work environment harassment exists when job conditions interfere with job performance. Components of hostile working conditions include demeaning comments, suggestive gestures, threats, propositions, bribes, and sexual assault. The work performance of victims drops, and they may quit their jobs. Targets also suffer physically (headaches, sleep loss, nausea, eating disorders) and psychologically (depression, fear, a sense of helplessness).

Discrimination is putting members of selected groups, such as women, minorities, disabled employees, older workers, and homeless people, at a disadvantage. Such negative treatment is generally based on stereotypes and prejudice (e.g., older workers can't learn new skills, Hispanics are lazy). Because of the passage of antidiscrimination laws and changes in societal values, employment discrimination is generally expressed subtly through such behaviors as dismissing the achievements of people of color and women, avoiding members of low-status groups, and hiring and promoting those of similar backgrounds.[10]

Destructive behaviors are all too common in modern organizations. Twenty percent of one sample reported being the targets of uncivil messages in a given week. There were 15,000 incidents of violence resulting in time away from work in one 12-month period, and assaults and suicides account for 13% of all deaths on the job. Fifty to sixty percent of female students and employees report being the targets of harassing actions. Unemployment rates are significantly higher for minorities and women, and people of color continue to earn less than white men.[11]

Fortunately, leaders like those described in the "Agenda for Change" chapter end case can significantly reduce the rate of destructive behaviors by actively seeking to prevent and control them. Moral leaders

1. Create zero-tolerance policies that prohibit antisocial actions. (We'll take a closer look at codes of ethics later in the chapter.) They insist on employee-to-employee civility, forbid aggression and sexual harassment, and prohibit discrimination.

2. Obey guidelines. As noted earlier, leaders are powerful role models. Zero-tolerance policies will have little effect if leaders do not follow the rules they set. Ironically, leaders are most likely to violate standards because they believe that they are exceptions to the rules (see the discussion of unhealthy motivations in Chapter 2). Furthermore, because they are in positions of power, leaders are freer to act uncivilly, to bully others, or to offer favors in return for sex.

3. Constantly monitor for possible violations. Destructive behavior may be hidden from the view of top leaders. Some managers are good at "kissing up and kicking down," for example. They act respectfully toward superiors while bullying employees and treating them with disrespect. Ethical leaders actively seek feedback from employees further down the organizational hierarchy. They conduct 360% reviews that allow employees to rate their supervisors and provide channels (human relations departments, open door policies) for reporting misbehaviors. Those who come forward with complaints are protected from retribution.

4. Move quickly when standards are violated. Ethical leaders quickly investigate charges of sexual harassment and discrimination, for instance, and don't hesitate to punish offenders. They recognize that failing to act sends the wrong message, undermining ethical climate. If left unchecked, incivility escalates into aggression. A culture of aggression forms when abusive members are allowed to act as role models. Victims of sexual harassment won't come forward if they think that their leaders won't respond. Patterns of discrimination perpetuate themselves unless leaders intervene.

5. Address the underlying factors that trigger destructive actions. Moral leaders try to screen out potential employees who have a history of destructive behavior. They also try to eliminate situational elements that produce antisocial

action. Important contextual triggers include unpleasant working conditions, job stress, oppressive supervision, perceived injustice, and extreme competitiveness.[12]

INTEGRITY

Integrity is ethical soundness, wholeness, and consistency.[13] All units and organizational levels share a commitment to high moral standards, backing up their ethical talk with their ethical walk. Consistency increases the level of trust, encouraging members and units to be vulnerable to one another. They are more willing to share undistorted information, negotiate in good faith, take risks, share authority for making decisions, collaborate, and follow through on promises. Organizational productivity and performance improve as a result (see Chapter 6).

According to business ethicist Lynn Paine, managers who act with integrity see ethics as a driving force of an enterprise. These leaders recognize that ethical values largely define what an organization is and what it hopes to accomplish. They keep these values in mind when making routine decisions. Their goal? To help constituents learn to govern their own behavior by following these same principles. Paine believes that any effort to improve organizational integrity must include the following elements:[14]

There are sensible, clearly communicated values and commitments. These values and commitments spell out the organization's obligations to external stakeholders (customers, suppliers, neighbors) while appealing to insiders. In highly ethical organizations, members take shared values seriously and don't hesitate to talk about them.

Company leaders are committed to and act on the values. Leaders consistently back the values, use them when making choices, and determine priorities when ethical obligations conflict with one another. For example, former Southwest Airlines president Herb Kelleher put a high value both on the needs of his employees and on customer service. However, it's clear that his workers came first. He didn't hesitate to take their side when customers unfairly criticized them. Such principled leadership was missing at Arthur Andersen. Andersen accountants certified the financial statements of Quest, Waste Management, Boston Chicken, Global Crossing, WorldCom, and the Baptist Foundation of Arizona, which were all found guilty of accounting fraud. They were reluctant to challenge the accounting practices of clients because they didn't want to lose lucrative consulting contracts with these organizations. Andersen's managing partners dissolved the firm after executives were convicted for obstruction of justice for shredding Enron documents.[15]

The values are part of the routine decision-making process and are factored into every important organizational activity. Ethical considerations shape such activities as planning and goal setting, spending, the gathering and sharing of information, evaluation, and promotion.

Systems and structures support and reinforce organizational commitments. Systems and structures, such as the organizational chart, how work is processed, budgeting procedures, and product development, serve the organization's values. (I'll have more to say about the relationship between ethics and structure later in the chapter.)

Leaders throughout the organization have the knowledge and skills they need to make ethical decisions. Organizational leaders make ethical choices every day. To demonstrate integrity, they must have the necessary skills, knowledge, and experience (see our discussion of ethical development in Chapter 2). Ethics education and training must be part of their professional development.

Paine and other observers warn us not to confuse integrity with compliance. Ethical compliance strategies are generally responses to outside pressures such as media scrutiny, the U.S. Sentencing Commission guidelines, or the Sarbanes–Oxley Act. Under these federal guidelines, corporate executives can be fined and jailed not only for their ethical misdeeds but also for failing to take reasonable steps to prevent the illegal behavior of employees. Although compliance tactics look good to outsiders, they don't have a lasting impact on ethical climate.[16] Consider the ethics programs of many *Fortune 1000* companies, for example. Nearly all of the nation's largest firms have ethical strategies in place, including formal ethics codes and policies, ethics officers, and systems for registering and dealing with ethical concerns and complaints. However, most of these programs have minimal influence on company operations. Many ethics officials devote only a small portion of their time to their ethical duties, and some complaint hotlines are rarely used. CEOs typically discuss ethical topics with their ethics officers only once or twice a year, attend no meetings focusing primarily on ethics, and rarely communicate to employees about ethics. Followers generally don't receive more than one ethical message annually, and one-fifth to one-third of lower-level workers receive no ethics training at all in a given year.[17] A similar compliance focus is found in Canadian firms.[18]

The contrast between compliance and integrity is reflected in the model of corporate moral development offered by Eric Reidenbach and Donald Robin.[19] These theorists argue that organizations can be classified according to their level of ethical progress. Stage I *amoral organizations* occupy the lowest level on the hierarchy. Such companies largely ignore ethical concerns, focusing solely on productivity and profit. To them, fines and penalties are the cost of doing business. Dishonest telemarketing firms fall into this category. Next up are Stage II *legalistic organizations,* in which leaders equate ethics with following societal rules and want to protect their organizations from harm. Large tobacco companies, such as R. J. Reynolds, Philip Morris, and Brown & Williamson, are Stage II organizations that believe that there is nothing wrong with selling cigarettes because such activity is not prohibited by law.

Responsive organizations (Stage III) are concerned about external stakeholders and with being seen as responsible corporate citizens. Yet they often find themselves reacting to ethical problems rather than anticipating them before they occur. Proctor & Gamble's reaction to the toxic shock syndrome of the 1980s is typical of responsive organizations. When notified of the possible link between Rely tampons and toxic shock, the company bought back all unsold products and sponsored research into the disease at the Centers for Disease Control. *Emergent ethical organizations* (Stage IV) are more advanced than their Stage III counterparts because these groups actively manage their cultures to improve ethical climate. They create a variety of ethical vehicles (handbooks, policy statements, ombudspersons) to shape and communicate important values and standards. Johnson & Johnson, Lockheed Martin, and Sara Lee are Stage IV organizations that go to great lengths to emphasize that ethics and not just profits should guide corporate activities.

The highest level of moral development is the Stage V *ethical organization.* Groups in this stage model integrity. Company officers and employees select core values and use these principles in everything from strategic planning to hiring and firing. Furthermore, they try to anticipate ethical problems that might arise. Examples of contemporary Stage V corporations are hard to find, but Reidenbach and Robin point to Sir Adrian Cadbury as a model of how to incorporate ethics into organizational operations. The founder of Britain's Cadbury chocolates was confronted with the choice of whether to supply Christmas tins to English soldiers during the Boer War. Cadbury (a Quaker) opposed the war but realized that his employees and the soldiers would be hurt if he turned down the contract. He resolved the problem by providing the chocolates at cost. His employees were then paid, but Sir Adrian didn't benefit personally from the contract.[20]

PROCESS FOCUS (CONCERN FOR MEANS AND ENDS)

Concern for how an organization achieves its goals is another important indicator of a healthy ethical climate. In far too many organizations, leaders set demanding performance goals but intentionally or unintentionally ignore how these objectives are to be reached. Instead, they pressure employees to produce sales and profits by whatever means possible. Followers then feel powerless and alienated, becoming estranged from the rest of the group. Sociologists use the term *anomie* to refer to this sense of normlessness and unease that results when rules lose their force.[21] Anomie increases the likelihood that group members will engage in illegal activities and reduces their resistance to demands from authority figures who want them to break the law. Loss of confidence in the organization may also encourage alienated employees to retaliate against coworkers and the group as a whole.

Leaders can address the problem of anomie by making sure that goals are achieved through ethical means. False promises cannot be used to land accounts, all debts must be fully disclosed to investors, kickbacks are prohibited, and so on. They can also make a stronger link between means and ends through ethics programs that address all aspects of organizational ethical performance.

STRUCTURAL REINFORCEMENT

An organization's structure shouldn't undermine the ethical standards of its members, but as I noted in our discussion of integrity, it should encourage higher ethical performance on the part of both leaders and followers. Three elements of an organization's structure have a particularly strong impact on moral behavior:

1. *Monetary and nonmonetary reward systems.* Organizations often encourage unethical behavior by rewarding it.[22] Consider the case of the software company that paid programmers $20 to correct each software bug they found. Soon programmers were deliberately creating bugs to fix! A visit to the local 10-minute oil change shop provides another example of the impact of misplaced rewards. Some lube and oil franchises pay managers and employees based in part on how many additional services and parts they sell beyond the basic oil change. As a consequence, unscrupulous mechanics persuade car owners to buy unneeded air filters, transmission flushes, and wiper blades. It is not always easy to determine all the consequences of a particular reward system. However, ethical leaders make every effort to ensure that desired moral behaviors are rewarded, not discouraged.

2. *Performance and evaluation processes.* Performance and evaluation processes must reflect the balance between means and ends described earlier, monitoring both *how* and *whether* goals are achieved. Ethically insensitive monitoring processes fail to detect illegal and immoral behavior and may actually make such practices more likely. As noted earlier, when poor behavior goes unpunished, followers may assume that leaders condone and expect such actions. Salomon, Inc., described at the end of Chapter 2, is a case in point. Failure to swiftly punish star performers Paul Mozer and Jack Grubman cost the company millions and eventually led to its demise.[23]

3. *Decision-making rights and responsibilities.* Ethical conduct is more likely when workers are responsible for ethical decisions and have the authority to choose how to respond. Leaders at ethical organizations do all they can to ensure that those closest to the process or problem can communicate their concerns about ethical issues. These managers also empower followers to make and implement their choices. Unfortunately, employees with the most knowledge are often excluded from the decision-making process or lack the power to follow through on their choices. Such was the case in the *Columbia* shuttle explosion profiled in Chapter 8. Higher-ranking NASA officials dismissed the concerns of lower-level managers.

SOCIAL RESPONSIBILITY

Concern for those outside the organization is another sign of a healthy ethical climate. Ethical organizations recognize that they have obligations to their communities. For example, responsible corporations engage in "triple bottom line" accounting.[24] They evaluate their success not just on financial results but also on their social and environmental performance. Good corporate citizens send volunteers to Habitat for Humanity building projects, sponsor food drives, set up philanthropic organizations to give money to needy causes, and so forth.[25] At the same time, they address environmental problems by taking such steps as capping plant emissions, using recycled components, creating less toxic products, reducing oil consumption, and buying from environmentally friendly suppliers. For example, Starbucks incorporates social responsibility into its corporate values. One of its guiding principles is "sustaining coffee communities." Another is "contributing positively to communities and the environment." Individual stores are free to promote local charities through volunteer hours, store products, and cash contributions. Corporate headquarters supports literacy programs and disaster relief. To measure its progress, the firm commissions an annual social responsibility report that indicates whether the company is reaching its social goals.[26] (More examples of socially responsible corporations can be found in the discussion of corporate values to follow.)

Recognizing the legitimate claims of stakeholders is key to social responsibility. Stakeholders are any group affected by the organization's policies and operations. Organizational stakeholders might include shareholders, suppliers, competitors, customers, creditors, unions, governments, local communities, and the general public.[27] Stakeholder theorists argue that organizational leaders have an ethical obligation to consider such groups because they have intrinsic value and ought to be treated justly. Reaching out to these parties contributes to the common good of society.[28] Socially responsible organizations try to identify all stakeholders and their interests. They try to be accountable to these groups, cooperating with them whenever possible and minimizing the negative impact of organizational activities. When needed, these organizations engage in dialogue with their critics, as Nike did after years of ignoring public outcry about conditions at its overseas suppliers. The firm invited human rights, labor, and environmental officials to company headquarters to discuss international worker issues.[29]

Climate-Building Tools

To build or create ethical organizational climates, leaders rely heavily on three tools: core values, codes of ethics, and ethical learning.

DISCOVERING CORE VALUES

Identifying and applying ethical values is an important step to creating a highly moral climate. Leaders promoting integrity first define and then focus attention on central ethical values. I noted in Chapter 3 that comparing responses on a standardized value list can be a way to clarify group and organizational priorities. In this section, I will introduce additional strategies specifically designed to reveal shared values, purposes, and assumptions.

Core Ideology

Management experts James Collins and Jerry Porras use the term *core ideology* to refer to the central identity or character of an organization. The character of outstanding companies remains constant even as these firms continually learn and adapt. According to Collins and Porras, "truly great companies understand the difference between what should never change and what should be open for change, between what is genuinely sacred and what is not."[30]

Core values are the first component of core ideology. (See Box 9.3 for some examples.) One way to determine whether a value is sacred to your organization is to ask, "What would happen if we were penalized for holding this standard?" If you can't honestly say that you would keep this value if it cost your group market share or profits, then it shouldn't show up on your final list. To determine who should be involved in spelling out core values, Collins and Porras recommend the Mars Group technique described in Box 9.4.

Core purpose is the second part of an organization's ideology. *Purpose* is the group's reason for being that reflects the ideals of its members. Here are some examples of corporate purpose statements:[31]

> To be the world's best staffing services company and to be recognized as the best. (Kelly Services)
>
> Bring to the world pharmaceutical and health care products that improve lives and deliver outstanding value to our customers and shareholders. (Wyeth)
>
> To bring inspiration and innovation to every athlete in the world. (Nike)
>
> To be the most powerful one-stop shop to connect people with the wonders of modern technology. (Radio Shack)
>
> To simply delight you . . . every day. (Sara Lee)
>
> Dedication to the highest quality of Customer Service delivered with a sense of warmth, friendliness, individual pride, and Company Spirit. (Southwest Airlines)

Asking the "Five Whys" is one way to identify organizational purpose. Start with a description of what your organization does and then ask why that

Box 9.3

Core Values

Eaton Corporation

- Make our customers the focus of everything we do
- Recognize our people as our greatest asset
- Treat each other with respect
- Be fair, honest, and open
- Be considerate of the environment and our communities
- Keep our commitments
- Strive for excellence

Levi Strauss

- **Empathy**—Walking in other people's shoes
- **Originality**—Being authentic and innovative
- **Integrity**—Doing the right thing
- **Courage**—Standing up for what we believe

Amgen Inc.

- Be science-based
- Compete intensely and win
- Create value for patients, staff, and stockholders
- Be ethical
- Trust and respect each other
- Ensure quality
- Work in teams
- Collaborate, communicate, and be accountable

Denny's

- Giving our best
- Appreciating others
- A can-do attitude

First Horizon National Corporation

- Exceptional teamwork
- Individual accountability
- Absolute determination
- Knowing our customers
- Doing the right thing

SOURCE: Abrahams, J. (2007). *101 mission statements from top companies.* Berkeley, CA: Ten Speed Press.

CODES OF ETHICS

Codes of ethics are among the most common ethics tools. Companies listed on the New York Stock Exchange and the Nasdaq are required to have them, and under the Sarbanes–Oxley Act, public firms must disclose whether they have a code for their senior executives.[33] Many government departments, professional associations, social service agencies, and schools have developed codes as well. Nevertheless, formal ethics statements are as controversial as they are popular. Skeptics make these criticisms:[34]

- Codes are too vague to be useful.
- Codes may not be widely distributed or read.
- Most codes are developed as public relations documents designed solely to improve an organization's image.
- Codes don't improve the ethical climate of an organization or produce more ethical behavior.
- Codes often become the final word on the subject of ethics.
- Codes are hard to apply across cultures and in different situations.
- Codes often lack adequate enforcement provisions.
- Codes often fail to spell out which ethical obligations should take priority, or they put the needs of the organization ahead of those of society as a whole.
- Adherence to codes often goes unrewarded.

The experience of Enron highlights the shortcomings of formal ethical statements. Company officials had a "beautifully written" code of ethics that specifically prohibited the off-the-books financial deals that led to its bankruptcy (see Chapter 1).[35] Unfortunately, these same executives convinced the board of directors to waive this prohibition.

Defenders of ethical codes point to their potential benefits. First, a code describes an organization's ethical stance both to members and to the outside world. Newcomers, in particular, look to the code for guidance about an organization's ethical standards and potential ethical problems they may face in carrying out their duties. Second, a formal ethics statement can improve the group's image while protecting it from lawsuits and further regulation. In the case of wrongdoing, an organization can point to the code as evidence that the unethical behavior is limited to a few individuals and not the policy of the company as a whole. Third, referring to a code can encourage followers and leaders to resist unethical group and organizational pressures. Fourth, a written document can have a direct, positive influence on ethical behavior. Students who sign honor codes, for example, are significantly less likely to plagiarize and cheat on tests.[36] (See Case Study 9.1 for a closer look at the problem of academic cheating.) Employees in companies with formal codes of ethics judge themselves, their coworkers, and their leaders to be more ethical than workers in companies that don't have codes. Members of code organizations believe that their organizations are more supportive of ethical behavior and express a higher level of organizational commitment.[37]

CASE STUDY 9.1
Cutting Corners at the University

Academic cheating—claiming someone else's work as your own—has reached epidemic proportions among college students in the United States and Canada. Donald McCabe, a Rutgers professor who studies cheating, found that 21% of the 40,000 American and Canadian undergraduates he surveyed acknowledged at least one instance of serious cheating on a test, and 51% admitted to serious cheating on written work. In another study, 56% of graduate business students and 47% of nonbusiness graduate students reported that they had cheated at least once in the past year. Some cases of cheating have made the headlines. Thirty-four students at Duke University's School of Business were convicted of cheating. Freshmen at the Air Force Academy shared answers on a test of basic military knowledge. Would-be dentists in New Jersey falsified records to certify that they could do root canals and extractions.

Technology has helped drive up the rate of cheating. The World Wide Web enables students to cut and paste sentences and paragraphs into their written work and to purchase papers online. Cheaters can send homework answers as computer files and use their cell phones and personal digital assistants to instant message answers to classmates during exams. (Some universities now ban such devices from test sites.)

Students report tremendous pressure to succeed. Cheating, then, appears to be a means to an end, helping undergraduates get jobs and to make it into graduate school and helping graduate students move on to better positions. Offenders often go unpunished. Those who don't cheat are at a disadvantage and may be seen as naive because they won't manipulate the system. According to McCabe, "There's this feeling that everybody else does it and I would be a fool if I didn't. I'm getting left behind."[1] This perception is bolstered by well-publicized examples of corporate fraud and cheating in athletics.

Many students aren't clear as to what constitutes cheating. If they are used to working in teams, they may think its okay to work together on an individual assignment, for instance. Others may not realize it is important to cite every source. Then, too, there are students who think of cheating as a personal matter. They don't believe that copying test questions or downloading material from the Internet is a problem for others. However, widespread cheating reduces the value of every degree granted by an institution, and dishonest habits established in school can carry over after graduation. There have been reports of police recruits and paramedics using notes and stolen exams to pass cardiopulmonary resuscitation and emergency medical tests. Coast Guard personnel have been charged with cheating on pilot license exams. And no one wants a root canal performed by a dentist who didn't master this procedure while in school.

Alarmed by the rise in academic dishonesty, your college or university president has created an Integrity Task Force to come up with a plan for reducing cheating among students at your school. The president has asked you to serve as a representative on this panel. What suggestions would you make to the rest of the group?

NOTE

1. Shrieves, L. (2007, February 22). Cheating's waters run deep and dirty. *Orlando Sentinel*. Retrieved December 4, 2007, from Newspaper Source database, para. 18.

SOURCES

Burling, S. (2006, September 19). Preparing for the world of business; Survey: M.B.A. students more likely to cheat. *The Philadelphia Inquirer,* p. A01. Retrieved December 4, 2007, from LexisNexis Academic database.

Cheating is a personal foul. (n.d.). Retrieved September 25, 2001, from http://www .nocheating.org/adcouncil/research/cheatingbackgrounder.html.

Gulli, C., Kohler, N., & Patriquin, M. (2007, February 12). The great university cheating scandal. *Maclean's*. Retrieved December 4, 2007, from LexisNexis Academic database.

Oh, H. (2006, February 6). Biz majors get an F for honesty. *Business Week*. Retrieved December 4, 2007, from LexisNexis Academic database.

Universities retreat in war on cheating. (2000, August 25). Retrieved September 25, 2000, from http://www.ncpa.org/pi/edu/jan890.html.

There's no doubt that a code of ethics can be a vague document that has little impact on how members act. A number of organizations use these statements for purposes of image, not integrity. They want to appear concerned about ethical issues while protecting themselves from litigation. Just having a code on file, as in the case of Enron, doesn't mean that it will be read or used. Nonetheless, creating an ethical statement can be an important first step on the road to organizational integrity. Although a code doesn't guarantee moral improvement, it is hard to imagine an ethical organization without one. Codes can focus attention on important ethical standards, outline expectations, and help people act more appropriately. They have the most impact when senior executives make them a priority and follow their provisions while rewarding followers who do the same.

Communication ethicist Richard Johannsen believes that many of the objections to formal codes could be overcome by following these guidelines:[38]

- Distinguish between ideals and minimum conditions. Identify which parts of the statement are goals to strive for and which are minimal or basic ethical standards.

- Design the code for ordinary circumstances. Members shouldn't have to demonstrate extraordinary courage or make unusual sacrifices in order to follow the code. Ensure that average employees can follow its guidelines.

- Use clear, specific language. Important abstract terms such as "reasonable," "distort," and "falsify" should be explained and illustrated.

- Prioritize obligations. Which commitments are most important to the client? The public? The employer? The profession?

- Protect the larger community. Don't protect the interests of the organization at the expense of the public. Speak to the needs of outside groups.

- Focus on issues of particular importance to group members. Every organization and profession will face particular ethical dilemmas and temptations. For instance, lawyers must balance duties to clients with their responsibilities as officers of the court. Doctors try to provide the best care while health maintenance organizations pressure them to keep costs down. The code should address the group's unique moral issues.

- Stimulate further discussion and modification. Don't file the code away or treat it as the final word on the subject of collective ethics. Use it to spark ethical discussion and modify its provisions when needed.

- Provide guidance for the entire organization and the profession to which it belongs. Spell out the consequences when the business or nonprofit as a whole acts unethically. Who should respond and how? What role should outside groups (professional associations, accrediting bodies, regulatory agencies) play in responding to the organization's ethical transgressions?

- Outline the moral principles behind the code. Explain *why* an action is right based on ethical standards (communitarianism, utilitarianism, altruism) like those described in Chapter 5.

- Encourage widespread input. Draw on all constituencies, including management, union members, and professionals, when developing the provisions of the code.

- Back the code with enforcement. Create procedures for interpreting the code and applying sanctions. Ethics offices and officers should set up systems for reporting problems, investigating charges, and reaching conclusions. Possible punishments for ethical transgressions include informal warnings, formal reprimands that are entered into employment files, suspensions without pay, and terminations.

Most codes of ethics address the following:[39]

- *Conflicts of interest.* Conflicts of interest arise when an employee benefits at the expense of the organization or can't exercise independent judgment because of an investment, activity, or association. Even the appearance of a conflict of interest is problematic.
- *Records, funds, and assets.* Organizations must keep accurate records and protect funds and other assets. Such records (including financial statements) must meet state and federal regulations.
- *Information.* In for-profit organizations, employees can be liable if they or even their families reveal confidential information that undermines performance or competitive advantage. In the public sector, codes of ethics encourage employees to share rather than to withhold information from the public.
- *Outside relationships.* This category addresses contact with customers, suppliers, competitors, contractors, and other outside individuals and organizations. Includes prohibitions against bad-mouthing the competition, price fixing, and the sharing of sensitive information.
- *Employment practices.* Covers discrimination, sexual harassment, drug use, voluntary activities, and related human resource issues.
- *Other practices.* Sets policies related to a variety of other topics, including health and safety, the use of technology, the environment, political activities, and the use of organizational assets for personal benefit.

If you're interested in developing or refining a code of ethics, you can use the examples in Box 9.5 as a model.

CONTINUOUS ETHICAL IMPROVEMENT

The Need for Continuous Ethical Learnings

Total quality management (TQM) is a buzzword at thousands of firms in Japan, the United States, and other countries. TQM describes a continuous improvement process designed to reduce product defects, improve response times, and eliminate waste. The TQM movement is founded on the belief that organizations, like individuals, learn through experience, observation, training, and other means. Although all organizations learn, some learn faster and more efficiently than others, a characteristic that gives them a competitive edge. Those that learn quickly produce better products in less time while responding to demographic shifts and technological advances. High-tech firms are particularly aware of the importance of rapid learning. They scramble to stay ahead in the development of memory chips, cell phones, software, and other products.

Organizations ought to be as concerned about continuous ethical improvement, what I'll call total ethical management (TEM), as they are about improving products and services.[40] Three factors should encourage ongoing ethical learning: risk, lingering ethical weaknesses, and change. Let's take a closer look at each.

Box 9.5

Ethics Codes

A SAMPLER

Conflicts of Interest (Cummins Engine Co.)

All of Cummins' employees are expected to use non-discriminatory practices throughout the supplier selection process. Every employee is expected to avoid any situation in which his or her interests (or those of his or her family) may conflict with the interests of the company. Every employee with a financial interest in any actual or potential supplier or customer must disclose that interest to his or her supervisor immediately and, if applicable, in his or her annual Ethics Certification Statement.

In general, employees should neither accept nor offer gifts to customers or suppliers unless the gifts are designated as part of a recognized business event.

Gifts exceeding US $50 in value may be given or accepted only with the concurrence of an employee's supervisor. All gifts (except minor promotional token items) not reported and approved by the employee's supervisor must be reported annually on the Ethics Certification Statement.

Records, Funds, and Assets (Honeywell)

Honeywell's financial, accounting, and other reports and records will accurately and fairly reflect the transactions and financial condition of the company in reasonable detail, and in accordance with generally accepted and company-approved accounting principles, practices and procedures, and applicable government regulations.

Protecting Information (Coca-Cola)

Safeguard the Company's nonpublic information, which includes everything from contracts and pricing information to marketing plans, technical specifications, and employee information.

Outside Relationships (Eaton)

Competition—We respect the rights of competitors, customers, and suppliers. The only competitive advantages we seek are those gained through superior research, engineering, manufacturing, and marketing. We do not engage in unfair or illegal trade practices.

Employment Practices (Cummins Engine Co.)

Treatment of Each Other at Work

Each employee will treat every other employee, customer, vendor, and others met in the course of work with dignity and respect. Harassment of any type in the workplace will not be tolerated.

Box 9.5 (Continued)

Other Practices (PPG)

Political Activity Policy

1. Each employee is encouraged to participate in the electoral process at all levels of government by voting and supporting candidates and issues of his or her choice.

2. No employee shall, directly or indirectly, contribute or expend any of the Company's money, property, services or other things of value for any use prohibited by laws regulating the electoral process or the political activity of corporations.

SOURCES: Center for the Study of Ethics in the Professions at Illinois Institute of Technology. Retrieved December 13, 2007, from http://ethics.iit.edu/codes; The Coca-Cola Code of Business Conduct. Retrieved April 3, 2008, from http://www.thecoca-colacompany.com/ourcompany/business_conduct.html.

Risk. As we've seen, serious ethical misbehavior can threaten the very survival of an organization. Accounting fraud is a quick path to corporate bankruptcy, malfeasance in government agencies leads to budget reductions, and contributions dry up when the leaders of social service agencies and religious groups live like royalty. Managerial misconduct (whether motivated by poor judgment or criminal intent) is now a leading cause of business crises. No type of organization, be it religious, humanitarian, business, government, or military, is exempt from ethical failure.

On a more positive note, there is evidence that moral organizations can be extremely effective, as noted in the introduction. The Body Shop, Ben & Jerry's, Tom's of Maine, the Herman Miller Company, and ServiceMaster are highly successful as well as highly ethical. Shared values can increase productivity by focusing the efforts of employees and by encouraging supervisors to empower their subordinates. Having a good reputation attracts customers, clients, and investors and forms the basis for long-term relationships with outside constituencies.[41]

Ethical Weakness. Organizations can never claim to have arrived when it comes to ethical development. There will always be room for improvement. In addition, the same inconsistencies that plague individual leaders are found in the climate of entire organizations. Starbucks, which I cited earlier as a positive example, has been criticized for not paying coffee growers enough. Valuable rainforest has been destroyed in order to grow its coffee beans.

Change. Organizational leaders must recognize that they operate in constantly shifting environments. Competitors, suppliers, government regulations, and public tastes are always changing. Each change, in turn, brings new ethical challenges. Take the case of genetically altered foods. Opponents are raising moral objections to these products. They worry about their safety and their impact on the environment. Critics believe that biotechnology companies are putting the health of consumers and the future of native plants and animals at risk. Leaders of biotech companies must now publicly acknowledge and respond to these arguments.

Like the environments in which they live, organizations themselves are in a constant process of transformation. New employees join, divisions reorganize, companies become publicly owned, and products and services are added or dropped. Each change alters the ethical landscape. Consider the impact of a changing workforce, for instance. As more women and minorities join an organization, leaders need to focus more attention on diversity issues. They must consider such questions as "How do we make all individuals feel like valued team members?" "How do we ensure that everyone has an equal chance of being promoted, regardless of background?" "How far do we go to meet the needs of subgroups (working mothers, nonnative speakers, and religious minorities)?" (We'll start to develop some answers to these questions in the next chapter.)

Enhancing Organizational Ethical Learning

Ethical development, like other forms of organizational learning, is more likely under the right conditions. Key factors that spur organizational learning and continuous ethical improvement include the following.[42]

Scanning Imperative. Ethical learners look outside the immediate group for information. They continually scan the environment for emerging ethical issues that might affect the organization in the future. Global warming is one such issue. In just the past few years, organizations of all kinds have had to determine how they can reduce their carbon emissions. Ongoing learners monitor newspapers and trade journals to identify questionable industry practices and consider the ethical impact of entering a new market or introducing a new product (see our earlier discussion of genetically altered foods). In addition, moral leaders look closely at what other organizations do to prevent and to manage ethical problems. Organizational learning theorists call this process benchmarking. In benchmarking, groups identify outstanding organizations and isolate the practices that make them so effective. They then adapt these practices to their own organizations.[43]

Information on effective ethical practices can be found in a variety of sources. You may want to draw on these as you identify ethical benchmarks. Managerial texts and business ethics books include examples of moral and immoral behavior, sample ethics codes, and case studies. There are also two academic journals—the *Journal of Business Ethics* and *Business Ethics Quarterly*—devoted exclusively to ethics in the workplace. Information on corporate mission and values, social responsibility, academic cheating, religion and ethics, and other ethical topics can be found on a host of Web sites.

Performance Gap. A performance gap is the distance between where an organization is and where it would like to be. Martin Marietta is one example of an organization that recognized its ethical failings and took steps to correct them. The defense contractor, under investigation for improper billings in the mid-1980s, responded by highlighting its code of conduct, starting an ethics training program, developing a system for reporting ethical concerns, and rewarding executives for moral behavior. As a result, the company (which later merged with Lockheed) improved its compliance with federal regulations and reduced the number of ethical complaints filed by employees. The firm also prevented a number of potential crises stemming from bad management, safety problems, and discrimination.

Some organizations turn their moral failures into case studies. At West Point, Army instructors use the massacre of civilians at My Lai during the Vietnam War to teach ethical principles to cadets. Organizations don't have to wait for an ethical disaster to strike to identify performance gaps, of course. Ethics audits (surveys that measure employee perceptions of values and corporate behavior), ethics hotlines, and focus groups track the moral climate of the group as a whole. Ethics items on performance appraisal forms provide data on individual performance.

Climate of Openness. Openness is, first of all, the free flow of information. In open organizations, leaders make a conscious effort to reduce barriers of all kinds between individuals and units. In this environment, new ideas are more likely to develop and then to be shared throughout the group as a whole. Learning leaders put few restrictions on what can be shared, rotate people between divisions, set up forums for sharing ideas, and form multidepartment task forces. In addition, they create formal (company-wide forums, idea fairs) and informal (employee cafeterias, celebrations) settings where members can meet and share information about projects, procedures, and ethics.

Openness also refers to the type of communication that occurs between group members. In learning organizations, people engage in dialogue (see Chapter 8). They recognize that they can glean important information from anyone, regardless of status. When they interact, members treat others as equals and are more interested in understanding than in being understood. They work together to create shared meaning.

Ethical dialogue can be facilitated through designated dialogue sessions. In these gatherings, members meet to engage in open communication about moral questions. Dialogue sessions work best when attendees complete assigned readings in advance, meet in a quiet setting, convene at a round table or in a circle to emphasize equality, and suspend their opinions and judgments.[44]

Continuous Education. Continuous education reflects the organization-wide commitment to the never-ending process of learning. Organizations that value learning will make it a priority everywhere, not just in the training department. These groups (a) support on-the-job training (such as when an experienced worker helps a new hire resolve an ethical problem), (b) hold retreats, (c) encourage networking and dialogue, and (d) send people to conferences, classes, and workshops to learn more about ethics.

Involved Leadership. Leaders play a critical role in driving continuous ethical improvement. The key is hands-on involvement. Involved leaders are students. They encourage the learning of others by first learning themselves. If they want to promote diversity, for instance, they are the first to take diversity training. They continue to be involved in the learning process by interacting with followers, visiting job sites, and holding forums on ethical issues.

System Perspective. The system perspective refers to seeing the big picture, to recognizing that organizations are highly interdependent. Ongoing ethical learners try to anticipate the ethical implications of their decisions for those in other divisions. A big-picture leader may be tempted to "dump" an incompetent employee onto another department but recognizes that this strategy benefits her unit at the expense of another. The productivity of the organization as a whole suffers because this ineffective person is still on the payroll. With this in mind, she confronts the problem employee immediately.

The open communication climate described earlier facilitates system thinking. Communicating across boundaries helps members develop a better understanding of the ethical problems faced by other units and learn how their actions may result in moral complications for others.

Implications and Applications

- As a leader, you will serve as an ethics officer of your organization, exercising influence by the example you set for followers.
- Create a positive ethical climate that encourages moral decision making and behavior.
- Organizations have varying ethical orientations that affect their ethical decision making and behavior. Climates marked by self-interest are most likely to encourage unethical behavior.

- Combat the shadow side of organizational life by creating zero-tolerance policies for incivility, aggression, sexual harassment, discrimination, and other destructive actions.
- Integrity develops through clearly communicated values and commitments, leaders who are committed to these values, application of the values to routine decisions, systems and structures that support organizational commitments, and members who are equipped to make wise ethical choices.
- Don't confuse compliance with integrity. Compliance protects an organization from regulation and public criticism but has little impact on day-to-day operations. Integrity is at the center of an organization's activities, influencing every type of decision and activity.
- Pay close attention to how your organization achieves its goals. Failure to do so will create anomie and undermine ethical performance.
- Reinforce ethical commitments in your organization through the design of monetary and nonmonetary reward systems, performance and evaluation processes, and allocation of decision-making authority.
- Ethical organizations recognize their obligations to their communities, demonstrating concern for social and environmental performance. Help your organization act in a socially responsible manner by honoring your ethical obligation to stakeholder groups.
- Shared values are essential to any healthy ethical climate. Help your organization identify these values through the use of task forces, employee meetings, and other means.
- Useful codes of ethics can play an important role in shaping ethical climate. Make sure they define and illustrate important terms and address the problems faced by the members of your particular organization. View ethics statements as discussion starters, not as the final word on the topic of organizational morality.
- Risk, lingering ethical weaknesses, and constant change create a demand for continuous organizational ethical development.
- The ethical learning capacity of your organization will be determined by the presence or absence of such factors as scanning the environment, recognizing performance gaps, open communication, continuous education, involved leadership, and system thinking.

For Further Exploration, Challenge, and Self-Assessment

1. Select a well-known senior executive and determine whether this person should be classified as ethical, hypocritical, ethically neutral, or unethical. Provide evidence to support your conclusion.

2. Analyze the ethical climate of your organization. In your paper, consider the following questions: How would you classify its ethical orientation? What stage of moral development is it in? Overall, would you characterize the climate as positive or negative? Why? What factors shape the moral atmosphere? What role have leaders played in its formation and maintenance? What steps does it take to deal with misbehaviors? Does the organization consider both means

and ends? How does the group's structure reinforce (or fail to reinforce) espoused values and ethical behavior? What inconsistencies do you note? Write up your findings.

3. Discuss each of the following statements in a group or, as an alternative, argue for and against each proposition in a formal debate. Your instructor will set the rules and time limits. Refer to Box 8.3 ("Argumentativeness Scale") and Box 8.4 ("Common Fallacies") in the previous chapter for more information on constructing effective arguments.

    Pro or con: Organizations are less ethical now than they were 10 years ago.

    Pro or con: Formal codes of ethics do more harm than good.

    Pro or con: Ethical businesses are more profitable over the long term.

    Pro or con: Organizational values can't be developed; they must be uncovered or discovered instead.

    Pro or con: An organization's purpose has to be inspirational.

    Pro or con: An organization can change everything except its core values and purpose.

4. Write a research paper on one form of destructive behavior in the workplace. Conclude with suggestions to help leaders curb this type of behavior.

5. Compare and contrast an organization that has a climate of integrity with one that pursues ethical compliance.

6. Describe a time when you experienced anomie in an organization. What factors led to your feelings of powerlessness and alienation? How did anomie influence your behavior?

7. Develop a shared set of values for your class using strategies presented in the chapter.

8. Evaluate an ethical code based on chapter guidelines. What are its strengths and weaknesses? How useful would it be to members of the organization? How could the code be improved? What can we learn from this statement?

CASE STUDY 9.2

Chapter End Case:
The High Cost of Ethical Neutrality

Few leaders have risen so far and fallen so fast as former Hewlett Packard CEO Carleton (Carly) Fiorina. A medieval history and philosophy major in college, Fiorina abandoned her plans to become a lawyer after graduation and earned an MBA instead. Once she entered business, she quickly became a superstar. At AT&T she rose from a low-level sales manager to president of North American sales. When AT&T spun off Lucent Technologies, she became the new company's leader of sales and marketing. Lucent's revenue and stock values soared during her time there, and she was named as *Fortune* magazine's most powerful female American executive in 1998.

In 1999 Fiorina was hired as CEO of technology giant Hewlett Packard, becoming the first woman to head a Dow 30 company. Fiorina was a celebrity CEO. She starred in company commercials and recruited entertainment stars such as Matt Damon, Ben Affleck, and Sheryl Crow to promote HP products. Her image appeared regularly on the cover of business magazines. She became known by her first name only, like Michael Jordan and Martha Stewart.

Carly took over an organization that had been both highly profitable and highly regarded for decades. The company went 63 years without an annual loss and was one of the first to offer employees such benefits as profit sharing, catastrophic insurance, and tuition assistance. Founders Bill Hewlett and Dave Packard created a strong ethical culture built on a set of values known as the "HP Way." These principles included trusting employees, treating everyone with respect, sound finances, technical excellence, teamwork, thrift, humility, and hard work. However, by the late 1990s, profits dipped, and board members believed that HP had become a bloated bureaucracy. They hired Fiorina to streamline the company and improve its earnings and stock price.

Carly believed that employees who clung to company's past and the HP Way put the company at risk. She instituted three major changes. First, she shifted priority from nurturing employees (what Bill and Dave believed was key to HP's earlier success) to financial performance. Revenue growth and earnings became the primary focus. In one of her first meetings with her top managers, Carly interrupted a presentation to say, "Let me make something very clear. You will make your numbers. There will be no excuses. And if you can't make your numbers, I will find someone who can."[1] Second, the CEO replaced Hewlett Packard's annual profit sharing plan with an incentive program tied to reaching certain company-wide benchmarks. Salespeople, who had been salaried, now earned commissions. Third, she consolidated divisions (which had operated like independent companies in part to maintain the firm's person-centered culture) under her authority.

Employee satisfaction plummeted, particularly after employees failed to receive any bonuses and Carly ordered the largest layoff in company history. Current and past workers rebelled when Fiorina launched merger talks with Compaq computer in 2002. They feared that Hewlett Packard's culture wouldn't be able to survive the influx of so many new workers. Fiorina prevailed in a bitter stockholder and court fight with Walter Hewlett, Bill Hewlett's oldest son, but only barely. The company's stock value and employee morale continued to drop after the merger. Carly began to fight with the HP board over future plans for reorganization and executive appointments. In early 2005 she was fired, abruptly ending her reign as the most powerful businesswoman in the United States. Mark Hurd, who focuses on operations and shuns the media spotlight, replaced Fiorina, and the firm's stock price and employee morale have rebounded.

The business and popular press blamed Fiorina's dismissal on poor execution. A dynamic, charismatic speaker, she appeared to be better at creating and selling her vision than at running day-to-day operations. However, her failure can also be explained from an ethical vantage point. Carly demonstrated all the characteristics of an ethically neutral leader. To begin, she was seen (fairly or not) as self-centered. She rarely mixed with employees and seemed to overlook the fact that her plans had human costs. (The Compaq merger meant the loss of thousands of jobs, for example.) Fiorina was quick to blame others for failure rather than take personal responsibility. Her publicity efforts and downward communication style made her appear proud, not humble.

There is evidence that Carly's single-minded focus on making the numbers undermined HP's ethical standards. Salespeople began to engage in "channel stuffing," offering discounts or other incentives to get buyers to purchase more in the current quarter than they originally planned. This practice boosts current revenue at the expense of future sales. Similar practices contributed to the collapse of Lucent after Fiorina left for Hewlett Packard. Financial analysts, who used to consider HP a model of integrity, began to question HP's quarterly reports. Changing the reward system encouraged salespeople to focus on volume, bringing in orders on low-margin items to boost their income instead of selling more profitable products that would benefit the company in the long run. Individual rewards also undermined HP's collaborative culture, which up to that point had emphasized teamwork. Consolidating divisions increased Carly's power, making it harder for followers to question her bottom-line focus.

The most damage to Hewlett Packard's ethical reputation came after Fiorina was dismissed, although she helped set this crisis in motion. A board member leaked information on board deliberations to the press during the Compaq merger battle. Fiorina and her successor as board chair, Patricia Dunn, authorized investigations to identify the source of the leaks. Under Dunn's direction, private investigators spied on board members and obtained information about journalists under false pretenses, an illegal practice called pretexting. Dunn was forced out, and the state of California, the Securities and Exchange Commission, and Congress investigated. Charges against Dunn were dropped, but the company's former chief ethics officer and two private investigators pled guilty to misdemeanor fraud charges.

The scandal marked a new ethical low for the company. Once noted for its ethical reputation, HP now served as a bad example. The chair of the House Energy and Commerce subcommittee, which investigated the pretexting scandal, summed up the firm's new image this way: "For the highest-ranking officials of a company like Hewlett Packard to be aware of and seemingly approve of this kind of activity I do not think speaks well of their value system or their culture."[2]

NOTES

1. Burrows, P. (2003). *Backfire: Carly Fiorina's high stake battle for the soul of Hewlett Packard.* New York: Wiley, p. 141.

2. Nakashima, E. (2006, September 26). Between the lines of HP's spy scandal. *The Washington Post.* Retrieved September 28, 2006, from http://WashingtonPost.com, para. 24.

DISCUSSION QUESTIONS

1. What are the dangers associated with celebrity CEOs? The advantages? Do the advantages outweigh the disadvantages?

2. Do you think Carly could have introduced major changes without undermining Hewlett Packard's ethical values? How?

3. How can a leader focus attention on the bottom line without encouraging unethical behavior?

4. How much blame do you assign to the Hewlett Packard board for what happened during Fiorina's tenure as CEO?

5. Can you think of other examples of ethically neutral leaders? What impact did they have on their organizations?

6. How can the leaders of Hewlett Packard restore the company's ethical reputation?

7. What leadership ethics lessons do you take from this case?

SOURCES

Adapted from Johnson, C. E. (in press). The rise and fall of Carly Fiorina: An ethical case study. *Journal of Leadership and Organizational Studies.*

See also:

Guynn, J. (2006, September 23). A tale of two bosses at scandal-scarred HP. *San Francisco Chronicle,* pp. C1, C3.

Malone, M. S. (2007). *Bill & Dave: How Hewlett and Packard built the world's greatest company.* New York: Portfolio.

CASE STUDY 9.3

Chapter End Case: Agenda for Change at the Air Force Academy

U.S. service academies attract many of the nation's top high school students who hope to become the next generation of military leaders. Cadets are nominated by members of their congressional delegations and must be fit as well as smart. Once enrolled, they combine strenuous physical training with a demanding academic program. Plebes pledge to follow stringent honor codes that prohibit such behaviors as drinking, drug use, cheating, and breaking curfew.

Unfortunately, would-be leaders at the service academies don't always live up to their lofty reputations or follow the codes of ethics of their institutions. Nowhere is this more apparent than at the Air Force Academy. In 2002, current and former female cadets approached Colorado congressional representatives and the Air Force with complaints that academy officers mishandled charges of sexual assault. Not only did officials fail to prosecute the rapists, these women claimed, but also those who filed reports were punished for minor rule infractions. Investigations were shoddy, with complainants facing retribution from their immediate superiors and shunning by fellow plebes. In some cases, the victims dropped out of school while the offenders were promoted.

Allegations of widespread sexual crimes against women sparked three investigations and led to the replacement of top academy officials. Investigators found that the academy had been a hostile environment for women since female cadets were first admitted in 1981. The academy was male dominated, showed little concern for the welfare of female officers, and seldom put women in leadership positions. Retention rates for female cadets were lower, even though women on average had higher grades than their male counterparts. For years, a sign reading "Bring Me Men" greeted visitors to the school. In addition, the problem of sexual assault was widespread. Fifty-six cases were investigated in one 10-year period, with many more going unreported. Victims were fearful that they would find their Air Force careers cut short if they came forward. Top officials were unaware that abuse was so pervasive.

The Air Force took a number of steps called the "Agenda for Change" to root out sexual crime at the academy and to restore the school's luster. In addition to removing top officials, the academy took down the offensive "Bring Me Men" sign and renewed its emphasis on character. Colonel Debra Gray was named vice commandant, making her the first woman to occupy a top spot at the academy. (She has since retired.) Minor infractions are now covered by a "blanket amnesty." This means, for example, that a victim won't be punished for drinking if the rape took place at a drinking party. Fliers advertise a sexual assault hotline that cadets can call at any hour of the night or day to seek advice, ask questions, or report sex crimes. Victims are assigned an advocate and receive immediate medical care and counseling. If the victim reports the incident to authorities, she is assigned two advisors to help her through the system.

The centerpiece of the Agenda for Change is an aggressive training and prevention program. Cadets receive 70 hours of education about sexual assault, harassment, accountability, and substance abuse, training that begins immediately after they arrive on campus. Each squadron has a representative who trains fellow cadets and polices potentially harassing behavior.

The Agenda for Change appears to be having a positive impact. A follow-up Department of Defense survey found that fewer women reported being sexually harassed or assaulted at the Air Force Academy than at West Point or the Naval Academy. Women at the Colorado Springs campus said that they were much more likely to report such behaviors and were less fearful of reprisal. They also noted that the environment for women had improved. Nevertheless, sexist behavior is still a problem at all the academies. Most female cadets surveyed said that they had experienced crude and offensive behavior.

DISCUSSION PROBES

1. Should we expect cadets at service academies to behave more ethically than students at other colleges or universities? Is such an expectation realistic?

2. Cadets at the Air Force Academy are in violation of the honor code if they fail to report violators. Is this requirement ethical?

3. Do you blame top leaders for being unaware of the extent of the sexual assault problem on a campus? Why or why not?

4. How well is your campus dealing with issues of sexual harassment and assault? What additional steps should be taken?

5. Why do you think the Agenda for Change is working? Are there elements of the agenda that could be adapted for use on your campus?

6. What more needs to be done at the academies to reduce sexist behavior?

7. What leadership ethics lessons do you take from this case?

SOURCES

Air Force's top officers say academy problems endemic. (2003, June 2). *The Colorado Springs Gazette*. Retrieved July 21, 2003, from http://web12.epnet.com/citation.

Janofsky, M. (2003, March 8). Top Air Force officer, at academy, issues warning. *The New York Times*, p. A13.

Janofsky, M. (2003, April 1). Academy's top general apologizes to cadets. *The New York Times*, p. A14.

O'Driscoll, P., & Kenworthy, T. (2003, June 27). Cadets march into new academy. *USA Today*, p. 6A.

Olson, B. (2006, July 9). Air Force learns lesson: Cadets get the message about harassment. *Baltimore Sun*. Retrieved December 4, 2007, from Newspaper Source database.

Olson, B. (2007, October 28). Mids hear frank talk on sexual assault. *Baltimore Sun*. Retrieved December 4, 2007, from Newspaper Source database.

Schemo, D. J. (2003, May 22). Women at West Point face tough choices on assaults. *The New York Times*, p. A16.

Schemo, D. J. (2003, June 7). Policy shift on handling of complaints at academy. *The New York Times*, p. A1.

Schemo, D. J. (2003, July 12). Ex-superintendent of Air Force Academy is demoted in wake of rape scandal. *The New York Times*, p. A7.

Schemo, D. J. (2003, July 13). Academy cadet chief backs rape report disclosures. *The New York Times*, p. A16.

Study concluded Air Force Academy hostile to women for 25 years. (2003, June 16). *The Colorado Springs Gazette*. Retrieved July 21, 2003, from http://epnet.com/citation.

White, J. (2005, December 23). Air Force Academy shows improvement. *The Washington Post*, p. A02. Retrieved December 4, 2007, from LexisNexis Academic database.

Notes

1. Trevino, L. K., Hartman, L. P., & Brown, M. (2000). Moral person and moral manager: How executives develop a reputation for ethical leadership. *California Management Reviews, 42,* 128–133; Trevino, L. K., Brown, M., & Pincus, L. (2003). A qualitative investigation of perceived executive ethical leadership: Perceptions from inside and outside the executive suite. *Human Relations, 56,* 5–37; Brown, M. E., Trevino, L. K., & Harrison, D. (2005). Ethical leadership: A social learning perspective for construct development and testing. *Organizational Behavior and Human Decision Processes, 97,* 117–134; Brown, M. E., & Trevino L. K. (2006). Ethical leadership: A review and future directions. *Leadership Quarterly, 17,* 595–616.

2. Trevino, Hartman, & Brown; Trevino, L. K., & Nelson, K. A. (2004). *Managing business ethics: Straight talk about how to do it right* (3rd ed.). Hoboken, NJ: Wiley, Ch. 9.

3. Pacanowsky, M. E., & O'Donnell-Trujillo, N. (1983). Organizational communication as cultural performance. *Communication Monographs, 5,* 126–147.

4. Victor, B., & Cullen, J. B. (1988). The organizational bases of ethical work climates. *Administrative Science Quarterly, 33,* 101–125; Victor, B., & Cullen, J. B. (1990). A theory and measure of ethical climate in organizations. In W. C. Frederic & L. E. Preston (Eds.), *Business ethics: Research issues and empirical studies* (pp. 77–97). Greenwich, CT: JAI; Cullen, J. B., Victor, B., & Bronson, J. W. (1993). The ethical climate questionnaire: An assessment of its development and validity. *Psychological Reports, 73,* 667–674.

5. Fritzsche, D. J. (2000). Ethical climates and the ethical dimension of decision making. *Journal of Business Ethics, 24,* 125–140; Peterson, D. K. (2002). The relationship between unethical behavior and the dimensions of the Ethical Climate Questionnaire. *Journal of Business Ethics, 41,* 313–326; Cullen, J. B., Parboteeah, K. P., & Victor, B. (2003). The effects of ethical climates on organizational commitment: A two-study analysis. *Journal of Business Ethics, 46,* 127–141; Sims, R. L., & Keon, T. L. (1997). Ethical

work climate as a factor in the development of person–organization fit. *Journal of Business Ethics, 16,* 1095–1105; Trevino, L. K., Butterfield, K. D., & McCabe, D. L. (1998). The ethical context in organizations: Influences on employee attitudes and behaviors. *Business Ethics Quarterly, 8,* 447–476.

   6.   Griffin, R. W., & O'Leary-Kelly, A. M. (Eds.). (2004). *The dark side of organizational behavior.* San Francisco: Jossey-Bass; Mumford, M. D., Gessner, T. L., Connelly, M. S., O'Conner, J. A., & Clifton, T. (1993). Leadership and destructive acts: Individual and situational influences. *Leadership Quarterly, 4,* 115–147.

   7.   Pearson, C. M., & Porath, C. L. (2004). On incivility, its impact and directions for future research. In R. W. Griffin & A. M. O'Leary-Kelly (Eds.), *The dark side of organizational behavior* (pp. 131–158). San Francisco: Jossey-Bass; Porath, C. L., & Erez, A. (2007). Does rudeness really matter? The effects of rudeness on task performance and helpfulness. *The Academy of Management Journal, 50,* 1181–1197.

   8.   Buss, A. H. (1961). *The psychology of aggression.* New York: Wiley.

   9.   Levy, A. C., & Paludi, M. A. (2002). *Workplace sexual harassment* (2nd ed.). Upper Saddle River, NJ: Prentice Hall.

   10.   Diboye, R. L., & Halverson, S. K. (2004). Subtle (and not so subtle) discrimination in organizations. In R. W. Griffin & A. M. O'Leary-Kelly (Eds.), *The dark side of organizational behavior* (pp. 404–425). San Francisco: Jossey-Bass.

   11.   Pearson, C. M., & Porath, C. I. (2005). On the nature, consequences and remedies of workplace incivility: No time for "nice"? Think again. *Academy of Management Executive, 19,* 7–18; U.S. Department of Labor Bureau of Labor Statistics. (2007, August 9). Retrieved December 13, 2007, from http://dol.gov/dolfaq/dolfaq.asp; Ilies, R., Hauserman, N., Schwochau, S., & Stibal, J. (2003). Reported incidence rates of work-related sexual harassment in the United States: Using meta-analysis to explain reported rate disparities. *Personnel Psychology, 56,* 607–651; Diboye & Halverson.

   12.   Baron, R. A. (2004). Workplace aggression and violence: Insights from basic research. In R. W. Griffin & A. M. O'Leary-Kelly (Eds.), *The dark side of organizational behavior* (pp. 23–61). San Francisco: Jossey-Bass.

   13.   A number of authors use the term *integrity* to describe ideal managers and organizations. See the following:

   >   Pearson, G. (1995). *Integrity in organizations: An alternative business ethic.* London: McGraw-Hill.

   >   Petrick, J. A. (1998). Building organizational integrity and quality with the four Ps: Perspectives, paradigms, processes, and principles. In M. Schminke (Ed.), *Managerial ethics: Moral management of people and processes* (pp. 115–131). Mahwah, NJ: Erlbaum.

   >   Solomon, R. C. (1992). *Ethics and excellence: Cooperation and integrity in business.* New York: Oxford University Press.

   >   Srivastva, S. (Ed.). (1988). *Executive integrity.* San Francisco: Jossey-Bass.

   14.   Paine, L. S. (1996, March–April). Managing for organizational integrity. *Harvard Business Review,* pp. 106–117.

   15.   Toffler, B. L., & Reingold, J. (2003). *Final accounting: Ambition, greed, and the fall of Arthur Andersen.* New York: Broadway.

   16.   Weaver, G. R., Trevino, L. K., & Cochran, P. L. (1999). Integrated and decoupled corporate social performance: Management commitments, external pressures, and corporate ethics practices. *Academy of Management Journal, 42,* 539–552.

17. Weaver, G. R., Trevino, L. K., & Cochran, P. L. (1999). Corporate ethics practices in the mid-1990s: An empirical study of the Fortune 1000. *Journal of Business Ethics, 18,* 283–294.

18. Lindsay, R. M., & Irvine, V. B. (1996). Instilling ethical behavior in organizations: A survey of Canadian companies. *Journal of Business Ethics, 15,* 393–407.

19. Reidenbach, R. E., & Robin, D. P. (1991). A conceptual model of corporate moral development. *Journal of Business Ethics, 1,* 273–284.

20. Cadbury, A. (1987, September–October). Ethical managers make their own rules. *Harvard Business Review,* pp. 69–73.

21. Cohen, D. V. (1993). Creating and maintaining ethical work climates: Anomie in the workplace and implications for managing change. *Business Ethics Quarterly, 3,* 343–358.

22. James, H. S. (2002). Reinforcing ethical decision-making through organizational structure. *Journal of Business Ethics, 28,* 43–58.

23. Useem, M. (1998). *The leadership moment: Nine stories of triumph and disaster and their lessons for us all.* New York: Times Business, Ch. 7.

24. Panchak, P. (2002). Time for a triple bottom line. *Industry Week,* p. 7; Robins, F. (2006). The challenge of TBL: A responsibility to whom? *Business and Society Review, 111,* 1–14.

25. Kotler, P., & Lee, N. (2005). *Corporate social responsibility: Doing the most good for your company and your cause.* Hoboken, NJ: Wiley.

26. Information on the social responsibility audit called "Living Our Values" can be found on the Starbucks Web site.

27. Buchholz, R. A., & Rosenthal, S. B. (2005). Toward a conceptual framework for stakeholder theory. *Journal of Business Ethics, 58,* 137–148; Sims, R. R. (2003). *Ethics and corporate social responsibility: Why giants fall.* Westport, CT: Praeger.

28. Donaldson, T., & Preston, L. E. (1995). The stakeholder theory of the corporation: Concepts, evidence, and implications. *Academy of Management Review, 20,* 65–91; Cooper, S. (2004). *Corporate social performance: A stakeholder approach.* Burlington, VT: Ashgate; Goodpaster, K. E. (1991). Business ethics and stakeholder analysis. *Business Ethics Quarterly, 1,* 53–27; Philips, R. (2003). *Stakeholder theory and organizational ethics.* San Francisco: Berrett-Koehler.

29. Zadek, S. (2004, December). The path to corporate responsibility. *Harvard Business Review,* pp. 125–132.

30. Collins, J. C., & Porras, J. I. (1996, September–October). Building your company's vision. *Harvard Business Review,* p. 66.

31. Kuczmarski, S. S., & Kuczmarski, T. D. (1995). *Values-based leadership.* Englewood Cliffs, NJ: Prentice Hall.

32. Kuczmarski & Kuczmarski.

33. Paine, L., Deshpande, R., Margolis, J. D., & Bettcher, K. E. (2005, December). Up to code. *Harvard Business Review,* pp. 122–133.

34. For more information on the pros and cons of codes of conduct, see the following:

> Darley, J. M. (2001). The dynamics of authority influence in organizations and the unintended action consequences. In J. M. Darley, D. M. Messick, & T. R. Tyler (Eds.), *Social influences on ethical behavior in organizations* (pp. 37–52). Mahwah, NJ: Erlbaum.

Mathews, M. C. (1999). Codes of ethics: Organizational behavior and misbehavior. In W. C. Frederick & L. E. Preston (Eds.), *Business ethics: Research issues and empirical studies* (pp. 99–122). Greenwich, CT: JAI Press.

Metzger, M., Dalton, D. R., & Hill, J. W. (1993). The organization of ethics and the ethics of organizations: The case for expanded organizational ethics audits. *Business Ethics Quarterly, 3*(1), 27–43.

Trevino, L. K., Butterfield, K. D., & McCabe, D. L. (1998). The ethical context in organizations: Influences on employee attitudes and behaviors. *Business Ethics Quarterly, 8,* 447–476.

Wright, D. K. (1993). Enforcement dilemma: Voluntary nature of public relations codes. *Public Relations Review, 19,* 13–20.

35. Countryman, A. (2001, December 7). Leadership key ingredient in ethics recipe, experts say. *The Chicago Tribune,* pp. B1, B6.

36. McCabe, D., & Trevino, K. L. (1993). Academic dishonesty: Honor codes and other contextual influences. *Journal of Higher Education, 64,* 522–569.

37. Adams, J. S., Taschian, A., & Shore, T. H. (2001). Codes of ethics as signals for ethical behavior. *Journal of Business Ethics, 29,* 199–211; Valentine, S., & Barnett, T. (2003). Ethics code awareness, perceived ethical values, and organizational commitment. *Journal of Personal Selling & Sales Management, 23,* 359–367.

38. Johannsen, R. L. (2002). *Ethics in human communication* (5th ed.). Prospect Heights, IL: Waveland, Ch. 1.

39. Hopen, D. (2002). Guiding corporate behavior: A leadership obligation not a choice. *Journal for Quality & Participation, 25,* 15–19.

40. For more information on the link between learning and organizational integrity, see Petrick, J. A. (1998). Building organizational integrity and quality with the four Ps: Perspectives, paradigms, processes, and principles. In M. Schminke (Ed.), *Managerial ethics: Moral management of people and processes* (pp. 115–131). Mahwah, NJ: Erlbaum.

41. Paine, L. S. (1997). *Cases in leadership, ethics, and organizational integrity: A strategic perspective.* Boston: Irwin McGraw-Hill, p. 1.

42. Learning factors taken from DiBella, A., & Nevis, E. C. (1998). *How organizations learn: An integrated strategy for building learning capability.* San Francisco: Jossey-Bass; DiBella, A. J., Nevis, E. C., & Gould, J. M. (1996). Organizational learning as a core capability. In B. Moingeon & A. Edmondson (Eds.), *Organizational learning and competitive advantage* (pp. 38–55). London: Sage.

43. Camp, R. C. (1989). *Benchmarking: The search for industry best practices that lead to superior performance.* Milwaukee, WI: Quality Press.

44. Brown, J. (1995). Dialogue: Capacities and stories. In S. Chawla & J. Renesch (Eds.), *Learning organizations: Developing cultures for tomorrow's workplace* (pp. 153–164). Portland, OR: Productivity Press.

10

Meeting the Ethical Challenges of Diversity

For all practical purposes, all business today is global.

—Business professor Ian Mitroff

Human beings draw close to one another by their common nature, but habits and customs keep them apart.

—Confucian saying

What's Ahead

In this chapter, we examine the problems and opportunities posed by cultural and other differences. Leaders have an ethical obligation to foster diversity in their organizations. At the same time, they must master the ethical challenges of leadership in a global society. Ethical global leaders acknowledge the dark side of globalization and recognize the impact of ethical diversity. They understand the relationship between cultural values and ethical choices, seek ethical common ground, and develop strategies for making choices in cross-cultural settings.

Promoting Diversity in the Organization: An Ethical Imperative

Globalization may be the most important trend of the 21st century. We now live in a global economy shaped by multinational corporations, international travel, the Internet, immigration, and satellite communication systems. Greater cultural diversity is one product of globalization. Nonwhites account for most of the population growth in the United States. In other industrialized nations, most new workers are immigrants or members of groups currently underrepresented in the workplace. Italy will need 350,000 new migrants each year to maintain its working-age population at 1995 levels, for example, and Germany will need 500,000. However, cultural diversity isn't the only reason that the workforce is becoming more heterogeneous. Women are participating in the labor force at historically high rates, no longer dropping out after marriage. Sixty-three percent of women with children under age 6 in the United States work outside the home, 65% in Canada. Governments around the world have instituted laws that prohibit discrimination against racial minorities, women, gays and lesbians, the disabled, older workers, and others.[1]

In light of these trends, diversity expert Taylor Cox concludes that managing diversity is the core of modern organizational leadership. Cox and others define managing diversity or diversity management as taking advantage of the benefits of a diverse workforce while coping with the problems (such as the misunderstanding and conflict described in Case Study 10.1) that can arise when people from different backgrounds work together. The goal is to enable all employees, regardless of ethnicity, age, gender, sexual orientation, or physical ability, to achieve their full potential and to contribute to organizational goals and performance.[2]

CASE STUDY 10.1
Diversity Pushback

Like many other small colleges located in rural areas, Tyler University has struggled to diversify its student population. College officials find it hard to recruit minorities from urban areas. The local population is overwhelmingly white, and students of color feel isolated, far from their home communities and urban amenities. The few students of color on campus are largely exchange students from the Far East.

Under pressure from Tyler's board of trustees to diversify the student body, President Nick Hope has begun the "Tyler Forward" program. This program pays all expenses (tuition, room, and board) for 15 students of color. The students have their own advisor, who counsels them on academic issues and helps them deal with the unique problems they face as minorities on Tyler's campus. Initial indications are that students in the program are successfully adjusting to college life.

The faculty supports President Hope's initiative. However, many white students (who heard about the program only after it was launched) are not. They are bitter about the fact that Tyler Forward students are receiving a free education when they are taking out thousands of dollars in loans. They see little value in investing so much money in the program when the funds could be used to keep tuition costs down for everyone. Others think that the campus is already diverse because it includes people from a variety of geographic regions, interests, family backgrounds, physical and mental abilities, and personalities. The more cynical believe that Tyler Forward is just a token effort to improve the college's image.

Groups of students have been expressing their displeasure through campus Internet bulletin boards, comments to instructors, and appointments with administrators. President Hope has called a "town hall" meeting where he will explain and defend the Tyler Forward program and take questions.

DISCUSSION PROBES

1. What mistakes, if any, did President Hope make in rolling out the Tyler Forward program?

2. What messages should the president communicate during the meeting?

3. What questions or objections can Hope expect? How should he respond?

4. Should the president call on others to help him present the program?

5. What suggestions would you have for Tyler University to ensure Forward's success in the years to come?

SOURCE: Fictional case adapted from real-life events.

Researchers and organizational leaders have discovered that there are many benefits to a diverse workforce. Diverse organizations are more innovative, make better decisions (see our discussion of minority influence in Chapter 8), have lower absentee and turnover rates, attract higher-quality employees, improve their public image, and gain market share.[3] These benefits make the "business case" for encouraging diversity. However, the best reason for promoting diversity is that it is the right thing to do based on the ethical perspectives described in Chapter 5. In addition to doing more good than harm (utilitarianism), honoring differences recognizes the dignity of individuals (Kant), promotes justice (Rawls), and builds community (communitarianism). Helping followers of all kinds reach their full potential also reflects love of neighbor (altruism).

Although fostering diversity is an ethical imperative, there are significant barriers to carrying out this task. Prejudice, stereotypes, and ethnocentrism are important attitudinal obstacles *Prejudice* is the prejudgment of out-group members based on prior experiences and beliefs. Prejudice is universal, but the degree of prejudice varies from person to person, ranging from slight bias to extreme prejudice such as that displayed by racist skinheads. Negative prejudgments can be dangerous because they produce discriminatory behavior. For instance, police in many urban areas believe that African Americans are more likely to commit crimes. As a consequence, officers are more likely to stop and question black citizens, particularly young men, and to use force if they show the slightest sign of resistance.[4]

Stereotyping is process of classifying group members according to their perceived similarities while overlooking the individual differences. For example, Asian Americans have strong technical but not managerial skills. As a result, some organizations are eager to hire Asian Americans as engineers but are reluctant to put them in managerial roles. Because of perceptual biases, stereotypes are particularly devastating to marginalized groups. The natural tendency is to blame our failures on outside factors and to attribute our success to internal factors. The opposite is true when we evaluate the behavior of low-status groups. When we fall short, we blame other people, bad luck, bad weather, and other external forces. When we succeed, we point to our knowledge, character, skills, motivation, and training. Conversely, when members of marginalized groups fail, it is their laziness, low intelligence, or poor character that is to blame. When they succeed, however, we give the credit to the help they get from others rather than to their individual skills and effort.[5]

Ethnocentrism is the tendency to see the world from our cultural group's point of view. From this vantage point, our customs and values then become the standard by which the rest of the world is judged. Our cultural ways seem natural; those of other groups fall short. According to cross-cultural communication experts William Gudykunst and Young Yun Kim, a certain degree of ethnocentrism is inevitable.[6] Ethnocentrism can help a group band together and survive in the face of outside threats. However, ethnocentrism is a significant barrier to cross-cultural communication and problem solving. High levels of ethnocentrism can lead to the following problems:

- Inaccurate attributions about the behavior of those who differ from us (we interpret their behavior from our point of view, not theirs)
- Expressions of disparagement or animosity (ethnic slurs, belittling nicknames)
- Reduced contact with outsiders
- Indifference and insensitivity to the perspectives of members of marginalized groups
- Pressure on other groups to conform to our cultural standards
- Justification for war and violence as a means of expressing cultural dominance

Examples of ethnocentrism abound. For many years, the Bureau of Indian Affairs made assimilation its official policy, forcing Native Americans to send their children to reservation schools, where they were punished for speaking their tribal languages. Government officials in Australia kidnapped aboriginal children and placed them with white families. In other instances, well-meaning people assume that their values and practices are the only "right" ones. Many early missionaries equated Christianity with Western lifestyles and required converts to dress, live, think, and worship like Europeans or North Americans.

Organizations (often unconsciously) erect barriers to diversity through routine practices. These can include (1) inaccessible facilities that make it hard for disabled people to enter workplaces, movie theaters, churches, and other buildings; (2) long work weeks and evening and weekend hours, which increase stress for working mothers; (3) an emphasis on self-promotion, which makes people from cultures such as Japan and China that value modesty uncomfortable; and (4) informal networks that exclude minorities, women, the disabled, and others from information and contacts for promotion.[7]

Overcoming the barriers described here begins with addressing our attitudes. According to Gudykunst and Kim, we can reduce our levels of negative prejudice, stereotyping, and ethnocentrism by committing ourselves to the following:

Mindfulness. In most routine encounters, we tend to operate on "autopilot" and perform our roles mechanically, without much reflection. When we're engaged in such mindless interaction, we're not likely to challenge the ethnocentric assumption that ours is the only way to solve problems. Mindfulness is the opposite of mindlessness. When we're mindful, we pay close attention to our attitudes and behaviors. Three psychological processes take place.[8]

The first is *openness to new categories.* Being mindful makes us more sensitive to differences. Instead of lumping people into broad categories based on age, race, gender, or role, we make finer distinctions within these classifications.

We discover that not all student government officers, retirees, engineers, Japanese exchange students, and professors are alike.

The second psychological process involves *openness to new information.* Mindless communication closes us off to new data, and we fail to note the kinds of cultural differences I described earlier. We assume that others hold the same ethical values. In mindful communication, we pick up new information as we closely monitor our behavior along with the behavior of others.

The third psychological process is *recognizing the existence of more than one perspective.* Mindlessness results in tunnel vision that ignores potential solutions. Mindfulness, on the other hand, opens our eyes to other possibilities. For example, there can be more than one way to make and implement ethical choices.

Dignity and Integrity. Dignity and integrity ought to characterize all of our interactions with people of other cultures. We maintain our own dignity by confronting others who engage in prejudicial comments or actions; we maintain the dignity of others by respecting their views. Respect doesn't mean that we have to agree with another's moral stance. But when we disagree, we need to respond in a civil, sensitive manner.

Moral Inclusion. As we saw in Chapter 4, widespread evil occurs when groups have been devalued or dehumanized. This sanctioning process is called moral exclusion.[9] Exclusionary tactics include biased evaluation of women and minorities, hostility, contempt, condescension, and double standards (one for insiders, another for outsiders). Moral inclusiveness rejects exclusionary tactics of all kinds. If we're dedicated to inclusiveness, we'll apply the same rules, values, and standards to those outside our group as we do to our fellow group members.

By committing ourselves as leaders to mindful communication, the dignity of others, and moral inclusion, we can reduce ethnocentrism and prejudice in the group as a whole. Using morally inclusive language and disputing prejudiced statements, for instance, improves ethical climate because followers will be less likely to attack other groups in our presence. However, if we don't speak out when followers disparage members of out-groups, the practice will continue. We'll share some of the responsibility for creating a hostile atmosphere.

In addition to addressing attitudes about diversity, we can initiate diversity programs. Diversity initiatives address the organizational obstacles to diversity described earlier, highlight the importance of diversity, prevent discrimination, and build diversity practices into routine processes and operations. Effective diversity initiatives include (a) the involvement of senior management (taking the lead in diversity projects, hiring consultants, participating in diversity training and programs); (b) education and training featuring seminars and workshops that help employees understand the value of a diverse workforce, overcome prejudice and discrimination, and develop the skills they need to lead multicultural teams; (c) creating diversity action plans for business units and the entire organization; (d) holding managers accountable for diversity results; (e) offering flexible work arrangements (telecommuting, job sharing, working at home, part-time employment) to accommodate the needs of diverse employees; and (f) providing career development opportunities for members of marginalized groups that increase the likelihood of promotion and entry into management.[10] (Complete the self-assessment in Box 10.1 to determine your perceptions of the diversity climate of your organization and your level of comfort with diversity issues.)

Mastering the Ethical Challenges of Leadership in a Global Society

So far we've focused on our ethical obligation to foster diversity within our organizations. However, globalization means that we also have to master the ethical challenges of leading across national and cultural boundaries. Meeting these challenges begins with acknowledging the dark side of the globalization process and recognizing the impact of ethical diversity.

THE DARK SIDE OF GLOBALIZATION

Supporters of globalization point to its benefits. Free trade produces new wealth by opening up international markets, they argue. At the same time, the costs of goods and services drop. Cheaper, faster means of communication and travel encourage unprecedented cross-cultural contact.[11] The greater flow of information and people puts pressure on repressive governments to reform.

Critics of globalization paint a much bleaker picture. They note that global capitalism encourages greed rather than concern for others. Ethical and spiritual values have been overshadowed by the profit motive. Local cultural traditions and the environment are being destroyed in the name of economic growth. The gap between the rich and poor keeps growing.[12]

Debate over whether the benefits of globalization outweigh its costs is not likely to end anytime soon. This much is clear, however: As leaders, we need to give serious consideration to the dark side of the global society in order to help prevent ethical abuse. With that in mind, let's take a closer look at how leaders cast the shadows I outlined in Chapter 1 in a global environment.

The Global Shadow of Power

In the modern world, a leader's power is no longer limited by national boundaries. Increasing interdependence brought about by the integration of

Box 10.1

Self-Assessment

THE DIVERSITY PERCEPTIONS SCALE

Respond to each item by placing a check in the appropriate box. 1 = *strongly disagree,* 6 = *strongly agree.*

1. I feel that I have been treated differently here because of my race, gender, sexual orientation, religion, or age. (Reverse)

   1   2   3   4   5   6

2. Managers here have a track record of hiring and promoting employees objectively, regardless of their race, gender, sexual orientation, religion, or age.

   1   2   3   4   5   6

3. Managers here give feedback and evaluate employees fairly, regardless of employees' race, gender, sexual orientation, religion, age, or social background.

   1   2   3   4   5   6

4. Managers here make layoff decisions fairly, regardless of factors such as employees' race, gender, age, or social background.

   1   2   3   4   5   6

5. Managers interpret human resource policies (such as sick leave) fairly for all employees.

   1   2   3   4   5   6

6. Managers give assignments based on the skills and abilities of employees.

   1   2   3   4   5   6

7. Management here encourages the formation of employee network support groups.

   1   2   3   4   5   6

8. There is a mentoring program in use here that identifies and prepares all minority and female employees for promotion.

   1   2   3   4   5   6

9. The "old boys' network" is alive and well here. (Reverse)

   1   2   3   4   5   6

10. The company spends enough money and time on diversity awareness and related training.

    1   2   3   4   5   6

Box 10.1 (Continued)

11. Knowing more about cultural norms of diverse groups would help me be more effective in my job.

    1   2   3   4   5   6

12. I think that diverse viewpoints add value.

    1   2   3   4   5   6

13. I believe diversity is a strategic business issue.

    1   2   3   4   5   6

14. I feel at ease with people from backgrounds different from my own.

    1   2   3   4   5   6

15. I am afraid to disagree with members of other groups for fear of being called prejudiced. (Reverse)

    1   2   3   4   5   6

16. Diversity issues keep some work teams here from performing to their maximum effectiveness. (Reverse)

    1   2   3   4   5   6

Scoring

This scale measures two dimensions—the organizational and the personal—which each contain two factors as follows:

I. Organizational dimension
   a. Organizational fairness factor (items 1–6)
   b. Organizational inclusion factor (items 7–10)

II. Personal dimension
   c. Personal diversity value factor (items 11–13)
   d. Personal comfort with diversity (items 14–16)

Reverse scores on items 1, 9, 15, and 16. Then add up your responses to all 16 items (maximum score 96). The higher your total score, the more positive your view of the diversity climate. Similarly, the higher your score on each of the item subsets described above, the more positive your perceptions on that factor.

SOURCE: Reprinted from Mor Barak, M. (2005). *Managing diversity: Toward a globally inclusive workplace.* Thousand Oaks, CA: Sage, pp. 293–294. Used by permission.

markets, communication systems, computers, and financial institutions means that the actions of one leader or nation can have a dramatic impact on the rest of the world. Pulitzer Prize–winning foreign affairs correspondent Thomas Friedman points to the collapse of Thailand's currency in 1997 as an example of just how integrated the international economy has become.[13] When the value of the Thai baht plunged, Southeast Asia went into a deep recession that drove down world commodity prices. The Russian economy, which is heavily based on exports of oil and other commodities, then collapsed. Investors sold off their holdings to cover their losses in Southeast Asia and Russia. This massive sell-off forced the Brazilian government to raise interest rates as high as 40% to retain economic capital. Some frightened investors sought safety in U.S. treasury bonds, driving down interest rates and undermining the financial standing of many U.S. mutual funds and banks.

Ethical leadership in the multinational context must take into account the potential, far-ranging consequences of every choice. Shadows fall when leaders forget this fact. For example, the U.S. government refused for decades to increase mileage requirements for trucks and automobiles, which contributed to global warming. Saudi Arabia's unwillingness to ban terrorist groups contributed to the World Trade Center and Bali bombings.

Concentration of power is a byproduct of globalization that increases the likelihood of abuse. The United States is a case in point. Critics accuse the world's only superpower of throwing its political and military weight around. Corporations also wield great influence in the global marketplace. Multinational companies have more economic clout than many nations. According to one estimate, 53 of the world's 100 largest economies are corporations.[14]

The Global Shadow of Privilege

As noted earlier, globalization appears to be increasing, not decreasing, the gap between the haves and have-nots. Between 1960 and 1995, the income gap between the world's richest and poorest people more than doubled.[15] So far, leaders of wealthy nations have been more interested in promoting the sale of their goods than in opening up their markets to poorer countries. Privileged nations also consume more, which leads to environmental damage in the form of logging, oil drilling, and mineral extraction. This damage has a disproportionate impact on the disadvantaged. Whereas the wealthy can move to cleaner areas, the poor cannot. Instead, poor citizens must deal with the loss of hunting and fishing grounds, clean air, and safe water.

Leaders will continue to cast shadows unless they take steps to make globalization more equitable. To do so, they must (a) put the common (international) good above private gain or self- or national interest, (b) create a global economy that recognizes the interconnectedness of all peoples and the importance of sustaining the environment, (c) practice restraint and moderation in the consumption of goods, and (d) seek justice and compassion by helping marginalized groups.[16]

The Global Shadow of Mismanaged Information

Deceit is all too common on the international stage. Nations routinely spy on each other for economic and military purposes and do their best to deceive their enemies. Businesses from industrialized countries frequently take advantage of consumers in economically depressed regions. Take the marketing of infant formula, for example. United Nations experts estimate that the lives of a million and a half babies could be saved every year if they were adequately breast-fed rather than bottle-fed.[17] As an added benefit, poor households could then spend their money on other pressing needs. Despite the adoption of the International Code of Marketing Breast-Milk Substitutes in 1981, formula manufacturers continue to engage in a variety of deceptive sales practices. These include claiming that baby formula is equal to or better than breast-feeding; playing on women's fears that they won't produce enough milk; representing healthy, thriving babies on packaging (in impoverished countries, babies often sicken and die when formula is mixed with polluted water); disguising salespeople as health workers; and gaining medical endorsement by providing free samples to hospitals and gifts to doctors.

In addition to casting shadows through deception, global leaders also cast shadows by withholding information. They don't feel as much obligation to share information about safety problems and environmental hazards with foreign nationals as they do with their own citizens. They are guilty of extracting information from poor countries, giving little in return. For example, clinical drug trials in undeveloped countries produce data that goes back to company headquarters in Europe or the United States. Weaker countries are given little support in their efforts to develop their own research facilities.[18]

The Global Shadow of Inconsistency

Economic and social disparities make it hard for leaders of multinational firms and nonprofits to act consistently. For instance, what are "fair" wages and working conditions in a developing nation? Do these workers deserve the same safety standards as employees in an industrialized country? Should drugs that are banned in the United States for their undesirable side effects be sold in countries where their potential health benefits outweigh their risks? Should a multinational follow the stringent pollution regulations of its home country or the lower standards of a host nation? All too often global leaders answer these questions in ways that cast shadows on disadvantaged world citizens. They pay the bare minimum to workers in developing countries, pay less attention to safety and environmental problems in overseas locations, dump dangerous products they can't sell in their homelands, and so on.

The shadow of inconsistency grows deeper and longer when leaders ignore human rights abuses and buy the favor of corrupt officials in order to benefit from the status quo. Such was the case with Shell Nigeria. Nigeria has huge oil reserves (24–25 billion gallons) that account for 80–90% of its exports. Such natural bounty should bring prosperity, but it does not. The country's political and military leaders (rated as some of the most corrupt in the world) siphon off most oil revenue; little goes to its poor and indigenous peoples. When dissidents demanded that a larger share of oil revenue return to communities around drilling sites, Shell Nigeria leaders supported government efforts to repress the rebellion. They refused to intervene when two ethnic leaders were falsely convicted and hanged by the military regime. Shell learned from its ethical missteps in Nigeria, however. After meeting with its critics and stakeholder groups around the world, it rewrote its operating principles to emphasize commitment to human rights and the environment.[19]

The Global Shadow of Misplaced and Broken Loyalties

Traditional loyalties are eroding in an integrated world. In the past, national leaders were expected to meet the needs of their citizens. Now, because their actions affect the lives of residents of other nations, they must consider their duties to people they may never meet. Failure to do so produces shadow in the form of environmental damage, poverty, hunger, and the widening income gap.[20]

Broken loyalties cast shadows in a global society just as they do in individual leader–follower relationships. Many poorer world citizens feel betrayed by the shattered promises of globalization. Trade barriers remain in place, and special interests in wealthy nations continue to receive favored treatment. Economic exploitation adds to this sense of betrayal. Low labor costs drive the investments of many multinational companies. Executives at these firms are continually on the lookout for cheaper labor, so they transfer production to even more economically depressed regions.

The Global Shadow of Irresponsibility

Globalization increases the breadth of leaders' responsibilities because they are accountable for the actions of followers in many different geographic locations. Like local leaders, they can't be blamed for all the misdeeds of their followers. Yet they should be held to the same set of responsibility standards outlined in our discussion of the shadow side of leadership in Chapter 1. In order to cast light instead of shadow, global leaders must do the following:

1. *Take reasonable efforts to prevent followers' misdeeds.* Fostering a consistent, ethical organizational climate in every location can prevent many moral abuses. Integrity and a clear set of guiding values should be as characteristic of branch offices as they are of headquarters. This can be done by (a) clearly stating organizational values, (b) communicating these values to all branches through print and electronic media and training programs, (c) letting business partners know about standards, and (d) translating ethical behavior into performance standards and then evaluating followers based on those criteria.[21]

2. *Acknowledge and address ethical problems wherever they occur.* Geographic and cultural distance makes it easy for global leaders to deny responsibility for the misbehavior of followers. Subcontractors often get the blame for low wages and poor working conditions at foreign manufacturing facilities. More responsible firms acknowledge their duty to adequately supervise the activities of their contractors.

3. *Shoulder responsibility for the consequences of their directives.* Wise global leaders recognize that in trying to do the right thing, they might end up producing some unintended negative consequences. Take well-intentioned efforts to eliminate child labor, for instance. Removing children from the factory floor in developing countries can do significant harm. Poor children are an important source of income for their families. When fired from their manufacturing jobs, they often are forced into prostitution or begging. Levi Strauss realized that eliminating child laborers from its Bangladesh plants could do damage to both the children and their families. After identifying workers under age 14 (the international standard for child labor), company officials asked their contractors to remove these children from the production line while continuing to pay their wages. Levi Strauss covered the kids' school costs (tuition, uniforms, books) and agreed to rehire them when they reached age 14.[22]

4. *Admit their duties to followers.* Multinational leaders have obligations to all their followers, regardless of citizenship or ethnic and cultural background, and to the communities where they operate. Shell Nigeria tried to deny any responsibility for human rights abuses, claiming that it had no right to interfere in local affairs. However, the company regularly intervened in Nigerian politics in order to try to reduce the amount of oil royalties it owed the government.

5. *Hold themselves to the same standards as followers.* Leaders are not above the values, rules, and codes of conduct they impose on their global organizations. While they hold diverse followers to consistent standards, ethical leaders also live up to the same guidelines.

LEADERSHIP AND ETHICAL DIVERSITY

Along with taking stock of the potential moral pitfalls of globalization, leaders need to recognize that cultural diversity makes the always-difficult process of ethical decision making even harder. Every ethnic group, nation, and religion approaches moral dilemmas from a different perspective. (See the "Leadership Ethics at the Movies" case in Box 10.2 for a vivid demonstration of this fact.) What is perfectly acceptable to members of one group may raise serious ethical concerns for another. Consider the differing responses to these common ethical problems.[23]

Bribery. Spurred by reports that ExxonMobil had paid $59 million to Italian politicians in order to do business in that country, Congress passed the Foreign Corrupt Practices Act of 1977, which forbids U.S. corporations from exchanging money or goods for something in return. Those guilty of bribery can be fined and sent to prison. Malaysia has even stricter bribery statutes, executing corporate officers who offer and accept bribes. On the other hand, bribery is a common, accepted practice in many countries in Africa, Asia, and the Middle East. In recognition of this fact, small payments to facilitate travel and business in less developed nations are permitted under the Corrupt Practices Act.

False Information. Mexico and the United States might be geographic neighbors, but citizens of these countries react differently to deception. In one encounter, American businesspeople were offended when their Mexican counterparts promised to complete a project by an impossible deadline. The Mexicans, on the other hand, viewed their deception as a way to smooth relations between the two sides while protecting their interests.

Intellectual Property Rights. Copyright laws are rigorously enforced in many Western nations but are less binding in many Asian countries. In fact, piracy is legal in Thailand, Indonesia, and Malaysia.

Gender Equality. Treatment of women varies widely. Denmark and Sweden have done the most to promote gender equality, whereas Japan and Saudi Arabia offer some of the stiffest resistance to women's rights. In Japan, women are expected to care for the home and are excluded from leadership positions in government and business. In Saudi Arabia, women (who must wear traditional garb) aren't allowed to drive or form relationships with non-Muslim men.

The challenges posed by cultural variables can discourage leaders from making reasoned moral choices. They may decide to cling to their old ways of thinking or blindly follow local customs. Cultural relativism ("When in Rome do as the Romans do") is an attractive option for many. Nevertheless, being in a new

---

Box 10.2

Leadership Ethics at the Movies

LETTERS FROM IWO JIMA

Key Cast Members: Ken Watanabe, Kazunari Ninomiya, Tsuyoshi Ihara, Rho Kase, Shidou Nakamura

Synopsis: Tells the story of the World War II battle for Iwo Jima from the vantage point of the Japanese soldiers assigned the hopeless task of defending the island from an overwhelming American invasion force. The invaders expect a quick victory. Instead, the defenders, under the leadership of General Tadamichi Kuribayashi (Watanabe), resist for 40 days. Their code of honor, along with the belief that the Americans kill their captives, drives the Japanese soldiers and officers to fight to the death or to take their own lives instead of surrendering. Both sides display both brutality and compassion. Director Clint Eastwood created this film as a companion to *Flags of Our Fathers,* which examines the battle and its aftermath from the American perspective.

Rating: R for graphic war violence

Themes: differing cultural value patterns, ethnocentrism, prejudice, stereotypes, universal values and virtues, transformational leadership

---

culture or working with a diverse group of followers doesn't excuse leaders from engaging in careful ethical deliberation. Just because a culture has adopted a practice doesn't make it right. Female circumcision may still be carried out in parts of Africa, but the vast majority of those in the West are appalled by this custom.

Fortunately, we can expand our capacity to act ethically in a global society and, brighten the lives of diverse groups of followers. To do so, we have to deepen our understanding of the relationship between cultural differences and ethical values. Then we need to search for moral common ground and identify strategies for making decisions in cross-cultural settings.

Cultural Differences and Ethical Values

DEFINING CULTURE

The same factors that make up an organization's culture—language, rituals, stories, buildings, beliefs, assumptions, power structures—also form the cultures of communities, ethnic groups, and nations. Cultures are comprehensive, incorporating both the visible (architecture, physical objects, nonverbal behavior) and the invisible (thoughts, attitudes, values). In sum, a culture is "the total way of life of a people, composed of their learned and shared behavior patterns, values, norms, and material objects."[24]

Several features of cultures are worth noting in more detail. These elements include the following:

- *Created.* Ethnocentrism would have us believe that ours is the only way to solve problems. In fact, there are countless ways to deal with the environment, manage interpersonal relationships, produce food, and cope with death. Each cultural group devises its own way of responding to circumstances.
- *Learned.* Elements of culture are passed on from generation to generation and from person to person. Cultural conditioning is both a formal and informal process that takes place in every context—homes, schools, playgrounds, camps, games. The most crucial aspects of a culture, such as loyalty to country, are constantly reinforced. Patriotism in the United States is promoted through high school civics classes, the singing of the national anthem at sporting events, flags flying on everything from pickup trucks to skyscrapers and giant construction cranes, and Fourth of July and Memorial Day programs.
- *Shared.* The shared nature of culture becomes apparent when we break the rules that are set and enforced by the group. There are negative consequences for violating cultural norms of all types. Punishments vary depending on the severity of the offense. For example, you might receive a cold stare from your professor when your cell phone goes off in class. However, you may face jail time if you break drug laws.
- *Dynamic.* Cultures aren't static but evolve. Over time, the changes can be dramatic. Compare the cultural values of the *Leave It to Beaver* television show with those found in modern situation comedies. The world of the Cleavers (a wholesome, two-parent family with a well-dressed, stay-at-home mom) has been replaced by portrayals of unmarried friends, single parents, blended families, and gay partners.

Ethical decisions and practices are shaped by widely held cultural values. Although each culture has its own set of ethical priorities, researchers have discovered that ethnic groups and nations hold values in common. As a result, cultures can be grouped according to their value orientations. These orientations help explain ethical differences and enable leaders to predict how members of other cultural groups will respond to moral dilemmas. In this section of the chapter, I'll describe two widely used cultural classification systems. Before we examine them, however, there are four cautions to keep in mind. First, all categories are gross overgeneralizations. They describe what most people in that culture value. Not all U.S. residents are individualistic, for example, and not all Japanese citizens are collectivists. However, *in general,* more Americans put the individual first, whereas more Japanese emphasize group relations. Second, scholars may categorize the same nation differently and have not studied some regions of the world (such as Africa) as intensively as others (Europe, Asia, and the United States). Third, political and cultural boundaries aren't always identical. For instance, the Basque people live in both France and Spain. Fourth, as noted earlier, cultures are dynamic, so values change. A society may change its ethical priorities over time.

PROGRAMMED VALUE PATTERNS

Gert Hofstede of the Netherlands conducted an extensive investigation of cultural value patterns.[25] According to Hofstede, important values are "programmed" into members of every culture. He surveyed more than 100,000, IBM employees in 50 countries and three multicountry regions to uncover these value dimensions. He then checked his findings against those of other researchers who studied the same countries. Four value orientations emerged:

Power Distance. The first category describes the relative importance of power differences. Status differences are universal, but cultures treat them differently. In high–power distance cultures (Philippines, Mexico), inequality is accepted as part of the natural order. Leaders enjoy special privileges and make no attempt to reduce power differentials; however, they are expected to care for the less fortunate. Low–power distance cultures (Ireland, New Zealand), in contrast, are uneasy with large gaps in wealth, power, privilege, and status. Superiors tend to downplay these differences and strive for a greater degree of equality.

Individualism Versus Collectivism. Hofstede's second value category divides cultures according to their preference for either the individual or the group. Individualistic cultures put the needs and goals of the person and her or his immediate family first. Members of these cultures see themselves as independent actors. In contrast, collectivistic cultures give top priority to the desires of the larger group (extended family, tribe, community). Members of these societies stress connection instead of separateness, putting a high value on their place in the collective. Think back to your decision to attend your current college or university. As a resident of Canada or the United States, you probably asked friends, high school counselors, and family members for advice, but in the end, you made the choice. In a collectivistic society such as Taiwan, Peru, or Pakistan, your family or village might well make this decision for you. There's no guarantee that you would have even gone to college. Families with limited resources can afford to send only one child to school. You might have been expected to go to work to help pay for the education of a brother or sister.

Masculinity Versus Femininity. The third dimension reflects attitudes toward the roles of men and women. Highly masculine cultures such as Japan, Venezuela, and Italy maintain clearly defined sex roles. Men are expected to be decisive, assertive, dominant, ambitious, and materialistic; women are encouraged to serve. They are to care for the family, interpersonal relationships, and the weaker members of society. In feminine cultures such as Finland, Denmark, and the Netherlands, the differences between the sexes are blurred. Both men and women can be competitive and caring, assertive and nurturing. These cultures are more likely to stress interdependence, intuition, and concern for others.

Uncertainty Avoidance. This dimension describes the way in which cultures respond to uncertainty. Three indicators measure this orientation: anxiety level, widely held attitudes about rules, and employment stability. Members of high–uncertainty avoidance societies (Greece, Portugal, Japan) feel anxious about uncertainty and view it as a threat. They believe in written rules and regulations, engage in more rituals, and accept directives from those in authority. In addition, they are less likely to change jobs and view long-term employment as a right. People who live in low–uncertainty avoidance cultures (Ireland, Hong Kong, Sweden) are more comfortable with uncertainty, viewing ambiguity as a fact of life. They experience lower stress and are more likely to take risks such as starting a new company or accepting a new job in another part of the country. These people are less reliant on written regulations and rituals and are more likely to trust their own judgments instead of obeying authority figures.

Hofstede argues that value patterns have a significant impact on ethical behavior.[26] For example, masculine European countries give little to inter--national development programs but invest heavily in weapons. Feminine European nations do just the opposite. High–uncertainty avoidance cultures are prone to ethnocentrism and prejudice because they follow the credo, "What is different is dangerous." Low–uncertainty avoidance cultures follow the credo, "What is different is curious," and are more tolerant of strangers and new ideas.

Of the four value dimensions, individualism versus collectivism has attracted the most attention. Scholars have used this dimension to explain a variety of cultural differences, including variations in ethical behavior. Management professors Stephen Carroll and Martin Gannon report that individualistic countries prefer universal ethical standards such as Kant's categorical imperative.[27] Collectivistic societies take a more utilitarian approach, seeking to generate the greatest good for in-group members. Citizens of these nations are more sensitive to elements of the situation. To see how these orientations affect ethical decisions, let's return to the four dilemmas I introduced earlier in the chapter.

- *Bribery.* Payoffs tend to be more common in collectivistic nations and may be a way to meet obligations to the community. In some cases, there are laws against the practice, but they take a back seat to history and custom. Individualistic nations view bribery as a form of corruption; payoffs destroy trust and benefit some companies and people at the expense of others.

- *False information.* Individualists are more likely to lie in order to protect their privacy; collectivists are more likely to lie in order to protect the group or family. This accounts for the conflict between the Mexican and U.S. businesspeople described earlier. Mexicans, who tend to have a collectivistic orientation, promise what they can't deliver in order to reduce tensions between their in-group and outsiders. Americans (among the world's most individualistic peoples) condemn this practice as deceptive and therefore unethical. Individualists and collectivists also express disagreement differently. For instance, Germans and Americans don't hesitate to say "no" directly to another party. Japanese may answer by saying "that will be difficult" rather than by offering an out-and-out refusal. This indirect strategy is designed to save the face or image of the receiver.
- *Intellectual property rights.* Whereas individuals own the rights to their creative ideas in individualistic societies, they are expected to share their knowledge in collectivistic nations. Copyright laws are a Western invention based on the belief that individuals should be rewarded for their efforts.
- *Gender equality.* Resistance to gender equality is strongest in collectivistic nations such as Saudi Arabia and Japan. Women are seen as an out-group in these societies. Many men fear that granting women more status (better jobs, leadership positions) would threaten group stability. Individualistic nations are more likely to have laws that promote equal opportunity, although in many of these countries (such as the United States) women hold fewer leadership positions than men and continue to earn less.

In addition to shaping our moral choices, both individualism and collectivism create *ethical blind spots.* Being self- or group-focused can make us particularly susceptible to certain types of ethical abuses. Turn to Box 10.3 for one list of the ethical problems associated with individualism and collectivism.

PROJECT GLOBE

Project GLOBE (Global Leadership and Organizational Behavior Effectiveness) is an international effort involving 170 researchers who have gathered data from more than 17,000 managers in 62 countries. The researchers hope to better equip global managers by identifying the relationship between cultural values and effective leadership behaviors. Like Hofstede, the GLOBE researchers identify power distance, uncertainty avoidance, gender differentiation (masculinity and femininity), and individualism versus collectivism as important cultural dimensions. However, they extend Hofstede's list by including the following:[28]

In-Group Collectivism. This dimension describes the degree to which societal members take pride in their small groups, families, and organizations. In-group collectivism differs from Hofstede's collectivism dimension, which describes maintaining harmony and cooperation throughout society as a

Box 10.3

Ethical Disadvantages of Collectivism and Individualism

University of Illinois psychology professor Harry Triandis argues that there are ethical strengths and weaknesses associated with collectivism and individualism. In general, collectivism is better for interpersonal relationships but poses a danger when members deal with outsiders. Individualism promotes human rights, creativity, and achievement but undermines social connections. Some of the specific ethical disadvantages of collectivism and individualism are outlined here:

Ethical Disadvantages of Collectivism

> Suppression of individual thought and innovation
>
> Undermining of the self-esteem of some members
>
> Encouragement of blind obedience to authoritarian groups and leaders
>
> Harsh treatment of out-groups (e.g., discrimination, ethnic cleansing)
>
> Human rights abuses
>
> Wife beating and killing
>
> Continual feuds between groups
>
> Hoarding of information by the in-group

Ethical Disadvantages of Individualism

> High crime rates
>
> Selfishness and narcissism
>
> Extreme competitiveness
>
> Violence
>
> Suicide and drug abuse
>
> Aggression
>
> Materialism
>
> Lack of concern about the common good

SOURCE: Triandis, H. C. (1995). *Individualism and collectivism.* Boulder, CO: Westview, Ch. 7.

whole. Being a member of a family, close group, or employing organization is very important to members of in-group collectivist societies (Iran, India, China), and they have high expectations of other group members. People living in countries that score low on this dimension, such as Denmark, Sweden, and New Zealand, don't have similar expectations of friends and family.

Assertiveness. Assertiveness is the extent to which a culture encourages individuals to be tough, confrontational, and competitive, as opposed to modest and tender. Spain and the United States rate high on this dimension; Sweden and New Zealand rate low. Those in highly assertive societies have a take-charge attitude and value competition. They are not particularly sympathetic to the weak and less fortunate. Members of less assertive cultures place more value on empathy, loyalty, and solidarity.

Future Orientation. This is the extent to which a society fosters and reinforces such future-oriented activities as planning and investing (Singapore, Switzerland, the Netherlands) rather than immediate gratification (Russia, Argentina, Poland).

Performance Orientation. This is the degree to which a society encourages and rewards group members for improving performance and demonstrating excellence. In places such as Hong Kong, Singapore, and the United States, training and development are valued and people take initiative. Citizens prefer a direct communication style and feel a sense of urgency. In countries such as Russia, Italy, and Argentina, people put loyalty and belonging ahead of performance. They are uncomfortable with feedback and competition and put more weight on someone's family and background than on performance.

Humane Orientation. Humane orientation is the extent to which a culture encourages and honors people for being altruistic, caring, kind, fair, and generous. Support for the weak and vulnerable is particularly high in countries such as Malaysia, Ireland, and the Philippines. People are usually friendly and tolerant and may develop patronage and paternalistic relationships with their leaders. In contrast, power and material possessions motivate people in the former West Germany, Spain, and France. Self-enhancement takes precedence. Individuals are to solve their own problems; children are expected to be independent.

It is clear that differences on these values dimensions can cause some serious ethical conflicts. Those scoring high on in-group collectivism see no problem in hiring friends and family members even when more qualified candidates are available, a fact that will trouble those who believe that members of their in-groups should not expect preferential treatment (see the "Family Values or Nepotism?" scenario in the chapter end case). People oriented toward the future will save and invest. They will condemn those who live in the moment and spend all they earn. Competition, direct communication, power, and personal advancement are applauded in assertive, performance-oriented, less humane groups. These elements are undesirable to people who put more value on harmony, cooperation, family, and concern for others.

Although there is plenty of evidence of ethical diversity in the GLOBE study, there are also signs of common ethical ground. As I noted in Chapter 6, the GLOBE researchers discovered that many of the characteristics associated with transformational leadership—motive arouser, foresight, encouraging, dynamic, motivational, trustworthy, positive, confidence builder, communicative—are admired across cultures (though to varying degrees).[29] (For a closer look at the relationship between cultural dimensions and followership, see Box 10.4.) In another study, researchers from Florida Atlantic, the University of Maryland, and Wayne State University analyzed the GLOBE data to determine whether there are aspects of ethical leadership that are important for effective leadership across cultures. Four attributes emerged, although the extent to which each is endorsed and how each is implemented varies across cultures.[30] Character and integrity (consistency, virtue) were rated as important, as were altruism, collective motivation (putting the interests of the group ahead of personal interests), and encouraging and empowering (helping followers feel competent). Taken together, these dimensions describe positive, people-oriented leadership that respects the rights and dignity of others. The fact that observers from many different cultural backgrounds agree on the attributes of ethical leadership suggests that there are common ethical standards shared by all cultures. We'll take a closer look at those standards in the next section.

Standing on Moral Common Ground

Confronted with a wide range of ethical values and standards, a number of philosophers, business leaders, anthropologists, and others opt for ethical relativism. In ethical relativism, there are no universal moral codes or standards. Each group and society is unique. Therefore, members of one culture can't pass moral judgment on members of another group.

I'll admit that, at first glance, ethical relativism is appealing. It avoids the problem of ethnocentrism while simplifying the decision-making process. We can concentrate on fitting in with the prevailing culture and never have to pass judgment. On closer examination, however, the difficulties of ethical relativism become all too apparent.[31] Without shared standards, there's little hope that the peoples of the world can work together to address global problems. There may be no basis on which to condemn the evil of notorious leaders who are popular

---

Box 10.4

Focus on Follower Ethics

FOLLOWER OBLIGATIONS IN CROSS-CULTURAL LEADER–FOLLOWER RELATIONSHIPS

Both the Hofstede and GLOBE studies are based on the premise that a leader's success depends on how well she or he complements the cultural values of subordinates. Leaders who violate the expectations of followers are not likely to succeed, as in the case of the Irish manager (from a low–uncertainty avoidance culture) who fails to give clear instructions to his employees in Greece (a high–uncertainty avoidance culture). Power distance has a particularly strong impact on follower expectations of leaders. Those in low–power distance societies want their leaders to be democratic and may rebel if not consulted about important decisions. Those in medium–power distance cultures such as the United States want to be consulted but will tolerate autocratic leadership at times. Those in high–power distance cultures expect their superiors to act unilaterally. To them, the ideal superior is a benevolent authoritarian figure.

The subordinate's responsibility in cross-cultural leader–follower relationships has been largely overlooked. Cultural differences don't excuse followers from their ethical obligations to their leaders. They have a duty to try to help the leader succeed, even when the leader violates cultural expectations at first. They should seek to understand as well as to be understood, determining how the leader's cultural values influence her or his leadership behaviors and ethical decisions. Together with their leaders, they should ask what each party can contribute to the relationship based on his or her cultural background. Both leaders and followers can learn from the insights of the other cultural group. In the end, they can develop synergistic relationships that generate better-than-anticipated results.

Sources

Adler, N. J. (2002). *From Boston to Beijing: Managing with a world view.* Cincinnati: South-Western.

Deresky, H. (2003). *International management: Managing across borders and cultures.* Upper Saddle River, NJ: Prentice Hall, Ch. 11.

Hofstede, G. (1980, Summer). Motivation, leadership, and organization: Do American theories apply abroad? *Organizational Dynamics,* pp. 42–63.

---

in their own countries. Furthermore, the standard of cultural relativism obligates us to follow (or at least not to protest against) abhorrent local practices such as the killing of brides by their in-laws in the rural villages of Pakistan. Without universal rights and wrongs, we have no basis on which to contest such practices.

I believe that there is ethical common ground that can help us address the dark side of globalization. In fact, the existence of universal standards has enabled members of the world community to punish crimes against humanity and to create the United Nations and its Universal Declaration of Human Rights. Responsible multinational corporations such as the Body Shop, Nike, and Starbucks adhere to widely held moral principles as they conduct business in a variety of cultural settings. In this final section, I'll describe five different approaches to universal ethics: a Global Ethic, Eight Global Values, the Peace Ethic, the Global Business Standards Codex, and the Caux Principles. Any one of these approaches could serve as a worldwide standard. As you read each description, look for commonalties. Then decide for yourself which approach or combination of approaches best captures the foundational values of humankind.

A GLOBAL ETHIC

Many of the world's conflicts center around religious differences: Hindu versus Muslim, Protestant versus Catholic, Muslim versus Jew. However, these hostilities didn't prevent 6,500 representatives from a wide range of religious faiths from reaching agreement on a global ethic.[32] A council of former heads of state and prime ministers then ratified this statement. Delegates of both groups agreed on two universal principles. First, every person must be treated humanely regardless of language, skin color, mental ability, political beliefs, or national or social origin. Every person and group, no matter how powerful, must respect the dignity of others. Second, "what you wish done to yourself, do to others" (or the Golden Rule). These two foundational principles, in turn, lead to the following ethical directives or imperatives:

- Commitment to a culture of nonviolence and respect for all life
- Commitment to a culture of solidarity and a just economic order (do not steal, deal fairly and honestly with others)
- Commitment to a culture of tolerance and truthfulness
- Commitment to a culture of equal rights and partnership between men and women (avoid immorality; respect and love members of both genders)

EIGHT GLOBAL VALUES

Rushworth Kidder and his colleagues at the Institute for Global Ethics identified eight core values that appear to be shared the world over. They isolated these values after conducting interviews with 24 international "ethical thought leaders."[33] Kidder's sample included United Nations officials, heads of states, university presidents, writers, and religious figures drawn from such nations as the United States, Vietnam, Mozambique, New Zealand, Bangladesh,

Britain, China, Sri Lanka, Costa Rica, and Lebanon. Each interview ran from 1 to 3 hours and began with this question: "If you could help create a global code of ethics, what would be on it?" These global standards emerged:

- *Love:* Spontaneous concern for others, compassion that transcends political and ethnic differences
- *Truthfulness:* Achieving goals through honest means, keeping promises, being worthy of the trust of others
- *Fairness (justice):* Fair play, evenhandedness, equality
- *Freedom:* The pursuit of liberty, right of free expression and action, and accountability
- *Unity:* Seeking the common good; cooperation, community, solidarity
- *Tolerance:* Respect for others and their ideas; empathy, appreciation for variety
- *Responsibility:* Care for self, the sick and needy, the community, and future generations; responsible use of force
- *Respect for life:* Reluctance to kill through war and other means

Kidder and his fellow researchers don't claim to have discovered the one and only set of universal values, but they do believe that they have established ethical common ground. Kidder admits that the eight values are ordinary rather than unique, but the fact that the list contains few surprises is evidence these standards are widely shared.

THE PEACE ETHIC

Communication professor David Kale argues that peace ought to be the ultimate goal of all intercultural contact because living in peace protects the worth and dignity of the human spirit.[34] Conflicts are inevitable. Nevertheless, with the help of those in leadership roles, peoples and nations can learn to value the goals of other parties even in the midst of their differences. There are four principles of the Peace Ethic:

Principle 1: Ethical communicators address people of other cultures with the same respect they desire themselves. Verbal and psychological violence, like physical violence, damages the human spirit. Demeaning or belittling others makes it hard for people to live at peace with themselves or their cultural heritage.

Principle 2: Ethical communicators describe the world as they see it as accurately as possible. Perceptions of what truth is vary from culture to culture, but all people, regardless of their cultural background, should be true to the truth as they perceive it. Lying undermines trust that lays the foundation for peace.

Principle 3: Ethical communicators encourage people of other cultures to express their cultural uniqueness. Individuals and nations have the right to hold and express different values and beliefs, a principle enshrined in the United Nations

Universal Declaration of Human Rights. As leaders, we shouldn't force others to adopt our standards before allowing them to engage in dialogue.

Principle 4: Ethical communicators strive for identification with people of other cultures. We should seek mutual understanding and common ethical ground whenever possible. Incidents of racial harassment at colleges and universities are unethical, according to this principle, because they lead to division rather than peace.

THE GLOBAL BUSINESS STANDARDS CODEX

Harvard business professor Lynn Paine and her colleagues argue that world-class corporations base their codes of ethics on a set of eight universal, overarching ethical principles.[35] Paine's group compiled these guidelines after surveying a variety of global and corporate codes of conduct and government regulations. The researchers offer their Global Business Standards Codex as a benchmark for those who want to conform to universal standards of corporate conduct.

I. *Fiduciary principle.* Act on behalf of the company and its investors. Be diligent and loyal in carrying out the firm's business. As a trustee, be candid (open and honest).

II. *Property principle.* Respect and protect property and the rights of its owners. Don't steal or misuse company assets, including information, funds, and equipment. Avoid waste and take care of property entrusted to you.

III. *Reliability principle.* Honor all commitments. Keep promises and follow through on agreements even when they are not in the form of legally binding contracts.

IV. *Transparency principle.* Do business in a truthful manner. Avoid deceptive acts and practices and keep accurate records. Release information that should be shared in a timely fashion but maintain confidentiality and privacy as necessary.

V. *Dignity principle.* Respect the dignity of all who come in contact with the corporation, including employees, suppliers, customers, and the public. Protect their health, privacy, and rights. Avoid coercion. Promote human development instead by providing learning and development opportunities.

VI. *Fairness principle.* Deal fairly with everyone. Engage in fair competition, provide just compensation to employees, and be even-handed in dealings with suppliers and corporate partners. Practice nondiscrimination in both employment and contracting.

VII. *Citizenship principle.* Act as a responsible member of the community by (a) obeying the law, (b) protecting the public good (not engaging in corruption, protecting the environment), (c) cooperating with public authorities, (d) avoiding improper involvement in politics, and (e) contributing to the community (e.g., economic and social development, giving to charitable causes).

VIII. *Responsiveness principle.* Engage with groups (neighborhood groups, activists, customers) that may have concerns about the company's activities. Work with other groups to better society while not usurping the government's role in protecting the public interest.

THE CAUX PRINCIPLES

The Caux Round Table is made up of business executives from the United States, Japan, and Europe who meet every year in Caux, Switzerland. Round Table members hope to set a world standard by which to judge business behavior. Their principles are based on twin ethical ideals. The first is the Japanese concept of *kyosei,* which refers to living and working together for the common good. The second is the Western notion of human dignity, the sacredness and value of each person as an end rather than as a means to someone else's end.[36]

Principle 1. The responsibilities of corporations: Beyond shareholders toward stakeholders. Corporations have a responsibility to improve the lives of everyone they come in contact with, starting with employees, shareholders, and suppliers, and then extending out to local, national, regional, and global communities.

Principle 2. The economic and social impact of corporations: Toward innovation, justice, and world community. Companies in foreign countries should not only create jobs and wealth but also foster better social conditions (education, welfare, human rights). Corporations have an obligation to enrich the world community through innovation, the wise use of resources, and fair competition.

Principle 3. Corporate behavior: Beyond the letter of law toward a spirit of trust. Businesses ought to promote honesty, transparency, integrity, and keeping promises. These behaviors make it easier to conduct international business and to support a global economy.

Principle 4. Respect for rules: Beyond trade friction toward cooperation. Leaders of international firms must respect both international and local laws in order to reduce trade wars and to promote the free flow of goods and services.

Principle 5. Support for multilateral trade: Beyond isolation toward world community. Firms should support international trading systems and agreements and eliminate domestic measures that undermine free trade.

Principle 6. Respect for the environment: Beyond protection toward enhancement. A corporation ought to protect and, if possible, improve the physical environment through sustainable development and cutting back on the wasteful use of natural resources.

Principle 7. Avoidance of illicit operations: Beyond profit toward peace. Global business leaders must ensure that their organizations aren't involved in such forbidden activities as bribery, money laundering, support of terrorism, drug trafficking, and organized crime.

After spelling out general principles, the Caux accord applies them to important stakeholder groups. Leaders following these standards hope to (a) treat customers and employees with dignity, (b) honor the trust of investors, (c) create relationships with suppliers based on mutual trust, (d) engage in just behavior with competitors, and (e) work for reform and human rights in host communities.

Making Ethical Choices in Culturally Diverse Settings: Integrated Social Contracts Theory

The universal principles described in the last section play an important role when we are faced with making ethical decisions involving more than one culture. According to business ethicists Thomas Donaldson and Thomas Dunfee, we need to hold fast to global principles while we take local values into account.[37] Their Integrated Social Contracts Theory (ISCT) provides one set of guidelines for balancing respect for ethical diversity with adherence to universal ethical standards.

ISCT is based on the idea of social contracts—agreements that spell out the duties of institutions, communities, and societies. The theory is integrated because it incorporates two kinds of contracts: macrosocial and microsocial. *Macrosocial* contracts are broader and lay the foundation for how people interact with one another. The requirement that the government protect its citizens and the belief that employers should respect the rights of workers are examples of ideal contracts. *Microsocial* contracts govern the relationships between the members of specific groups (local towns, regions, nations, companies, professions). These contacts are revealed by the norms of the group. For example, those who participate in auctions must adhere to the norms of the auction community, which include revealing whether participants have the means to back up their bids and not interfering with others who are making bids. Community contracts are considered authentic or binding if members of the group have a voice in the creation of the norms, members can exit the group if they disagree with prevailing norms, and the norms are widely recognized and practiced by group members. Under these standards, prohibitions against free speech in countries ruled by repressive regimes would not be authentic because citizens had no say in creating these rules and can't leave the community if they want.

Local communities have a great deal of latitude or *moral free space* to create their own rules, and these norms should be respected whenever possible. An Indonesian manager participating in an Australian real estate auction should obey the Australian auction norms, for instance. However, universal principles such as those described in the previous section (what Donaldson and Dunfee call *hypernorms*) take priority when global principles clash with community standards. Exploitation of workers (excessive hours, low pay, imprisonment, sexual abuse) might be the norm in some developing countries. But such practices should be rejected because they violate hypernorms that urge us to respect the dignity of other human beings, treat them fairly and humanely, and follow the Golden Rule.

To make decisions following ISCT guidelines, follow these steps:

1. Identify all relevant stakeholders or communities.

2. Determine whether these communities are legitimate (do they allow voice and exit by members?).

3. Identify authentic norms (those that are widely known and shared).

4. Determine whether the norms are legitimate (do not conflict with hypernorms).

5. Resolve any conflicts between legitimate norms. (If both sets of norms do not conflict with universal standards, go with the option that is dominant—the one accepted by the larger community).

You can practice these steps by applying them to the "Google Meets the Great Firewall of China" case at the end of the chapter, which involves the difficult ethical choices facing American technology companies operating under a communist regime.

Implications and Applications

- Fostering diversity is not just good business strategy; it is an ethical imperative for leaders.
- Prejudice, stereotypes, and ethnocentrism are barriers to diversity and lead to moral abuses. You can avoid casting shadows if you commit yourself to mindfulness, human dignity, and moral inclusiveness.
- Acknowledging the dark side of globalization reduces the likelihood of ethical abuse on the world stage. As a leader in a global environment, you must take additional care to avoid casting shadows of power, privilege, mismanaged information, inconsistency, misplaced and broken loyalties, and irresponsibility.
- Cultural differences make ethical decisions more difficult. Nevertheless, resist the temptation to revert to your old ways of thinking or to blindly follow local customs. Try instead to expand your capacity to act ethically in multicultural situations.
- Understanding the relationship between cultural differences and ethical values can help you predict how members of that group will respond to moral questions.
- Two popular cultural value classification systems are Hofstede's programmed values (power distance, individualism versus collectivism, masculinity versus femininity, uncertainty avoidance) and the GLOBE cultural dimensions, which include Hofstede's categories along with in-group collectivism, assertiveness, future orientation, performance orientation, and humane orientation.

- Universal standards can help you establish common ground with diverse followers. These shared standards can take the form of religious commitments, global values, a commitment to peace, or world business standards.
- To make ethical decisions in cross-cultural settings, take both local values and global principles into account. Follow community norms except when they conflict with universal moral standards.

For Further Exploration, Challenge, and Self-Assessment

1. Distribute the Diversity Perceptions Scale assessment to other members of your organization and discuss your responses. What factors contributed to your organizational and personal perceptions? What can you do to boost your individual and collective scores?

2. Form groups and debate the following proposition: "Overall, globalization does more harm than good."

3. Brainstorm a list of the advantages and disadvantages of ethical diversity. What conclusions do you draw from your list?

4. Using the Internet, compare press coverage of an international ethical issue from a variety of countries. How does the coverage differ and why?

5. Rate yourself on one or both of the cultural classification systems described in the chapter. Create a value profile of your community, organization, or university. How well do you fit in?

6. Analyze the cultural values that probably influenced the ethical decision of a prominent leader.

7. Is there a common morality that peoples of all nations can share? Which of the global codes described in the chapter best reflects these shared standards and values? If you were to create your own declaration of global ethics, what would you put on it?

CASE STUDY 10.2

Chapter End Case: Google Meets the Great Firewall of China

The Chinese Internet market is exploding. The number of Internet-connected computers in China has doubled in the past few years, and only the United States has more Internet users. To enter this lucrative market, Microsoft, Yahoo, Cisco Systems, Google, and other American technology firms must participate in the communist government's censorship program, which has been dubbed the "Great Firewall of China." Thirty thousand censors monitor Web sites and Internet traffic to determine whether users are breaking the law by defaming the government, divulging state secrets, or promoting separatist movements. Chinese officials ban such "subversive" material as government criticism, pornography, and information about Tibet, Taiwanese independence, and the Falun Gong religious sect.

American firms have done their part to shore up the Great Firewall. Cisco and Sun Microsystems sell China's government networking hardware that allows officials to filter out content. Yahoo gave Chinese authorities the e-mail address of a journalist who is now serving a 10-year prison term for writing about human rights abuses. MSN denies access to individual blogs at the government's request. Google blocks content that Beijing deems controversial. For example, Westerners using the search term "Tiananmen" get images of protesters being overrun by tanks in 1989. In China, the same search may generate an image of a U.S. official posing for a snapshot in Tiananmen Square.

Google has taken the most criticism for supporting China's censorship efforts. The company's decision to censor appears to contradict its motto to "do no evil" and undermines its efforts to provide unlimited access to information. Google justifies its decision by arguing that censorship is the lesser of two evils. "Filtering our search results clearly compromises our mission," the firm admits, "but failing to offer Google search at all to a fifth of the world's population, however, does so far more severely."[1] Critics do not agree. Iowa Republican Congressman Jim Leach argued that Google's actions turned it into a "functionary of the Chinese government."[2] California representative Tom Lantos, a Holocaust survivor, compared Google and other high-tech firms to American companies that did business in Nazi Germany. Some in Congress believe that the U.S. government ought to intervene by preventing American companies from working with repressive regimes. For example, American firms would have to locate their computer hardware outside China, curtail exports to countries that censor online material, and agree to a shared code of Internet conduct.

Even if U.S. technology giants continue to obey Chinese Internet laws, it's not clear that China's Great Firewall can survive in the long run. Censors will be hard pressed to keep up with the rapid growth of blogs, computers, and Internet cafes.

The Freegate Network enables Chinese users to circumvent filters by connecting directly to U.S. servers, and the Tor network, based in Boston, allows them to send messages anonymously. Furthermore, the Web has already played a role in opening up Chinese society. Chinese Web users have more access to information from outside China than ever before. They have also used the Internet to publicize national incidents, such as a toxic chemical spill and the severe acute respiratory syndrome (SARS) outbreak, that were censored in the mainstream Chinese press.

DISCUSSION PROBES

1. Google argues that filtering Internet content is less damaging than pulling out of the Chinese market. Do you agree?

2. Use the steps of the Integrated Social Contracts Theory decision-making process to determine whether American high-tech firms participate in the Great Firewall of China. What do you conclude?

3. Should the U.S. government pass legislation banning corporations from participating in censorship programs sponsored by foreign governments?

4. Is Web censorship ever justified? Are there some topics that should be filtered?

5. What leadership ethics lessons do you take from this case?

NOTES

1. Grossman, L., & Beech, H. (2006, February 13). Google under the gun. *Time.* Retrieved December 20, 2007, from Business Source Complete database, para. 5.

2. Silla, B., Knight, D., & Fang, B. (2006, February 27). Learning to live with big brother. *U.S. News & World Report.* Retrieved December 20, 2007, from Business Source Complete database, para. 7.

SOURCES

Einhorn, B. (2006, August 11). Search engines censured for censorship. *Business Week Online.* Retrieved December 20, 2007, from Business Source Complete database.

Levy, S. (2006, February 13). Google and the China syndrome. *Newsweek.* Retrieved December 20, 2007, from Business Source Complete database.

The party, the people and the power of cyber-talk. (2006, April 29). *Economist.* Retrieved December 20, 2007, from Business Source Complete database.

CASE STUDY 10.3

Chapter End Case:
Ethical Diversity Scenarios

Family Values or Nepotism?

A number of companies in India will hire the children of employees once a child has completed his or her schooling. The firms honor this commitment even though more qualified applicants are available. This benefit is extremely valuable in a country where jobs are often hard to find. Also, many Indians believe that the West has allowed economic considerations to break up families. Although this practice is popular among employees, it would be considered nepotism in the United States and violates the principle of equal opportunity. The Equal Employment Opportunity Commission would fine U.S. companies making such commitments.

As a manager, how should you react to Indian nepotism? Should you refuse to accept Indian companies as partners or suppliers unless they cease this practice?

SOURCE: Donaldson, T. (1996, September–October). Values in tension: Ethics away from home. *Harvard Business Review, 74,* 48–57.

The Case of the Disguised Leader

You are the new director of overseas operations for a small cargo airline. The company's most profitable international contract is with the government of Kuwait. You are planning your first visit to that country to see Kuwaiti operations firsthand. The problem is that you are a woman traveling to a male-dominated Muslim society. Kuwaiti officials object to women in leadership roles. The CEO of your firm suggests that you let your male deputy act as the leader (meeting with government authorities and company employees, conducting negotiations) when you travel to the Middle East. That way, the Kuwaitis won't be offended, and the contract probably will be renewed. Of course, you would resume your regular duties when you left the region.

Would you take the CEO's advice? Why or why not?

Hazardous Material Labels

Governments in most industrialized countries require manufacturers to place safety labels on containers of hazardous materials and ban the importation of unmarked products. These labels inform users about the content of the materials, how to use them, and what to do in the case of an accident. Government authorities in many developing nations aren't as likely to require such labels. Managers who purchase unlabeled containers from vendors in developing countries may not be sure what they are buying but, even more importantly, are putting their employees at risk. Workers could harm themselves while using the products on a daily basis and don't know how to respond in the case of an accident involving the materials.

Requiring suppliers in poor nations to place safety labels on their containers significantly boosts their costs. They have to spend significant time and money to gather and communicate such information and may be annoyed by having to comply with what they perceive as "petty demands." A significant number of suppliers may seek out more accepting customers instead. The additional administrative costs are passed onto the buyer, which can put the purchaser at a competitive disadvantage. Some purchasing managers try to lower their costs and maintain their relationships with suppliers by buying unlabeled materials for use in international facilities where safety labels aren't required.

As a purchasing manager in a multinational firm, would you require your suppliers in developing countries to label their hazardous materials? Would you use unlabeled hazardous materials in countries where the law allows?

SOURCE: Reynolds, S. J. (2003). A single framework for strategic and ethical behavior in the international context. *Business Ethics Quarterly, 13,* 361–379.

The Regime Change

You are the plant manager at a large clothing manufacturing facility in a small Central American country. Your Canadian company has invested heavily in the plant over the past decade and offers the best wages and working conditions in this impoverished region. Recently the host nation's parliamentary democracy was overthrown in a military coup. The new president has assured you that your plant can continue to operate without government interference. At the same time, he is moving aggressively against his opponents by shutting down newspapers, jailing dissidents, and placing former government officials under house arrest. Upcoming trials could mean lengthy sentences for the accused and, in some cases, death sentences.

Should your plant continue to operate under the new regime? What recommendation would you make to company officials at company headquarters?

Tainted Amnesty

The dictator of a small, war-torn African nation has agreed to go into exile and let opposition forces take power. His departure will not only end the fighting but also open the door to international humanitarian aid and investment for a country that has been largely reduced to rubble. The dictator will leave only if the international community assures him that he will never be prosecuted by an international court of law for crimes committed during his regime. News sources report that thousands of citizens were kidnapped and killed during his reign of terror. He will be relocating with millions looted from the state treasury.

As a diplomat, would you encourage your national government to agree to the dictator's demand for amnesty?

Notes

1. Mor Barak, M. E. (2005). *Toward a globally inclusive workplace.* Thousand Oaks, CA: Sage; Konrad, A. M. (2006). Leveraging workplace diversity in organizations. *Organization Management Journal, 3,* 164–189; Scully, S. (2001, March 13). Minorities gain ground on whites in '00 census. *The Washington Times,* p. A1. Retrieved December 13, 2007, from Newspaper Source database.

2. Cox, T. (1993). *Cultural diversity in organizations: Theory, research and practice.* San Francisco: Berrett-Koehler; Cox, T. (2001). *Creating the multicultural organization: A strategy for capturing the power of diversity.* San Francisco: Jossey-Bass.

3. See the following:

> Hays-Thomas, R. (2004). Why now? The contemporary focus on managing diversity. In M. S. Stockdale & F. J. Crosby (Eds.), *The psychology and management of workplace diversity* (pp. 3–30). Malden, MA: Blackwell.
>
> Konrad.
>
> Koonce, R. (2001, December). Redefining diversity. *Training and Development,* pp. 22–28.
>
> Kossek, E. E., Lobel, S. A., & Brown, J. (2006). Human resource strategies to manage workplace diversity: Examining the "business case." In A. M. Konrad, P. Prasad, & J. K. Pringle (Eds.), *Handbook of workplace diversity* (pp. 53–74). London: Sage.
>
> Mor Barak.

4. Drummond, T. (2000, April 3). Coping with cops. *Time,* pp. 72–73.

5. Brown, R. (1995). *Prejudice: Its social psychology.* Oxford, UK: Blackwell; Fiske, S. T. (1998). Stereotyping, prejudice, and discrimination. In D. T. Gilbert, S. T. Fiske, & G. Lindzey (Eds.), *The handbook of social psychology* (Vol. 2, pp. 357–411). Boston: McGraw-Hill.

6. Gudykunst, W. B., & Kim, Y. Y. (1997). *Communicating with strangers: An approach to intercultural communication* (3rd ed.). New York: McGraw-Hill; Gudykunst, W. B., Ting-Toomey, S., Suydweeks, S., & Stewart, L. P. (1995). *Building bridges: Interpersonal skills for a changing world.* Boston: Houghton Mifflin.

7. Cox (1993), Ch. 13.

8. Langer, E. J. (1989). *Mindfulness.* Reading, MA: Addison-Wesley.

9. Opotow, S. (1990). Moral exclusion and injustice: An introduction. *Journal of Social Issues, 46*(1), 1–20.

10. Mor Barak; Cox (2001); Morrison, A. M. (1996). *The new leaders: Guidelines on leadership diversity in America.* San Francisco: Jossey-Bass; Konrad.

11. Tavis, T. (2000). The globalization phenomenon and multinational corporate developmental responsibility. In O. F. Williams (Ed.), *Global codes of conduct: An idea whose time has come* (pp. 13–36). Notre Dame, IN: University of Notre Dame Press; Dunning, J. H. (2003). Overview. In J. H. Dunning (Ed.), *Making globalization good: The moral challenges of global capitalism* (pp. 11–40). Oxford, UK: Oxford University Press.

12. Muzaffar, C. (2002). Conclusion. In P. F. Knitter & C. Muzaffar (Eds.), *Subverting greed: Religious perspectives on the global economy* (pp. 154–172). Maryknoll, NY: Orbis; Ritzer, G. (2004). *The globalization of nothing.* Thousand Oaks, CA: Pine Forge; Dunning, J. H. (2000). Whither global capitalism? *Global Focus, 12,* 117–136.

13. Friedman, T. (2000). *The Lexus and the olive tree* (Expanded ver.). New York: Anchor.

14. Melloan, G. (2004, January 6). Feeling the muscle of the multinationals. *Wall Street Journal,* p. A19. Retrieved April 11, 2008, from ProQuest Newspaper database.

15. Statistics taken from Singer, P. (2002). *One world: The ethics of globalization.* New Haven, CT: Yale University Press.

16. Muzaffar.

17. Richter, J. (2001). *Holding corporations accountable: Corporate conduct, international codes and citizen action.* London: Zed.

18. Karim, A. (2000, June 23). Globalization, ethics, and AIDS vaccines. *Science,* pp. 21–29.

19. Manby, B. (1999). The role and responsibility of oil multinationals in Nigeria. *Journal of International Affairs, 53,* 281–301; Murphy, C. (1999, March 15). The most twisted economy on the planet. *Fortune,* pp. 42–43; Donaldson, T., & Dunfee, T. W. (1999). *Ties that bind: A social contracts approach to business ethics.* Boston: Harvard Business School Press.

20. Ethicist Peter Singer (2002) believes that loyalty to traditional nation-state is obsolete.

21. Solomon, C. M. (2001). Put your ethics to a global test. In M. H. Albrecht (Ed.), *International HRM: Managing diversity in the workplace* (pp. 329–335). Oxford, UK: Blackwell.

22. Donaldson, T. (1996, September–October). Values in tension: Ethics away from home. *Harvard Business Review,* pp. 48–57.

23. Carroll, S. J., & Gannon, M. J. (1997). *Ethical dimensions of management.* Thousand Oaks, CA: Sage.

24. Rogers, E. M., & Steinfatt, T. M. (1999). *Intercultural communication.* Prospect Heights, IL: Waveland, p. 79.

25. Hofstede, G. (1984). *Culture's consequences.* Beverly Hills, CA: Sage; Hofstede, G. (1991). *Cultures and organizations: Software of the mind.* London: McGraw-Hill.

26. Hofstede, G. (2001). Difference and danger: Cultural profiles of nations and limits to tolerance. In M. H. Albrecht (Ed.), *International HRM: Managing diversity in the workplace* (pp. 9–23). Oxford, UK: Blackwell.

27. Carroll and Gannon.

28. Javidan, M., & House, R. J. (2001). Cultural acumen for the global manager: Lessons from Project GLOBE. *Organizational Dynamics, 29,* 289–305; House, R. J., Hange, P. J., Javidan, M., Dorfman, P. W., & Gupta, V. (Eds.). (2004). *Culture, leadership, and organizations: The GLOBE study of 62 societies.* Thousand Oaks, CA: Sage.

29. Den Hartog, D. N., House, R. J., Hange, P. U., Ruiz-Quintanilla, S. A., & Dorfman, P. W. (1999). Culture-specific and cross-culturally generalizable implicit leadership theories: Are attributes of charismatic/transformational leadership universally endorsed? *Leadership Quarterly, 10,* 219–257.

30. Resick, C. J., Hange, P. J., Dickson, M. W., & Mitchelson, J. K. (2006). A cross-cultural examination of the endorsement of ethical leadership. *Journal of Business Ethics, 63,* 345–359.

31. Talbot, M. (1999). Against relativism. In J. M. Halstead & T. H. McLaughlin (Eds.), *Education in morality* (pp. 206–217). London: Routledge.

32. Kung, H. (1998). *A global ethic for global politics and economics.* New York: Oxford University Press; Kung, H. (1999). A global ethic in an age of globalization. In G. Enderle (Ed.), *International business ethics: Challenges and approaches* (pp. 19–127). Notre Dame, IN: University of Notre Dame Press; Kung, H. (2003). An ethical framework for the global market economy. In J. H. Dunning (Ed.), *Making globalization good: The moral challenges of global capitalism* (pp. 146–158). Oxford, UK: Oxford University Press.

33. Kidder, R. M. (1994). *Shared values for a troubled world: Conversations with men and women of conscience.* San Francisco: Jossey-Bass.

34. Kale, D. W. (1994). Peace as an ethic for intercultural communication. In L. A. Samovar & R. E. Porter (Eds.), *Intercultural communication: A reader* (7th ed., pp. 435–444). Belmont, CA: Wadsworth.

35. Paine, L., Deshpande, R., Margolis, J. D., & Bettcher, K. E. (2005, December). Up to code: Does your company's conduct meet world-class standards? *Harvard Business Review,* pp. 122–133.

36. Caux Round Table. (2000). Appendix 26: The Caux principles. In O. F. Williams (Ed.), *Global codes of conduct: An idea whose time has come* (pp. 384–388). Notre Dame, IN: Notre Dame University Press.

37. Donaldson, T., & Dunfee, T. W. (1994). Toward a unified conception of business ethics: Integrative social contracts theory. *Academy of Management Review, 19,* 252–284; Donaldson & Dunfee (1999).

Epilogue

It's only fair to tell you fellows now that we're not likely to come out of this.

—Captain Joshua James, speaking to
his crew during the hurricane of 1888

Captain Joshua James (1826–1902) is the "patron saint" of the search and rescue unit of the U.S. Coast Guard. James led rescue efforts to save sailors who crashed off the shores of Massachusetts. When word came of shipwreck, James and his volunteer crew would launch a large rowboat into heavy seas. James would keep an eye out for the stricken vessel as his men rowed, steering with a large wooden rudder. During his career, he never lost a crewman or a shipwrecked person who had been alive when picked up. The captain's finest hour came during a tremendous storm in late November 1888. Over a 24-hour period, James (62 years old at the time) and his men rescued 29 sailors from five ships.

Philip Haillie, who writes about James in his book *Tales of Good and Evil, Help and Harm,* argues that we can understand James's courageous leadership only as an extension of his larger community. James lived in the town of Hull, a tiny, impoverished community on the Massachusetts coast. Most coastal villages of the time profited from shipwrecks. Beachcombers would scavenge everything from the cargo to the sunken ship's timbers and anchors. Unscrupulous people called "mooncussers" would lure boats aground. On dark, moonless nights, they would hang a lantern from a donkey and trick sea captains into sailing on to the rocks.

Unlike their neighbors up and down the coast, the people of Hull tried to stop the carnage. They built shelters for those who washed ashore, cared for the sick and injured, protested against shipping companies and insurers who sent inexperienced captains and crews into danger, and had their lifeboat always at the ready. During the storm of 1888, citizens burned their fences to light the way for Captain James, his crew, and victims alike. According to Haillie,

> Many of the other people of Hull tore up some picket fences near the crest of the hill and built a big fire that lit up the wreck and helped the lifesavers to avoid the flopping, slashing debris around the boat. The loose and broken spars of a ruined ship were one of the main dangers lifesavers had to face. But the sailors on the wrecked ship needed the firelight too. It showed them what the lifesavers were doing, and what they could do to help them. And it gave them hope: It showed them that they were not alone.[1]

The story of Captain James and his neighbors is a fitting end to this text. In their actions, they embodied many of the themes introduced earlier: character; values; good versus evil; moral action; altruism; cooperation; transformational, authentic, and servant leadership; social responsibility; and purpose. The captain, who lost his mother and baby sister in a shipwreck, had one mission in life: saving lives at sea. Following his lead, residents took on nearly insurmountable challenges at great personal cost. They recognized that helpers often need help. By burning their fences, these followers (living in extremely modest conditions) cast a light that literally made the difference between life and death. But like other groups of leaders and followers, they were far from perfect. In the winter hurricane season, the village did its best to save lives. In the summer, pickpockets (helped by a corrupt police force) preyed on those who visited the town's resorts. The dark side of Hull shouldn't diminish the astonishing feats of Captain James and his neighbors, however. Haillie calls what James did during the storm of 1888 an example of "moral beauty."

> And moral beauty happens when someone carves out a place for compassion in a largely ruthless universe. It happened in the French village of Le Chambon during the war, and it happened in and near the American village of Hull during the long lifetime of Joshua James.
>
> It happens, and it fails to happen, in almost every event of people's lives together—in streets, in kitchens, in bedrooms, in workplaces, in wars. But sometimes it happens in a way that engrosses the mind and captivates memory. Sometimes it happens in such a way that the people who make it happen seem to unify the universe around themselves like powerful magnets. Somehow they seem to redeem us all from deathlike indifference. They carve a place for caring in the very middle of the quiet and loud storms of uncaring that surround—and eventually kill—us all.[2]

Notes

1. Haillie, P. (1997). *Tales of good and evil, help and harm.* New York: HarperCollins, p. 146.
2. Haillie, p. 173.

References

Abrahams, J. (2007). *101 mission statements from top companies.* Berkeley, CA: Ten Speed Press.

Adams, G. B., & Balfour, D. L. (1998). *Unmasking administrative evil.* Thousand Oaks, CA: Sage.

Adams, J. S., Taschian, A., & Shore, T. H. (2001). Codes of ethics as signals for ethical behavior. *Journal of Business Ethics, 29,* 199–211.

Adler, J. (2002, December 23). A cardinal offense. *Newsweek,* p. 5.

Adler, N. J. (2002). *From Boston to Beijing: Managing with a world view.* Cincinnati: South-Western.

Air Force's top officers say academy problems endemic. (2003, June 2). *The Colorado Springs Gazette.* Retrieved July 21, 2003, from http://web12.epnet.com/citation

Alderman, H. (1997). By virtue of a virtue. In D. Statman (Ed.), *Virtue ethics* (pp. 145–164). Washington, DC: Georgetown University Press.

Alexander, C. (1999). *The* Endurance: *Shackleton's legendary Antarctic expedition.* New York: Alfred A. Knopf.

Alford, C. F. (1997). *What evil means to us.* Ithaca, NY: Cornell University Press.

Allport, G. (1961). *Pattern and growth in personality.* New York: Holt, Rinehart & Winston.

Amichai-Hamburger, Y. (2003). Understanding social loafing. In A. Sagie, S. Stashevsky, & M. Koslowsky (Eds.), *Misbehaviour and dysfunctional attitudes in organizations* (pp. 79–102). New York: Palgrave Macmillan.

Anand, V., Ashforth, B. E., & Joshi, M. (2004). Business as usual: The acceptance and perpetuation of corruption in organizations. *Academy of Management Executive, 18,* 39–53.

Anderssen, E., & Aphonso, C. (2007, September 15). Should our daughter get the needle? *The Globe and Mail,* p. A1+. Retrieved October 8, 2007, from LexisNexis Academic database.

Arendt, H. (1964). *Eichmann in Jerusalem: A report on the banality of evil.* New York: Viking.

Arias, D. C. (2006, August). New vaccine for cervical cancer virus raises access questions. *Nation's Health,* pp. 1, 41. Retrieved October 8, 2007, from LexisNexis Academic database.

Aristotle. (350 B.C.E./1962). *Nichomachean ethics* (Martin Ostwald, Trans.). Indianapolis, IN: Bobbs-Merrill.

Ashmos, D. P., & Duchon, D. (2000). Spirituality at work: A conceptualization and measure. *Journal of Management Inquiry, 9,* 134–145.

Aspinwall, L. G., & Staudinger, U. M. (Eds.). (2002). *A psychology of human strengths: Fundamental questions about future directions for a positive psychology.* Washington, DC: American Psychological Association.

Austin Peterson, L. (2007, January 30). Merck lobbies to require cervical-cancer vaccine for school girls. *The Associated Press State & Local Wire.* Retrieved March 13, 2007, from LexisNexis Academic database.

Avolio, B. J., & Gardner, W. L. (2005). Authentic leadership development: Getting to the root of positive forms of leadership. *Leadership Quarterly, 16,* 315–340.

Avolio, B. J., Gardner, W. L., Walumbwa, F. O., Luthans, F., & May, D. R. (2004). Unlocking the mask: A look at the process by which authentic leaders impact follower attitudes and behaviors. *Leadership Quarterly, 15,* 801–823.

Avolio, B. J., & Locke, E. E. (2002). Contrasting different philosophies of leader motivation: Altruism versus egoism. *Leadership Quarterly, 13,* 169–191.

Barker, L., Johnson, P., & Watson, K. (1991). The role of listening in managing interpersonal and group conflict. In D. Borisoff & M. Purdy (Eds.), *Listening in everyday life: A personal and professional approach* (pp. 139–157). Lanham, MD: University Press of America.

Baron, R. A. (2004). Workplace aggression and violence: Insights from basic research. In R. W. Griffin & A. M. O'Leary-Kelly (Eds.), *The dark side of organizational behavior* (pp. 23–61). San Francisco: Jossey-Bass.

Barrett, J. (2003, July 18). Q&A: Clearly there is a problem here. *Newsweek* (Web exclusive). Retrieved September 2, 2003, from LexisNexis Academic database.

Barry, V. (1978). *Personal and social ethics: Moral problems with integrated theory.* Belmont, CA: Wadsworth.

Bartholomew, C. S., & Gustafson, S. B. (1998). Perceived leader integrity scale: An instrument for assessing employee perceptions of leader integrity. *Leadership Quarterly, 9,* 143–144.

Bass, B. M. (1990). *Bass & Stogdill's handbook of leadership* (3rd ed.). New York: Free Press.

Bass, B. M. (1995). The ethics of transformational leadership. In J. Ciulla (Ed.), *Ethics: The heart of leadership* (pp. 169–192). Westport, CT: Praeger.

Bass, B. M. (1996). *A new paradigm of leadership: An inquiry into transformational leadership.* Alexandria, VA: U.S. Army Research Institute for the Behavioral and Social Sciences.

Bass, B. M., & Avolio, B. J. (1993). Transformational leadership: A response to critiques. In M. M. Chemers & R. Ayman (Eds.), *Leadership theory and research: Perspectives and directions* (pp. 49–80). San Diego: Academic Press.

Bass, B. M., Avolio, B. J., Jung, D. I., & Berson, Y. (2003). Predicting unit performance by assessing transformational and transactional leadership. *Journal of Applied Psychology, 88,* 207–218.

Bass, B. M., & Steidlmeier, P. (1999). Ethics, character, and authentic transformational leadership behavior. *Leadership Quarterly, 10,* 181–217.

Batson, C. D., Van Lange, P. A. M., Ahmad, N., & Lishner, D. A. (2003). Altruism and helping behavior. In M. A. Hogg & J. Cooper (Eds.), *The Sage handbook of social psychology* (pp. 279–295). London: Sage.

Bazar, E. (2005, December 27). Advertisers catch the school bus: Signs generate cash, criticism for local districts. *USA Today,* p. 3A.

Bazerman, M. H. (1986). *Management in managerial decision making.* New York: Wiley.

Bedian, A. G. (2007). Even if the tower is "ivory," it isn't "white": Understanding the consequences of faculty cynicism. *Academy of Management Learning and Education, 6,* 9–32.

Bell, M. A. (1974). The effects of substantive and affective conflict in problem-solving groups. *Speech Monographs, 41,* 19–23.

Bell, M. A. (1979). The effects of substantive and affective verbal conflict on the quality of decisions of small problem-solving groups. *Central States Speech Journal, 3,* 75–82.

Bellah, N., Madsen, R., Sullivan, W. M., Swidler, A., & Tipton, S. M. (1991). *The good society.* New York: Vintage.

Belmonte, K. (2007). *William Wilberforce: A hero for humanity.* Grand Rapids, MI: Zondervan.

Bennis, W., & Nanus, B. (2003). *Leaders: Strategies for taking charge.* New York: Harper Business Essentials.

Bennis, W. G., & Thomas, R. J. (2002). *Geeks and geezers: How era, values, and defining moments shape leaders.* Boston: Harvard Business School Press.

Bentham, J. (1948). *An introduction to the principles of morals and legislation.* New York: Hafner.

Berry, J. (2007, July 18). A cardinal's shameless struggle for survival. *The Boston Globe,* p. A15. Retrieved September 23, 2007, from LexisNexis Academic database.

Bing, S. (2000). *What would Machiavelli do? The ends justify the meanness.* New York: HarperBusiness.

Bird, F. B. (1996). *The muted conscience: Moral silence and the practice of ethics in business.* Westport, CT: Quorum.

Biz Briefs. (2004, January 5). *Television Week.* Retrieved August 2, 2007, from LexisNexis Academic database.

Block, P. (1996). *Stewardship: Choosing service over self-interest.* San Francisco: Berrett-Koehler.

Block, S., Chu, K., & Edelman, A. (2007, April 25). How students borrow for college could soon change. *USA Today,* p. 1B. Retrieved October 8, 2007, from LexisNexis Academic database.

Booker, K. (2001, May 28). The chairman of the board looks back. *Fortune,* pp. 63–76.

Bordas, J. (1995). Becoming a servant-leader: The personal development path. In L. Spears (Ed.), *Reflections on leadership* (pp. 149–160). New York: Wiley.

Boston Globe Investigative Staff. (2002). *Betrayal: The crisis in the Catholic Church.* Boston: Little, Brown.

Brissett, D., & Edgley, C. (Eds.). (1990). The dramaturgical perspective. In D. Brissett & C. Edgley (Eds.), *Life as theater: A dramaturgical sourcebook* (2nd ed., pp. 1–46). New York: Aldine de Gruyter.

Brokaw, C. (2007, January 9). S. Dakota plans to provide free cervical cancer vaccine. *The Associated Press State & Local Wire.* Retrieved March 13, 2007, from LexisNexis Academic database.

Brown, D. J., Scott, K. A., & Lewis, H. (2004). Information processing and leadership. In J. Antonakis, A. T. Cianciolo, & Sternberg, R. J. (Eds.), *The nature of leadership* (pp. 125–147). Thousand Oaks, CA: Sage.

Brown, J. (1995). Dialogue: Capacities and stories. In S. Chawla & J. Renesch (Eds.), *Learning organizations: Developing cultures for tomorrow's workplace* (pp. 153–164). Portland, OR: Productivity Press.

Brown, M. E., & Trevino, L. K. (2006). Ethical leadership: A review and future directions. *Leadership Quarterly, 17,* 595–616.

Brown, M. E., Trevino, L. K., & Harrison, D. (2005). Ethical leadership: A social learning perspective for construct development and testing. *Organizational Behavior and Human Decision Processes, 97,* 117–134.

Brown, R. (1995). *Prejudice: Its social psychology.* Oxford, UK: Blackwell.

Brown, R. P. (2003). Measuring individual differences in the tendency to forgive: Construct validity and links with depression. *Personality and Social Psychology Bulletin, 29,* 759–771.

Bruhn, J. G. (2001). *Trust and the health of organizations.* New York: Kluwer/Plenum.

Buber, M. (1970). *I and thou.* (R. G. Smith, Trans.). New York: Charles Scribner's Sons.

Buchholz, R. A., & Rosenthal, S. B. (2005). Toward a conceptual framework for stakeholder theory. *Journal of Business Ethics, 58,* 137–148.

Burdick, G. (2007, September 16). Armed teachers? Just think about the scenarios. *The Oregonian,* p. D5.

Burling, S. (2006, September 19). Preparing for the world of business; Survey: M.B.A. students more likely to cheat. *The Philadelphia Inquirer,* p. A01. Retrieved December 4, 2007, from LexisNexis Academic database.

Burnett, J. (2002, April 22). James Burnett looks at how the Catholic Church might salvage its tainted reputation. *PR Week,* p. 17.

Burns, J. M. (1978). *Leadership.* New York: Harper & Row.

Burns, J. M. (2003). *Transforming leadership: A new pursuit of happiness.* New York: Atlantic Monthly Press.

Burrows, P. (2003). *Backfire: Carly Fiorina's high stake battle for the soul of Hewlett Packard.* New York: Wiley.

Buss, A. H. (1961). *The psychology of aggression.* New York: John Wiley & Sons.

Byrne, J. (1999). *The notorious career of Al Dunlap in the era of profit-at-any-price.* New York: HarperCollins.

Cadbury, A. (1987, September–October). Ethical managers make their own rules. *Harvard Business Review,* pp. 69–73.

Camp, R. C. (1989). *Benchmarking: The search for industry best practices that lead to superior performance.* Milwaukee, WI: Quality Press.

Campaign contributions from big oil sharply influenced votes on clean energy. (2006, November 1). *U.S. Newswire.* Retrieved June 19, 2007, from LexisNexis Academic database.

Cancer vaccines. (2007, April 13). *Drug Week.* Retrieved October 8, 2007, from LexisNexis Academic database.

Carroll, S. J., & Gannon, M. J. (1997). *Ethical dimensions of management.* Thousand Oaks, CA: Sage.

Carson, T. (2007, September 20). Pistol-packing teacher sues. *Herald Sun,* p. 41. Retrieved October 27, 2007, from LexisNexis Academic database.

Carver, C. S., & Scheier, M. F. (2005). Optimism. In C. R. Snyder & S. J. Lopez (Eds.), *Handbook of positive psychology* (pp. 231–243). Oxford, UK: Oxford University Press.

Carville, J. (2000). *Stickin': The case for loyalty.* New York: Simon & Schuster.

Casarjian, R. (1992). *Forgiveness: A bold choice for a peaceful heart.* New York: Bantam.

Cavanagh, G. F., & Moberg, D. J. (1999). The virtue of courage within the organization. In M. L. Pava & P. Primeaux (Eds.), *Research in ethical issues in organizations* (Vol. 1, pp. 1–25). Stamford, CT: JAI Press.

Caux Round Table. (2000). Appendix 26: The Caux principles. In O. F. Williams (Ed.), *Global codes of conduct: An idea whose time has come* (pp. 384–388). Notre Dame, IN: Notre Dame University Press.

Center for the Study of Ethics in the Professions at Illinois Institute of Technology. Retrieved December 13, 2007, from http://ethics.iit.edu/codes

Chaleff, I. (2003). *The courageous follower: Standing up to & for our leaders* (2nd ed.). San Francisco: Berrett-Koehler.

Chan, A., Hannah, S. T., & Gardner, W. L. (2005). Veritable authentic leadership: Emergence, functioning, and impacts. In W. L. Gardner, B. J. Avolio, & F. O. Walumbwa (Eds.), *Authentic leadership theory and practice: Origins, effects and development* (pp. 3–41). Amsterdam: Elsevier.

Chan, W. (1963). *The way of Lao Tzu.* Indianapolis, IN: Bobbs-Merrill.

Chang, K. (2007, August 20). Caution over damage to *Endeavour* illustrates changes at space agency. *The New York Times,* p. A12. Retrieved November 22, 2007, from LexisNexis Academic database.

Cheating is a personal foul. (n.d.). Retrieved September 25, 2001, from http://www.nocheating.org/adcouncil/research/cheatingbackgrounder.html

Chen, A., Lawson, R. B., Gordon, L. R., & McIntosh, B. (1996). Groupthink: Deciding with the leader and the devil. *Psychological Record, 46,* 581–590.

Chrislip, D. D. (2002). *The collaborative leadership fieldbook.* San Francisco: Jossey-Bass.

Chrislip, D. D., & Larson, C. E. (1994). *Collaborative leadership: How citizens and civic leaders can make a difference.* San Francisco: Jossey-Bass.

Christians, C. G., Rotzell, K. B., & Fackler, M. (1999). *Media ethics* (3rd ed.). New York: Longman.

Cissna, K. N., & Anderson, R. (1994). Communication and the ground of dialogue. In R. Anderson, K. N. Cissna, & R. C. Arnett (Eds.), *The reach of dialogue: Confirmation, voice, and community* (pp. 9–3). Cresskill, NJ: Hampton.

Ciulla, J. (Ed.). (2004). *Ethics: The heart of leadership.* Westport, CT: Praeger.

Ciulla, J. B. (2004). Leadership ethics: Mapping the territory. In J. B. Ciulla (Ed.), *Ethics: The heart of leadership* (pp. 3–24). Westport, CT: Praeger.

Clark, K. (2001, December 31). Nothing but the plane truth. *U.S. News & World Report.* Retrieved October 3, 2007, from Business Source Complete database.

The Coca-Cola Code of Business Conduct. Retrieved April 3, 2008, from http://www.thecoca-colacompany.com/ourcompany/business_conduct.html

Cohen, D. V. (1993). Creating and maintaining ethical work climates: Anomie in the workplace and implications for managing change. *Business Ethics Quarterly, 3,* 343–358.

Cohen, L. R., & Undis, D. J. (2006, March/April). New solution to the organ shortage. *Saturday Evening Post.* Retrieved January 7, 2008, from Academic Source Premier database.

Colby, A., & Damon, W. (1992). *Some do care: Contemporary lives of moral commitment.* New York: Free Press.

Colby, A., & Damon, W. (1995). The development of extraordinary moral commitment. In M. Killen & D. Hart (Eds.), *Morality in everyday life: Developmental perspectives* (pp. 342–369). Cambridge, UK: Cambridge University Press.

Colle, Z. (2007, April 21). Evidence of cover-up key to Tillman hearings. *The San Francisco Chronicle,* p. A1. Retrieved June 5, 2007, from LexisNexis Academic database.

Colle, Z., & Collier, R. (2007, April 25). Lawmakers see cover-up, vow to probe Tillman death. *The San Francisco Chronicle*, p. A1. Retrieved June 5, 2007, from LexisNexis Academic database.

Collier, R., & Epstein, E. (2007, March 27). Tillmans assail Pentagon report. *The San Francisco Chronicle*, p. A1. Retrieved June 5, 2007, from LexisNexis Academic database.

Collins, J. (2001). *Good to great*. New York: HarperBusiness.

Collins, J. (2001, January). Level 5 leadership: The triumph of humility and fierce resolve. *Harvard Business Review*, pp. 67–76.

Collins, J. C., & Porras, J. I. (1996, September–October). Building your company's vision. *Harvard Business Review*, pp. 65–77.

Comte-Sponville, A. (2001). *A small treatise on the great virtues: The uses of philosophy in everyday life*. New York: Metropolitan.

Connelly, S., Helton-Fauth, W., & Mumford, M. D. (2004). A managerial in-basket study of the impact of trait emotions on ethical choice. *Journal of Business Ethics, 51*, 245–267.

Conrad, C., & Poole, M. S. (1998). *Strategic organizational communication: Into the twenty-first century* (4th ed.). Fort Worth, TX: Harcourt Brace.

Cooper, H. (2007, April 13). Darfur collides the Olympics, and China yields. *The New York Times*, p. A1. Retrieved September 7, 2007, from LexisNexis Academic database.

Cooper, C. D., Scandura, T. A., & Schriesheim, C. A. (2005). Looking forward but learning from our past: Potential challenges to developing authentic leadership theory and authentic leaders. *Leadership Quarterly, 16*, 475–493.

Cooper, S. (2004). *Corporate social performance: A stakeholder approach*. Burlington, VT: Ashgate.

Cooperman, A. (2003, July 19). Catholic bishops look for leadership: Abuse scandal reshaping hierarchy. *The Washington Post*, p. A7.

Cornwell, R. (2007, April 26). Secrets and lies: How war heroes returned to haunt Pentagon. *The Independent* (London). Retrieved June 5, 2007, from LexisNexis Academic database.

Countryman, A. (2001, December 7). Leadership key ingredient in ethics recipe, experts say. *The Chicago Tribune*, pp. B1, B6.

Covey, S. (1989). *The seven habits of highly effective people*. New York: Simon & Schuster.

Cox, T. (1993). *Cultural diversity in organizations: Theory, research and practice*. San Francisco: Berrett-Koehler.

Cox, T. (2001). *Creating the multicultural organization: A strategy for capturing the power of diversity*. San Francisco: Jossey-Bass.

Craigie, F. C. (1999). The spirit and work: Observations about spirituality and organizational life. *Journal of Psychology and Christianity, 18*, 43–53.

Crosariol, B. (2005, November 21). The diminishing allure of rock-star executives. *Globe and Mail Update*. Retrieved June 5, 2007, from LexisNexis Academic database.

Cullen, J. B., Parboteeah, K. P., & Victor, B. (2003). The effects of ethical climates on organizational commitment: A two-study analysis. *Journal of Business Ethics, 46*, 127–141.

Cullen, J. B., Victor, B., & Bronson, J. W. (1993). The ethical climate questionnaire: An assessment of its development and validity. *Psychological Reports, 73*, 667–674.

Czubaroff, J. (2000). Dialogical rhetoric: An application of Martin Buber's philosophy of dialogue. *Quarterly Journal of Speech, 2*, 168–189.

Darley, J. M. (1996). How organizations socialize individuals into evildoing. In D. M. Messick & A. E. Tenbrunsel (Eds.), *Codes of conduct: Behavioral research into business ethics* (pp. 12–43). New York: Russell Sage Foundation.

Darley, J. M. (2001). The dynamics of authority influence in organizations and the unintended action consequences. In J. M. Darley, D. M. Messick, & T. R. Tyler (Eds.), *Social influences on ethical behavior in organizations* (pp. 37–52). Mahwah, NJ: Erlbaum.

Day, L. A. (2003). *Ethics in media communications: Cases & controversies* (4th ed.). Belmont, CA: Wadsworth/Thompson.

Dean, J. W., Brandes, P., & Dharwadkar, R. (1998). Organizational cynicism. *Academy of Management Review, 23,* 341–352.

De George, R. T. (1995). *Business ethics* (4th ed.). Englewood Cliffs, NJ: Prentice Hall.

DeGroot, T., Kiker, D. S., & Cross, T. C. (2000). A meta-analysis to review organizational outcomes related to charismatic leadership. *Canadian Journal of Administrative Sciences, 17,* 356–371.

Den Hartog, D. N., House, R. J., Hanges, P. U., Ruiz-Quintanilla, S. A., & Dorfman, P. W. (1999). Culture-specific and cross-culturally generalizable implicit leadership theories: Are attributes of charismatic/transformational leadership universally endorsed? *Leadership Quarterly, 10,* 219–257.

DePree, M. (1989). *Leadership is an art.* New York: Doubleday.

DePree, M. (2003). Servant-leadership: Three things necessary. In L. C. Spears & M. Lawrence (Eds.), *Focus on leadership: Servant-leadership for the 21st century.* New York: Wiley.

Deresky, H. (2003). *International management: Managing across borders and cultures.* Upper Saddle River, NJ: Prentice Hall.

DiBella, A., & Nevis, E. C. (1998). *How organizations learn: An integrated strategy for building learning capability.* San Francisco: Jossey-Bass.

DiBella, A. J., Nevis, E. C., & Gould, J. M. (1996). Organizational learning as a core capability. In B. Moingeon & A. Edmondson (Eds.), *Organizational learning and competitive advantage* (pp. 38–55). London: Sage.

Diboye, R. L., & Halverson, S. K. (2004). Subtle (and not so subtle) discrimination in organizations. In R. W. Griffin & A. M. O'Leary-Kelly (Eds.), *The dark side of organizational behavior* (pp. 404–425). San Francisco: Jossey-Bass.

Dirks, K. T. (1999). The effects of interpersonal trust on work group performance. *Journal of Applied Psychology, 84,* 445–455.

Donaldson, T. (1996, September–October). Values in tension: Ethics away from home. *Harvard Business Review,* pp. 48–57.

Donaldson, T., & Dunfee, T. W. (1994). Toward a unified conception of business ethics: Integrative social contracts theory. *Academy of Management Review, 19,* 252–284.

Donaldson, T., & Dunfee, T. W. (1999). *Ties that bind: A social contracts approach to business ethics.* Boston: Harvard Business School Press.

Donaldson, T., & Preston, L. E. (1995). The stakeholder theory of the corporation: Concepts, evidence, and implications. *Academy of Management Review, 20,* 65–91.

Dreher, R. (2002, January 15). Boston travesty. *National Review* [Online]. Retrieved November 15, 2003, from LexisNexis Academic database.

Driscoll, J. W. (1978). Trust and participation in organizational decision making as predictors of satisfaction. *Academy of Management Journal, 21,* 44–56.

Drummond, T. (2000, April 3). Coping with cops. *Time,* pp. 72–73.

Duchon, D., & Plowman, D. A. (2005). Nurturing the spirit at work: Impact on work unit performance. *Leadership Quarterly, 16,* 807–833.

Dukerich, J. M., Nichols, M. L., Elm, D. R., & Voltrath, D. A. (1990). Moral reasoning in groups: Leaders make a difference. *Human Relations, 43,* 473–493.

Dunning, J. H. (2000). Whither global capitalism? *Global Focus, 12,* 117–136.

Dunning, J. H. (2003). Overview. In J. H. Dunning (Ed.), *Making globalization good: The moral challenges of global capitalism* (pp. 11–40). Oxford, UK: Oxford University Press.

Eberly, D. E. (1994). *Building a community of citizens: Civil society in the 21st century.* Lanham, MD: University Press of America.

Einhorn, B. (2006, August 11). Search engines censured for censorship. *Business Week Online.* Retrieved December 20, 2007, from Business Source Complete database.

Eisenberg, N. (2000). Emotion, regulation, and moral development. *Annual Review of Psychology, 51,* 665–697.

Elangovan, A. R., & Shapiro, D. L. (1998). Betrayal of trust in organizations. *Academy of Management Review, 23,* 547–566.

Ellenwood, S. (2006). Revisiting character education: From McGuffey to narratives. *Journal of Education, 187,* 21–43.

Enright, R. D., Freedman, S., & Rique, J. (1998). The psychology of interpersonal forgiveness. In R. D. Enright & J. North (Eds.), *Exploring forgiveness* (pp. 46–62). Madison: University of Wisconsin Press.

Enright, R. D., & Gassin, E. A. (1992). Forgiveness: A developmental view. *Journal of Moral Education, 21,* 99–114.

Esser, J. K. (1998). Alive and well after 25 years: A review of groupthink research. *Organizational Behavior and Human Decision Processes, 73,* 116–141.

Etzel, B. (2002, July 1). WorldCom's wrong number. *Investment Dealers' Digest,* pp. 9–12. Retrieved July 21, 2003, from LexisNexis Academic database.

Etzioni, A. (1993). *The spirit of community: The reinvention of American society.* New York: Touchstone.

Etzioni, A. (Ed.). (1995). *New communitarian thinking: Persons, virtues, institutions, and communities.* Charlottesville: University Press of Virginia.

Etzioni, A. (Ed.). (1995). *Rights and the common good: A communitarian perspective.* New York: St. Martin's.

Etzioni, A. (1996). *The new golden rule: Community and morality in a democratic society.* New York: Basic Books.

Fairholm, G. W. (1996). Spiritual leadership: Fulfilling whole-self needs at work. *Leadership & Organization Development Journal, 17*(5), 11–17.

The fallen. (2003, January 13). *Business Week.* Retrieved August 2, 2007, from LexisNexis Academic database.

Farmer, P. (2007, September 4). Commentary. *Forbes.com.* Retrieved October 3, 2007, from LexisNexis Academic database.

Fiol, C. M., Harris, D., & House, R. J. (1999). Charismatic leadership: Strategies for effecting social change. *Leadership Quarterly, 1,* 449–482.

Fisher, R., & Ury, W. (1991). *Getting to yes* (2nd ed.). New York: Penguin.

Fisher, S. (2007, September). Flying off into the sunset. *Costco Connection,* pp. 17–19.

Fisher, W. (1987). *Human communication as narration: Toward a philosophy of reason, value, and action.* Columbia: University of South Carolina Press.

Fiske, S. T. (1993). Controlling other people: The impact of power on stereotyping. *American Psychologist, 48,* 621–628.

Fiske S. T. (1998). Stereotyping, prejudice, and discrimination. In D. T. Gilbert, S. T. Fiske, & G. Lindzey (Eds.), *The handbook of social psychology* (Vol. 2, pp. 357–411). Boston: McGraw-Hill.

Fitzpatrick, D. (2005, May 12). "Aw-shucks" president embodies Southwest style. *Pittsburgh Post-Gazette.* Retrieved October 3, 2007, from Newspaper Source database.

Fletcher, G. (1993). *Loyalty: An essay on the morality of relationships.* New York: Oxford University Press.

Flippen, A. R. (1999). Understanding groupthink from a self-regulatory perspective. *Small Group Research, 3,* 139–165.

Ford, C. V. (1996). *Lies! Lies! Lies! The psychology of deceit.* Washington, DC: American Psychiatric Press.

Foster, R. J. (1978). *Celebration of discipline: The path to spiritual growth.* New York: Harper & Row.

Freedman, S., Enright, R. D., & Knutson, J. (2005). A progress report on the process model of forgiveness. In E. L. Worthington Jr. (Ed.), *Handbook of forgiveness* (pp. 393–406). New York: Routledge.

French, R. P., & Raven, B. (1959). The bases of social power. In D. Cartwright, *Studies in social power* (pp. 150–167). Ann Arbor: University of Michigan, Institute for Social Research.

Friedman, T. (2000). *The Lexus and the olive tree* (Expanded ver.). New York: Anchor.

Fritzsche, D. J. (2000). Ethical climates and the ethical dimension of decision making. *Journal of Business Ethics, 24,* 125–140.

Fromm, E. (1964). *The heart of man: Its genius for good and evil.* New York: Harper & Row.

Frosch, D. (2007, April 20). Ex-Chief at Quest found guilty. *The New York Times,* p. C1.

Fry, L. W. (2003). Toward a theory of spiritual leadership. *Leadership Quarterly, 14,* 693–727.

Fry, L. W., Vitucci, S., & Cedillo, M. (2005). Spiritual leadership and army transformation: Theory, measurement, and establishing a baseline. *Leadership Quarterly, 16,* 835–862.

Garcia-Zamor, J. C. (2003). Workplace spirituality and organizational performance. *Public Administration Review, 63,* 355–363.

Gardner, J. (1995). Building a responsive community. In A. Etzioni (Ed.), *Rights and the common good: The communitarian perspective* (pp. 167–178). New York: St. Martin's.

Gardner, W. L., Avolio, B. J., Luthans, F., May, D. R., & Walumbwa, F. O. (2005). "Can you see the real me?" A self-based model of authentic leader and follower development. *Leadership Quarterly, 16,* 343–372.

Garvin, D. A. (1993, July–August). Building a learning organization. *Harvard Business Review,* pp. 78–91.

Gaudine, A., & Thorne, L. (2001). Emotion and ethical decision-making in organizations. *Journal of Business Ethics, 31,* 175–187.

Gettleman, J. (2007, September 3). Chaos in Darfur on rise as Arabs fight with Arabs. *The New York Times,* p. A1. Retrieved September 8, 2007, from LexisNexis Academic database.

Giacalone, R. A., & Jurkiewicz, C. L. (2003). Right from wrong: The influence of spirituality on perceptions of unethical business activities. *Journal of Business Ethics, 46,* 85–97.

Giacalone, R. A., & Jurkiewicz, C. L. (2003). Toward a science of workplace spirituality. In R. A. Giacalone & C. L. Jurkiewicz (Eds.), *Handbook of workplace spirituality and organizational performance* (pp. 3–28). Armonk, NY: M.E. Sharpe.

Gibb, J. R. (1961). Defensive communication. *Journal of Communication, 11–12*, 141–148.

Gilbert, J. A., & Tang, T. L. (1998). An examination of organizational trust antecedents. *Public Personnel Management, 27*, 321–338.

Gilbert, N. (2003, August 22). Darkness in the Catholic confessional. *The New York Times Higher Education Supplement*, p. 18.

Gioia, D. A. (1992). Pinto fires and personal ethics: A script analysis of missed opportunities. *Journal of Business Ethics, 11*, 379–389.

Glanz, W. (2003, August 27). NASA ignored dangers to shuttle, panel says. *The Washington Times*, p. A1. Retrieved September 2, 2003, from LexisNexis Academic database.

Goff, S. (2007, May 30). Solo apologizes, but won't play for U.S. vs. Norway. *The Washington Post*, p. D05. Retrieved October 25, 2007, from LexisNexis Academic database.

Gold, J. (2005, December 22). Judge orders Lucent to pay $224 million to Winstar creditors. *Associated Press State & Local Wire*. Retrieved July 11, 2007, from LexisNexis Academic database.

Goldberg, M. (1997). Doesn't anybody read the Bible anymo'? In O. F. Williams (Ed.), *The moral imagination: How literature and films can stimulate ethical reflection in the business world* (pp. 19–32). Notre Dame, IN: Notre Dame Press.

Goodman, E. (2002, October 6). Freeze-frame nation. *The Oregonian*, p. C3.

Goodpaster, K. E. (1991). Business ethics and stakeholder analysis. *Business Ethics Quarterly, 1*, 53–27.

Gordon, M. (2006, June 9). Role of directors is piece of puzzle as scandal over stock options widens. *Associated Press Financial Wire*. Retrieved June 20, 2007, from LexisNexis Academic database.

Gordon, M. (2006, December 12). Toll of options timing scandal heavy in 2006; more cases expected next year. *Associated Press Financial Wire*. Retrieved June 20, 2007, from LexisNexis Academic database.

Gorovitz, S. (Ed.). (1971). *Utilitarianism: Text and critical essays*. Indianapolis, IN: Bobbs-Merrill.

Gouran, D. S., & Hirokawa, R. Y. (1986). Counteractive functions of communication in effective group decision making. In R. Y. Hirokawa & M. S. Poole (Eds.), *Communication and group decision making* (pp. 81–89). Beverly Hills, CA: Sage.

Gouran, D. S., Hirokawa, R. Y., Julian, K. M., & Leatham, G. B. (1993). The evolution and current status of the functional perspective on communication in decision-making and problem-solving groups. *Communication Yearbook, 16*, 573–576.

Grady, D. (2007, March 6). A vital discussion, clouded. *The New York Times*, p. F5. Retrieved October 8, 2007, LexisNexis Academic database.

Graen, G. B., & Cashman, J. F. (1975). A role-making model of leadership in formal organizations. In J. G. Hunt & L. L. Larson (Eds.), *Leadership frontiers* (pp. 143–165). Kent, OH: Kent State University Press.

Graen, G. B., & Scandura, T. (1987). Toward a psychology of dyadic organizing. *Research in Organizational Behavior, 9*, 175–208.

Graen, G. B., & Uhl-Bien, M. (1998). Relationship-based approach to leadership. Development of leader–member exchange (LMX) theory of leadership over 25 years:

Applying a multi-level multi-domain perspective. In F. Dansereau & F. J. Yammarino (Eds.), *Leadership: The multiple-level approaches* (pp. 103–158). Stamford, CT: JAI Press.

Grahame, L. J. (2007, October 23). Ryan out as coach of U.S. women. *Los Angeles Times*, p. D6. Retrieved October 25, 2007, from LexisNexis Academic database.

Greenleaf, R. K. (1977). *Servant leadership.* New York: Paulist Press.

Griffin, R. W., & O'Leary-Kelly, A. M. (Eds.). (2004). *The dark side of organizational behavior.* San Francisco: Jossey-Bass.

Grose, T. K. (2003, September 1). Can the manned space program find a new, revitalizing mission in the wake of the *Columbia* tragedy? *U.S. News & World Report*, p. 36.

Grossman, L., & Beech, H. (2006, February 13). Google under the gun. *Time.* Retrieved December 20, 2007, from Business Source Complete database.

Grow, B., Foust, D., Thornton, E., Farzad, R., McGregor, J., Zegle, S., et al. (2007, January 15). Out at Home Depot. *Business Week*, pp. 56–62. Retrieved January 22, 2007, from Business Source Premier database.

Gudykunst, W. B., & Kim, Y. Y. (1997). *Communicating with strangers: An approach to intercultural communication* (3rd ed.). New York: McGraw-Hill.

Gudykunst, W. B., Ting-Toomey, S., Suydweeks, S., & Stewart, L. P. (1995). *Building bridges: Interpersonal skills for a changing world.* Boston: Houghton Mifflin.

Gulli, C., Kohler, N., & Patriquin, M. (2007, February 12). The great university cheating scandal. *Maclean's.* Retrieved December 4, 2007, from LexisNexis Academic database.

Gumbel, P. (2004, July 5). Villain or fall guy? *Time Canada.* Retrieved August 2, 2007, from LexisNexis Academic database.

Guroian, V. (1996). Awakening the moral imagination. *Intercollegiate Review, 32,* 3–13.

Guth, W. D., & Tagiuri, R. (1965, September–October). Personal values and corporate strategy. *Harvard Business Review*, pp. 123–132.

Guynn, J. (2006, September 23). A tale of two bosses at scandal-scarred HP. *The San Francisco Chronicle*, pp. C1, C3.

Guyon, J. (2002, October 14). The king and I. *Fortune* (Europe), p. 38. Retrieved July 21, 2003, from LexisNexis Academic database.

Guyon, J. (2005, October 31). The coming storm over a cancer vaccine. *Fortune*, pp. 123–130. Retrieved March 13, 2007, from LexisNexis Academic database.

Hackman, M. Z., & Johnson, C. E. (2003). *Leadership: A communication perspective* (4th ed.). Prospect Heights, IL: Waveland.

Hackman, M. Z., & Johnson, C. E. (2008). *Leadership: A communication perspective* (5th ed.). Prospect Heights, IL: Waveland.

Haillie, P. (1979). *Lest innocent blood be shed: The story of the village of Le Chambon and how goodness happened there.* New York: Harper & Row.

Hallie, P. (1997). *Tales of good and evil, help and harm.* New York: HarperCollins.

Hanna, S. T., Lester, P. B., & Vgelgesang, G. R. (2005). Moral leadership: Explicating the moral component of authentic leadership. In W. L. Gardner, B. J. Avolio, & F. O. Walumbwa (Eds.), *Authentic leadership theory and practice: Origins, effects and development* (pp. 43–81). Amsterdam: Elsevier.

Hart, D. K. (1992). The moral exemplar in an organizational society. In T. L. Cooper & N. D. Wright (Eds.), *Exemplary public administrators: Character and leadership in government* (pp. 9–29). San Francisco: Jossey-Bass.

Harvey, J. (1988). *The Abilene paradox and other meditations on management.* New York: Simon & Schuster.

Harvey, J. B. (1999). *How come every time I get stabbed in the back my fingerprints are on the knife?* San Francisco: Jossey-Bass.

Harvey, P., Martinko, M. J., & Gardner, W. L. (2006). Promoting authentic behavior in organizations: An attributional perspective. *Journal of Leadership and Organizational Studies, 12,* 1–11.

Hauerwas, S. (1981). *A community of character.* Notre Dame, IN: University of Notre Dame Press.

Hays, K. (2007, May 24). Linda Lay files against forfeiture. *The Houston Chronicle,* Business, p. 3. Retrieved June 19, 2007, from LexisNexis Academic database.

Hays-Thomas, R. (2004). Why now? The contemporary focus on managing diversity. In M. S. Stockdale & F. J. Crosby (Eds.), *The psychology and management of workplace diversity* (pp. 3–30). Malden, MA: Blackwell.

Henderson, D. (2006, May 19). Federal advisers back cervical cancer vaccine. *The Boston Globe.* Retrieved March 13, 2007, from Newspaper Source database.

Hersh, P. (2007, September 30). Women's team facing turmoil. *Los Angeles Times,* p. D1. Retrieved October 25, 2007, from LexisNexis Academic database.

Higgins, M. W. (2003, May 13). A Canadian expert on the Vatican examines the sex abuse scandal. *Maclean's,* p. 48.

Hilzenrath, D. S. (2003, September 2). Rescue of *Columbia* a hindsight dream. *The Washington Post,* p. A8.

Hoffman, M. (2000). *Empathy and moral development: Implications for caring and justice.* Cambridge, UK: Cambridge University Press.

Hofstede, G. (1980, Summer). Motivation, leadership, and organization: Do American theories apply abroad? *Organizational Dynamics,* pp. 42–63.

Hofstede, G. (1984). *Culture's consequences.* Beverly Hills, CA: Sage.

Hofstede, G. (1991). *Cultures and organizations: Software of the mind.* London: McGraw-Hill.

Hofstede, G. (2001). Difference and danger: Cultural profiles of nations and limits to tolerance. In M. H. Albrecht (Ed.), *International HRM: Managing diversity in the workplace* (pp. 9–23). Oxford, UK: Blackwell.

Hoge, W. (2007, September 6). U.N. chief sees protests and refugees in Sudan. *The New York Times,* p. A15. Retrieved September 7, 2007, from LexisNexis Academic database.

Hoge, W. (2007, September 7). Sudan officials and rebels to discuss peace in Darfur. *The New York Times,* p. 12. Retrieved September 7, 2007, from LexisNexis Academic database.

Hollander, E. P. (1992, April). The essential interdependence of leadership and followership. *Current Directions in Psychological Science,* pp. 71–75.

Hopen, D. (2002). Guiding corporate behavior: A leadership obligation not a choice. *Journal for Quality & Participation, 25,* 15–19.

Hornstein, H. A. (1996). *Brutal bosses and their prey.* New York: Riverhead.

Horovitz, B. (2002, October 11). Scandals grow out of CEOs warped mind-set. *USA Today,* pp. 1B–2B.

House, R. J., Hange, P. J., Javidan, M., Dorfman, P. W., & Gupta, V. (Eds.). (2004). *Culture, leadership, and organizations: The GLOBE study of 62 societies.* Thousand Oaks, CA: Sage.

How green is your Apple? (2006, August 26). *Economist.* Retrieved March 15, 2007, from Business Source Premier database.

Howell, J., & Avolio, B. J. (1992). The ethics of charismatic leadership: Submission or liberation? *Academy of Management Executive, 6,* 43–54.

Huffington, A. (2003). *Pigs at the trough: How corporate greed and political corruption are undermining America.* New York: Crown.

Ilies, R., Hauserman, N., Schwochau, S., & Stibal, J. (2003). Reported incidence rates of work-related sexual harassment in the United States: Using meta-analysis to explain reported rate disparities. *Personnel Psychology, 56,* 607–651.

Ilies, R., Morgeson, F. P., & Nahrgang, J. D. (2005). Authentic leadership and eudemonic well-being: Understanding leader–follower outcomes. *Leadership Quarterly, 16,* 373–394.

Illinois yields to NCAA, will retire mascot. *The Washington Post,* p. E02. Retrieved September 29, 2007, from LexisNexis Academic database.

Inch, E. S., Warnick, B., & Endres, D. (2006). *Critical thinking and communication: The use of reason in argument* (5th ed.). Boston: Pearson.

Infante, D. (1988). *Arguing constructively.* Prospect Heights, IL: Waveland.

Infante, D. A., & Rancer, A. S. (1982). A conceptualization and measure of argumentativeness. *Journal of Personality Assessment, 46,* 72–78.

Infante, D., & Rancer, A. (1996). Argumentativeness and verbal aggressiveness: A review of recent theory and research. In B. Burleson (Ed.), *Communication yearbook 19* (pp. 319–351). Thousand Oaks, CA: Sage.

James, H. S. (2000). Reinforcing ethical decision-making through organizational structure. *Journal of Business Ethics, 28*(1), 43–58.

Janis, I. (1971, November). Groupthink: The problems of conformity. *Psychology Today,* pp. 271–279.

Janis, I. (1982). *Groupthink* (2nd ed.). Boston: Houghton Mifflin.

Janis, I. (1989). *Crucial decisions: Leadership in policymaking and crisis management.* New York: Free Press.

Janis, I., & Mann, L. (1977). *Decision making.* New York: Free Press.

Janofsky, M. (2003, March 8). Top Air Force officer, at academy, issues warning. *The New York Times,* p. A13.

Janofsky, M. (2003, April 1). Academy's top general apologizes to cadets. *The New York Times,* p. A14.

Jarvie, J. (2007, September 20). In La., thousands to rally for "Jena Six." *Los Angeles Times,* p. A12. Retrieved September 21, 2007, from LexisNexis Academic database.

Javidan, M., & House, R. J. (2001). Cultural acumen for the global manager: Lessons from Project GLOBE. *Organizational Dynamics, 29,* 289–305.

Jennings, M. M. (2006). *The seven signs of ethical collapse: How to spot moral meltdowns in companies . . . before it's too late.* New York: St. Martin's Press.

Jensen, J. V. (1996). Ethical tension points in whistleblowing. In J. A. Jaksa & M. S. Pritchard (Eds.), *Responsible communication: Ethical issues in business, industry, and the professions* (pp. 41–51). Cresskill, NJ: Hampton.

Johannsen, R. L. (1991). Virtue ethics, character, and political communication. In R. E. Denton (Ed.), *Ethical dimensions of political communication* (pp. 69–90). New York: Praeger.

Johannsen, R. L. (2002). *Ethics in human communication* (5th ed.). Prospect Heights, IL: Waveland.

Johnson, C. E. (1997, Spring). A leadership journey to the East. *Journal of Leadership Studies, 4,* 82–88.

Johnson, C. E. (2000). Emerging perspectives in leadership ethics. *Proceedings of the International Leadership Association,* pp. 48–54.

Johnson, C. E. (2000). Taoist leadership ethics. *Journal of Leadership Studies, 7,* 82–91.

Johnson, C. E. (2002). *Enron's ethical collapse: Lessons from the top.* Paper delivered at the National Communication Association convention, New Orleans, LA.

Johnson, C. E. (2003). Enron's ethical collapse: Lessons for leadership educators. *Journal of Leadership Education, 2.* Retrieved February 7, 2004, from http://www.fhsu.edu/jole/issues/archive_index.html

Johnson, C. E. (2007). Best practices in ethical leadership. In J. A. Conger & R. E. Riggio (Eds.), *The practice of leadership: Developing the next generation of leaders* (pp. 150–171). San Francisco: Jossey-Bass.

Johnson, C. E. (2007). *Ethics in the workplace: Tools and tactics for organizational transformation.* Thousand Oaks, CA: Sage.

Johnson, C. E. (in press). The rise and fall of Carly Fiorina: An ethical case study. *Journal of Leadership and Organizational Studies.*

Johnson, C. E., & Hackman, M. Z. (1997). *Rediscovering the power of followership in the leadership communication text.* Paper presented at the National Communication Association convention, Chicago.

Johnson, C. E., & Hackman, M. Z. (2002). *Assessing ethical competence.* Paper presented at the National Communication Association convention, Atlanta, GA.

Johnson, D. W., & Johnson, R. (1989). *Cooperation and competition: Theory and research.* Edina, MN: Interaction Book Company.

Johnson, D. W., & Johnson, R. (2000). *Joining together: Group theory and group skills* (7th ed.). Boston: Allyn & Bacon.

Johnson, D. W., & Johnson, R. (2005). Training for cooperative group work. In M. A. West, D. Tjosvold, & K. G. Smith (Eds.), *The essentials of teamworking: International perspectives* (pp. 131–147). West Sussex, UK: Wiley.

Johnson, D. W., Maruyama, G., Johnson, R., Nelson, D., & Skon, L. (1981). Effects of cooperative, competitive, and individualistic goal structures on achievement: A meta-analysis. *Psychological Bulletin, 82,* 47–62.

Johnson, D. W., & Tjosvold, D. (1983). *Productive conflict management.* New York: Irvington.

Johnson, J. (1993). Functions and processes of inner speech in listening. In D. Wolvin & C. G. Coakley (Eds.), *Perspectives in listening* (pp. 170–184). Norwood, NJ: Ablex.

Johnson, J. (2007). Dinged up *Endeavour* returns. *Los Angeles Times,* p. A10. Retrieved November 22, 2007, from LexisNexis Academic database.

Johnson, J., & Orange, M. (2003). *The man who tried to buy the world: Jean-Marie Messier and Vivendi Universal.* New York: Portfolio.

Johnson, M. (1993). *Moral imagination: Implications of cognitive science for ethics.* Chicago: University of Chicago Press.

Johnson, M. (2007, April 11). Nation's largest student-loan provider settles in loan scandal. *The Associated Press State & Local Wire.* Retrieved October 8, 2007, from LexisNexis Academic database.

Johnston, D. (1995, April 25). Terror in Oklahoma: The overview. *The New York Times,* p. A1.

Johnston, J. (2007, April 16). Our very modern dilemma. *Daily Mail.* Retrieved March 13, 2007, from Newspaper Source database.

Jones, L. B. (1996). *The path: Creating your mission statement for work and for life.* New York: Hyperion.

Jones, P. E., & Roelofsma, P. H. M. P. (2000). The potential for social contextual and group biases in team decision-making: Biases, conditions and psychological mechanisms. *Ergonomics, 43,* 1129–1152.

Jones, R. G. (2007, September 19). In Louisiana, a tree, a fight and a question of justice. *The New York Times,* p. A14. Retrieved September 21, 2007, from LexisNexis Academic database.

Jones, R. G. (2007, September 20). Protest in Louisiana case echoes the civil rights era. *The New York Times,* p. A15. Retrieved September 21, 2007, from LexisNexis Academic database.

Jones, T. M. (1991). Ethical decision making by individuals in organizations: An issue-contingent model. *Academy of Management Review, 15,* 366–395.

Jonsen, A. R., & Toulmin, S. (1988). *The abuse of casuistry: A history of moral reasoning.* Berkeley: University of California Press.

Judge, W. Q. (1999). *The leader's shadow: Exploring and developing executive character.* Thousand Oaks, CA: Sage.

Julavits, R. (2003, March 28). NASD's Grubman probe going up the ladder. *American Banker,* p. 20. Retrieved July 21, 2003, from LexisNexis Academic database.

Jung, C. B. (1933). *Modern man in search of a soul.* New York: Harcourt.

Jurkiewicz, C. L., & Giacalone, R. A. (2004). A values framework for measuring the impact of workplace spirituality on organizational performance. *Journal of Business Ethics, 49,* 129–142.

Kale, D. W. (1994). Peace as an ethic for intercultural communication. In L. A. Samovar & R. E. Porter (Eds.), *Intercultural communication: A reader* (7th ed., pp. 435–444). Belmont, CA: Wadsworth.

Kant, I. (1964). *Groundwork of the metaphysics of morals* (H. J. Ryan, Trans.). New York: Harper & Row.

Kanter, R. M. (1979, July–August). Power failure in management circuits. *Harvard Business Review,* pp. 65–75.

Kanungo, R. N., & Conger, J. A. (1990). The quest for altruism in organizations. In S. Srivastra & D. L. Cooperrider (Eds.), *Appreciative management and leadership* (pp. 228–256). San Francisco: Jossey-Bass.

Kanungo, R. N., & Mendonca, M. (1996). *Ethical dimensions of leadership.* Thousand Oaks, CA: Sage.

Karau, S. J., & Williams, K. D. (1995). Social loafing: Research findings, implications, and future directions. *Current Directions in Psychological Science, 4,* 134–140.

Karau, S. J., & Williams, K. D. (2001). Understanding individual motivation in groups: The Collective Effort Model. In M. E. Turner (Ed.), *Groups at work: Theory and research* (pp. 113–141). Mahwah, NJ: Erlbaum.

Karim, A. (2000, June 23). Globalization, ethics, and AIDS vaccines. *Science,* pp. 21–29.

Katz, F. E. (1993). *Ordinary people and extraordinary evil: A report on the beguilings of evil.* Albany: State University of New York Press.

Kekes, J. (1991). Moral imagination, freedom, and the humanities. *American Philosophical Quarterly, 28,* 101–111.

Kekes, J. (2005). *The roots of evil.* Ithaca, NY: Cornell University Press.

Kellerman, B. (2004). *Bad leadership: What it is, how it happens, why it matters.* Boston: Harvard Business School Press.

Kelley, R. (1992). *The power of followership.* New York: Doubleday/Currency.

Kelley, R. (1998). Followership in a leadership world. In L. C. Spears (Ed.), *Insights on leadership: Service, stewardship, spirit and servant-leadership* (pp. 170–184). New York: Wiley.

Keltner, D., Langner, C. A., & Allison, M. L. (2006). Power and moral leadership. In D. L. Rhode (Ed.), *Moral leadership: The theory and practice of power, judgment, and policy* (pp. 177–194). San Francisco: Jossey-Bass.

Kernis, M. H. (2003). Toward a conceptualization of optimal self-esteem. *Psychological Inquiry, 14,* 1–26.

Kidder, R. M. (1994). *Shared values for a troubled world: Conversations with men and women of conscience.* San Francisco: Jossey-Bass.

Kidder, R. M. (1995). *How good people make tough choices: Resolving the dilemmas of ethical living.* New York: Fireside.

Kidder, R. M. (2005). *Moral courage.* New York: William Morrow.

Kidder, T. (2003). *Mountains beyond mountains.* New York: Random House.

Kievra, B. (2007, January 12). Creditors challenge bankruptcy protection; Malden Mills accused of deceit, misconduct. *Worcester Telegram & Gazette,* p. E1. Retrieved July 12, 2007, from LexisNexis Academic database.

Kinsley, M. (2007, September 15). The wacky world of student loans. *The Washington Post,* p. A17. Retrieved October 8, 2007, from LexisNexis Academic database.

Kirkland, R. (2002). Self-fulfillment through selflessness: The moral teachings of the Daode Jing. In M. Barnhart (Ed.), *Varieties of ethical reflection: New directions for ethics in a global context* (pp. 21–48). Lanham, MD: Lexington.

Kiuchi, T., & Shireman, B. (2002). *What we learned in the rainforest: Business lessons from nature.* San Francisco: Berrett-Koehler.

Klenke, K. (2005). The internal theater of the authentic leader: Integrating cognitive, affective, conative and spiritual facets of authentic leadership. In W. L. Gardner, B. J. Avolio, & F. O. Walumbwa (Eds.), *Authentic leadership theory and practice: Origins, effects and development* (pp. 43–81). Amsterdam: Elsevier.

Kohlberg, L. A. (1984). *The psychology of moral development: The nature and validity of moral stages* (Vol. 2). San Francisco: Harper & Row.

Kohlberg, L. A. (1986). A current statement on some theoretical issues. In S. Modgil & C. Modgil (Eds.), *Lawrence Kohlberg: Consensus and controversy* (pp. 485–546). Philadelphia: Palmer.

Konrad, A. M. (2006). Leveraging workplace diversity in organizations. *Organization Management Journal, 3,* 164–189.

Koonce, R. (2001, December). Redefining diversity. *Training and Development,* pp. 22–28.

Kossek, E. E., Lobel, S. A., & Brown, J. (2006). Human resource strategies to manage workplace diversity: Examining the "business case." In A. M. Konrad, P. Prasad, & J. K. Pringle (Eds.), *Handbook of workplace diversity* (pp. 53–74). London: Sage.

Kotler, P., & Lee, N. (2005). *Corporate social responsibility: Doing the most good for your company and your cause.* Hoboken, NJ: Wiley.

Kotter, J. P. (1990). *A force for change: How leadership differs from management.* New York: Free Press.

Kouzes, J. M., & Posner, B. Z. (2003). *Credibility: How leaders gain and lose it, why people demand it.* San Francisco: Jossey-Bass.

Kouzes, J. M., & Posner, B. (2007). *The leadership challenge* (4th ed.). San Francisco: Jossey-Bass.

Kramer, R. M., & Cook, K. S. (Eds.). (2004). *Trust and distrust in organizations: Dilemmas and approaches.* New York: Russell Sage Foundation.

Kramer, R. M., & Tyler, T. R. (Eds.). (1996). *Trust in organizations: Frontiers of theory and research.* Thousand Oaks, CA: Sage.

Krugan, P. (2006, October 20). Incentives for the dead. *The New York Times,* p. A23. Retrieved June 20, 2007, from LexisNexis Academic database.

Kuczmarski, S. S., & Kuczmarski, T. D. (1995). *Values-based leadership.* Englewood Cliffs, NJ: Prentice Hall.

Kung, H. (1998). *A global ethic for global politics and economics.* New York: Oxford University Press.

Kung, H. (1999). A global ethic in an age of globalization. In G. Enderle (Ed.), *International business ethics: Challenges and approaches* (pp. 19–127). Notre Dame, IN: University of Notre Dame Press.

Kung, H. (2003). An ethical framework for the global market economy. In J. H. Dunning (Ed.), *Making globalization good: The moral challenges of global capitalism* (pp. 146–158). Oxford, UK: Oxford University Press.

Lacayo, R., & Ripley, A. (2002, December 30). Persons of the year. *Time,* pp. 30–60.

Langer, E. J. (1989). *Mindfulness.* Reading, MA: Addison-Wesley.

Larson, L. (2007, October 16). Disarming only amplifies the likelihood of violence. *The Oregonian,* p. D5.

Leary, W. E., & Schwartz, J. (2006, July 4). Shuttle launching set for today despite broken foam. *The New York Times,* p. A11. Retrieved November 22, 2007, from LexisNexis Academic database.

Leslie, L. Z. (2000). *Mass communication ethics: Decision-making in postmodern culture.* Boston: Houghton Mifflin.

Levine, S., & Hamil, H. (2007, January 12). Wave of support for HPV vaccination of girls. *The Washington Post.* Retrieved March 13, 2007, from Newspaper Source database.

Levy, A. C., & Paludi, M. A. (2002). *Workplace sexual harassment* (2nd ed.). Upper Saddle River, NJ: Prentice Hall.

Levy, S. (2006, February 13). Google and the China syndrome. *Newsweek.* Retrieved December 20, 2007, from Business Source Complete database.

Lewis, C. S. (1946). *The great divorce.* New York: Macmillan.

Lewis, M. (1989). *Liar's poker.* New York: Norton.

Liedtke, M. (2006, November 9). Chummy CEOs now part of Silicon Valley's backdating club. *Associated Press Financial Wire.* Retrieved June 20, 2007, from LexisNexis Academic database.

Lindsay, R. M., & Irvine, V. B. (1996). Instilling ethical behavior in organizations: A survey of Canadian companies. *Journal of Business Ethics, 15,* 393–407.

Lipman-Blumen, J. (2005). *The allure of toxic leaders: Why we follow destructive bosses and corrupt politicians—and how we can survive them.* Oxford, UK: Oxford University Press.

Liptak, A. (2002, April 18). Judge blocks U.S. bid to ban suicide law. *The New York Times,* p. A16.

Lipton, E. (2007, September 3). Safety agency failing consumers? *The International Herald Tribune,* p. 15. Retrieved November 5, 2007, from LexisNexis Academic database.

Lisman, C. D. (1996). *The curricular integration of ethics: Theory and practice.* Westport, CT: Praeger.

Lister, S. (2006, February 16). Let people sell their kidneys for transplant, say doctors. *The Times* (London), p. 31. Retrieved January 7, 2008, from Academic Source Premier database.

Longman, J. (2007, October 23). After haunting loss, U.S. fires women's coach. *The New York Times*, p. D6. Retrieved October 25, 2007, from LexisNexis Academic database.

Loomis, C. J., & Kahn, J. (1999, January 11). Citigroup: Scenes from a merger. *Fortune,* pp. 76–83. Retrieved July 21, 2003, from LexisNexis Academic database.

Lowe, K. B., & Kroeck, K. G. (1996). Effectiveness correlates of transformational and transactional leadership: A meta-analytic review. *Leadership Quarterly, 7,* 385–425.

Lublin, J. S. (2006, October 12). Executive pay soars despite attempted restraints. *Associated Press Financial Wire.* Retrieved January 22, 2007, from LexisNexis Academic database.

Maas, A., & Clark, R. D. (1984). Hidden impact of minorities: Fifteen years of minority influence research. *Psychological Bulletin, 95,* 428–445.

MacIntyre, A. (1984). *After virtue: A study in moral theory* (2nd ed.). Notre Dame, IN: University of Notre Dame Press.

Malden Mills (Television series episode). (2002, March 24). *60 Minutes.* CBS Television.

Malden Mills withdraws controversial plan for executive bonuses. (2007, February 6). *Associated Press State & Local Wire.* Retrieved July 12, 2007, from LexisNexis Academic database.

Malone, M. S. (2007). *Bill & Dave: How Hewlett and Packard built the world's greatest company.* New York: Portfolio.

Manby, B. (1999). The role and responsibility of oil multinationals in Nigeria. *Journal of International Affairs, 53,* 281–301.

Manning, J. (2007, May 16). Riders throttle safety legislation. *The Oregonian.* Retrieved November 5, 2007, from NewsBank database.

Manning, J., Walth, B., & Goldsmith, S. (2007, May 17). Deceptively dangerous: Why ATVs keep killing. *The Oregonian.* Retrieved November 5, 2007, from NewsBank database.

Manz, C. C., & Neck, C. P. (1995). Teamthink: Beyond the groupthink syndrome in self-managing work teams. *Journal of Managerial Psychology, 1,* 7–15.

Manz, C. C., & Sims, H. P. (1989). *Superleadership: Leading others to lead themselves.* Upper Saddle River, NJ: Prentice Hall.

Martin, J., & Powers, M. E. (1983). Truth or corporate propaganda: The value of a good story. In L. R. Pondy, P. J. Frost, G. Morgan, & T. C. Dandridge (Eds.), *Organizational symbolism* (pp. 93–107). Greenwich, CT: JAI Press.

Mathews, M. C. (1999). Codes of ethics: Organizational behavior and misbehavior. In W. C. Frederick & L. E. Preston (Eds.), *Business ethics: Research issues and empirical studies* (pp. 99–122). Greenwich, CT: JAI Press.

May, D. R., Chan, A. Y. L., Hodges, T. D., & Avolio, B. J. (2003). Developing the moral component of authentic leadership. *Organizational Dynamics, 32,* 247–260.

Mayer, R. C., & Gavin, M. B. (2005). Trust in management and performance: Who minds the shop while the employees watch the boss? *Academy of Management Journal, 48,* 874–888.

McCabe, D., & Trevino, K. L. (1993). Academic dishonesty: Honor codes and other contextual influences. *Journal of Higher Education, 64,* 522–569.

McCauley, C. D., & Van Velsor, E. (Eds.). (2004). *The Center for Creative Leadership handbook of leadership development* (2nd ed.). San Francisco: Jossey-Bass.

McCullough, M. E., Pargament, K. I., & Thoresen, C. E. (2000). The psychology of forgiveness: History, conceptual issues, and overview. In M. E. McCullough, K. I. Pargament, & C. E. Thoresen (Eds.), *Forgiveness: Theory, research, and practice* (pp. 1–14). New York: Guilford.

McCullough, M. E., Sandage, S. J., & Worthington, E. L. (1997). *To forgive is human: How to put your past in the past.* Downers Grove, IL: InterVarsity Press.

Meilander, G. (1986). Virtue in contemporary religious thought. In R. J. Nehaus (Ed.), *Virtue: Public and private* (pp. 7–30). Grand Rapids, MI: Eerdmans.

Melloan, G. (2004, January 6). Feeling the muscle of the multinationals. *Wall Street Journal,* p. A19. Retrieved April 11, 2008, from ProQuest Newspaper database.

Messick, D. M., & Bazerman, M. H. (1996, Winter). Ethical leadership and the psychology of decision making. *Sloan Management Review, 37*(2), 9–23.

Metaxas, E. (2007). *Amazing grace: William Wilberforce and the heroic campaign to end slavery.* San Francisco: Harper San Francisco.

Metzger, M., Dalton, D. R., & Hill, J. W. (1993). The organization of ethics and the ethics of organizations: The case for expanded organizational ethics audits. *Business Ethics Quarterly, 3*(1), 27–43.

Miller, L., & France, D. (2003, March 4). Sins of the father. *Newsweek,* p. 42.

Milloy, R. E. (2000, June 21). 2 Sides give 2 versions of facts in Waco suit. *The New York Times,* p. A14.

Mirvis, P. H. (1997). "Soul work" in organizations. *Organization Science, 8,* 193–206.

Mishra, R. (2003, August 27). Probe hits NASA in crash of shuttle. *The Boston Globe.* Retrieved September 2, 2003, from LexisNexis Academic database.

Mitchell, S. (1988). *Tao te ching.* New York: Harper Perennial.

Moorhead, G., Neck, C. P., & West, M. S. (1998). The tendency toward defective decision making within self-managing teams: The relevance of groupthink for the 21st century. *Organizational Behavior and Human Decision Processes, 73,* 327–351.

Mor Barak, M. E. (2005). *Toward a globally inclusive workplace.* Thousand Oaks, CA: Sage.

Morrell, M., Capparell, S., & Shackleton, A. (2001). *Shackleton's way: Leadership lessons from the great Antarctic explorer.* New York: Viking.

Morris, J. A., Brotheridge, C. M., & Urbanski, J. C. (2005). Bringing humility to leadership: Antecedents and consequences of leader humility. *Human Relations,* pp. 1323–1350.

Morrison, A. M. (1996). *The new leaders: Guidelines on leadership diversity in America.* San Francisco: Jossey-Bass.

Morrow, L. (2003). *Evil: An investigation.* New York: Basic Books.

Moscovici, S., Mugny, G., & Van Avermaet, E. (Eds.). (1985). *Perspectives on minority influence.* Cambridge, UK: Cambridge University Press.

Moxley, R. S., & Pulley, M. L. (2004). Hardships. In C. D. McCauley & E. Van Velsor (Eds.), *The Center for Creative Leadership handbook of leadership development* (2nd ed., pp. 183–203). San Francisco: Jossey-Bass.

Mozingo, J., & Spano, J. (2007, July 15). $660 million in priest abuses. *Los Angeles Times,* p. A1. Retrieved September, 2007, from LexisNexis Academic database.

Mulligan, T. S. (2006, May 26). The Enron verdicts. *Los Angeles Times,* p. A1. Retrieved June 19, 2007, from LexisNexis Academic database.

Mumford, M. D., Gessner, T. L., Connelly, M. S., O'Conner, J. A., & Clifton, T. (1993). Leadership and destructive acts: Individual and situational influences. *Leadership Quarterly, 4,* 115–147.

Murphy, C. (1999, March 15). The most twisted economy on the planet. *Fortune,* pp. 42–43.

Murphy, J. G. (2003). *Getting even: Forgiveness and its limits.* Oxford, UK: Oxford University Press.

Muzaffar, C. (2002). Conclusion. In P. F. Knitter & C. Muzaffar (Eds.), *Subverting greed: Religious perspectives on the global economy* (pp. 154–172). Maryknoll, NY: Orbis.

Nakashima, E. (2006, September 26). Between the lines of HP's spy scandal. *The Washington Post.* Retrieved September 28, 2006, from http://WashingtonPost.com

Nanus, B. (1992). *Visionary leadership.* San Francisco: Jossey-Bass.

Narell, M. (2007, May 16). Dr. Paul Farmer and philanthropy for global health. *On Philanthropy.* Retrieved October 3, 2007, from http://www.onphilanthropy.com

Nash, L. L. (1989). Ethics without the sermon. In K. R. Andrews (Ed.), *Ethics in practice: Managing the moral corporation* (pp. 243–257). Boston: Harvard Business School Press.

Nash, L. L. (1990). *Good intentions aside: A manager's guide to resolving ethical problems.* Boston: Harvard Business School Press.

Nemeth, C., & Chiles, C. (1986). Modeling courage: The role of dissent in fostering independence. *European Journal of Social Psychology, 18,* 275–280.

Neumeister, L. (2006, January 6). U.S. appeals court upholds Martha Stewart's conviction. *Associated Press Worldstream.* Retrieved August 14, 2007, from LexisNexis Academic database.

Nichols, M. L., & Day, V. E. (1982). A comparison of moral reasoning of groups and individuals on the "defining issues test." *Academy of Management Journal, 24,* 21–28.

Not for sale at any price. (2006, April 8). *The Lancet,* p. 1118. Retrieved January 7, 2008, from Academic Source Premier database.

O'Driscoll, P., & Kenworthy, T. (2003, June 27). Cadets march into new academy. *USA Today,* p. 6A.

Oh, H. (2006, February 6). Biz majors get an F for honesty. *Business Week.* Retrieved December 4, 2007, from LexisNexis Academic database.

Olson, B. (2006, July 9). Air Force learns lesson: Cadets get the message about harassment. *Baltimore Sun.* Retrieved December 4, 2007, from Newspaper Source database.

Olson, B. (2007, October 28). Mids hear frank talk on sexual assault. *Baltimore Sun.* Retrieved December 4, 2007, from Newspaper Source database.

Opotow, S. (1990). Moral exclusion and injustice: An introduction. *Journal of Social Issues, 46,* 1–20.

Pacanowsky, M. E., & O'Donnell-Trujillo, N. (1983). Organizational communication as cultural performance. *Communication Monographs, 5,* 126–147.

Padilla, A., Hogan, R., & Kaiser, R. B. (2007). The toxic triangle: Destructive leaders, susceptible followers, and conducive environments. *The Leadership Quarterly, 18,* 176–194.

Paine, L. S. (1996). Moral thinking in management: An essential capability. *Business Ethics Quarterly, 6,* 477–492.

Paine, L. S. (1996, March–April). Managing for organizational integrity. *Harvard Business Review,* pp. 106–117.

Paine, L. S. (1997). *Cases in leadership, ethics, and organizational integrity: A strategic perspective.* Boston: Irwin McGraw-Hill.

Paine, L., Deshpande, R., Margolis, J. D., & Bettcher, K. E. (2005, December). Up to code. *Harvard Business Review,* pp. 122–133.

Palmer, P. (1996). Leading from within. In L. C. Spears (Ed.), *Insights on leadership: Service, stewardship, spirit, and servant-leadership* (pp. 197–208). New York: Wiley.

Panchak, P. (2002). Time for a triple bottom line. *Industry Week*, p. 7.

Pappano, L. (2007, July 29). Lessons from the loan scandal. *The New York Times*, Education Life Supplement, p. 16. Retrieved October 8, 2007, from LexisNexis Academic database.

Parker, C. P., Baltes, B. B., & Christiansen, N. D. (1997). Support for affirmative action, justice perceptions, and work attitudes: A study of gender and racial-ethnic group differences. *Journal of Applied Psychology, 82*(3), 376–389.

The party, the people and the power of cyber-talk. (2006, April 29). *Economist*. Retrieved December 20, 2007, from Business Source Complete database.

Paulson, M. (2003, July 1). Florida Bishop O'Malley seen choice to lead Boston diocese has strong record on abusive priests in 2 assignments. *The Boston Globe*, p. A1.

Paulson, M., & Farragher, T. (2003, August 24). Ex-priest Geoghan attacked, dies. *The Boston Globe*, p. A1.

Pearson, C. M., & Porath, C. L. (2004). On incivility, its impact and directions for future research. In R. W. Griffin & A. M. O'Leary-Kelly (Eds.), *The dark side of organizational behavior* (pp. 131–158). San Francisco: Jossey-Bass.

Pearson, C. M., & Porath, C. I. (2005). On the nature, consequences and remedies of workplace incivility: No time for "nice"? Think again. *Academy of Management Executive, 19,* 7–18.

Pearson, G. (1995). *Integrity in organizations: An alternative business ethic.* London: McGraw-Hill.

Peck, M. S. (1983). *People of the lie: The hope for healing human evil.* New York: Touchstone.

Perkins, D. N. T. (2000). *Leading at the edge.* New York: AMACOM.

Perry, A. (2007, March 19). A war without end gets worse. *Time*. Retrieved September 3, 2007, from LexisNexis Academic database.

Perry, A. (2007, May 7). How to prevent the next Darfur. *Time*. Retrieved September 9, 2007, from LexisNexis Academic database.

Peters, T. (1992). *Liberation management.* New York: Ballantine.

Peterson, C., & Seligman, M. E. P. (2004). *Character strengths and virtues: A handbook and classification.* Oxford, UK: Oxford University Press.

Peterson, D. K. (2002). The relationship between unethical behavior and the dimensions of the Ethical Climate Questionnaire. *Journal of Business Ethics, 41,* 313–326.

Petrick, J. A. (1998). Building organizational integrity and quality with the four Ps: Perspectives, paradigms, processes, and principles. In M. Schminke (Ed.), *Managerial ethics: Moral management of people and processes* (pp. 115–131). Mahwah, NJ: Erlbaum.

Petrou, M., & Savage, L. (2006, December 11). Genocide in slow motion. *Macleans*. Retrieved September 9, 2007, from LexisNexis Academic database.

Pfeffer, J. (1992, Winter). Understanding power in organizations. *California Management Review, 34*(2), 29–50.

Phelps, D. (2006, October 6). A quiet Viking sniffed out a stock-option scandal. *Minneapolis Star Tribune*. Retrieved June 20, 2007, from LexisNexis Academic database.

Philips, R. (2003). *Stakeholder theory and organizational ethics.* San Francisco: Berrett-Koehler.

Piliavin, J. A., & Chang, H. W. (1990). Altruism: A review of recent theory and research. *American Sociological Review, 16,* 27–65.

Pollack, A., & Saul, S. (2007, February 21). Lobbying for vaccine to be halted. *The New York Times*, p. C1. Retrieved March 13, 2007, from LexisNexis Academic database.

Porath, C. L., & Erez, A. (2007). Does rudeness really matter? The effects of rudeness on task performance and helpfulness. *The Academy of Management Journal, 50,* 1181–1197.

Potter, R. B. (1972). The logic of moral argument. In P. Deats (Ed.), *Toward a discipline of social ethics* (pp. 93–114). Boston: Boston University Press.

Powers, C. W., & Vogel, D. (1980). *Ethics in the education of business managers.* Hasting-on-Hudson, NY: Institute of Society, Ethics and the Life Sciences.

Price, T. L. (2006). *Understanding ethical failures in leadership.* Cambridge, UK: Cambridge University Press.

Pringle, P. (2007, April 24). Probe into student lending spotlights dual role of U.S. *Los Angeles Times*, p. B1. Retrieved October 8, 2007, from LexisNexis Academic database.

Race, justice and Jena: Black leadership in America. (2007, September 29). *The Economist.* Retrieved October 1, 2007, from LexisNexis Academic database.

Rampersad, A. (1997). *Jackie Robinson.* New York: Alfred A. Knopf.

Ransley, C., & Spy, T. (Eds.). (2004). *Forgiveness and the healing process: A central therapeutic concern.* New York: Brunner-Routledge.

Rawls, J. (1971). *A theory of justice.* Cambridge, MA: Belknap.

Rawls, J. (1993). *Political liberalism.* New York: Columbia University Press.

Rawls, J. (1993). Distributive justice. In T. Donaldson & P. H. Werhane (Eds.), *Ethical issues in business: A philosophical approach* (pp. 274–285). Englewood Cliffs, NJ: Prentice Hall.

Rawls, J. (2001). *Justice as fairness: A restatement* (E. Kelly, Ed.). Cambridge, MA: Belknap.

Reave, L. (2005). Spiritual values and practices related to leadership effectiveness. *Leadership Quarterly, 16,* 655–687.

Red, C., & Kennedy, H. (2007, September 28). Jena suspect freed. *Daily News.* Retrieved October 1, 2007, from LexisNexis Academic database.

Reeves, E. (2007, Summer). Genocide without end?: The destruction of Darfur. *Dissent,* pp. 9–13.

Reid, C. (2007, April 29). Organ donation group spurs debate. *The State* (Columbia, SC). Retrieved January 7, 2008, from Newspaper Source database.

Reidenbach, R. E., & Robin, D. P. (1991). A conceptual model of corporate moral development. *Journal of Business Ethics, 1,* 273–284.

Resick, C. J., Hange, P. J., Dickson, M. W., & Mitchelson, J. K. (2006). A cross-cultural examination of the endorsement of ethical leadership. *Journal of Business Ethics, 63,* 345–359.

Rest, J. (1986). *Moral development: Advances in research and theory.* New York: Praeger.

Rest, J. R. (1993). Research on moral judgment in college students. In A. Garrod (Ed.), *Approaches to moral development* (pp. 201–211). New York: Teachers College Press.

Rest, J. R. (1994). Background: Theory and research. In J. R. Rest & D. Narvaez (Eds.), *Moral development in the professions: Psychology and applied ethics* (pp. 1–25). Hillsdale, NJ: Erlbaum.

Rest, J. R., & Narvaez, D. (1991). The college experience and moral development. In W. M. Kurtines & J. L. Gewirtz (Eds.), *Handbook of moral behavior and development. Vol. 2: Research* (pp. 229–245). Hillsdale, NJ: Erlbaum.

Rest, J., Narvaez, D., Bebeau, M. J., & Thoma, S. J. (1999). *Postconventional moral thinking: A neo-Kohlbergian approach*. Mahwah, NJ: Erlbaum.

Reynolds, S. J. (2003). A single framework for strategic and ethical behavior in the international context. *Business Ethics Quarterly, 13,* 361–379.

Richter, J. (2001). *Holding corporations accountable: Corporate conduct, international codes and citizen action*. London: Zed.

Ricks, D. (2007, February 11). Push for mandatory cervical cancer vaccine. *Newsday.* Retrieved March 13, 2007, from Newspaper Source database.

Ritzer, G. (2004). *The globalization of nothing*. Thousand Oaks, CA: Pine Forge.

Roberto, M. A. (2005). *Why great leaders don't take yes for an answer*. Upper Saddle River, NJ: Wharton School Publishing.

Robertson, C. (2005, Spring). Organ advertising: Desperate patients solicit volunteers. *The Journal of Law, Medicine & Ethics,* pp. 170–174. Retrieved January 7, 2008, from Academic Source Premier database.

Robins, F. (2006). The challenge of TBL: A responsibility to whom? *Business and Society Review, 111,* 1–14.

Rogers, E. M., & Steinfatt, T. M. (1999). *Intercultural communication*. Prospect Heights, IL: Waveland.

Rokeach, M. (1973). *The nature of human values*. New York: Free Press.

Roloff, M. E., & Paulson, G. D. (2001). Confronting organizational transgressions. In J. M. Darley, D. M. Messick, & T. R. Tyler (Eds.), *Social influences on ethical behavior in organizations* (pp. 53–68). Mahwah, NJ: Erlbaum.

Rosenfeld, P., Giacalone, R. A., & Riordan, C. A. (1995). *Impression management in organizations: Theory, measurement, practice*. London: Routledge.

Rothwell, J. D. (1998). *In mixed company: Small group communication* (3rd ed.). Fort Worth, TX: Harcourt Brace.

Ruibal, S., & Steeg, J. L. (2007, October 1). Solo's outburst draws strong reaction; U.S. teammates shun goalkeeper. *USA Today,* p. 8C. Retrieved October 25, 2007, from LexisNexis Academic database.

Ruschman, N. L. (2002). Servant-leadership and the best companies to work for in America. In L. C. Spears & M. Lawrence (Eds.), *Focus on leadership: Servant-leadership for the twenty-first century* (pp. 123–139). New York: Wiley.

Sachs, J. (2007, May 27). Sharing the wealth. *Time,* p. 81.

Sanford, N., & Comstock, C. (Eds.). (1971). *Sanctions for evil*. San Francisco: Jossey-Bass.

Saul, S., & Pollack, A. (2007, February 17). Furor on rush to require cervical cancer vaccine. *The New York Times,* p. A1. Retrieved March 13, 2007, from LexisNexis Academic database.

Sawyer, K. (2003, August 24). Shuttle's "smoking gun" took time to register. *The Washington Post,* p. A1.

Scelfo, J. (2007, May 14). Accidents will happen. *Newsweek,* p. 59. Retrieved November 5, 2007, from LexisNexis Academic database.

Schemo, D. J. (2003, May 22). Women at West Point face tough choices on assaults. *The New York Times,* p. A16.

Schemo, D. J. (2003, June 7). Policy shift on handling of complaints at academy. *The New York Times,* p. A1.

Schemo, D. J. (2003, July 12). Ex-superintendent of Air Force Academy is demoted in wake of rape scandal. *The New York Times,* p. A7.

Schemo, D. J. (2003, July 13). Academy cadet chief backs rape report disclosures. *The New York Times,* p. A16.

Schultz, B. (1982). Argumentativeness: Its effect in group decision-making and its role in leadership perception. *Communication Quarterly, 3,* 368–375.

Scully, S. (2001, March 13). Minorities gain ground on whites in '00 census. *The Washington Times,* p. A1. Retrieved December 13, 2007, from Newspaper Source database.

Seeger, M. W., & Ulmer, R. R. (2001). Virtuous responses to organizational crisis: Aaron Feuerstein and Milt Cole. *Journal of Business Ethics, 31,* 369–376.

Seston, A. (2006, December 6). AIDS day draws attention to epidemic. *The Daily Cardinal.* Retrieved June 13, 2007, from LexisNexis Academic database.

Shackleton, E. (1998). *South: A memoir of the* Endurance *voyage.* New York: Carroll & Graf.

Shady practices taint college loan business. (2007, April 24). *USA Today,* p. 10A. Retrieved October 8, 2007, from LexisNexis Academic database.

Shared sacrifice? Not for these airline executives. (2006, February 2). *USA Today.* Retrieved June 9, 2007, from LexisNexis Academic database.

Shinn, A. (2007, October 28). ATV "non-recall" reveals Consumer Safety Board's constraints. *The Washington Post,* p. A01. Retrieved November 5, 2007, from LexisNexis Academic database.

Shockley-Zalabak, P., Ellis, K., & Winograd, G. (2000). Organizational trust: What it means, why it matters. *Organizational Development Journal, 18,* 35–47.

Shrieves, L. (2007, February 22). Cheating's waters run deep and dirty. *Orlando Sentinel.* Retrieved December 4, 2007, from LexisNexis Academic database.

Shriver, D. W. (1995). *An ethic for enemies: Forgiveness in politics.* New York: Oxford University Press.

Silla, B., Knight, D., & Fang, B. (2006, February 27). Learning to live with big brother. *U.S. News & World Report.* Retrieved December 20, 2007, from Business Source Complete database.

Simons, M. (2007, February 28). 2 face trials at The Hague over atrocities in Darfur. *The New York Times,* p. A3.

Sims, R. L., & Keon, T. L. (1997). Ethical work climate as a factor in the development of person–organization fit. *Journal of Business Ethics, 16,* 1095–1105.

Sims, R. R. (2003). *Ethics and corporate social responsibility: Why giants fall.* Westport, CT: Praeger.

Singer, P. (2002). *One world: The ethics of globalization.* New Haven, CT: Yale University Press.

Skoloff, B. (2006, April 29). Both Limbaugh and prosecutors can declare victory in deal. *The Associated Press.* Retrieved June 18, 2007, from LexisNexis Academic database.

Skrzycki, C. (2007, July 10). ATV industry plays the China card. *The Washington Post,* p. D02. Retrieved November 5, 2007, from LexisNexis Academic database.

Sleeth, P. (2007, October 3). Teacher goes public in fight to pack pistol. *The Oregonian.* Retrieved October 27, 2007, from Newspaper Source database.

Smith, D. H. (1993). Stories, values, and patient care decisions. In C. Conrad (Ed.), *The ethical nexus* (pp. 123–148). Norwood, NJ: Ablex.

Smith, T. (1999). Justice as a personal virtue. *Social Theory & Practice, 25,* 361–384.

Snyder, C. R., & Lopez. S. J. (2005). *Handbook of positive psychology.* Oxford, UK: Oxford University Press.

Solomon, C. M. (2001). Put your ethics to a global test. In M. H. Albrecht (Ed.), *International HRM: Managing diversity in the workplace* (pp. 329–335). Oxford, UK: Blackwell.

Solomon, R. C. (1992). *Ethics and excellence: Cooperation and integrity in business.* New York: Oxford University Press.

Spears, L. (1998). Introduction: Tracing the growing impact of servant-leadership. In L. C. Spears (Ed.), *Insights on leadership* (pp. 1–12). New York: Wiley.

Srivastva, S. (Ed.). (1988). *Executive integrity.* San Francisco: Jossey-Bass.

Stanley, D. J., Meyer, J. P., & Topolnytsky, L. (2005). Employee cynicism and resistance to organizational change. *Journal of Business and Psychology, 19,* 429–459.

Staub, E. (1989). *The roots of evil: The origins of genocide and other group violence.* Cambridge, UK: Cambridge University Press.

Stecklow, S. (2006, July 20). How one company played with timing of stock options. *Associated Press Financial Wire.* Retrieved June 20, 2007, from LexisNexis Academic database.

Sternberg, R. J. (2002). Smart people are not stupid, but they sure can be foolish. In R. Sternberg (Ed.), *Why smart people can be so stupid* (pp. 232–242). New Haven, CT: Yale University Press.

Stewart, D. R. (2006, June 1). Southwest staff "family": The airline's corporate culture is tied to its success. *Tulsa World.* Retrieved October 3, 2007, from Newspaper Source database.

Street, M. D. (1997). Groupthink: An examination of theoretical issues, implications, and future research suggestions. *Small Group Research, 28,* 72–93.

Study concluded Air Force Academy hostile to women for 25 years. (June 16, 2003). *The Colorado Springs Gazette.* Retrieved July 21, 2003, from http://epnet.com/citation

Sweeping up the street. (2003, May 12). *Business Week,* p. 114. Retrieved July 21, 2003, from LexisNexis Academic database.

Talbot, M. (1999). Against relativism. In J. M. Halstead & T. H. McLaughlin (Eds.), *Education in morality* (pp. 206–217). London: Routledge.

Tangney, J. P. (2000). Humility: Theoretical perspectives, empirical findings and directions for future research. *Journal of Social and Clinical Psychology, 19,* 70–82.

Tavis, T. (2000). The globalization phenomenon and multinational corporate developmental responsibility. In O. F. Williams (Ed.), *Global codes of conduct: An idea whose time has come* (pp. 13–36). Notre Dame, IN: University of Notre Dame Press.

Tenbrunsel, A. E., & Messick, D. M. (2004). Ethical fading: The role of self-deception in unethical behavior. *Social Justice Research, 17,* 223–236.

Thoma, S. J. (2006). Research on the defining issues test. In M. Killen & J. G. Smetana (Eds.), *Handbook of moral development* (pp. 67–91). Mahwah, NJ: Erlbaum.

Thomas, G. (2000, January 10). The forgiveness factor. *Christianity Today,* pp. 38–43.

Thoresen, C. E., Harris, H. S., & Luskin, F. (2000). Forgiveness and health: An unanswered question. In M. E. McCullough, K. I. Pargament, & C. E. Thoresen (Eds.), *Forgiveness: Theory, research and practice* (pp. 254–280). New York: Guilford.

Time to outlaw sweetheart IPOs. (2003, May 16). *Rocky Mountain News,* p. 46A. Retrieved February 7, 2004, from LexisNexis Academic database.

Timmons, H., Cohn, L., McNamee, M., & Rossant, J. (2002, August 5). Citi's sleepless nights. *Business Week,* pp. 42–43. Retrieved July 21, 2003, from LexisNexis Academic database.

Tivnan, E. (1995). *The moral imagination*. New York: Routledge, Chapman, and Hall.

Toffler, B. L., & Reingold, J. (2003). *Final accounting: Ambition, greed, and the fall of Arthur Andersen*. New York: Broadway.

Tourish, D., & Pinnington, A. (2002). Transformational leadership, corporate cultism and the spirituality paradigm: An unholy trinity in the workplace? *Human Relations, 55*, 147–172.

Trevino, L. K., Brown, M., & Pincus, L (2003). A qualitative investigation of perceived executive ethical leadership: Perceptions from inside and outside the executive suite. *Human Relations, 56*, 5–37.

Trevino, L. K., Butterfield, K. D., & McCabe, D. L. (1998). The ethical context in organizations: Influences on employee attitudes and behaviors. *Business Ethics Quarterly, 8*, 447–476.

Trevino, L. K., Hartman, L. P., & Brown, M. (2000). Moral person and moral manager: How executives develop a reputation for ethical leadership. *California Management Reviews, 42*, 128–133.

Trevino, L. K., & Nelson, K. A. (2004). *Managing business ethics: Straight talk about how to do it right* (3rd ed.). Hoboken, NJ: Wiley.

Trevino, L. K., & Weaver, G. R. (2003). *Managing ethics in business organizations: Social scientific perspectives*. Stanford, CA: Stanford University Press.

Triandis, H. C. (1995). *Individualism and collectivism*. Boulder, CO: Westview.

Tropman, J. (2003). *Making meetings work: Achieving high quality group decisions* (2nd ed.). Thousand Oaks, CA: Sage.

Turner, L. (2007, July 18). China's deadly scheme to harvest organs. *The Globe and Mail* (Canada), p. A23. Retrieved January 7, 2008, from Academic Source Premier database.

Turner, N., Barling, J., Epitropaki, O., Butcher, V., & Milner, C. (2002, April). Transformational leadership and moral reasoning. *Journal of Applied Psychology, 87*, 304–311.

Ulmer, R. R., & Seeger, M. W. (2000). Communication ethics and the Malden Mills disaster. In G. L. Peterson (Ed.), *Communicating in organizations* (2nd ed., pp. 191–194). Boston: Allyn & Bacon.

Universities retreat in war on cheating. (2000, August 25). Retrieved September 25, 2000, from http://www.ncpa.org/pi/edu/jan890.html

U.S. Department of Labor Bureau of Labor Statistics. (2007, August 9). Retrieved December 13, 2007, from http://dol.gov/dolfaq/dolfaq.asp

Useem, M. (1998). *The leadership moment: Nine stories of triumph and disaster and their lessons for us all*. New York: Times Books.

Valentine, S., & Barnett, T. (2003). Ethics code awareness, perceived ethical values, and organizational commitment. *Journal of Personal Selling & Sales Management, 23*, 359–367.

Varachaver, N. (2004, November 11). Glamour! Fame! Org charts! *Fortune*. Retrieved June 5, 2007, from Academic Search Premier database.

Vecchio, R. P. (1982). A further test of leadership effects due to between-group variation and in-group variation. *Journal of Applied Psychology, 67*, 200–208.

Velasquez, M. G. (1992). *Business ethics: Concepts and cases* (3rd ed.). Englewood Cliffs, NJ: Prentice Hall.

Verhovek, S. H. (1993, April 22). Death in Waco: F. B. I. saw the ego in Koresh, but not a willingness to die. *The New York Times*, p. A1.

Victor, B., & Cullen, J. B. (1988). The organizational bases of ethical work climates. *Administrative Science Quarterly, 33,* 101–125.

Victor, B., & Cullen, J. B. (1990). A theory and measure of ethical climate in organizations. In W. C. Frederic & L. E. Preston (Eds.), *Business ethics: Research issues and empirical studies* (pp. 77–97). Greenwich, CT: JAI Press.

Waddock, S. A., & Graves, S. B. (1997). The corporate social performance–financial performance link. *Strategic Management Journal, 18,* 303–319.

Waldman, D. A., Bass, B. M., & Yammarino, F. J. (1990). Adding to contingent-reward behavior: The augmenting effect of charismatic leadership. *Group and Organizational Studies, 15,* 381–394.

Waller, J. (2007). *Becoming evil: How ordinary people commit genocide and mass killing* (2nd ed.). Oxford, UK: Oxford University Press.

Walters, R. (2007, September 26). Justice in Jena. *The New York Times,* p. A27. Retrieved October 1, 2007, from LexisNexis Academic database.

Warnke, G. (1993). *Justice and interpretation.* Cambridge: MIT Press.

Wayne, L. (2005, March 8). Boeing chief is ousted after admitting affair. *The New York Times,* p. A1. Retrieved July 27, 2005, from LexisNexis Academic database.

Weaver, G. R., Trevino, L. K., & Cochran, P. L. (1999). Corporate ethics practices in the mid-1990s: An empirical study of the Fortune 1000. *Journal of Business Ethics, 18,* 283–294.

Weaver, G. R., Trevino, L. K., & Cochran, P. L. (1999). Integrated and decoupled corporate social performance: Management commitments, external pressures, and corporate ethics practices. *Academy of Management Journal, 42,* 539–552.

Weidlich, T., & Calkins, L. B. (2006, October 24). Skilling jailed 24 years. *National Post,* p. FP1. Retrieved June 19, 2007, from LexisNexis Academic database.

Werhane, P. (1999). *Moral imagination and management decision-making.* New York: Oxford University Press.

White, B. J., & Prywes, Y. (2007). *The nature of leadership: Reptiles, mammals, and the challenge of becoming a great leader.* New York: AMACOM.

White, J. (2005, December 23). Air Force Academy shows improvement. *The Washington Post,* p. A02. Retrieved December 4, 2007, from LexisNexis Academic database.

Williams, K. D., Harkins, S. G., & Karau, S. J. (2003). Social performance. In M. A. Hogg & J. Cooper (Eds.), *The Sage handbook of social psychology* (pp. 327–346). London: Sage.

Wilmot, W. W., & Hocker, J. L. (2001). *Interpersonal conflict* (6th ed.). New York: McGraw-Hill Higher Education.

Wolvin, A. D., & Coakley, G. C. (1993). A listening taxonomy. In A. D. Wolvin & C. G. Coakley (Eds.), *Perspectives in listening* (pp. 15–22). Norwood, NJ: Ablex.

Woodruff, P. (2001). *Reverence: Renewing a forgotten virtue.* Oxford, UK: Oxford University Press.

Worthington, E. L. Jr. (2005). Initial questions about the art and science of forgiving. In E. L. Worthington (Ed.), *Handbook of forgiveness* (pp. 1–13). New York: Routledge.

Wright, D. K. (1993). Enforcement dilemma: Voluntary nature of public relations codes. *Public Relations Review, 19,* 13–20.

Zadek, S. (2004, December). The path to corporate responsibility. *Harvard Business Review,* pp. 125–132.

Zhu, W., May, D. R., & Avolio, B. J. (2004). The impact of ethical leadership behavior on employee outcomes: The roles of psychological empowerment and authenticity. *Journal of Leadership and Organizational Studies, 11,* 16–26.

Zimbardo, P. G. (2007). *The Lucifer effect: Understanding how good people turn evil.* New York: Random House.

Zinnbauer, B. J., & Pargament, K. I. (2005). Religiousness and spirituality. In R. F. Paloutzian & C. L. Park (Eds.), *Handbook of the psychology of religion and spirituality* (pp. 21–42). New York: Guilford.

Zuckerbrod, N. (2007, April 19). Student loan probe moves Congress to act. *Associated Press Online.* Retrieved October 8, 2007, from LexisNexis Academic database.

Index

About the Author

Craig E. Johnson is a professor of leadership studies at George Fox University, Newberg, Oregon. He directs the university's Doctor of Management program and teaches graduate and undergraduate courses in leadership, ethics, and leadership communication. He is the author of *Ethics in the Workplace: Tools and Tactics for Organizational Transformation* (also published by Sage) and the co-author, with Michael Z. Hackman, of *Leadership: A Communication Perspective.* His research findings have been published in the *Journal of Leadership Education, Journal of Leadership Studies, Journal of Leadership and Organizational Studies, Communication Quarterly, Communication Reports,* and *Communication Education.* Johnson is active in the International Leadership Association and the Academy of Management. He has held a variety of volunteer leadership positions in religious and nonprofit organizations and has participated in educational and service trips to Kenya, Rwanda, New Zealand, Brazil, and Honduras.